"If you find yourself arguing endlessly over what is fair, moral or ethical, I urge you to read Cliff Stromberg's book, which expertly and thoughtfully provides valuable suggestions for how we can improve respectful dialogue with one another, mindful that there are no perfect answers."

> —Myron Frans, former head of Minnesota Department of Management and Budget, and former Vice President for Finance and Operations, University of Minnesota

"Reminding us of the many ambiguities inherent in our moral judgments, and providing a healthy dose of humility for the next time we jump to conclusions, Stromberg also throws us a timely anchor as we navigate this era of relativism, confirming the timeless hierarchy of facts over feelings in moral arguments."

> —Jeffrey Balser, M.D., Ph.D., President and CEO of Vanderbilt University Medical Center

How Do You Know What's Right?

Thinking, Deciding, and Persuading

CLIFF STROMBERG

Hardcover edition ISBN-13: 978-1-953943-75-0
Paperback edition ISBN-13: 978-1-953943-76-7
Ebook edition ISBN-13: 978-1-953943-77-4

LCCN Imprint Name: Rivertowns Books
Library of Congress Control Number: 2026932144

Rivertowns Books are available from all bookshops, other stores that carry books, online retailers, and directly from the publisher. Visit our website at www.rivertownsbooks.com. Retailer and consumer orders, inquiries about discounts for bulk purchases, and other correspondence may be addressed to:

Rivertowns Books
240 Locust Lane
Irvington NY 10533
Email: info@rivertownsbooks.com

For my wife, Ava Feiner,
our children, Kim Stromberg Waldmann
and Eric Stromberg,
their loving spouses and radiant children,
and my parents, Greta and George Stromberg

Contents

Introduction

ARE YOU A GOOD AND MORAL PERSON? Do you have good values? You probably say Yes, although if you're like most of us, you're also aware of how you fall short at times.

But suppose you had to explain to someone with different ideas *why* your ways of deciding tough issues of morals or values are right. Would you say that you just try to follow the Bible's teachings? Or that you adopt reasonable moral principles and follow them consistently no matter what? Or that you follow your gut and do what feels right in a given situation? Or that you try to assess what's the best outcome for most of the affected people? Or that you just seek to behave consistently with the values of the finest people you know?

These are all good starting points, but what if they conflict with one another? And what if your approach doesn't persuade someone else who really matters in the situation? Fulfilling good values and moral conduct isn't just a matter of having a kind heart and a benevolent will. Achieving good also requires *skillful reasoning and sensible problem solving*. It entails astute assessment of facts, emotions, and psychology, as well as wisdom in weighing choices and the ability to explain them to others.

What approach you take to advancing your values and moral ideas really matters, for several reasons.

First, morality and values are core elements of our identity—who we are and seek to be as individuals. Think of the common refrain, "I just couldn't live with myself if I acted that way." How we make moral choices and implement our values deeply affects our sense of self.

Second, the values we embrace and the way we decide moral issues lead to importantly different actions with serious effects on those we care about or engage with—and on our society.

And third, not infrequently, we disagree with others about questions of values and morals, and so we must argue these issues to resolve disputes. Moral and value-laden questions have enormous emotional significance in our lives; relationships can be sustained, eroded, or fractured by how well such arguments are conducted.

The fact is that most of us spend an awful lot of time arguing. We argue with family, friends, coworkers, and people in our community. We listen to politicians and media pundits argue endlessly—and we mentally argue back at the laptop, tablet, phone, or TV. We even argue with ourselves about what opinion we should hold or what to do in a touchy situation.

Many arguments are about usual day-to-day matters without profound moral dimensions (like whether you can afford to put a new roof on the house, or whether a proposed new project at work makes sense). But research has shown that a significant portion of all the conversations people engage in relate to judging good or bad conduct. Just for example:

- When is it okay to break a promise?
- Should you respect a person's "right to their own opinion"—even if the opinion is really ugly?
- Should you report bad behavior at work—even if it's by a friend?
- What matters more—a good intent or the practical consequences of your action?
- Is there a moral right to decent health care?
- What does "being fair" mean in a given situation?
- Is affirmative action in college admissions and hiring right?
- Do we have a moral duty to open our nation's borders to immigrants and refugees?
- Are all morals relative—just a matter of having different values?
- What makes one a "good person"?
- What would it take for us to create a decent society?
- What moral values should we teach our children?

These are hard questions, and they deserve deep personal reflection. After you decide what you think is the right thing to do, you often face the even tougher challenge of convincing others. You may need to persuade an annoyed spouse that you weren't "selfish" or "mean" to a relative. You may have to persuade your boss that you were right to reveal to a customer a mistake made by your company. You may need to convince a friend that they shouldn't "talk trash" about another, even if it's true. You may want to convince your town council that removing certain kinds of books from the school library is or isn't the right thing to do.

This book is about how we think about issues of morals and values, and how you can more productively engage with others about them. It deals with feelings —even strong feelings—but it also explores the role of rational reasoning about morals and values. When it comes to convincing others, it won't work simply to shout, "You have bad values" or "That's just immoral." You need to provide reasons, explanations, justifications. And that requires an organized framework for understanding how values, morals, reasons, facts, and human psychology interact. This book aims to help you with that.

Let's first note one of the most challenging features of morality: Moral choices almost always involve multiple factors, not just one pristine, righteous principle. That means that when you argue with someone about a moral issue, the first task is to pinpoint the real "fulcrum" around which the disagreement pivots.

Take this example: Suppose that Sean is accused of having reneged on a promise not to reveal something bad that Joe did. Sean might defend himself in many ways:

- Disagreement about facts: "Hey, that's not true—I never said I wouldn't tell."

- Different definitions/meanings: "I said I wouldn't talk about what happened, but it was never a promise."

- No intent to deceive: "I promised, but I didn't know that later I'd be forced to tell."

- Different norms: "All of us promise a lot of stuff, but we don't really expect everybody to follow through."

- Varying duties: "I'd never welch on a promise to a real friend—but I hardly know Joe."

- Stronger obligations: "Yes, I promised not to tell what Joe did—but lying when the police came to my house would be a crime."

- Good excuse: "Sure I promised, but then I found out that Joe was badmouthing me at work—so to heck with him."

- Social good: "I promised Joe, but then I heard that he was going to swindle lots of people, so I felt like I needed to tell."

- Upholding a principle: "I should never have promised. Agreeing to hide a bad thing is bad itself."

Each of these reasons rests on an implicit moral principle. But note how each takes you down a different pathway with its own implied values, relevant facts, justifications, and potential rebuttals.

Today, one common response to a moral claim is, "You and I are different and have different values, so you can't judge me." But that's unrealistic. If you live in society, you judge—and are judged—every day. People routinely say things like "She's not being sincere," "He's too ambitious and cutthroat," or "He didn't really mean to hurt anybody's feelings." Moral judgment is part of being human and living in a social group; you can't avoid it. The challenge is to judge with a proper balance of humility, honor, empathy, reasons, and realism—what might be called a degree of wisdom.

In this book, I'll ask you, the reader, a lot of questions. That's because issues of values and morals often come to us as questions, dilemmas, stories, or conundrums. I surely don't have answers to all the challenges I pose. But by asking yourself these questions, you can perform a sort of self-diagnosis, learning how your mind and heart move from factor to factor as you arrive at a conclusion. That self-understanding can help you become a more morally effective person, one whose results better accord with your actual beliefs.

This book revolves around two key concepts: *morals* and *values*. They often get conflated. Suppose you ask someone an essentially moral question like "For really heinous crimes, do you believe in prison terms without any chance of parole?" They may respond Yes and refer to retribution, or No and refer to forgiveness—and then say, "Those are just my *values*." But the concepts of morality and values, while related, are different.

Values are broader than morality. Each of us cares about a set of core things we believe are important to a good life; these are called values. Common values include things like family, achievement, faith, community, patriotism, health, leisure, autonomy, self-understanding, new experiences, and a better way of life for our children.

People are often conflicted about the source of their values. On the one hand, they feel that they have autonomy and can choose their values, and they hold others accountable for their choices. But on the other hand, people often say, "That's just the way I was raised"—as if their values were inevitable and unchanging. As we'll see later, some values are strongly influenced by inborn genetic and personality dispositions, but people still modify some values during their lives. Your values are not a random hodgepodge that you're totally free to mix and match. Research has shown that a person's values tend to coalesce into relatively predictable patterns, forming a *value matrix*. Some values just naturally tend to go together. For example, political liberals and conservatives tend to hold high somewhat different values—even on seemingly nonpolitical matters.

Morality involves the subset of value-laden judgments that guide us in deciding what is right and wrong. Morality can include right *belief* (e.g., Is it a moral duty to love God, respect reason, etc.?), but largely involves right *conduct* toward others. And morality can be extended to other important questions, such as: What is our duty to create a moral society, and what principles should that embody? Values and morality flow together in interesting ways, some of which we'll explore in this book. Obviously, the values you hold most dear affect the moral judgments you make. For example, if you value avoiding harm over personal autonomy, you might make the hard moral decision to take the car keys away from your 90-year-old father, whose eyesight and reflexes are very poor. Conversely, your moral judgments flow back and affect your values. For example, suppose you decide that it's morally wrong that some folks you know are so relentlessly focused on their careers that they ignore their children, who then get into real trouble. That might bring you to recalibrate the value you place on ambition versus family in your own life.

But values and morality also differ importantly. Embracing a given value doesn't mean you believe others should rank competing values exactly as you do. If I am a violinist or a painter, I wouldn't expect my friend who is an accountant and a sports fanatic to place the same value on experiencing the arts. But morality is different. If I believe that it is wrong for me to do *x*, I also believe it's wrong for you to do *x* (assuming the same circumstances). Conversely, I can't believe that it's immoral for you to flat-out lie to our manager at the company, but it's fine for me to do so. People often resist this inherent meaning of morality as rationally obligatory on all similarly situated people because they think that is "intolerant" and means you are "imposing" your morals on others. That is not so. I can believe fervently that something is right and moral, *and that you should see that, too*—but also believe that society rightly allows you to disagree. And then, of course, some things are so widely viewed as immoral that society does bar them. (In Chapter 8, we'll explore the overlapping mandates of customs, morality, and law.)

A term often used interchangeably with morals is *ethics*. But there are differences, and ethics has a wider range of meanings. (See the Notes at the back of this book.) Morals are largely personal and social judgments that are informally enforced through social interactions. (A relatively small subset of moral rules are established in law, such as the prohibitions on theft or fraud). But a "code of ethics" refers to rules of conduct that are formally enforced by a professional or business organization and go beyond morality to define what behavior is expected in a particular context. Sometimes, as with the term "bioethics," ethics denotes an amalgam of moral principles, social practices, values, and legal requirements. And there are other fields of ethics—like "Christian Ethics" and "Jewish Ethics," with their own vast literatures encompassing religious beliefs, church teachings, and group practices.

In this book, I'll explore morality and then values, in roughly the following ways.

First, we'll ask what morality really is, how it developed in humanity, and how it routinely develops in children. Then I'll outline the main moral frameworks that have evolved in philosophy and practical thinking in Western culture. These include the approaches of relying on Biblical teachings; following moral feelings or "sentiments"; adhering to good moral principles regardless of consequences; stressing the actual good and bad effects on all the affected people; and just trying to emulate what a "virtuous person" would do.

Then I'll examine the revealing research about the biological and psychological bases of moral judgments, which also helps explain how political liberals and conservatives differ in their moral approaches. I'll describe the different meanings of "fairness"—a concept that has enormous impact on public policy issues like access to health care, diversity, tax rates, immigration, and law enforcement. As we'll see, issues such as these involve both moral questions and matters of fact, prediction, reasons, and rationality. This book is designed to help you navigate better through such issues.

Fundamentally, morality is a set of competencies to guide people toward living honorably and cooperatively in society. But then one might ask: Why don't we just act morally all the time? Historically, the most common answer was: because we are selfish and ruled by emotion. True, but that's only part of the answer. As we will see, there are many other reasons we don't act morally. They include moral blind spots, mistaken facts, moral confusion or bias, moral stasis, misleading words, deceptive metaphors, thinking errors (illogic), diffused responsibility, convenient excuses, bad economic or other incentives, and social conformity. We'll explore many of these.

Then we'll turn to values, and investigate what they are, how they relate to one another, and how your personality shapes your values. We'll see that contrary to popular wisdom, people's values and self-interests are not the same, and in fact are often in tension. We'll see what causes people to change their values. Then we'll show how people's values are logically organized into a matrix—which helps us understand why people who feel strongly about *a* tend also to care about *z*—even if the two things might otherwise seem unrelated. We will navigate through surprising research showing that psychological differences help explain why political conservatives and liberals come to weigh values differently.

These are deep waters indeed, and the rivers of thought we'll explore traverse many disciplines, including paleoanthropology, human development, psychology, neuroscience, sociology, philosophy, economics, business ethics, and even math and game theory. I can't capsulize here even the top one percent of the fascinating research in these fields. But I'll outline some key findings and the guidance they point toward. (Some sources for quotes, research findings, or ideas are stated in the text, but many are not. The Notes at the back of the book provide the sources for each and further elaborations for some. One of the first notes, under the heading "A Note on What's Missing," mentions some of the aspects of morality that I have *not* explored in this book.)

Sharpening your tools for thinking and arguing about values and morals can help you a lot in life. Shouting matches charging people with having "bad values" or "lacking morals" rarely yield good results. Instead, knowing how to engage around values and morals in a skillful way can help one save a marriage, avoid losing a friend, reach wiser decisions at work, and be a better citizen in our democracy.

I know you will argue such issues often. I hope this book helps you do it well.

1

Morality and Human Nature

"**T**HE NEED OF AN EXTERNAL MORAL ORDER is one of the deepest needs of our [human] breast." So said the influential psychologist and philosopher William James, and daily life confirms this. Our days are punctuated by the clarion calls of moral judgments: "You owe her an apology," "The doctor should be more empathic," and "Mortgage practices are unethical." People care about what they see as right, decent, or fair. We may not like people who self-righteously moralize, but we aspire to act morally and feel ashamed when we don't.

Research studies confirm the commonsense fact that people spend a good bit of their time in conversation commenting on the good and bad actions of others. But what do we mean by "morality"? A leading theorist says: "This question seems as if it could be answered by any intelligent person until he actually tries to answer it. Then a funny thing happens. If you start by saying 'Morality is . . . ' nothing you say afterward seems to be quite right." But let's try!

Morality generally involves at least three core questions: (1) What is right conduct? (2) What does it take to be a virtuous or moral person? (3) Accordingly, what are the features of a good and moral society? Which question you stress can lead to different views of morality. But most share the core concept that morality involves "principles concerning the distinction between right and wrong or good and bad behavior."

Morality is fundamentally a social concept—it focuses on conduct toward others. "Morality is primarily concerned with the behavior of people insofar as that behavior affects others," and "morality has the goal of limiting the amount of evil or harm suffered." Hence, while moral systems cite many goals, the two most important are avoiding harm and practicing altruism (helping others even when you don't benefit). Psychologist Joshua Greene says, "The essence of morality is altruism, unselfishness, a willingness to pay a personal cost to benefit others," and evolutionary scholar Michael Tomasello calls sympathy and altruism "the *sine qua non* of all things moral."

Many religious people may find this concept woefully limited, believing that morality also must include purely inner values like faith, piety, and humility before God, quite apart from conduct toward others. Some humanists may say that morality should focus on fostering the "flourishing" of one's innate capacities, and more broadly, that "morality is about human well-being. All our moral ideas, such as justice, fairness, compassion, virtue, tolerance, freedom . . . stem from a fundamental human concern with what is best for us and how we ought to live."

At its core, morality remains a social concept. Think about how necessarily shrunken would be the moral life of a lifelong hermit who never interacted with others. He might be pious, but most of what we mean by morality would be irrelevant to his life. Most experts stress the critical role of morality in sustaining social cohesion. As Patricia Churchland says, "Morality is the set of shared attitudes and practices that regulate individual behavior to facilitate cohesion and well-being among individuals in the group." Greene offers this nutshell definition: "Morality is a set of psychological adaptations that allow otherwise selfish individuals to reap the benefits of [social] cooperation." In this sense, morality is seen as a "theory of rational behavior," because widespread violations lead to worse outcomes for all. Morality evinces "shared values that demonstrate one's continued identification with the moral community." Rabbi Jonathan Sacks goes further, saying, "Morality achieves something almost miraculous, and fundamental to human achievement. . . . It creates trust." Thus, "society is constituted by a shared morality."

But the social expectations for moral conduct can be complicated. For example, good conduct toward others doesn't always earn praise. We don't laud a traffic cop as moral because she routinely prevents cars from running over pedestrians; that's just her job. Usually, you get moral credit only for what are called "supererogatory" acts (i.e., ones "beyond the call of duty"), like stopping by the roadside to help someone whose car won't function. Even then, it might at times be deemed morally wrong to perform such acts. Suppose a man swims out to sea to save a drowning man, risking drowning himself and leaving his own wife and four children with no income. Is that morally right or wrong?

Beyond social expectations, morality plays a strong role in self-identity, what kind of person we want to be. "Identity is a tapestry of beliefs about the self, many of which are moral beliefs." Thus, "if you're engaged in a moral conversation, your discussion is always—whether overtly or covertly—about identity issues." This is revealed whenever a person says, "Oh, I couldn't live with myself if I did that." Such a statement reflects the key role of moral character in self-conception and self-worth. As we will see later, it also reflects the way we struggle to reconcile our character with challenging situations. And researchers find that "moral character traits are among the most important determinants of the overall impression that people form about you."

Morality is also about what someone holds to be sacred, which could include such things as religion, family, patriotism, rationality, or the environment. With those potent identity issues in play, no wonder arguments about morality often have a strong emotional valence. As psychologist Jonathan Haidt says, "We're born to be righteous, but we have to learn what, exactly, people like us should be righteous about." And part of feeling righteous about something is that you really want others to agree.

As we try to get a handle on the idea of morality, we often resort to metaphors—which can both help and deceive. We use physical metaphors like "staying on the straight and narrow," not "crossing the line," and not "falling into sin"—which imply that being moral is an obvious posture and it's easy to tell when we fall out of it. But we also talk about moral "principles" and "judgments," which implies a more reasoned, effortful process than just not falling. We talk about "pure" motives, as if any taint were abnormal. We speak of "low morals" or a "higher moral sense," as if morals were arrayed on a single, unchanging scale, like musical notes. But then we talk about the "decline in morals" and a "moral crisis" or the "evolution of morals," which suggests that morality changes over time. It seems hard to fix on just the right metaphor.

There is no avoiding the fact that morality has many dimensions. As we'll see in this book, there are roles in morality for faith and inspiration, for one's gut feelings, for a good heart and good intent, for reason, for principles and rules, for assessing consequences, for practicality and weighing competing factors, for obeying social customs, and for both consistency and exceptions to consistency. Thus, as Tomasello says, "Human morality is not a monolith but a motley, patched together from a variety of different sources . . . during the several million years of human evolution. . . . Human beings today thus enter into each and every social interaction with selfish me-motives, sympathetic you-motives, egalitarian motives, group minded we-motives, and a tendency to follow whatever cultural norms are in effect." And yet, when we make moral decisions, we try to do so in a coherent way that can be justified to and persuade others. In later chapters, we'll explore how to do that.

But first: How exactly did this mosaic of morality develop in human nature?

The Evolution of Morality

IN THE WESTERN RELIGIOUS TRADITION, morality is usually seen as a product of twin concepts: (1) God created humans in His own image and endowed them with a moral soul, but (2) We are sinful or imperfect, and must struggle against our human flaws in order to act morally as God ordains. So, in arguing about morality, we often appeal to what people "inherently" are. We aspire to be good but shouldn't expect people routinely to act contrary to their "human nature." But what exactly is that human nature?

It's a very big question, one that has been answered in several ways over the millennia. Even before the birth of modern science, philosophers portrayed morality as the use of reason to overcome our "animal passions," such as greed, envy, and anger. Humans were seen as often blind to their true interest in achieving wisdom and "the good." They were inherently selfish satisfiers of their animal desires, only tenuously restrained by moral rules, reason, and custom. The Greek philosopher Plato famously depicted the soul as a chariot with the charioteer of reason heroically straining to reconcile two powerful horses, base appetites and morality. But in the 18th century, the influential philosopher David Hume declared that "reason is and ought only to be the slave of the passions." Over the last 150 years, we have tended to define human nature in scientific terms, as greatly influenced by evolutionary processes. And in our own day, social scientists have portrayed morality as just "a thin veneer" hiding an otherwise selfish and brutish nature. But, as we will see, this "veneer theory" of morals turns out to be a simplistic and mistaken concept.

Today, more than a century and a half after Charles Darwin's pioneering work in formulating the theory of evolution, most thinkers take it for granted that human nature has been powerfully shaped by eons of evolution, in which behaviors that are "adaptive"—that is, beneficial to survival—were "selected" and preserved. So, to understand how people's moral machinery functions, we must reverse-engineer it, asking, "How could the moral mechanisms we now see in humans have evolved?" As Darwin wrote in his notebook, "He who understand[s] [the] baboon would do more toward [understanding] metaphysics than [studying the philosopher, John] Locke."

But if we seek to discover how morality evolved in humans by studying other species, what behavior in them should we regard as displaying a moral sense? What, exactly, is "moral behavior" in animals?

Many researchers have tackled this problem. In their effort to define morality in terms that could apply to other species of animals, most experts start with behaviors such as cooperation, unselfishness, empathy, and altruism.

You might assume that such behaviors are quintessentially human. Yet researchers have observed what they call cooperative and even self-sacrificing behavior in species as diverse as ants, bats, fish, birds, and small mammals. The keys to these behaviors seem to be support of kin, reciprocal altruism toward some others, and "coalitionary support" when threatened by outsiders. In some species, this involves food sharing under a tit-for-tat regime with kin or colony mates. As Patricia Churchland concludes: "In the wild as well as captivity, [some species of] mammals and birds behave in ways that *can reasonably be considered in the moral category,* such as consolation of the defeated, reconciliation after a row, food sharing and orphan adoption."

Note the cautious italicized wording. Ascribing morality to nonhuman animals is a tricky philosophical matter. While some scholars see such behavior as within a broad category of morality, most ascribe such behaviors simply to self-protection strategies or to genetically selected affinity for kin, tribe, or colony. These behaviors are helpful to other animals in ways we consider moral when humans perform them, but calling them "morality" may be circular, human-centric reasoning. If x in humans takes on meaning as a moral kind of behavior, and x is observed in ants, then—presto—ants must possess morality, too! That begs the very question we are trying to answer, which is whether *x* has a similar *motive or meaning* to the ant—a question that seems fundamentally unanswerable.

Those who reject equating humans' social sacrifices with those of ants might still admit that both species evolved in groups that reward helpful social behavior, some of which we now call "moral." But ants apparently can't choose to act immorally (selfishly to the detriment of the colony), while humans can and often do. Isn't that one meaningful difference?

A leading researcher concludes that dogs know when their misbehavior is disapproved by their owners—but he sees no evidence of what we would call guilt or shame. And dog trainers reportedly say that you must discipline bad behavior right away; the dog cannot "hold" the concept of having acted badly for long. Apes seem to make up with one another after behaving selfishly, perhaps to reduce group tension, but it's unclear if they experience guilt or shame apart from wanting peace.

Hence, most scholars hedge by saying things, such as "lots of animals display *building blocks* of empathic states"—thus not claiming that we can know whether their inner feelings actually resemble ours. In the view of philosopher Thomas Nagel, altruism is not just any self-sacrificing behavior that an organism engages in, but only the kind that is "motivated . . . by the *belief* that someone will benefit or avoid harm by it." Jesse Prinz notes that "reciprocal altruism is actually rare in other animals" because it "carries fairly demanding cognitive prerequisites" (such as assessing risk, judging intent, recalling prior exchanges, planning acts). Darwin saw this long ago: "Any animal whatever, endowed with well-marked social instincts, would inevitably acquire a moral sense or conscience, *as soon as its intellectual powers had become as well developed, or nearly as well-developed, as in man.*" So those who have studied the question generally agree there's a major difference in kind and degree between the morality of humans and that of other animals.

Indeed, only very limited moral behavior has been observed even in our closest kin—chimpanzees, bonobos, and great apes. The leading researcher Frans de Waal has documented "the exchange of food for grooming in chimpanzees," calling it "reciprocal altruism." But apes don't seem to cooperate much with one another, other than through the behavioral "golden triad of grooming, food sharing and coalitionary support [in fights]." They will ally to defend their infants, or to fend off a dominant male. But evidence of reciprocity or fairness

("You shared yesterday; I will share with you today") is rarely seen. Moreover, caged chimps usually *will not* pull a lever to get food for others in addition to themselves, though there are different reported results. Some researchers report that monkeys will starve themselves and not grab food rather than cause shocks to be administered to cagemates.

This limited expression of behaviors we humans see as moral may be because chimps live in pretty brutal male-hierarchical troops, in which punishment, violence, and tension are the norm. As de Waal vividly states, "Chimpanzee group life is a [constant] market in power, sex, support, influence and hostility." Only occasionally do chimps cooperate, such as to resist an aggressor or to hunt monkeys. Other than that, little cooperative activity has ever been observed among apes, despite experimental efforts to enable it. As Tomasello says, for example, "It is inconceivable that you would ever see two chimpanzees carrying a log together." Others report that in general, "chimps simply do not seem to care about the welfare of unrelated group members."

But de Waal sees things more positively, noting that chimpanzees will help a friend in a fight, and console one who lost. He interprets such behaviors as demonstrating that "the building blocks of morality clearly predate humanity. We recognize this in other primate relatives, with empathy being most conspicuous in the bonobo and reciprocity in the chimpanzee." He also sees them as having "primitive social rules" for policing bad behavior. And one widely noted (but also questioned) study reported that monkeys—an earlier species than chimps—displayed a rudimentary sense of "fairness" and would refuse a piece of cucumber if another monkey was given a better "treat"—a grape.

However, even bonobos, the hippie-love-child cousins of chimps and us, who are promiscuous in sharing sex and grooming, don't display much cooperation or what we recognize as moral behavior. Basically, de Waal seems to say that apes have the building blocks for, but not truly evolved, morality. Others are even more skeptical. Christopher Boehm says that after decades of study, "I was looking for any sign of an incipient ape conscience and I didn't see it."

Morality as a Survival Strategy

HUMANS, IN CONTRAST TO THE OTHER GREAT APES, exhibit a dizzying array of cooperative, reciprocal, and altruistic behaviors. This brings us to ask, How and why did such behavior arise?

Many scholars believe that a "great leap forward" in human moral development occurred when sudden changes in African ecology forced humans to begin mate-paired foraging and clan hunting across the expanding savannah grasslands. Higher-value food sources (meat on the hoof rather than fruits) became abundant, but acquiring them required intensive cooperation. It became conducive to survival if you had genes enabling you to recognize and reciprocate empathy, cooperation, and bonding—and therefore engage in cooperative game-hunting forays. So, cooperation became a smart survival strategy. And bonding/empathy/altruism developed a powerful biological reinforcer, thought to be the hormone oxytocin (sometimes called the "love hormone"). Extensive recent research shows that people's propensity for trust and cooperation can be artificially manipulated by their exposure to oxytocin. One can "turn the behavioral response on or off like a garden hose."

Moral thinking as we understand it would have taken a long time to develop. Initially, as psychologist Paul Bloom notes, "there is a strong reproductive benefit to . . . favor friends and family over strangers and one would expect this to be incorporated as part of an innate moral sense." But over time, cooperation became even more powerful when extended to a larger group. Thus, "humans are inclined to come up with systems based on indirect reciprocity whenever they need 'insurance' against bad luck." If I share meat with you when I kill an animal but you fail, then next time when the situation is reversed, you'll share with me. This may be the ultimate solution to the question why selfishness alone didn't dominate human nature.

Scholars such as William Hamilton, Donald Campbell, Richard Alexander, and others resolved the "altruism paradox" by showing "through mathematical modeling that selfishly competing individuals could [prosper by making] . . . reasonable personal sacrifices if these benefited their own offspring." Sacrifice could benefit an individual (and his/her altruistic genes) if it engendered enough loyalty in others that they would help with hunting, defending against dangers, or feeding and caring for one's offspring if needed. James Q. Wilson vividly points out, "After a few thousand encounters with the saber tooth tiger, this primitive culture will probably consist disproportionately of people who are altruistic or fair or both. The others will have been eaten."

This gave rise, according to many scholars, to *reciprocal altruism*, which prospered genetically because it conferred survival advantages on the individual and its (genetic) kin group. As Darwin observed, "Selfish and contentious people will not cohere, and without coherence, nothing can be effected. A tribe rich in the above qualities [cooperation] would spread and be victorious over other tribes." And as Joshua Greene says, "Cooperation evolves not because it is 'nice' but because it confers a survival advantage." Reciprocal altruism has been documented in many small-scale hunter-gatherer cultures.

The key moral mechanisms that developed as a result of these evolutionary pressures were empathy, reciprocity, and fairness. Empathy is not, as people today tend to say, "feeling" what the other person feels. It is not "catching another's emotion (emotional contagion), but [rather, it is] responding emotionally to the perceived welfare of another." (For example, even if I hate snakes, I might empathize with a young boy whose pet snake just died.) As we've seen, reciprocity is also a key moral concept. And then there is fairness, a concept requiring pretty high cognitive functions, since it assesses the subject's *deservingness* in light of many past actions and present features. Overall, there are dozens of ways that humans, including children, engage in reciprocal cooperation where apes don't. As Tomasello observes, "human beings are biologically adapted for collaboration in a way that other great apes are not." Thus, the "morality of fairness . . . may well be confined to the human species," and "it is much more complex than the morality of sympathy."

The next evolutionary step was when these patterns of cooperative reciprocity and fairness were extended beyond the family to the larger social clan or grouping. This represented, according to evolutionary biologist Marc Hauser, the "signature of a uniquely human cognitive adaptation. Whereas we inherited a largely selfish nature from our ancestors, we also evolved a uniquely human psychology that predisposes us toward a different form of altruistic behavior—*strong reciprocity*."

Fast forward to the present: Most humans still view the core of morality as empathy, reciprocity, helping others, and fairness. Indeed, neuroimaging studies reveal that "cooperation is associated with heightened activity in the brain's reward regions." Normal people often experience a "warm glow" when they help others. In contrast, those who show aberrant blindness to others' feelings, selfishness (narcissism), and willingness to lie are known as psychopaths or sociopaths—meaning they have a *disease* that separates them from human normality. This sad defect in normal human capacity is thought to be largely heritable.

By the time modern humans emerged as a species, they were, as Tomasello says, "three-ways moral": They had "a morality of sympathy," "a morality of fairness," and "a morality of justice." In a similar vein, human development expert Elliot Turiel writes that humans have "a biologically based disposition for bonding and attachment . . . [that produces] four [elements] . . . of the moral life: sympathy toward the feelings and experiences of others, a sense of fairness, self-control to delay rewards and goals, and conscience or duty."

But morality requires not only good intent but also social enforcement of norms against bad behavior. Cooperation and selfless action for the group only continue to work if there are policing or punishment mechanisms against violators. Anthropologist Christopher Boehm has documented across many small-scale societies "how altruists are compensated" and how "free riders" are suppressed. Many additional tools developed: shaming, exclusion from the common pot, punishment, and finally, expulsion from the group. He concludes that "my database shows that everywhere hunter-gatherers do in fact readily punish their deviants" and non-cooperators. The threat of such punishments is itself a usually-effective deterrent that is learned and has "helped in significantly suppressing the frequency of genes that favor predatory . . . cheating." Thus, as Paul Zak notes, fairness and cheater detection are recognized as mechanisms needed to support reciprocal altruism.

Effective punishment for antisocial behavior was a common feature of early societies, and it could turn violent. But it was an essential tool for maintaining a successful society. Today, game theorists have used computer simulations to calculate just what ratio of "good" cooperators versus "bad" cheaters is necessary to sustain a cooperative group dynamic. With different good/bad ratios, a cascade toward morality of the group develops, or doesn't. When experimenters conduct such games with volunteers, they find that people will predictably sacrifice benefits to themselves to punish violators and preserve the fairness of the experimental "society." (More on that later.) Importantly, in the real world it has been found that "the societies in which people are most cooperative are also the societies in which people are most willing to punish people who are not cooperative."

In sum, the evolutionary dynamic of morality began with attachment/bonding and then empathy/altruism. Over time, it grew to encompass cooperation, keeping promises, respect for rules, a willingness to invest effort in punishing bad actors, a sense of conscience, guilt, shame, indignation at insult to the tribe, and a devotion to group integrity. As Churchland says, "Morality in humans . . . is intensely biological: [It is in] the platform that makes us want to be with others and find attachments rewarding, in the [neural] . . . circuitry that allows us to remember specific people and their actions, in the capacity for seeing others as having feelings and goals."

In today's wealthy, industrialized nations, we tend to see morality only in the positive, aspirational sense. We generally don't like to focus on morality as including harsh punishment of criminals or shunning of bad or flawed people. The punitive concepts of group shaming, ostracism, and revenge may even seem barbaric. But both history and scientific evidence suggest that their psychic sources are fundamental to morality. Indeed, "countless ethnographies have [confirmed] that punishment through shame, ostracism, scapegoating and outright violence is essential for maintaining egalitarianism and adherence to social norms in small-scale societies." Nicholas Christakis surveyed a range of cultures and concluded that in general, "cultures showing more punishment also showed more altruism." Of course, a low level of conduct requiring punishment might be a good index of social health.

Reciprocity and Moral Intuition

RECIPROCITY IS A CORE COMPONENT of the moral systems generated by evolutionary processes. We can see this in our everyday relations. We usually remember—emotionally—how others have treated us. As the ancient Roman leader Cicero said, "There is no duty more indispensable than that of returning a kindness. All men distrust one forgetful of a benefit." Indeed, when experiments test what happens when subjects engage in bargaining with those who violate reciprocity or make unfair offers, "[brain] imaging studies reveal significant activation of the anterior insula, an address in the brain known to play a role in negative emotions such as pain, distress, anger and especially disgust." In short, we get mad! Reciprocity is so much at the core of social relations that an affront to it feels existential.

In one of those unexpectedly wonderful connections between fields, modern computer simulations have been used by game theorists to analyze how prehistoric morality likely evolved and imprinted itself on our nature. When researcher Robert Axelrod conducted an "Olympiad" among competing computer games devised to win negotiations, one brilliant strategy beat out 62 others, yielding the most success and benefits overall. The winning strategy was incredibly simple: *tit-for-tat morality*—that is, *I do to you exactly what you did to me in your last move.* Under this code, deception or pure selfishness doesn't advantage you as the game progresses, whereas basic cooperation does.

Most people intuitively see the logic of this. As mathematician-economist-ethicist Kenneth Binmore concludes, "I don't believe this is because [people] . . . have a natural bent for metaphysics. I think it is because they recognize a principle that matches up with the fairness norms that they actually use every day in solving . . . the myriads of small coordination games of which daily life largely consists." It's the commonsense principle we use all the time: "Okay, I'll cover for you by working late Friday, but you gotta do the same for me some day next week."

Another key moral concept—fairness—is confirmed by a vast body of research. For example, in the "Ultimatum Game," one test subject (A) is given a sum of money like $100 and told that he can offer some part of it—or nothing—to another (B) who must take it or leave it (the ultimatum). But the catch is that A only gets to keep money *if B accepts the offer.*

Pure economic logic suggests that A should offer B just $1. After all, B is getting a buck for nothing, so why should he refuse? And A gets to maximize what he keeps ($99). But people are not just rational economic calculators. They feel morally "pissed off" by being treated unfairly when offered only $1 while the other person gets $99 that they didn't even earn! As a result, generally, B will refuse a deal in which they receive anything lower than about $25. (Interestingly, this norm varies by nation/culture, with people in some countries typically expecting the local equivalent of $40, while in others, they only expect $15. But everywhere, some degree of sharing is expected.)

People intuitively feel the importance of policing and reinforcing the concept of fairness. In effect, they will "pay" (by refusing the deal) to punish selfish bad actors who don't play fair. They are giving up a current benefit because of some sense that, in the long run, we are all better off if other people don't get away with being selfish.

Still more surprising are the results from a variant called the "Dictator Game." Here, A is given $100 and told that she can keep it or give some to B—but *there is no requirement that B must accept the offer.* Whatever A decides is final. Yet most A subjects do not wield this power selfishly. Paul Bloom reports that "there have been more than a hundred published studies of dictator games and it turns out that most people do give and the average gift is between 20 and 30 percent." Marc Hauser concludes that "in the same way that all humans share a universal grammar but speak [different languages] . . . all humans share a universal sense of distribution fairness, [adjusted by] cross cultural differences coupled to local quirks of exchange, justice, power and resource regulation." Within every culture, people still vary in their sharing propensity. What's more, a massive genetic study found that some 40 to 50 percent of the difference in sharing in such games is genetically predicted.

The same moral dynamic that works between individuals also influences societies. People expect benefits and burdens to be shared fairly. People will pay for shared public goods through taxation—but only if most other users also pay and there aren't too many who abuse the resources or are free riders. The town park is for walking and picnics, not permanent settlements. The county lake is for catch-and-release fishing, not commercial fishing. If sharing rules are broken, people will stop paying for these public amenities. Indeed, research confirms the correlation between a high level of willingness to pay for public goods and strong policing of the rules, across a range of nations.

So, the development of human moral capacity depends on many building blocks, including the abilities to have empathy and other-directed emotions, form a mental picture of actions, recall and keep score of others' behavior, exercise self-control, practice reciprocity, mind-read others' intent, conceive principles of fairness, and be willing to sanction bad actors.

We've covered a lot of terrain. The moral arguments we engage in can become complicated and subtle. But underlying them are a few ancient, genetically encoded values, including empathy, reciprocity, trustworthiness, and respect for the group and its rules. You feel them, and so does everyone else you may need to argue with, even if they hold differing ideas on how best to apply them. As Darwin said, "Ultimately, our moral sense or conscience becomes a highly complex sentiment—originating in the social instincts, largely guided by the approbation of our fellow men, ruled by reason, self-interest and in later times by deep religious feelings, and confirmed by instruction and habit."

There you have it—the many sources of the whole complex edifice of human morality.

What About God?

BEFORE WE LEAVE THIS EVOLUTIONARY DISCUSSION, I want to acknowledge that strong religious believers may feel that the preceding discussion is flawed. For them, there is a much truer and simpler answer to why humans evolved to have morality: We developed as God intended. God created humans in His own image, and ordained that we would strive to do right according to divine law. He allowed us free will, and we often fail in our calling. But morality is in mankind because God intended it to be thus.

Nothing in the preceding discussion is contrary to such belief. Many people with deep religious convictions consider the process of evolution as just one of the tools God used to help shape and form human beings, as well as other living things. But whether or not you share this belief, I hope you'll agree that, since our society includes both believers and nonbelievers (as well as many folks who are unsure), in order to resolve moral issues, we need to be able to engage with others whose deep beliefs differ from our own. We must understand and be able to explain the morality that our faith, our reason, or both, guide us to follow.

If Morality Is Innate, Why Isn't It the Same Everywhere?

OUR DISCUSSION OF HOW MORALITY EVOLVED suggests that its basic moral architecture has come to be innate in the human mind. As Churchland says, "Conscience is a brain construct rooted in our neural circuitry." But many generations grew up with a very different idea—that some societies were morally enlightened while others were primitive and barbaric. Most people believed that human life for eons was, in the immortal phrase of philosopher Thomas Hobbes, "solitary, poor, nasty, brutish and short"—until we created "enlightened" and "higher" civilizations.

But during the second half of the twentieth century, most thinking moved in a different direction, toward cultural and moral relativism, which holds that no culture is dramatically better or worse in moral terms than any other. The pendulum swing began with the realization that wealthy nations had a patronizing view of poorer ones' morality, often used to justify the exploitation involved in colonialism and imperialism. In time, the pendulum swung so far as to say that no morality can ever be deemed better than another. For example, to a British

Christian, polygamy was barbaric, but to an African Muslim, it was wise and socially admired. So, morality came to be viewed by many as just another variety of social custom.

Researchers in ethnography and sociology delighted in describing far-off cultures with "totally different" customs and morality. Leading anthropologists found the variety of specific moral customs more intriguing than the commonality of core principles. Given their professional orientation, scholars of culture generally resisted the idea of uniform biological drivers of human conduct, believing that culture was largely "constructed." Some prominent examples of that work have now been shown to be exaggerated or wrong. (See the Notes.) But moral relativism remains a popular doctrine.

However, relativism gives rise to several confusions that need to be dispelled. For example, in arguing about morals, people often confuse the concepts of *innateness* and *uniformity.* They assume that if morality is innate to humans, it would have to be uniform across cultures. And if morality is found to be largely uniform, then that must be because it's innate. But neither of these inferences is strictly justified.

As we've seen, almost surely the *capacity* for morality is innate in humans. But a given *set of moral rules* isn't necessarily so. A particular variant of the basic moral system might evolve as the best solution in given ecological and social conditions, which vary. It might be like the invention of boats. Only humans have the mental capacity to develop boats, and boat building is universal among societies with water access. Water called forth the innate human capacity to create boats—but what kind of boat depends on whether the people live near rivers, lakes, or oceans. Innate capacity and varied outputs aren't contradictory.

The analogy is often drawn between morality and grammar. Thus: "our moral faculty is equipped with a *universal moral grammar,* a tool kit for building specific moral systems." Words and specific rules of syntax vary across languages, but many linguists say that most languages share a "deep structure" with key features such as nouns, verbs, possessives, tenses, and so on. Likewise, all moralities contain features such as caring, reciprocity, truthfulness, sacredness, and justice.

Another common analogy is that morality is like a tool kit: People across cultures use different kinds of knives or saws or hammering tools. But these tools share common features because they solve common challenges. Likewise, morality must help solve common challenges embedded in social life, like keeping promises, reciprocity, unequal goods, safety, and punishment—but the specific tools might be locally adapted.

Many people make the added mistake of inferring that if morality isn't *precisely uniform*, that means there can be no objective moral values, no "universals." It turns out that whether that claim is true or false depends very much on the level of generality or detail you believe matters. For example, all societies sanction lying, stealing, and killing, but they may recognize different exceptions or excuses. Does that mean their morality is the same (at the level of principle) or different (specific exceptions)?

In reality, many elements of morality are virtually universal across cultures. Humans have developed remarkably similar moral principles because morality itself arose from universal needs in human groupings, such as mutual reliance, cooperation, value-exchange, and care for kin. And as we will see, when group-centric societies gave way to more individualistic societies, morality changed to reflect this change in values.

Therefore, it's misleading to frame the debate as between (1) "Morality is just social convention; look at the variety of moral beliefs" and (2) "Morality is innate; look at how much is universal." That framing succumbs to the classic "glass half full/half empty" fallacy. The glass can be *both* half full and half empty. Morality can be highly similar across individuals and societies at the level of major principles, and yet different at the level of some kinds of specific actions.

For example, it is shocking to Americans that in some societies, killing a woman for adultery is accepted as moral; female genital mutilation is accepted; and killing so-called infidels is venerated. As a member of American society, I believe that those practices are morally awful. But I can also recognize (without implying any equivalency) that some societies see it as shockingly immoral when Americans move far away and leave their elderly parents alone in a nursing home, or never go to church or believe in a deity, or tolerate high rates of crime and drug abuse among our adolescents.

If we focus on the differences among moral systems, we can fail to appreciate the strong cross-cultural patterns of respect for core moral principles. Instead, "we must look at the deep structure of human social contracts written into our genes." As philosopher Mary Warnock says, "Radical [moral] relativism denies what I have asserted, namely that there are shared and permanent values," and they are significant. In fact, some differences are noticeable precisely because they break the strong pattern of commonality, the blueprint given by our evolved nature.

What then are these more-or-less universal moral principles that virtually all human societies endorse?

All or almost all societies *value* and *respect* truthfulness, fulfilling promises, respecting elders, caring for spouses and children, loyalty to tribe/group/polity, fulfilling duty, empathy, kindness, fairness, reciprocity, humility, courtesy, diligence, reliability, adherence to principles, respecting sacred traditions, decency in public, helping those in need, courage, sacrifice for the group, and fairly enforcing rules against violators.

And conversely, all or almost all societies *condemn or punish* lying, cheating, stealing, adultery, obscenity, neglect of spouses or children, selfishness, disrespect of elders, laziness, arrogance, greed, cruelty, rape, murder, assault, defaming others, claiming unearned credit, disloyalty to tribe/group/polity, profaning sacred things, shirking duty, and endangering others.

There are at least several dozen important and virtually universal moral values identified by scholars who have surveyed many societies. So before we say that moral frameworks are just relative because they are not identical, let's acknowledge their enormous common ground.

Still, while almost all societies agree on many core moral principles, some disagree about which specific actions violate a given principle. Take this example: Abandoning one's children is universally condemned as immoral, but what constitutes "abandoning" varies. For example, consider the following list of behaviors. In your view, which of these qualify as "abandoning one's children"?

- A young woman determined to pursue an acting career gives her infant child to her mother to raise so that she will be free to accept roles no matter where they may take her.

- A British couple places their seven-year-old child in a prestigious but distant boarding school, and sees the child only a few times a year.

- A poor, rural African woman gives her child to a family in a far distant city which has better schools.

- An American woman who is a drug addict gives her child up for adoption because she knows she can't care for it.

- A single father learns he has a deadly degenerative disease, and to spare his son the pain of seeing him decline, he sends his son to live with his brother's family.

You might find all, or some, or none of these actions morally wrong. Yet the same underlying principle of "caring for one's children" governs, and requires a strong justification to depart from it. What does that say about whether human morality is more "universal" or more "relative"?

In our daily lives, we can't help but notice and think about even the relatively nuanced disagreements on moral issues we have with others. But that shouldn't cause us to ignore the remarkable consistency of basic moral principles across times and cultures.

And this general consistency is likely inevitable given our common human nature. Can you imagine a world of polyglot moral societies without any underlying similarity, in some of which treason is no big deal, or lying is rampant and respected, or stealing is an ongoing game everybody accepts? Can you imagine a society in which the highest moral goal is excellence in dominating others, grabbing as much as you can, and having a great sense of humor to mock the losers? Most likely, a society *couldn't* have developed in those ways for the obvious reason that it would be unstable and fall apart. As many scholars have suggested, our core moral values—empathy, fairness, reciprocity—developed because they are indispensable to social stability and survival. As C. S. Lewis said, "Think of a country where people were admired for running away in battle, or where a man felt proud of double-crossing all the people who had been kindest to him. You might as well try to imagine a country where two and two made five."

For a fascinating take on this, read Ken Binmore's *Natural Justice,* in which he shows that under the principles of game theory, every collaborative system seeks to achieve the talismanic "Nash Equilibrium," in which each participant's selfish strategy *cannot* be improved in relation to others' without destabilizing the whole system for all. For example, why is fairness a necessary rule? Binmore says, "I think we care because fairness is evolution's solution to the equilibrium selection problem for our ancestral game of life." Moreover, "since cultures vary, any *universal* principles of justice—its deep structure—presumably must be written into the genes we all share."

As you read this, you may find yourself wanting to push back. You may be thinking something like this: "How can you say that a society can't be stable without embodying fairness? What about the many societies across millennia in which slavery, treatment of women as chattel, genocide, gross inequality, and other kinds of cruelty prevailed and were accepted? These were stable societies with the worst kind of morals."

This is a fair point. But there are some responses. One might be that such societies existed, but many ultimately collapsed, and today they are becoming fewer and less extreme. Another might be that people in those societies recognized the same moral principles we do, but because of power and economic structures, they applied them to a much smaller group of recognized stakeholders. As they progressed, societies expanded the right to moral treatment from just wealthy in-group men, to all men, to women, to children, to animals, and even to future generations and the environment.

I confess I'm not satisfied with such answers. History shows that while some exceptionally repressive regimes are short-lived, other truly evil ones persist for a long time, if power can be maintained in the hands of a small group and/or there is a widely seductive ideology.

As we explore common moral principles, I should also acknowledge that this book addresses almost exclusively the framework of people who want to make good moral choices and are capable of doing so. There is a whole dimension of truly evil people and evil acts in the world that falls largely outside what I discuss.

How Does Morality Develop in Children?

WE'VE EXPLORED HOW MORALITY DEVELOPED in the human species, but what about those primitive little humans playing in the next room? Given morality's importance, it's no surprise that extensive research has been conducted on how morality develops in children and morphs as they grow into adults.

Thinking about morals in children was long dominated by researchers Jean Piaget and Lawrence Kohlberg. "Both held the view that moral judgments are handed down from society, refined as a function of experience (rewards and punishments), and based on the ability to reason through the terrain of moral dilemmas [and judge] . . . based on clearly defined principles." Piaget believed that in learning to comprehend morals, children progress through three cognitive stages, while Kohlberg discerned six stages, extending over a long period (perhaps through the mid teenage years). A key concept was that children first sense that their parents' authority defines what is good or bad by simple, fixed rules (like "Don't take your brother's food"). But as their minds develop, they gradually absorb broader moral principles ("Share fairly"). Finally, they learn to think for themselves about moral issues, referring to principles but also having the confidence to make exceptions to them ("I don't need to share this snack, because he doesn't like peanuts anyway"). As brain scientist Robert Sapolsky says, "The Kohlbergian emergence of increasingly complex stages of moral development is built on the Piagetian emergence of increasingly complex logical operations [in the child's mind]."

But this view has been challenged on several grounds. For example, Marc Hauser says that "even young children—well below the ages that would enter into Piaget's and Kohlberg's moral stages—recognize [moral issues like] the distinction between intentional and accidental actions . . . and intended and unforeseen consequences." The composite alternative explanation that emerges is roughly as follows.

Normal children by about age one or two understand the empathy and caring they receive from parents, and begin to develop their own capacity for empathy. They know that if a sibling cries, something must be upsetting it. They like being helped by parents, and they learn to like helping. They experience frustration and understand that others do, too. For example, it has been shown that young toddlers like and prefer dolls that are perceived to "help" another over those that "block" another. Very young children infer niceness or meanness even from abstract shapes that seem to be helping or hindering others. Humans evolved an "agent detection device" so that even small children infer that when an object moves in a nonlinear, unexpected way, there must be a conscious agent at work. And they think those agents should act nice. Even young children show some guilt over misbehavior and try to justify their actions. In sum, the child's "attachment [to parents] begets caring; [and] caring begets conscience."

Next, children develop what Tomasello calls "two person morality" based largely on the concepts of helping and fairness. They will help more if another child is younger or needy or helped them before. Young children oversimplify; they think fair means that every child gets the same thing. But as early as age three or so, they change and now expect to share equally the rewards of a task with children who also contributed, but not with others who didn't help at all. By age five, they will at times share even with people they have never met. And they understand the difference between intended and accidental harm. They also like to see rules obeyed; this shows that their good actions are appreciated by parents. This leads to self-identity: "I am a good child, because I act the way my parents want."

Initially, children can't distinguish between sensible rules and flawed ones. The mere fact that an adult states a rule establishes its moral worth. Children learn to experience guilt (for breaking moral rules) and shame (for breaking customs). But as any parent knows, children are not gentle little saints. They can be stubborn and selfish; they hide their crimes; they freely tattle on others; and they like to see "cheaters" get punished.

Gradually, children learn to broaden their moral views. They learn not just to rely on an external authority to define what is right, but to form moral principles on their own. Around age seven or eight, they might reason that, "The school has a rule not to share food with others. But Jane is my friend and eats at my house, and she lost her lunch, *so in this situation*, it's okay to break the rule and give her half my sandwich."

Researcher Elliot Turiel found that "over a period of more than twenty years, nearly 100 studies . . . [show] that children make judgments that differ" depending on the rather subtle factor of whether an action is immoral or just violates customs. Piaget and Kohlberg had reported that until age nine, children judge morality solely by consequences: If something hurts a person, it is bad. But more recent research shows that as early as age five, children can judge based on intent as well as consequences. They learn not just to follow rules but to balance factors ("I don't want to hurt Emma's feelings—but I still don't want her at my sleepover!"). Over time, "what grows in the child, and interacts with her moral judgments, are systems of self-control, emotion, numerical computation, and memory that [together] allow for more accurate bookkeeping [about consequences." Children also learn a great deal about kindness and fairness simply through play with other kids.

Some scholars report that stricter, more authority-based parenting styles tend to foster rule-based morality in children, while more lax or fluid parenting styles tend to encourage internalized, flexible morality. Many parents try to teach their children to derive inner satisfaction from acting morally, rather than relying on external dictates. Importantly, kids progress from a simple notion of fairness as meaning equal results, to fairness based on more nuanced criteria of deservingness in a given situation. And any parent knows that kids care deeply about anything that "just isn't fair!" As Pip says in Charles Dickens's *Great Expectations*, "In the little world in which children have their existence, there is nothing so finely perceived and finely felt as injustice."

In sum, in developing their concepts of morality, children start with empathy, progress to reciprocity and sharing, then to broader notions of fairness, and finally to the inner ability to think through moral issues in a flexible way. As Paul Bloom explains, children develop "some capacity to distinguish between kind and cruel actions; empathy and compassion; . . . a rudimentary sense of fairness . . . ; a . . . sense of justice; [and] a desire to see good actions rewarded and bad actions punished."

In time, children become, in Kohlberg's memorable phrase, little "moral philosophers." Then it should be easy for them to think through moral conundrums when they become adults, right? Well, that requires an organized moral framework, and that presents its own challenges and opportunities for each of us.

In the chapters that follow, I'll explore the leading moral frameworks that have won belief in Western culture.

2

Core Moral Frameworks:
Religion and Reason

TAKE A CLIPBOARD, GO OUT ON THE STREET, and ask random people, "Excuse me, I'm taking a survey: Can you tell me if stealing is wrong, and why?" You might get a few responses like "What are you, stupid?" or "What do I look like, a philosopher?" But more likely you'll hear answers like these:

"It's just wrong: 'Thou shalt not steal' is one of the Ten Commandments."

"Stealing is selfish—it hurts other people."

"Stealing breaks an important rule. If everybody did it, society would fall apart."

"People have a right not to be victims of theft."

"There might be rare exceptions—like if a family is starving and they steal from the rich—but otherwise it's almost always wrong."

"I don't know, stealing just feels evil."

There you have it—wisdom from sidewalk philosophers! They've done pretty well, too, because while entire libraries could be filled with books on moral philosophy, the six responses above encompass the main ways of judging moral conduct that have been devised over the millennia.

This chapter will explore the principal moral frameworks that have developed in Western thought. They're quite intriguing in themselves—and they draw you into very human dilemmas. Understanding them has practical value in everyday life for several good reasons.

First, if you want to be a decent, moral person, you'll need to make decisions in lots of tough situations. Life is just like that; it can't be avoided. And those situations will often present conundrums:

- Do you tell a "white lie" because it spares feelings (or maybe it's not so "white," and just serves your selfish purposes)?

- Do you report a coworker friend because he did something bad and reporting him is the right thing to do—or is that a personal betrayal?

- Do you have a duty to tell your cousin that her husband is cheating on her, or is that wrongful meddling?

- Do you secretly look at your teenager's computer, or is that an immoral invasion of privacy?

- Do you cheat on your taxes "a little"—because, after all, "everybody does it" and you don't want to be "the dummy"?

In deciding such things, you can just go with your gut and muddle through. But at some point, your conscience will ask, "Am I sure I'm doing the right thing? How can I decide between several actions when none of them feels exactly right?"

First, having a moral framework you understand and trust can help you make tough decisions like these, and be at greater peace with your conscience. Amusingly, the erudite website Stanford Encyclopedia of Philosophy states that "ethics is widely regarded as the most accessible branch of philosophy . . . because *many of its propositions are, seemingly, self-evident or trivial truths.*" Yet ethical choices are often neither self-evident nor trivial.

Second, moral frameworks help us be more effective. Nobody is morally perfect, and we all do unkind or dishonest things. But we don't want to compound that by doing what we intend as a good act only to find that it has the reverse effect. But unless you understand your moral framework—what factors you weigh most and what principles you're trying to uphold—you will stumble into that mistake.

Effective morality is an intellectual and social skill; it can be practiced and improved. Understanding your personal moral framework helps you hit the target you're aiming at. Let me use an analogy. Let's assume you want to be a really good parent. Fine, but unless you reflect on your core beliefs—when it's best to guide children or let them find their way; why you nurture or withhold; why you forgive or punish them—you won't wind up being the effective parent you want to be. Likewise, you will find it hard to be the kind of moral person you want to be unless you understand *why* you make moral choices as you do.

Third, moral frameworks focus on different elements of morality and so at times they can lead to very different actions. Yes, people acting within each framework can be good and moral. Yes, they frequently reach similar conclusions. But other times they differ—and that's why your framework matters. As you read about these frameworks, one or two may feel more sensible and virtuous to you than the others. It makes sense to pay attention to that feeling.

A final reason for learning about moral frameworks is that you'll often need to argue with others who have different moral viewpoints. Morals are not like food or movies, where we don't really care much if others have different tastes. On moral issues, people believe they are right *and that others ought to see that.* Strong disagreements create emotional divides. Understanding the moral frameworks we'll examine can be essential to conveying your convictions, bridging to another person's viewpoint, and perhaps finding common ground.

The goal of learning about moral frameworks is not necessarily for you to select one as the perfect framework to follow in all circumstances. In practice, all of us switch back and forth between moral frameworks while wrestling with significant challenges. Humans are not purists who routinely rely only on one approach, and that reveals a lot about morality. (We'll explore that in the chapters that follow.)

One simple tool for puzzling through a moral issue is to ask yourself questions such as these:

1. What do I feel about this situation? What does my gut tell me?

2. What's my main reason for seeing this action as good or bad?

3. What will be the consequences for people?

4. Can I think of a principle that could usually guide us well in this kind of situation?

5. Are there good exceptions to that principle or rule? Is this situation one of them?

6. What would a good person do here? How will I feel about myself if I do A or do B?

An interesting, if snarky, tidbit: Some studies have investigated whether being a professional moral philosopher who knows all about moral theories leads a person to be, well, more moral than the rest of us. They found that mostly the answer is . . . No. Apparently, knowing and doing are different.

The Historic Starting Point: Morality Based on Religion

THROUGH MOST OF RECORDED HISTORY, the main source of morality was belief in the mandates of the gods—or later, God. The earliest recorded systematic embodiments of morality are religious texts. Remarkably, across many times and cultures, the principal rule that emerged was the Golden Rule, stated in the New Testament (Matthew 7:22) thus: "As ye would that men do unto you, do ye also to them likewise." That of course echoed the far older Jewish tradition from which Christianity evolved, such as the command in Leviticus, "You shall not take vengeance or bear a grudge against any of your people but you shall love your neighbor as yourself." Or as Rabbi Hillel later said, "What is hateful to you, do not do to your fellow men. That is the entire Torah; the rest is commentary."

The same core value appears in the Islamic Hadith: "As you would have people do to you, do to them; and what you dislike to be done to you, do not do to them."

It is also embodied in Hindu texts: "One should never do that to another which one regards as injurious to one's own self. This, in brief, is the rule of dharma."

Likewise, the Buddha says: "Hurt not others in ways you yourself would find harmful."

And Taoism: "It is the way of the Tao . . . to recompense injury with kindness." And: "Regard your neighbor's gain as you gain, and your neighbor's loss as your loss."

And Confucius: "Never impose on others what you would not choose for yourself."

Not surprisingly, this maxim embodies the very principle of mutuality/reciprocity/tit-for-tat morality that we explored earlier and that is believed to have emerged in early humans. It's no wonder that the Golden Rule has been a source of moral inspiration for countless cultures and people through the ages.

However, the Golden Rule alone is not enough to guide us as we navigate life's challenges. First, we should embrace this nuance: "Do unto others as you would have them do unto you, *but bear in mind that they may want different things than you do.*" A driven man might feel that a friend is too focused on family and hobbies, and needs to "get some ambition" at work, but that may not be his friend's life goal. "Do unto others" really means "act toward them with the same spirit you would wish they had toward you," rather than "do the exact same thing you would want."

A great historical nugget is the story of a conversation between Alexander the Great and his mentor and military chief, Parmenion. Alexander had conquered much of the then-known world, far more than anyone before, and his troops, weary from a decade of battle far from home, yearned to turn back and were near revolt. Parmenion, the grizzled veteran of countless battles, advised him, "If I were Alexander, I would return home." To which Alexander replied "And if I were Parmenion, I would as well; but I am Alexander." Different strokes for different folks—which makes the practical application of the Golden Rule much more complicated.

Understanding the Golden Rule is easier than adhering to it. We all would wish to be treated with love, kindness, honesty, and respect. But few truly can come to "love thy neighbor as thyself," so each of us makes compromises, excuses, explanations. We decide that following the Golden Rule sometimes, in some situations, and only so far, is "good enough."

Over time, religious morality developed additional principles beyond the Golden Rule. In many ancient societies, these included observing the required rituals, paying obeisance to deities, and obeying civic authorities. In Judeo-Christian monotheism, religious morality came to mean more than just following set rituals, though that was still important. It meant attending to the spirit infused in the rules and thinking about how to be a righteous person who loved God and sought to follow his will. The Ten Commandments are not just about avoiding harm to others. They also include the commitment to love God ("Thou shalt not have strange Gods before me"), a mandate to respect God and sacred things ("Remember the Sabbath day, to keep it holy"), familial duties ("Honor thy father and thy mother"), and internal morality even apart from action ("Thou shalt not covet thy neighbor's wife [or goods]").

The moral teachings embraced by religion are not always consistent. The Bible, for example, is full not only of divine commands, but also stories, moral principles, learnings, and commentary, including wisdom written down, pruned, and assembled from at least 1200 BCE through about 400 CE and from diverse societies across the Middle East and the Levant. As a scholar of the Jewish Bible (Old Testament) says, "The editors of the Bible felt empowered to present a wide variety of ideas [from different cultures] . . . as part of their Israelite tradition." Scholars have noted many meaningful differences and contradictions among books of the Old Testament, among books of the New Testament, and between the Old and New, even when the New purports to quote or refer to the Old. These "points of difference can actually have an enormous significance for the interpretation of a book or the reconstruction of the history of ancient Israel or the life of the historical Jesus."

Furthermore, the Septuagint, the earliest existing compilation of the Old Testament in Greek from the historic Rabbinic Judaic text, actually contains several books that had not been in the older versions of the Bible. Conversely, many revelatory texts later contended to be accepted in the New Testament, and many of the Gnostic gospels and other texts were ignored or excluded from the Bible during the process by which the authority of the early Church coalesced. Church councils at Nicea, Laodicia, and Carthage through the fourth century CE resolved theological disputes and pruned and consolidated the canon of Scriptures—but significant inconsistencies remain. At the great council at Nicea in 325 CE (which gave rise to the authoritative Nicene Creed of the Catholic Church), many dozens of inspired writings contended to be included in the canon. Bishops tried to resolve this by voting, but there were many dissents. The Emperor Constantine, who presided, finally got impatient and demanded agreement, so some books were included and others discarded. But for decades after, various bishops convened their own councils to adopt an adjusted but agreed canon.

After all this, it isn't surprising that the moral rules or injunctions within the entire Bible are not all consistent. Most of the Bible is *not* said to be the word of God, or of Jesus, but rather is a compilation of history, stories, parables, psalms, and customs. The texts, even the core New Testament Gospels of Mathew, Mark, Luke, and John, diverge and sometimes contradict one another. In many places, the New Testament seeks to echo the Old Testament, but the quotation is demonstrably amiss, or the analogized event is quite different. As one scholar notes, "The Bible is a collection of texts, written over the course of more than a thousand years. It is neither systematic nor consistent, and it often expresses contradictory positions."

There are many who disagree, believing that the Bible is "inerrant" (accurate and compelling) in every word, and if it seems otherwise, that just reflects human limitations. Also, some evangelical Christians believe that the New Testament evidences a "new covenant" between God and humans that revokes the covenant established in the Old Testament. The earlier document is not binding so that, properly understood, there are no inconsistent moral injunctions. But millions of other Christians from various denominations disagree, believing, for example, that the New Testament fulfills, rather than abrogates, the bond to God in the Old Testament. As Jesus said in Matthew 5.17, he came to fulfill rather than abolish the Law and the Prophets. And of course, in the Jewish tradition, religious and moral authority can be derived not just from the written Torah, but the Midrash (Oral Torah), the rest of the Old Testament, the Rabbinic literature including the Talmud, including the Mishnah (Jewish oral law) and Gemara (commentaries)—and in some views, later authorities as well.

So, in interpreting the Bible or related religious texts as a sufficient guide to morals, we must have a good bit of humility. For example, if you are the average American Protestant trying to understand the literal words of Jesus, bear in mind that you are probably reading a seventeenth-century translation into English, of a Latin version, that was translated some centuries before from a Koine Greek version, that was translated centuries before that from Aramaic, the language Jesus almost surely spoke. Jesus' actual words are very important. As in any translation of a complex text from language to language to language, there are likely to be mistakes, arguable selections of synonyms, and loss or addition of connotative meanings. And the words of Jesus were themselves written down and codified in the Gospels four to six decades after his death by anonymous people who tried to recall them, or knew people who had recited his words to them. The spirit lives, but the words may vary.

As just one example, consider the commandment that is variously translated from the original Hebrew word *ratsach* as meaning "Thou shalt not *kill*" or

"Thou shalt not *murder*." Those are factually—and morally—different meanings. (The more generic Hebrew word for killing was *harag*.) Indeed, the Old Testament even contains two different versions of the Ten Commandments (in Exodus 20 and Deuteronomy 5). Many such Biblical inconsistencies are hardly just linguistic; they matter to theology and morals in important ways.

Also, deriving clear moral guidance from the Bible requires interpreting and reconciling conflicting mandates. We are instructed to forgive even repeated sinners and to show kindness to all—but also to slay unbelievers and idolators, stone to death women who are not virgin at marriage, kill disrespectful adult children, and visit the sins of the father unto the sons of the fourth generation. The Bible accepts and at times lauds acts of enslavement, treatment of women as chattel, eye-for-an-eye punishment, vengeance, genocide, and so on. The New Testament is suffused with the spirit of Christ, the doctrine of turning the other cheek, of love for all. And yet it includes death and destruction as instruments of divine judgment, and acceptance of war without mercy.

If one relies on the Bible as a complete guide to morals and the righteous life, there is still no way to avoid selecting, interpreting, and reconciling various moral injunctions. And significantly, the Bible contains many important stories, parables, and epigrammatic statements for which one must draw out the meaning. Some scholars believe that Jesus intentionally taught primarily by stories and parables to be pondered throughout life, rather than by simple lists of rules. Moreover, the Bible includes myriad statements about conduct that may be seen as just descriptive, not prescriptive—but how do we know which is which? And some are prescriptive but what we today call "prudential"—wise, but not actually commands of the Lord.

Beyond that, it is just hard to know what faithful adherence to the Biblical text would require in some of the challenges of modern life. Should doctors perform double-blind clinical studies, which may harm some people, in order to devise cures for many more? Should we explore space or instead leave other worlds as they are? Should we try to improve human health through genetic manipulation of the species? Should we try to develop artificial intelligence for the betterment of mankind, or does that risk the proper status of man as God's creation? How should we balance alleviation of poverty, economic growth, and impact on the environment? The authors of the Bible never confronted these questions, and they are not easy even for those today who have a sure base in their faith.

I have used Judeo-Christianity as the archetype of a religious source of moral principles. But of course, the Islamic, Hindu, Buddhist, and other traditions are rich sources for their believers and for other inquiring souls. Religious faith is the greatest fount of moral guidance for most people in the world. We must all respect the moral good that religious faith can achieve. But a degree of humility is due when one argues to others that by reading any religious text, one knows unerringly what God requires in a given situation. Perhaps part of humility is knowing that we are not unerring in *our reading* of God's will.

In addition, religious traditions and moralities differ. In the second half of the twentieth century, a common theme of scholarship was that we should move beyond parochial self-righteousness and realize that all religions are basically efforts to understand the same God. The metaphor of Huston Smith's long-running 1955 bestseller *The World's Religions* was that all religions are simply different paths up the steep mountain—but all lead to the same peak, God. He also used the metaphor of a musical chorus. Who sings the right notes? "We cannot know. All we can do is try to listen carefully and with full attention to each voice in turn as it addresses the divine."

Smith and others like him wanted to foster tolerant openness to a range of thought. But their message was often misunderstood as meaning "all religions are ultimately the same and their believers want the same things." That is just not so, and Smith's detailed explorations of religious differences show that.

For a revealing exploration of this idea, read Stephen Prothero's *God Is Not One*. Prothero doesn't argue that there is more than one deity, but that there are meaningful differences among religions. As he points out, each major religion starts by defining a central problem of human existence, which then entails pursuing a certain solution or goal. For Christianity, the core problem is sin, and accordingly, the goal is salvation. The challenge is different in the Jewish tradition: "In Christianity, sin is a fact of birth, whereas in Judaism, sin is a matter of choice." Meanwhile, in Buddhism, one does not seek atonement for sin at all. Instead, the core problem is suffering, and life's goal is to end suffering. In Islam, the key problem is pride, and the goal is righteous submission to Allah's will. In Hinduism, the core problem is *samsara*, the endless cycle of life, death and rebirth, and the goal is *moksha*, or release from this.

Obviously, these nutshell descriptions don't do justice to the world's great faiths, and teachers of each know so much more. But the key point is that religions offer different views of the existential challenge facing humankind, and of the relationship between the spiritual and public realms. For example, most Western societies are firmly committed to the distinction between a private spiritual realm and a public or governmental realm. But many (not all) Islamic nations do not believe that is right or proper, and hence maintain an official state religion.

Despite these differences among major religions, some surveys show that a significant segment of Americans hold that you can't be a moral person without believing in God. In a 2010 survey, this included 47 percent of Democrats and 64 percent of Republicans. (But more recent surveys show some decline in this viewpoint—with only about one third of Americans believing that.) This seems to reflect Nietzsche's epigram: "If God is dead, all is permitted." But is it true that religious faith is essential to moral thinking and behavior? As you consider all the people you know, are the religious ones virtuous and the nonreligious far less so? A major survey by the Pew Research Center found that religious and nonreligious people were remarkably similar in the principles they cited for their moral decisions. More generally, the evidence doesn't seem to support the idea that lack of religiosity results in evil. For example, the Nordic nations are now simultaneously among the least religious nations in the world and the least violent and most socially cooperative and altruistic. Surveys across more than 50 nations find about 24 percent of people saying they are not religious. A *majority* of people in Canada, Japan, Sweden, and Australia say they are not religious. Do you have the impression that these are among the *least* moral, most evil nations in the world? On some indices of social caring and collaboration, they rate especially high, not low.

I have kept short this thumbnail summary of religion as a fount of morality. Each major religious tradition has its own vast literature that helps guide believers to the right and true and good life. Our key point here is just that historically, religious belief has been by far the most important source of moral inspiration and guidance. It provides key spiritual principles. It harnesses a broad range of deep human emotions—fear, dread, aspiration, group love, altruism, identity, a desire for transcendence, and so on. Most of the other moral frameworks I'll describe below were developed by highly religious people who believed they were describing reasoned principles that guide people toward right conduct that is consistent with God's will.

To avoid misunderstanding, I'll also stress another point. This book focuses primarily (though not only) on the dimension of morality that involves right conduct toward others and in society. But many people believe that another dimension of morality also is critical—inward virtues like piety, humility, fortitude, and submission to God's will and plan for humankind. Religious scriptures and other writings in a number of traditions explore those concepts deeply, and they form a major part of what believers embrace and seek to practice.

From the Greeks to the Enlightenment

RELIGION, IN VARIOUS FORMS, represents the earliest recorded system of morality that shaped the thinking and behavior of human beings, and continues to hold enormous influence today. But another realm of thought emerged many centuries ago and has deeply influenced Western concepts of morality: the work of secular philosophers who plumbed the deep meanings of ideas like reason, duty, goodness, virtue, and justice.

I will now do something never before attempted in all of intellectual history: summarizing more than 2,000 years of Western moral thought (roughly 400 BCE to 1600 CE) in just three lines!

Sophists—Stoics—Socrates—Plato—Aristotle—Plotinus—Augustine
Boethius—Avicenna—Averroes—Anselm—Abelard—Maimonides
Aquinas—Duns Scotus—Erasmus—Bacon

There you go! I won't try to capsulize the towering achievements of these thinkers, though I will touch on some of them in the pages that follow. They refracted the lights of faith and reason through the lens of morals in profound ways. Vast periods of intellectual history were shaped by these thinkers. They provided many basic tools we still use—consciously or unconsciously—to puzzle through moral questions.

Several schools of Greek thinkers of the fifth and fourth centuries BCE pointed moral philosophy toward rational justification of moral choices. The Greeks focused on several key concepts. One was *eudaemonia*—achieving the good life, or flourishing. Another was *arete*, meaning virtue or excellence, or what we might call character. The Greeks felt that just as one can define excellence in an athlete, one should be able to define excellence in a moral person. A third key concept was *logos* or reason—the notion that unless a moral principle is consistent with reason, it can't be compelling to human beings. Indeed, various Greek philosophic schools "present themselves as a series of attempts to justify faith to reason." They believe that "the order of Nature is a moral order . . . [and that is] the most important truth about the world." And thus, "traditionally, [personal] conscience was given a cognitive status; it was regarded as a source of moral knowledge."

The Greeks also explicitly analogized the morality and justice of a society to that of an individual. The virtues of a good society are the same as those of a virtuous individual: rule by reason (rather than passions), fairness, moderation, piety, justice, and honor. But the Greeks also tended to be practical and raw in ways that strike many today as *not* virtuous. As just one example, Meno says that excellence for a political leader entails managing the city so that he benefits his friends, hurts his enemies, and brings no harm to himself. And bear in mind that "the Greeks" include perhaps a dozen philosophic schools (Cynics, Stoics, Sophists, Epicureans, Skeptics, Eleatics, Cyrenaics, Platonists, Aristotelians, and others) who vigorously disputed one another's basic premises—so generalizing about "the Greeks" can be misleading.

The later Greeks relied uniquely on the method of moral questioning that we now call "Socratic." Epitomized by some of the Dialogues of Plato (Socrates' pupil), this method is devoted less to declaring moral conclusions than to asking questions and wrestling with moral conundrums. To Plato, morality requires containing animal passions and using reason to lead the good life. Virtue is a matter of achieving the abstract ideals of reason, wisdom, and *arete*. The four "cardinal" (meaning "hinge" or "gating") virtues are wisdom, courage, moderation, and justice. (Yet in the *Republic*, Plato also allowed Thrasymachus to voice the more cynical view that morality is just a system of rules adopted by the weak to restrain the strong.)

In Aristotle, at times called the "father of ethics," morality became more practical. While Plato stressed the abstract "forms" of concepts like "the good," Aristotle sought to discern principles, rules, and empirical facts, seeking to answer the practical question: What do virtuous people agree about and act upon? He saw the virtuous person as acquiring "practical wisdom . . . through practice [and] . . . deliberative emotional and social skills." It is almost as if Aristotle, the son of a physician, sought to develop the science of a virtuous nature. As Aristotle said, "Neither by nature . . . nor contrary to nature, do the virtues rise in us; rather, we are adapted by nature to receive them, and [then] are made perfect by habit." That statement packs in a lot of concepts. Man is not just good "by nature." But neither are we unavoidably sinful. We have the reasoning capacity to discern and apply moral rules. But, as Aristotle said, "we are what we habitually do." You become a virtuous person by the hard work of acting virtuously day after day.

During what philosopher Karl Jaspers dubbed the Axial Age (the ninth to third centuries BCE), there was an efflorescence of religious and philosophical traditions across the world, not just in Greek philosophy, but also in the emergence of Buddhism, Confucianism, Zoroastrianism, Jainism, Taoism, the Hebrew Prophets, and other schools of thought. Those traditions also explored the deep questions of what it meant to live a good life, be a good person, and be in accord with the cosmos.

But then in the West, for almost a thousand years, people simply referred to "The Philosopher" without needing to say they meant Aristotle. Of who else could it seriously be said: "His writings extended nearly every domain of human learning"? Scholars say that lay thinking in the Middle Ages was fundamentally Aristotelian (i.e., fact or logic-based), until the Renaissance returned to the more Platonic (ideal-based) worldview. Of course, this vastly oversimplifies, but it contains at least a grain of truth. Both approaches still echo through the main modern theories of moral argument.

Importantly, as one scholar puts it, "Ethical debate resumed in the eighteenth century after more than a millennium during which the dominance of Christianity had silenced discussion of moral principles—the divine command morality of the scriptures being assumed, or claimed, to settle all matters of right and wrong and how to live." That statement may do a disservice to the deeply reasoned moral explorations in the theology of thinkers like Augustine and Aquinas, who both used and challenged Aristotle. But without question, in the eighteenth century, there was a flowering of alternative moral frameworks.

Rationalism: Kant's Moral Principles and Duties

DURING THE ENLIGHTENMENT of the seventeenth and eighteenth centuries, as traditional religious beliefs began to lose their exclusive authority in the West, two divergent theories of ethics emerged that have largely dominated moral debate down to our own times.

One was the *rationalist* or *deontological* (meaning "derived from duties") morality of Immanuel Kant. In Kant's framework, morality is embodied in immutable principles and clear duties that we find by reflecting upon what is ultimately rational. The second approach was the skeptical, *empiricist* theory of Thomas Hobbes, David Hume, Adam Smith, and others; they saw morals as based on practical "sentiments" rather than lofty principles.

In this chapter and the next, I'll discuss both the Kantian and Humean approaches at some length, because they continue to underlie how people argue moral issues in everyday life. Let's first explore Kant.

Kant's basic approach is easy to remember—because your mother likely was a Kantian! She probably told you something like this: "Think about what you're doing, meet your obligations, and always try to do the right thing. But then don't worry about what happens, because you can't control it!" This is morality based on good intentions, good principles, and duties—not the vagaries of consequences, intended and unintended.

In Kant's view, "the ground of [moral] obligation must be looked for, not in the nature of man nor in the circumstances of the world in which he is placed, but solely *a priori* in the concepts of pure reason." Kant believed that reason alone reveals which moral principles hold up and which don't. As one scholar notes, "For Kant, we are free [only] when the rules we choose for ourselves are rational ones." Moreover, Kant says that "virtue is the moral strength of a human being in obeying his duty" rather than allowing oneself to be "governed by feelings and inclinations." Hence Kant offered a clear moral principle: "I ought never to act except in such a way that I can also will that my maxim should become a universal law." In other words, devise rules that you and everyone else would want to live by, at all times and in all circumstances, and obey them.

Kant is a notoriously dense writer, and his thinking contains profound orbs within orbs. But as philosopher Bertrand Russell puckishly said, "[Kant] was like many people: in intellectual matters he was skeptical, but in moral matters, he believed implicitly in the maxims that he had imbibed at his mother's knee"— what is right is *always* right. As your mother might have asked, "How would you like it if everybody did what you just did?"

Kant's morality is supposed to be based on fixed rational principles, untainted by personal experiences or circumstances. That makes them "categorically" true—not "contingent" and variable. Kant aimed "to work out for once a pure moral philosophy . . . cleansed of everything that can only be empirical and appropriate to anthropology [i.e., mere cultural customs]." Thus, to Kant, anything other than universal rules would be contingent on transitory circumstances and thus not purely "rational." For example, he said that "I can lie [on occasion], but I can by no means will [desire] that lying should be a universal law, for with such a law, there would be no promises at all." If everyone lied, no one could trust anything. But Kant meant something more. Even if only some people lied and only some of the time, if lying was ever excused, morality would be variable, contingent, and hence not perfect and rational.

Kant's categorical principle is this: *It is always morally right to act according to a rule that you would want to become universal.* Thus, when facing a moral dilemma, you must cast aside how you feel about the people involved, their relation to you, whether they are worthy or not—and apply the general moral rule that would be right for all rational beings in similar circumstances. Kant declares that "we cannot do morality a worse service than by seeking to derive it by examples rather than [fixed rules]." As we will see, this demand for fixed rules causes people a lot of moral angst when they encounter situations where the gritty facts seem to undercut the morality of the nice abstract rule.

Another of Kant's key principles is that one must "act in such a way that you always treat humanity . . . never as a means, but always . . . as an end." In other words, respect people's autonomy and never use them as tools for your ends, even good ends. And the consequences of good actions are not your concern. Sometimes things turn out as hoped, sometimes not. All you can guarantee is your good intent. So "nothing in the world . . . can possibly be . . . called good without qualification except a *good will*." And a good will is not good because of its results or consequences. "[Even if your intent failed entirely] it would still shine like a jewel in its own right." This approach has become known as "non-consequentialism." (Mom again: "You can't control what happens!")

Kant's ethics "is often described as an ethics of duty." Thus, "virtue is the moral strength of a human being's will in fulfilling his duties, a moral constraint [arising] through his own lawgiving reason." In a nutshell, some duties are absolute and perfect, essentially negative duties like "Never kill." Positive duties are inherently imperfect, like "Help others, when you can." In Kant's view, a perfect duty can never bow to an imperfect one. Hence, you should not kill even a bad person to save a good one (except in self-defense). The corollary is that it's not even moral to kill one person to save 100. To many people, this is troubling.

Kant also said that one must act not simply according to the right moral rule, but "for the sake of" the rule. This is a subtle concept. It captures the idea that there is social value in reliable rules like "Don't steal," even if in some cases stealing might be justified. But what Kant really means is that following a rule is moral only if you act for the sake of your commitment to the rational rule, not for the sake of its specific effects. For example, a philanthropist is acting morally when he gives money to a university because it is right to support independent scholarship—even if he knows the university then funds scholars whose views the philanthropist hates.

The Kantian moral framework offers a number of benefits. Its dictates can be stated as clear, consistent rules that others can understand. The Kantian can claim to be a "rational" person if she follows those rules. She will likely be seen as "upright," never "wishy-washy." In this spirit, modern philosopher Bernard Gert even offered a short list of categorical rules that should appeal to us as universally moral.

Kantian thinking emphasizes the power of the individual to make moral choices based on reason. The value of this approach is buoyed by research suggesting that people tend to act more morally if they believe they have free will and choice.

Kantian moral rules offer the prospect of satisfying people's desire for reliable guides to life. We yearn for clear, unconditional moral laws that tie to the cosmos, resolve arguments with other humans, and leave us with inner peace. We tend to be skeptical of the person whose morals shift like the wind, who waffles or habitually responds to moral challenges by saying "It all depends on the situation." We're not sure we can rely on such people—and cooperative reliance is a key social purpose of morality. If it were possible in life, most people would want to say, "Those are my principles, and I stick to them no matter what." (Contrast this with the comedian Groucho Marx's quip: "Those are my principles, and if you don't like them, I have others!")

Interestingly, in a massive survey of the basic moral framework claimed by people in dozens of nations across the world, the United States had by far the greatest proportion of moral absolutists (Kantians). In this respect, the United States was the most "idealistic," and stood in contrast to most other wealthy nations.

The Kantian moral framework, then, has some clear advantages. But as a guide to life, critics find that it also has major flaws. Here are some.

CONSEQUENCES MATTER

By declaring that actual consequences are irrelevant to moral conduct, Kant ignores a lot of what people expect morality to achieve—good social relations. If I harm someone, telling them that I had a good intent usually won't cut it. Just consider our good buddy Blunto, who proclaims that he's moral because he always tells people the unvarnished truth. In real life, do we praise him because he tells people straight up that they are ugly or stupid? As a true Kantian, he says, "Consequences be damned." Does that make it morally necessary that I tell my elderly grandmother that she really annoys us when she can't remember things? That hardly seems moral.

In real life, the way we apply Kantian morality is inconsistent. Psychological research has confirmed the unsurprising fact that when we judge our own actions, we cut ourselves a lot of slack and cite our good intentions even when they cause harm. But when we judge other people's actions, we look at both intent *and* consequences. If a friend inserts himself into our spousal argument and makes it a lot worse, we say, "You should keep your nose out of our business," not "Well, you're a marvelous fellow for trying."

Moreover, critics charge that by insisting on consistency with universal laws, Kant is secretly using a consequentialist criterion of morals anyway. In effect, he is saying "we must obey the right principle of never lying even when a lie would be good—because in the long run, the consequences of people expecting to be lied to would be worse." So even a Kantian seems covertly to care about ultimate consequences.

WHY MUST FIXED, RATIONAL RULES GOVERN?

Critics also ask, "Is Kant's demand for absolute, fixed moral rules really required by reason, or is it just another moral choice?" How do we *know* that rules are better than feelings? As Churchland says, the effort to find invariable, perfect moral rules has "suffered a conspicuous lack of success." But we could all cite generally good *feelings*, like empathy, kindness, and forgiveness.

The reasons for Kant's insistence on reason aren't hard to find. He was a product of the eighteenth-century Enlightenment, which venerated reason above all. Reason was to liberate man from the vagaries of oppressive custom and lead to "autonomy." Believing that rationality is an attribute only of humans, Kant concluded that we have a duty to act in accordance with that rational nature. But why? Only humans have the will to wage organized war; does that mean we have a duty to use that natural capacity? Only humans write gross jokes about defecating; do we have a duty to do so? There is a missing step in logic here.

Critics also point out that the unbending commitment to rules can itself lead to morally bad acts. For example, since one categorical moral rule is never to lie, one must then tell the murderer who knocks on the front door that yes, his desired victim, your brother, is hiding in the hall closet. Conversely, a pure Kantian rule might cause some to *avoid* good deeds. Karl Marx reportedly refused to give to beggars, believing that universal charity would dull the proletariat's zeal to bring forth the revolution that was their true salvation. In Kant's system, there are no practicalities, no exceptions.

CONFLICTING RULES

Another criticism is that Kantian morality doesn't seem to help when one absolute moral rule conflicts with another. If I am a Kantian, I must never use people instrumentally, as tools rather than ends in themselves. That's a noble principle, but isn't it also moral to try to save lives?

Consider this real-world dilemma: If I'm a police chief, should I send in seven members of my SWAT team, risking their lives trying to rescue a single hostage being held by a killer? They are being "used"—yet I'm trying to save a life, and isn't that the duty of a police officer? Kant's rule-based regime seems unhelpful here.

As I noted before, Kant avoids this problem by his very abstract distinction between perfect and imperfect duties, but that doesn't seem to bear much relation to how people experience them in real life. Suppose that I fall out of a deep-sea fishing boat and my friend just decides to motor on, because he "promised" to return the boat on time. In Kant's scheme, this is okay—because the promise is a "perfect" duty, while the duty to help is a subordinate, "imperfect" duty. In reality, everyone would view my friend's action as deeply immoral.

DIFFERENT DUTIES

Many are also troubled because the concept of categorical (uniform) moral rules ignores the fact that people have different moral duties due to the multiple social roles they fulfill. Kant focused on perfect duties defined by the reasoning capacity we all share. But what of the special duties we take on in particular social roles? A moral person might say, "I think this law is irrational, but as a police officer [or judge], it's still my duty to enforce it"; or "As a Catholic, I think this doctrine is wrong, but as a professor at a state university, it's my obligation to teach about it." Isn't there a difference between what one believes personally to be moral or right, and the duties that arise when we undertake certain social roles?

And what of one's duties to family or lifelong friends? For a fascinating contrast, consider the difficult moral choices faced by men in two families because of their brothers' evil conduct. One was William Bulger, a respected lawyer, president of the Massachusetts State Senate for almost 20 years, and later president of the University of Massachusetts. His brother was the notorious organized crime boss Whitey Bulger, then on the FBI's Ten Most Wanted List. When police asked William if he knew where his fugitive brother was hiding, he refused to talk. A prosecutor called William before the grand jury and asked, "So just to be clear, you feel more loyalty to your brother than you did to the people of . . . Massachusetts?" The reply was amazing: "I never thought about it that way. But I do have an honest loyalty to my brother, and I care about him . . . It's my hope that I'm never helpful to anyone against him . . . I don't have an obligation to help everyone catch him."

In fact, a citizen who is called as a witness *does* have a legal duty not to conceal what they know, and as a lawyer William Bulger surely knew that. It's one price of living in a democracy with an organized judicial system. William could say, "Yes, I have that duty, but I'm going to violate it and accept the penalty." But he was just wrong to say the duty didn't exist.

The second man was the brother of Ted Kaczynski, the notorious and feared Unabomber, who over a period of years killed three people and injured more than 20 by sending explosive packages through the mail. He eluded the law for almost two decades until 1996, when his own brother recognized his writing style in some published screeds—and reported him to the FBI, leading to his trial and incarceration.

Two men; two criminal brothers; two different moral conclusions. When does your duty to help protect the public from harm outweigh your duty of loyalty to your brother? Which principle, if either, is inviolate?

EXCEPTIONS

Yet another criticism of Kantian morality is that every good moral rule ("Do not kill") has legitimate exceptions (". . . except in self-defense, or to stop violent crime, or in war"); and the exceptions have their own conditions (". . . but even then, don't use more force than is reasonably needed, and try to avoid collateral harm"). Thus, a loyal Kantian who wants to follow fixed rules that are moral in all situations would need to fashion a very detailed, complex moral playbook. That is not practical in everyday life.

These are not abstract problems. For example, over several decades the psychology and psychiatry professions have anguished over the so-called *Tarasoff* doctrine. Psychotherapists have a moral and legal duty not to reveal patient confidences. Revealing them would destroy the patient's sense of privacy and trust. But what if a patient tells the therapist that he is so pissed off at being stopped by police for traffic infractions that he may "blow away" the next cop that stops him? Should the therapist call the police? What if the patient says he may blow away a specific person, such as his boss?

In the seminal 1976 *Tarasoff* case, an obsessed man had killed his girlfriend, a university grad student, after having told his therapist that he might, and the court ruled that the therapist had a "duty to warn." Soon the California legislature passed a law confirming that a psychotherapist has a duty to warn or protect a third party if the therapist believes that the patient poses a serious risk of causing serious bodily injury to an identifiable person.

Just look at the complexities of this one exception to the moral rule of therapist confidentiality. The therapist must try to decide, among other things: (1) Is the threat real or just verbalized frustration? (2) Exactly how likely is the harm? (3) Is the harm minor or "serious"? (What about property damage like defacing a person's car?) (4) Is the likely victim known, or less easily identified ("those loud jerks on motorcycles")? (5) Who does the therapist warn? and (6) Is warning an identifiable victim enough—or should the therapist also call the police or seek involuntary hospitalization of the patient?

In 2006 and then again in 2013, the California legislature passed laws supposedly clarifying the *Tarasoff* duty, but after decades, much confusion remained. Even good rules tend to get more complicated when you try to operationalize what is right in varied situations. Again, the seemingly clear Kantian "universal law" cannot avoid the complex tangles that often confront us in real life.

THE LARGER FRAMEWORK

Some fault Kant's rigid "universal and always" moral rules for ignoring how individual acts relate to larger problems like inequality or poverty. Is it always right for a bank to follow a rigid and objective credit rating algorithm when making loans? If so, then young people or new immigrants striving to start a business will rarely get loans. Is it always right to allocate human organs to patients who are most likely to live long? If so, then certain ethnic and racial groups will get most of the available organs, while others get very few. Is it always right to be "consistent" in criminal sentencing? Then the convicted woman with five small children will be given the same prison sentence as a single male, potentially shattering the lives of six people at once. Is it more important to stick to the rule in all situations, or should we consider the effects on real people and their problems? Is the point of morality just feeling at peace with our principles—or actually creating a "good" result?

LACK OF REALISM

A final criticism of the Kantian approach is that it doesn't describe anything like the way people actually make moral decisions. Karen Stohr notes that to some, "Kant's theory has seemed overly abstract and even cold in its emphasis on rationality rather than emotion." It succumbs to what Jonathan Haidt calls "the rationalist delusion."

Experience shows that often, people don't follow logical rules; they have biases, feelings, and blind spots. They manufacture reasons to justify what feels right. Kant's rule regime also doesn't seem to explain the sudden and instinctive moral choices people make. Sometimes people dive into situations to help or save others, and sometimes they don't. During disasters, some people decide on the spot to go to the site and help others, but most of the time, they just go about their daily lives. People often lie and cheat in little ways, yet most of the time they don't. These people are not considering what universal rule would be best; they're just reacting to particular situations. Kant's unwavering, logic-based approach strikes many critics as being divorced from the reality of human nature.

RECONCILING INTENT AND IMPACT: THE DOCTRINE OF DOUBLE EFFECT

Many people attracted to the clarity of Kantian rationalism have tried to reconcile its emphasis solely on intent with the reality of a world in which effects matter to most people. One way out of this problem traces back to the "doctrine of double effect," formulated by the thirteenth-century Catholic theologian Thomas Aquinas.

Aquinas said that an act with some bad effect can still be moral if its main purpose is to achieve a good outcome and the bad consequence is just an unavoidable collateral effect (hence the "double effect"). This doctrine is widely recognized in criminal law, policing, bioethics, and military action, as well as everyday life. For example, it's usually immoral (and a crime) to knock a bystander to the ground, but it might be defensible if you are pushing them aside to save another person who fainted and is falling onto the subway tracks. It's viewed as ethical in double-blind medical trials to require half the participants (the control group) to undergo possibly unpleasant procedures without knowing whether they are getting the "real" treatment. They are being used in a way that Kantians normally consider immoral. But comparing groups who do and don't receive the real treatment is the only way to obtain reliable medical knowledge that can benefit *all* patients.

The doctrine of double effect recognizes that, if our moral system didn't accept causing any harm to anyone at any time, no matter the purpose or justification, we would wind up doing far less good in the world than we could.

But would it be moral for a physician to go even farther in using a person as a means to an end by pressuring her to donate a kidney to her sister who needs one to live? He is treating her as a tool—but ostensibly for a good cause. The doctrine of double effect clarifies the moral issue, but doesn't resolve it. Aquinas himself hedges about the acceptability of secondary effects, saying, "And yet though proceeding from a good intention, an act may be regarded as unlawful [if] it will be out of proportion to the end"—in other words, if you should have seen that greater harm would result. But how do we judge "proportion"? Those who would engage in so-called honor killing believe they are vindicating the paramount virtue of family honor and social order. How do we dissuade them morally?

Take yet another step. Morally, how can one *refuse* to use another person as a means if it will achieve a greater good? Marcus Luttrell, a heroic Navy SEAL who fought the Taliban in Afghanistan and was portrayed in the book and movie *Lone Survivor,* faced an impossible choice. He and his four-man team had to decide whether to kill an innocent goatherd who happened upon their unit and might reveal their location to the enemy. Since he was a noncombatant, they chose not to kill him. But when the herder did tell the Taliban the SEAL team's location, all except Luttrell were killed, along with a large helicopter rescue team. Luttrell's action was humane and heroic. But as he himself wonders, was it morally right?

The doctrine of double effect leads to countless conundrums, which have led many philosophers to critique it. Often in life, there may be several ways of attaining a given goal. They have uncertain chances of success and hard-to-predict side effects. So, knowing when to accept a bad side effect to get to a good result is rarely simple.

We might also question whether the doctrine of double effect really severs effect from intent. Consider the issue of physicians' compassionate assistance in a terminal patient's death. As ethicist Jonathan Baron writes, "Pennsylvania does not permit the use of lethal drugs such as morphine for the purpose of euthanasia, but it does permit the use of the same drugs for the purpose of pain relief. It is thus legal for a physician to give morphine to a dying patient, knowing that the drug will hasten death by suppressing respiration, and desiring that result, as long as the [main] 'intent' is to relieve pain." Is administering a lethal drug for the purpose of pain relief rather than for the purpose of ending life a distinction without a difference—if you know death will occur? Or is there still a moral difference?

For an especially consequential example of the tension between intent and effect, consider the moral quandary President Truman faced in deciding whether to approve the first use of the atomic bomb. At first blush, it seems horribly evil. Yet he sought to avoid the need to invade the Japanese homeland, a campaign that advisors predicted would result in hundreds of thousands of U.S. military deaths and several times that many Japanese deaths. Here are a few relevant facts: Some 30,000 had died in the battle for the insignificant rock known as Iwo Jima, and 130,000-240,000 died in the Japanese defense of

Okinawa. Perhaps 100,000 Japanese civilians died in the conventional fire-bombing of Tokyo in March 1945; then the U.S. firebombed 67 more Japanese cities in the succeeding few months, killing hundreds of thousands more. The Japanese still did not surrender.

How does all that affect the morality of killing an estimated 110,000–200,000 in the bombing of Hiroshima and Nagasaki, thereby ending the horrendous war, but beginning the nuclear age?

Here is another way to ask the question: Did Truman have a moral option *not* to try to save lives by using the atomic bomb? Would it have been moral for him to conclude, "Yes, the bomb will save a vast number of lives, but I couldn't live with myself if I ordered an atomic attack, and I value my moral virtue more than saving those lives"? Would such self-focus on virtue have been virtuous?

The question is complicated by further uncertainties. Some have claimed that Truman's action was a blunder: An offshore bomb test, they say, would have been enough to cause Japanese surrender, if the experimental bomb had detonated right. How sure about such alternative scenarios do you need to be for your decision *not* to drop the bomb to be moral? And as we assess Truman's decision with the value of hindsight, does it make any difference that we have now had 80 years without further use of nuclear weapons? Or, since that was unknowable to Truman, is it irrelevant to the Kantian "good will" of his decision at the time and thus its moral quality?

Defending Kant

Despite its flaws, the Kantian moral framework still has many adherents today, who say its supposed weaknesses are overstated. They point out that Kant doesn't totally ignore everyday duties, even "imperfect" ones. For example, Kant acknowledges that "to be kind where one can is a duty"; "to preserve one's life is a duty"; and even "to secure one's own happiness is a duty" (at least indirectly) because unhappy people may be tempted to do ill to others. So, Kant is not as rigid as some of his statements suggest.

Also, modern Kantians use his approach while accommodating the complexities of modern life. They preserve his emphasis on the moral value of good intent alone rather unpredictable consequences, but they allow flexibility. Thus, they argue that "[Kantian] Non-consequentialism does not deny that consequences can be a factor in determining the rightness of an act"—just that consequences shouldn't be the final measure.

To these Kantians, morality is derived from reason, but it is the reason of human beings who evolved to get along in cooperative social groups. They point out that one of the main functions of morality is to enable people to predict others' behavior, to rely on it, and thus to make social relations more stable. Clear Kantian rules may help people do that. For instance, if I know that most people in my society, even those I don't know, will refrain from treachery and theft, that encourages me to engage in new social and commercial relations. In this respect, the seemingly rigid, rule-based Kantian approach is practical and leads to good consequences. And Kant's cold "reason" wasn't immune to inspired emotion. He said, "Two things fill the mind with ever new and increasing admiration: the starry heavens above and the moral law within."

Still, you may be unconvinced that Kantian always-and-without-exception rules will work well in your life. If so, the next chapter offers two widely respected alternatives.

3

Moral Feelings and Utilitarianism

Hume and Moral Sentiments

"THERE HAS BEEN A CONTROVERSY STARTED OF LATE ... concerning the general foundation of morals; whether they be derived from reason, or from [emotional] sentiment; whether we attain the knowledge of them by a chain of argument and induction, or by an immediate feeling and finer internal sense." Thus did David Hume pose the question in 1748. Where Kant focused on abstract reason, the empiricist Hume argued that people arrive at knowledge only through the sensory "impressions" that come to us from the world. We form ideas that are internal—but imperfect—"copies" of those experiences. Then we learn from layer upon layer of perceptions and form ideas from them—and this, according to Hume, is the basis of rational judgment.

But what does that mean for morality? Hume said that one cannot "derive an ought from an is"—that is, infer what *should be* based on what *factually is so* at present. This has been widely viewed as creating an unbridgeable chasm between fact and value. (But see the Notes.) It implies that no matter how many facts one assembles about the evil effects of lying, rape, or torture, it wouldn't be enough to prove their *badness*—which is a moral overlay, not a pure deduction from facts.

Strictly logically, this may make sense. But for most people, this impossible gap between fact and value does not ring true.

Many have objected that sometimes you really can infer an "ought" from an "is." For example, the fact that a person is making a promise does mean that they ought to fulfill the promise (absent stronger moral reasons not to). The very meaning of the word "promise" is to commit to a moral obligation to do something. Denying that moral meaning would make "promise" an oxymoronic concept—the concept of a promise an oxymoron—a commitment that does not entail a commitment. It would be like saying, "Just because I love you doesn't mean I *ought to* care whether you live or die." Yes, actually, it does.

But Hume's point is right in some respects. The implication of "ought to" is far from clear in many instances where people try to derive value judgments from facts. For example, if someone says, "That man is hungry; you ought to give him money for food," or "That woman needs a job; you ought to hire her," the moral conclusion isn't irresistible, and you can imagine reasons to disagree (e.g., they are both bad criminals who don't deserve special treatment.)

Hume's insight is a useful corrective to conflating facts and values. It reminds us that asserting a moral obligation always requires providing a *reason* why it is so. Hume wanted to emancipate moral thinking from narrow social convention; he was in this sense a reformer. He rejected the idea that religious intolerance was right just because it was then common, or that since slavery was widely practiced, it must be moral. Instead, he made "an attempt to introduce the experimental Method of Reasoning into Moral Subjects." In his view, a science of man depended on "experience and observation" of how people actually judge moral questions, rather than just abstract philosophizing. He said, "Be a philosopher, but amid all your philosophy, be still a man."

So how to deal with the gap between facts and moral values? In Hume's view, morality is largely a matter of how you feel—your instinctive "sentiments." To many people, this seems wrong at first. My feeling of sympathy for someone stumbling and falling in the street might well be affected by whether they are pleasant-looking or disgusting—but surely that can't change the morality of helping them. But Hume believed that people have noble as well as base instincts, and that society can foster the former by paying attention to the role of emotions in morality.

Hume's point was that, in practice, people often do make moral judgments based on their "sentiments," that is, their gut instincts, rather than by rigorously applying abstract principles. (For a real-world example of the Humean "moral sentiments" way of thinking, consider the famous statement of President George W. Bush: "I don't spend a lot of time taking polls around the world to tell me what is the right way to act. I've just got to know how I feel.") As Hume said, pleasure and pain motivate us, and "it is for them to point out what we ought to do as well as to determine what we shall do." Thus, "morality is more properly felt than justified."

But it is important to realize that Hume did *not* mean "don't think about morals; just follow your gut." Hume agreed that there is a role for thinking as well as feeling. Thus, "*after* every circumstance, every relation is known, the judgment has *no further room to operate* . . . [so] the approbation or blame which then ensues cannot be the work of the judgment, but of the heart . . . an active feeling or sentiment." Rather conveniently for his theory, Hume also believed that emotion and reason usually do not diverge at the end of the day. On the contrary, "much reasoning should precede" moral judgment, and in the end, "reason and sentiment concur in almost all moral . . . conclusions." Thus, it has "seemed to many that much of [Hume's *Treatise*] . . . was not philosophy at all, but an early form of empirical psychology."

Hume has at least drawn attention to how many of us resolve a moral dilemma. We think: "Gee, what I told my boss was dead wrong. I should let him know. But he'll be real mad. Maybe it won't matter in the end, so I'll let it slide. But then I'll keep worrying about it, and if he finds out, he won't ever trust me again . . . Oh, what the heck, I'll just 'fess up.'" In real life, logical thinking, facts, duties, and emotional reactions all get intertwined. But in Hume's view, "sentiments" ultimately prevail.

Hume famously declared that "reason is and ought only to be the slave of the passions, and can never pretend to any other office than to serve and obey them." So, "the rules of morality are not conclusions of our reason." Hume was pointing toward an empirical assessment of how people form their moral judgments; he wasn't trying to justify irrational evil impulses. (Interestingly, Hume described himself as possessed of "great moderation in all my passions," and history records him as one of the few philosophers who was a very pleasant fellow. While proclaiming the supremacy of emotions, reportedly he was himself eminently reasonable. Go figure.)

Hume was a skeptic, stressing the limits of inductive generalizations. But in his moral theory, he confidently generalized:

> The same motives always produce the same actions. . . . Ambition, avarice, self-love, vanity, friendship, generosity, public spirit; these passions, mixed in various degrees and distributed through society, have been from the beginning of the world, and still are, the source of all actions and enterprises which have ever been observed among mankind. Would you [like to] know the sentiments, inclinations and course of life of the Greeks and Romans? . . . Mankind are so much the same, in all times and places, that history informs us of nothing new or strange. . . .

Following Hume, many philosophers and psychologists today believe that "moral sense or intuition is an initially more plausible description of what supplies many of our basic moral judgments than reason." Psychologist Jonathan Haidt says Hume began a "social intuitionist model of moral judgments" that is largely confirmed by modern research. As we'll see later in this chapter and in Chapter 6, Hume's empiricism is supported by extensive studies of the genetic, biological, and emotional drivers of what we usually think are our free and rational moral judgments.

The Enlightenment often portrayed emotions and reason as opposites always at war. That view remains popular in some circles. Centuries later, it was echoed by Rose Sayer, the Methodist missionary played by Katharine Hepburn in the movie *The African Queen,* who pithily informed the mechanic Charlie Alnutt, played by Humphrey Bogart, "Human nature, Mr. Alnutt, is what we are put into this world *to rise above.*" But to psychologists, this binary, Manichean view is inaccurate. Instead, they view emotions as "a meeting place of mind, body and behavior"—a place where thinking and feeling interact, leading to moral conclusions.

Of course, our personal "sentiments" don't just spring up randomly. As we saw, humans have some degree of "wired in" moral nature. Then we are influenced by the society we happen to be born into. For example, it has been found that individualistic societies tend to rely on moral suasion based on the feeling of guilt (my own conscience), while collectivist societies tend to rely more on shame (what my community will think). But either way, our moral judgments are influenced by our emotions.

What Research Tells Us About Emotions and Morals

HUME'S EMPIRICIST VIEW THAT MORALITY EMANATES from our inborn sentiments has been buttressed by psychological research over recent decades. As one expert concludes, "People make moral judgments quickly and emotionally," not based on careful moral calculations. This "social intuitionist" view of moral thinking, rather than a Kantian rationalist view, is now clearly ascendant. To begin, psychologists like Paul Rozin, Simone Schnall, and Jonathan Haidt have documented the "ick" factor in some moral judgments. We react emotionally to whether something disgusts us viscerally, and then we find reasons to condemn it morally. Thus, there is a primordial connection between our repulsion at things like spoiled food, carrion, or feces and our repulsion at some behaviors. This is why we say things like "Your behavior disgusts me," or "Your morals are repulsive." As Antonio Damasio notes, "Many of the actions in the human disgust program, including its typical facial expressions [screwing up one's nose, turning down the mouth] have been co-opted by a social emotion—*contempt*. Contempt is often a metaphor for moral disgust."

Neuroscientist Robert Sapolsky reports that the insular cortex in the brain lights up when we confront morally repulsive behavior, in the same way as when we eat rancid food. Thus, "someone does something lousy and selfish to you in a game, and the extent of insular and amygdaloid activation predicts how much outrage you feel and how much revenge you will take." Some things are seen as not only immoral, but also disgusting (sex between siblings, eating one's deceased pet dog, hitting a nun, stealing a ring from the finger of a dazed woman in a hospital bed). Our gut emotions tell us these acts are truly evil, even though their effects may be less harmful than lots of other bad acts we could list. Our gut is not always a reliable index to badness.

Relying on gut instincts when we make moral decisions doesn't mean that we will usually act meanly or selfishly. On the contrary, experience shows that the instinctive response of most people to seeing a person in need is a desire to help. Only a moment later does our reason tell us, "No, I better not get involved." Moreover, our gut reactions aren't random feelings but a system of socially reinforced responses.

Having studied these complexities, most psychologists today reject the "prevalent but useless dichotomy between cognition and emotion" in morals. Instead, emotion and cognition are intertwined. Indeed, leading researcher

Damasio concludes that without the aid of emotions, we would find it hard to make all the routine decisions required in life. Increasingly, research supports the general view, as described by Haidt, that "affect or 'feeling' is the first process [of decision]. It has primacy both because it happens first (it is part of perception and is therefore extremely fast) and because it is more powerful. . . . The thinking system is not equipped to lead—it simply doesn't have the power to make things happen—but it can be a useful adviser."

Haidt uses the metaphor that in making moral decisions, reason is a small rider atop a huge elephant of emotion—ultimately, the elephant is going where it wants to go. He says, "The first principle [of moral psychology is that] intuitions come first; strategic reasoning second." And Haidt sees that second step as largely "post hoc constructions made up on the fly."

Others, such as Paul Bloom, Marc Hauser, and Joshua Greene, regard this as too extreme. They point out that people genuinely wrestle with moral dilemmas, challenge their own intuitions, feel guilt and remorse, and sometimes change their judgments. Our moral thinking, then, is not all self-justification. There is a well-documented "dual process" of deciding, featuring both the quick and intuitive part and the slower, more deliberative part. This recalls Pascal's comment that "the two principles of truth, reason and sense, are not only both unreliable, but are engaged in mutual deception."

One reason to doubt that morals are driven only by emotion is that an emotion is too crude a tool—and the emotions in our tool kit are too few—to be relied on to resolve all the myriad moral situations we face. Think of this simple example: Emotionally, I get angry when someone hits me. Sure, I can be more or less mad, but that's about it. Yet I react in lots of very different, complex ways to being hit in various contexts: by a buddy slapping me on the back; by a drunk buddy who punches me; by a doctor hitting my knee to test it; by a stranger who obliviously runs into me on the street; by a friend with whom I'm boxing; by a boxer who strikes me with a "low blow"; by a criminal who's trying to steal my wallet; or by an opposing soldier in hand-to-hand combat in war. The moral judgments I apply in these situations are far more nuanced than just "more mad or less mad." Philosopher Jesse Prinz describes the process as involving a sequence: perception, judgment of meaning, categorization of the action, associated emotion, and moral conclusion.

We tend to think that emotion will drive us to do bad things (steal a woman's purse), while reason will restrain us (jail isn't much fun). But you could just as easily imagine even a criminal reasoning, "I can definitely get away with this crime," but then feeling that "I don't really want to steal from an old lady." Or rationally, a manager may know that her company needs to fire some employees in order to stay afloat, but emotionally, she can't bring herself to do it even though it is the "right" action to avoid even more layoffs. So, emotions can lead us toward morally good or bad actions—and the same is true of reasoning.

HOW DO WE BALANCE EMOTIONS AND REASON IN THE REAL WORLD?

The Humean view ("Go with your gut") is often considered more realistic than the Kantian ("Always follow the principle"). And sometimes, what feels right actually is right. But bear in mind that always following your gut will probably result in some troubling inconsistency.

Consider how the average person morally appraises these two situations: (1) A man sits calmly on the beach while observing a child drowning some way from shore; and (2) A man sits calmly on his sofa while watching a TV news clip of thousands of people starving in Africa.

To most people, the first man's conduct is horrible or at least disturbing, while the second is just another Tuesday night. Yet this contrast is difficult to defend as rational—surely if one has a moral duty to try to save one child, one has a duty to do something to save at least a few of the thousands. The theorists of reason twist themselves into pretzel shapes to reconcile this kind of contradiction. But the truth seems to be that for good or ill, we are emotional Humeans, and emotions dictate our response. Given human nature, the child nearby matters—but the distant multitudes, not so much. For evolutionary reasons, we feel immediate empathy for a person who is nearby and a member of our tribe, but less so for the world at large. We evolved to care about individuals, not vast populations. That's why charitable organizations find it more effective to ask for donations to help *one child* rather than thousands.

If you are a committed Humean empiricist, it seems that you must just accept this kind of irrationality attached to many of your moral intuitions. It's hard to deny the Humean view that people often make moral judgments by sensing their own gut instincts about right and wrong—and only then conjuring conscious reasons to support those instincts. But how satisfied are we with the results?

It's far from obvious that we are generally more moral when we think with our hearts rather than our heads.

Bloom goes farther in his book *Against Empathy*. He argues that even a supposedly "good" feeling like empathy is a badly flawed guide to morals. Empathy, he says, is different from compassion, and far different from morality. "It is reason [not empathy] that leads us to recognize, despite what our feelings tell us, that a child in a faraway land matters as much as our neighbor's child," or that drug research for disease is moral even though some people incur painful side effects. In such circumstances, Bloom says reason is a better guide than empathy to arriving at good results.

Similarly, Jonathan Baron has outlined many ways that "intuitions [feelings] cause trouble" in moral thinking about public policy issues. This is because we imagine our instincts to be more reliable than they are and allow vague feelings to become rules without exceptions. Are we sure that a "feeling" that the United States should always "help" by intervening in a foreign ethnic conflict will prove to be a reliable guide in the long run? The evidence from history is mixed at best. Baron also points out that our emotional fear of causing any harm sometimes leads to more harm, such as by not requiring vaccinations or not enacting tougher manufacturing safety regulations.

Even aside from empathy, our feelings can at times be poor guides to right conduct. Consider what you mean when you say that something is "only fair." Suppose that you buy one lottery ticket from your friend who bought ten, and yours wins. Do you have a moral duty to share the windfall with him, at least a little? (And what if he *gave you* the ticket?) If you are like many people, you say Yes, because it just feels right. Then how do you feel about the woman who buys a painting at a flea market and then finds it's a valuable work by a famous artist? Both seller and buyer were just mistaken. Should she go back and share her windfall with the vendor? What about someone who buys your house for $300,000, then luckily flips it a year later for $400,000; should they share some of their windfall? Does calling an event a "windfall" rather than a "profit" change anything morally?

Along the same lines, consider people's moral indignation about attorneys' fees in lawsuits. Many people instinctively feel that: (1) if they bring a lawsuit and win, the other side should pay their legal fees; (2) if they bring a lawsuit and lose, they shouldn't have to pay the other side's fees; (3) if they are sued and win, the other side should pay all legal fees; but (4) if they are sued and lose, each side should bear its own fees. There is no way to reconcile these feelings about what is morally fair—except by believing that "I am righteous, but you are not." This has been dubbed "bounded ethicality," meaning that we think ethically *up to a point only*—after which we don't. Instead, we just make up reasons to support what we feel. (More on that in Chapter 6.)

But all this still doesn't mean that reason is sidelined as irrelevant. Suppose someone shoves me from behind; my first reaction is anger—the offender is a jerk. Then I turn and see that he's a blind man, so my reason kicks in, and my moral outrage evaporates. Or consider what happens at work if I get angry about a subordinate who aggressively "questions my judgment." I don't just get mad; I start erecting all sorts of "rational" reasons why she is a bad person (she's too ambitious; she comes from a rich family and thinks she's better than others). But when I start venting to a colleague, I hear another side of the story: actually, she's a hard worker, collegial, always helps peers when they're in a jam, and she's just offering ideas that might help. Suddenly, my "reason" perceives "reasons" why my gut instinct may have been wrong. Thus, in real life, gut instinct and reason frequently play ping-pong with one another as we try to evaluate the moral quality of a situation.

Humeans say the Kantian approach to morality, centered on rigid rules and duties, isn't realistic. But a Humean approach that relies solely on emotion is equally unrealistic. People generally are not totally satisfied just following their gut instincts; they wrestle with their consciences, too. Heroes throughout history (Abraham, Moses, Agamemnon, Brutus, Hamlet, Othello, Raskolnikov, Lincoln, and the protagonist in every movie about a figure riddled by angst) have been portrayed as tormented by moral uncertainty, struggling with conscience, trying to figure out the right thing to do. We empathize with such heroes' moral struggles, because we have all experienced some of our own. We say things like "I hate to do it, but I'm supposed to," or "It's the right thing, but it just feels bad," or "I don't know, I need to figure that one out."

None of those examples reflect people simply following their gut instinct. Researchers have confirmed that "efforts to resolve such ambivalence are potentially difficult, protracted and aversive [i.e., painful]." Struggling with moral dilemmas is stressful. Yet we routinely engage in what one scholar calls "imaginative moral deliberation."

Not only that, but having made what we hope is the right moral decision, we defend ourselves as being rationally consistent. We try to explain why we acted one way in a given situation but the opposite way in another, by coming up with a sensible "rule." We feel that acting morally means that we should be able to justify our actions as based on more than just how we felt that day.

Hume focused on the constantly changing flux of perceptions, which provide no reliable moral principles. But psychologist William James proposed a more balanced view: "Hume says [the Self] is nothing but Diversity . . . whereas in truth it is that mixture of unity and diversity . . . [H]e denies this thread of resemblance, this core of sameness running through the ingredients of the Self." In reality, each of us continually works to "hold ourselves together," to form and sustain a sense of self as a moral being—which means finding ways to combine emotion with reason. We may succeed or fail to varying degrees, but we all try.

So, if you are a Humean follow-my-gut kind of person, you still probably wonder whether you're right when faced with a truly difficult moral dilemma. When that happens, gut instinct may not seem like enough, and you yearn for some kind of reliable, general moral guideline. Read on for another moral framework that promises such guidance.

Morality Based on the Greatest Good (Utilitarianism)

IN A MASSIVE 2020 SURVEY of philosophers worldwide, about one fifth believed that actions are right or wrong regardless of consequences (the Kantian approach), but a slightly greater percentage subscribed to the approach known as *consequentialism*. The most prominent version of consequentialism is the theory that emerged, in the nineteenth century, in the works of Jeremy Bentham, John Stuart Mill, Henry Sidgwick, and others—*utilitarianism*.

These thinkers sought a morality that was progressive, objective, and scientific. They wanted to place morality on solid ground that could be defended against those who thought it was little more than Humean sentiment, taste, or custom. As Jeremy Bentham famously enjoined, "Take reason, not custom, as your guide." But they also rejected the Kantian view that reason can only justify intentions, not effects, and that rules of conduct must be applied without exception. Bentham wrote that there couldn't be any absolute list of moral rules "because they are susceptible to no arrangement; they are a disorderly body, whose members are frequently in hostility with one another. . . . Most of them are characterized by that vagueness which is a convenient instrument to the poetical, but dangerous or useless to the practical moralist." Likewise, Sidgwick declared that his book *The Methods of Ethics* is "not, in the main, [either] metaphysical or psychological." It is neither Kant nor Hume. Instead, it seeks to ground morality "in the moral consciousness of mankind generally," and this led him to "Utilitarianism again, but on an intuitional basis."

So what solution did the utilitarians propose? That moral conduct requires us, given the facts of each situation, to do whatever *will bring the greatest happiness to the most affected people*. Note that in the word utilitarianism, "utility" has the meaning economists give it. It doesn't mean "usefulness" in merely the mechanical sense; instead, it means anything to which people attach value. Even some of its supporters agree that utilitarianism is an "awful name, suggesting [merely] a preoccupation with the mundanely functional," but it now has too much history to be abandoned.

This core idea is in stark contrast with Kantian views. Kant believed one must have the right motive and obey the right principle for the sake of the principle itself. By contrast, Mill wrote: "He who saves a fellow creature from drowning does what is morally right whether his motive be duty or hope of being paid." What matters is the good effect, not the motive.

But just what effects should we count in our moral calculus? Proponents of *act utilitarianism* believe you should assess solely the effects of your direct action in the given situation. Thus, if lying at a given time results in net good, do it.

Others endorse *rule utilitarianism*, acting based not only on the good effects of your specific act, but also its impact on maintaining social rules that cause overall good. Bentham said "the principle of utility . . . approves or disapproves of every action . . . *according to the tendency which it appears to have* to augment or diminish the happiness of the party whose interest is in question." Note the subtle difference here: Morality pivots on the apparent *tendency* of an action to do good, rather than its actual impact in a given case. In a sense, rule utilitarianism seeks to hybridize Kantian principles with utilitarian assessment of effects. So, whereas act utilitarianism "enjoins us, on every single occasion, to perform the act that will maximize total utility *on that occasion*, . . . [rule utilitarianism] tells us to act according to the rule that, when followed invariably, will maximize *total utility over time*."

These two kinds of utilitarianism can yield different conclusions. An example of rule utilitarianism in practice is the legal rule requiring the exclusion of illegally seized evidence from being presented in criminal trials. We adopt an absolute rule ("no illegally obtained evidence") even though it occasionally means that a really bad guy goes free and goodness is reduced. This is based on the rule utilitarian judgment that the overall social benefit of citizens feeling secure from illegal police searches while in their homes outweighs the cost of failing to convict some real criminals. And having adopted this legal rule, we don't make exceptions, even when a particular defendant is obviously guilty. (In this respect, it echoes the Kantian view.)

A further refinement is sometimes called *welfare utilitarianism*, which asks not just about the total net happiness resulting from a rule or act but whether it also contributes to a *just distribution* of happiness within society. The fact that strict utilitarianism seemed to pay no attention to inequalities troubled many people. It implied that a utilitarian should not care whether an action brings just one more unit of happiness to the richest person in the world or to an oppressed poor person. There is a partial response to this in the economic concept of *declining marginal utility*, which is essentially the idea that the more you have of something, the less each added increment means to you. Thus, since the same bag of groceries will make no difference to the rich family but a lot of difference to the poor one, if we have just one bag, we should give it to the poor. Welfare utilitarianism asks more broadly how we can take actions that not only increase overall happiness, but also achieve some decent distribution of happiness.

Sometimes, though not always, utilitarianism leads to different moral conclusions than would the frameworks of Kant or Hume. Consider criminal sentencing. From a utilitarian perspective, it might be justified for a judge to impose an especially harsh sentence for a given crime (say, spouse abuse or sex with minors) on a famous athlete, because the sentence will be widely publicized and have the good effect of deterring many others. But to a Kantian, this wrongly uses the athlete as a tool simply to achieve a larger purpose. And to a Humean, it may or may not feel right to hammer the athlete just because he happens to be famous.

For a more complex example, consider affirmative action in college admissions. To a utilitarian, providing a leg up for racial minorities may be a moral practice in order to overcome prior discrimination, foster hope and ambition, and build diverse leadership in social institutions. But to a pure Kantian, it is never moral to use some people (say, White) to their detriment as a mere tool or means to achieve benefits for others (say, Black). Some Kantians might bend and support affirmative action, by asserting that their will is good in seeking benefits for everyone (by making it possible for all to live in a more just society), but then they would fall hip-deep into measuring consequences, which the Kantian approach supposedly disavows. Meanwhile, some Humeans might say that it just feels wrong to penalize a college applicant because she is White, while other Humeans might say it feels wrong to perpetuate a system in which most Black students attend bad high schools and can't fairly compete for top college admissions.

The utilitarians reply that they have a potent tool for solving such conundrums: summing up the total good and bad consequences to all who are affected. You would try to measure the benefit to the favored minority students (times their number) versus the penalty to those they replace (times their number), and adjust for any good or bad effects on the rest of society. This seems sensible—but how in the world would you do it? And many still would not see this process as fair. (See the Notes.)

Consequentialism strives to provide a moral framework that is mathematical or scientific in its objectivity. One scholar describes it as "a moral doctrine which says that the right act in any given situation is the one that will produce the best overall outcome, as judged from an impersonal standpoint [and] which gives equal weight to the interests of everyone." As Mill said, when a person must choose between actions that benefit himself and those that benefit others, "utilitarianism requires him to be as strictly impartial as a disinterested and benevolent spectator." This means that one can't disregard the strong interests of others simply because you don't like their life choices—for example, if they are spoiled and wasteful rich people, religious fundamentalists living in a commune, political extremists, or alcoholics living on public welfare. Conversely, no extra weight is given to someone who has "good" desires, like composing symphonies rather than sitting on the sofa playing video games. Under the strict utilitarian model, every person's happiness is of equal worth (though at times utilitarians compromise on this).

The utilitarian goal of seeking the greatest good for the greatest number of people seems intuitively sensible, which is one reason utilitarianism continues to be influential. It helps to reconcile the painful fact that moral rules and moral duties often conflict with one another, leaving us confused. Should you miss your daughter's school play to visit your elderly mom who says she isn't feeling well? Should you let down your team at work who are crashing on a big project, because you promised to help a friend move out of her apartment? Do you become a whistleblower because, while the company duly paid your salary for 20 years and promoted you, now it's skimping on safety measures on its products?

At some point, simply invoking a Kantian "Do the right thing" or a Humean "Do what feels right" doesn't seem sufficient. You need to weigh competing good and bad effects, and utilitarianism provides a framework for doing so.

As Henry Sidgwick noted in his influential defense of utilitarianism, *The Methods of Ethics,* the recurring problem is the "dualism of practical reason"— that the "good thing" and the "right thing" may not always be the same, as when the good is not achievable. It may not be right to run into a blazing building when there is in fact no chance of saving anyone. To Sidgwick, one must always reason practically about what is moral. He said, "Reflection on Common Sense Morality . . . had continually brought home to me its character as a system of rules tending to the *promotion of general happiness.*" We need guidance on how to weigh two alternative good things, or two bad things, or things with varying degrees of goodness and badness. Utilitarianism offers a commonsense method: Assess the overall consequences to the happiness of the affected people.

In fact, taking anything *other than* the utilitarian approach would commit you to saying that "at times, my morality requires me to do things that I know are worse overall for the affected people." As the philosopher Philippa Foot observed, utilitarianism is "the rather simple thought that it can never be right to prefer a worse state of affairs to a better [one]." Who can argue with that? In fact, aren't there situations where it's immoral to *refuse to* harm one person if necessary to save a larger number of people (e.g., quarantining a person arriving in the country sick with a dread infectious disease)? In such situations, isn't the utilitarian rule the only one that makes sense?

Still, a number of objections to utilitarianism deserve to be considered seriously.

What kind of "greatest good"?

While the "greatest good" maxim may seem morally irresistible, to many it is not.

First, is the greatest happiness for the greatest number necessarily the right moral starting point? Some would argue that instead of maximum happiness and pleasure, our goal should be to execute God's will here on earth.

(It is reported that when someone proposed to Martin Luther that happiness was the true goal of life, he "violently rejected the idea, saying, '[No, it is] . . . suffering . . . the Cross.'") This has been the general stance of theocratic societies (ruled by priests or holy figures) throughout history.

Others may believe the ultimate goal of life is to maximize human achievement through ceaseless effort. Or that the goal should be ever more knowledge or enlightenment, even at the cost of struggle and perhaps suffering. Many people, such as research scientists, career military, and international relief workers, forsake elements of what most people see as happiness in service to an arduous mission. Utilitarians might argue that these are just different ways to seek "happiness," but that simply expands the term to mean almost anything, leading to the tautology that "happiness is whatever you actually do." Yet we know this isn't so, beginning with the fact that some people continually make themselves miserable.

Mill said that considering all the "evidence" of "fact and experience" led him to this analogy: "The only proof . . . that an object is visible is that people actually see it. . . . In like manner, . . . the sole evidence it is possible to produce that anything is desirable is that people do actually desire it." But this idea that whatever is desired is desirable and hence a "utility" has been criticized as logically flawed and circular by such distinguished thinkers as Bertrand Russell, G. E. Moore, Bernard Gert, and others. To Russell, this is "an argument so fallacious that it is hard to understand how he [Mill] can have thought it valid."

Mill was plainly wrong on this point. (See the Notes.) Visible means only that something can be or is seen; but desirable means not only that it can be desired but also that it is *worthy* of being desired. Some men desire exploitative, abusive, and even violent encounters with women—but no one would rightly say these are desires to which we should attach any moral weight. And consider the converse case: Aren't some things highly desirable even though people at a given time don't even think to desire them? For thousands of years, people never thought to attach value to clean air; it was everywhere. Today, in some nations, it is not. So we must consider what values are "in" or "out" of the utilitarian calculus by reference to more than what someone says is or is not desired.

Is utilitarianism just unrealistic?

Practicing utilitarian morality isn't easy, and sometimes it seems impossible. Logically, it requires us to assess not only the effects of our actions, but what would happen if we acted differently. This is a big job not entailed by the Kantian or Humean approaches. As Judea Pearl has said, "Counterfactuals are the building blocks of moral behavior. The ability to reflect on one's past actions and envision alternative scenarios is the basis of free will and social responsibility." Every moral judgment must consciously or unconsciously consider: What would happen if I did not do x, or if I did y instead of x?

Assessing those alternative scenarios could make moral calculations almost impossibly complex. But occasionally, it simplifies them. That is why a firing squad was long used for executions. The fact that several members of a firing squad all shoot toward the same convicted traitor blurs moral responsibility for the execution; no one knows for sure that their bullet caused death, and they do know that even if they hadn't fired or had missed on purpose, the person would have died anyway. Thus, the firing squad method enabled normal people to kill those deemed offenders without refusing on the spot or being endlessly tormented by moral qualms.

To a Kantian dedicated to good will, or a Humean reflecting on whether the action feels right, participating in the firing squad is horrible. To a utilitarian, his role does not have as much actual consequence, and hence, it carries less moral weight.

As I noted, a major criticism of the utilitarian approach is that it demands too much of people and thus is, in the words of philosopher Bernard Williams, merely "an ethics of fantasy." The requirement that we accord no special weight to our own interests and those of our family, and always do what's best for everyone overall, runs counter to many of our instincts and values. As psychologist Joshua Greene says, "The ideal utilitarian 'moral diet' is simply incompatible with the life for which our brains were designed. . . . [We] were not designed to care deeply about the happiness of strangers."

In addition, if taken literally, utilitarian ethics would require a brilliant medical researcher to work 18 hours every day and never take a vacation, because her personal comfort is so much less important to society than the cure for disease she is working to develop. It would mean that the typical well-to-do American family must give a very large part of their income every year to international relief organizations, because the suffering that money could alleviate for the poor is vastly greater than any pain from scrimping on luxuries experienced by the affluent family. This is just the argument advanced by philosopher Peter Singer, who says that giving away a lot of excess income isn't a just a *nice* thing to do—it's a moral *duty*.

If you think this level of altruism just isn't consistent with human nature, consider the case of Zell Kravinsky, a healthy man who donated a kidney to a stranger because their benefit obviously outweighed the risk of future harm to himself. (Oh, and this was after he had given away most of his $45 million fortune.) Some take this thinking even further and ask: How many saved lives would it take for me to be *required* to sacrifice my life? Or suppose a bird's life is only worth say one-millionth of a human life. Aren't I still morally required to offer up my life if it would somehow save a million birds? Silly, you say? Would you be more willing to risk your life to save 10,000 lovable golden retrievers or noble horses?

These are intriguing questions. But going down this reasoning path isn't a realistic expectation of most humans. Hence, some have argued that literal utilitarianism is not a practical moral system.

Personal Roles and Duties

A related criticism is that by requiring us to be impartial as between individuals, utilitarianism ignores so-called agent-relative values, and what you might call special duties. Don't our duties vary based on relationships and roles? Lying is bad, but isn't lying to my wife much worse than lying to a stranger? Are our moral principles so lofty that if your child and his friend both fall out of a boat, you must be impartial about which child to save? Do we expect a mother to march in to see her daughter's high school drama teacher and say that some other girl really deserves the lead in the school play? Should a well-to-do family never allow their child to apply to a fancy college because a more needy child would experience a bigger change in their life prospects if they took the slot? Put aside that these actions aren't true to human nature—would you even want them to be?

And what of roles beyond family? We expect people with certain social roles (priest, doctor, firefighter, accountant, judge) to perform with great fidelity to the special duties of those roles. But based on utilitarian principles, should they set aside such duties and just assess the costs and benefits of their action *to everyone*? Should a priest breach the confidence of the confessional and warn the police if the penitent says he is contemplating a crime? Should a firefighter refrain from running into a burning house if it belongs to a known drug dealer? Should an accountant "cook the books" of an unprofitable internet company if he thinks its products can someday "change the world"? Should the police phony-up evidence if they know the accused got away with prior crimes?

In cases like these, the proposed actions might have overall good effects for society. But isn't there something morally wrong in shedding your duties just because you predict that some greater good will result?

GOOD AND BAD DESIRES

As I noted, another main criticism of utilitarianism is that it tells us to weigh equally all sources of social satisfaction, regardless of their differing moral qualities. Bentham famously said, "Prejudice apart, the game of push-pin is of equal value with the arts and sciences." Thus, the strong desire of an addict who wants $100 to buy cocaine for his girlfriend must be weighed as heavily as the strong desire of a minister who wants $100 to buy a winter coat for a poor person. Obviously, some people strongly desire child pornography; do their desires count in the utilitarian algebra, or can we discard them from the outset?

Mill ultimately acknowledged that "some kinds of pleasure are more desirable and valuable than others." As he memorably said, "It is better to be a human being dissatisfied than a pig satisfied; better Socrates unsatisfied than a fool satisfied." Likewise, he said that "[while] I regard utility as the ultimate appeal on all ethical questions," still "it must be utility in the largest sense, grounded on the permanent interests of man as a progressive being." That makes utilitarianism more palatable but still leaves us asking how to identify the "permanent interests" of "progressive beings."

Bentham agreed that the "value of a pleasure or pain" experienced by a person is to be measured not only by its "intensity, its duration, its certainty . . . its remoteness, its fecundity"—but also by its "purity." On this basis, we can easily condemn child porn. But what of the spoiled rich guy who blows $100,000 hosting his posse at a fancy nightclub and spraying expensive champagne on the crowd, while people go hungry just down the street? Is it his money to spend however he likes, or is there something just wrong about this?

According to GiveWell, an organization that evaluates the finances of charities, if we give to the most efficient nonprofits across the world, we can expect to save a human life for about $2,500. We can give over time if we can't afford it all now. I've probably wasted $2,500 on stuff I didn't really need over the past year. Makes you think.

And in utilitarian calculus, how should we weigh the desire of most people to *live in a moral society* that reflects their values, even when it has no direct effect on them personally? Some people know they will never visit the Alaskan wilderness, but they want it preserved for others. Some people would never consume psychedelic drugs, but they want others to be able to. Some want a society that respects others' same-sex marriage; others find the idea a sacrilege. Do such people's feelings matter, or should we consider only the happiness of those most directly involved?

How do we measure Utility?

A utilitarian moralist needs to make interpersonal and intertemporal (across time) comparisons of utility. Utility is often said to mean happiness. But many philosophers give the concept more heft by saying it means enabling a person to "flourish" or "live a good life." Most economists find calculating utility less challenging than do philosophers. Economists assume that market prices and willingness to pay reveal the value people ascribe to competing goods, and they use time-based "discount rates" to compare the value of a given utility received in the future versus now. To an economist, utilitarianism implements the solid concept of "subjective expected utility" based on four components: "a cardinal utility function [i.e., happiness preferences come in quantumlike units]; an exhaustive set of alternative strategies [you assess every alternative to any choice]; a probability distribution . . . associated with each strategy [you know the likelihood of each outcome in advance]; and a policy of maximizing expected utility."

This all seems logical enough. But applying such complex calculations to moral decision-making assumes that normal people have an awful lot of time, mental energy, and predictive capacity as they make decisions in everyday life.

And there are other complications, too. For example, there's the fact that the willingness to pay for something and the ability to pay for it can be very different. Poor people desire many things they can't pay to obtain, like better local schools and safer neighborhoods, so the value they attach to them becomes "invisible" in a willingness-to-pay model. Many moralists believe that a broad distribution of happiness would be better than concentration in a few lucky people, even if the total units of happiness are the same. It's not clear whether or how classic utilitarianism supports this.

Furthermore, research by Jonathan Baron and Joshua Greene shows that when people think about what kind of utility (happiness) distribution would be fair in society, they have trouble decoupling the idea of utility from income. We can measure income, but how would we measure each family's happiness? The cognition, evaluation, and math required by utilitarianism is easier to imagine than to practice.

WHAT ABOUT RIGHTS?

I noted earlier that strict utilitarianism seems to ignore our social roles and duties. At times, it also seems to ignore people's rights, even fundamental rights.

Suppose that a small group of people want to practice an odd religion or publish extreme political screeds, and this is very upsetting to the vast majority. Is that a sufficient reason, based on utilitarian calculus, to limit the small group's rights? Under a utilitarian formula, one unit of disgust experienced by each of 100 million people would vastly outweigh even the 1,000 units of conviction held by each of 100 sect members (since 100 million is greater than 100 thousand). In effect, does that mean that strict utilitarianism would abolish freedom of religion or political belief?

The liberal reformer Mill himself sounded anti-utilitarian when he famously said that "the only purpose for which power can be rightfully exercised over a member of a civilized community against his will is to prevent harm to others." He wouldn't have allowed our hypothetical small sect to be banned, no matter how noxious it was to the majority. So does utilitarianism fly out the window as soon as someone invokes a right?

Well, in a limited sense, yes. The American Constitution was designed to ensure that minority rights in realms such as religion and speech *cannot* be outweighed by the majority's dislike, however intense. As philosopher Thomas Nagel argues, "A well designed set of political and social institutions should function as a moral buffer to protect personal life against the ravenous claims of impersonal [social] 'good,' and vice versa."

The utilitarian philosophers had to grapple with these practical issues. Both Bentham and Mill were social reformers ahead of their times, supporting women's rights, abolition of slavery, workers' rights, and prison reform. Mill admitted that a strict utilitarian approach would at times conflict with individual justice. Hence, "justice is a name for certain classes of moral rules, which concern the essentials of human well-being more nearly, and *are therefore of more absolute moral obligation, than any other rules* for the guidance of life." In this formulation, utilitarian principles are simply guides for "the best mode of managing some department of human affairs," but "*after justice has been assured* . . . [Thus], there are other goods besides happiness, and justice itself is a good." So, maybe utilitarianism does have room for rights that trump utility calculations.

Nonetheless, some believe utilitarianism remains fundamentally in tension with rights theory. Thus, "utilitarians make no room for justice," because they think "only of a single duty, to dump happiness wherever we most conveniently can." Others urge that in the end, rights can *only* be justified by utilitarian analysis—that it is better for society if individuals have certain protected rights, even if their exercise is at times obnoxious to most. Still others say that the importance of rights is sometimes overstated:

> Appeals to "rights" function as an intellectual free pass, a trump card that renders evidence [of social effects] irrelevant. Whatever you and your fellow tribes people feel, you can always posit the existence of a right that corresponds to your feelings. If you feel that abortion is wrong, you can talk about a "right to life." If you feel that outlawing abortion is wrong, you can talk about a "right to choose."

There's some validity to this argument—but not too much. Rights were created because the citizenry felt they were so important as to be quasi-sacred. We can disagree about what should become rights; but some are currently legally confirmed and others simply are not "rights," though people can keep fighting for them to be so. Rights embody utilities so weighty (e.g., freedom of religion) that we are willing to let an individual's choice outweigh even the majority's revulsion at some such choices. That isn't because the majority's interests are being quashed; it's because they also share an interest in being able to choose for themselves, and toleration protects that interest. So, one public interest is sacrificed—but only in aid of an even larger public interest.

We apply utilitarian thinking in many arenas of life, including law, health care, public benefits, and public safety—and we do this even when some people will suffer bad consequences or be deprived of what they see as their rights. For example:

- If a person has a highly infectious disease, they can be quarantined against their will, for the overall good of society.

- A mentally ill person can be involuntarily committed to an institution if they present a probable threat of violence to others.

- Some universities permit anonymous complaints of sexual violence or abuse on the ground that while this may be unfair to the accused, it is deemed more important not to discourage women from filing complaints to stop bad actors.

- Human organs are allocated among potential recipients based on a complex utilitarian scorecard of factors such as need, likely benefit, time waiting, and even race.

- Many government procurement programs include preferences for small or women-owned businesses, which means that the best-qualified vendor isn't always chosen, in order to build up the capacity of new and small businesses.

- Our tax rate system reflects the utilitarian view that it is better to tax the rich far more than the poor or middle class, up to the point when it causes the economy to stagnate, after which the net social benefit is reversed.

- We generally deny an elderly person the right to choose assisted suicide, even when it would bring them desired peace. This is because many believe it is immoral and others worry about potential abuses.

However, in other situations, we *reject* utilitarian principles. We affirm people's moral and legal rights regardless of whether on a net/net basis, society would be happier if they acted differently. Partly for this reason, it is often said that the U.S. Constitution is *intentionally anti-majoritarian.* For example:

- Even groups hated by the vast majority of people have the right to peaceful protest and speech.

- People have the right to practice their religion, even if most others find it odd or offensive.

- People have a right to pretrial bail in most cases, even though there is a risk that they will abscond and commit further crimes (as many do).

- Police or prosecutorial misconduct that violates the defendant's rights can lead to release of the accused, even if evidence of guilt is overwhelming and the accused may do future harm.

- People have a right to smoke tobacco products, even if it is likely to cause them cancer, and even if they are on Medicaid, so the public will pay their resulting medical costs.

Why are we such righteous utilitarians on some issues and so rights-oriented on others? Some would say that ultimately, all social rules derive from a utilitarian assessment. As Jonathan Baron argues, "The basic principles of traditional ethics look a lot like heuristics designed to achieve utility maximization." Still, as Jonathan Elster notes, "We judge some things as so weighty in overall value that we will not continually revisit the weighing/balancing process; we will deem them always to be issue-deciders or tiebreakers, and the word we use for these is 'rights.'" If this is roughly true, then utilitarianism is one major source of rights, but also a major default code judgment when rights don't govern.

How could you really implement utilitarianism?

The difficulties we've examined illustrate a core objection to utilitarianism—that it is just impractical. A person facing daily moral choices can't always (a) predict the effects of their decision, (b) identify all the affected people or groups, (c) weigh how much those people care about a given result, (d) by some unknown formula, calculate the net/net sum of good and evil resulting from a decision—and also calculate all this for each alternative choice in the situation. How in the world would one do that?

Moreover, massive research in behavioral economics and psychology has revealed all sorts of cognitive and affective biases that cause humans to be mistaken in calculating what utilitarianism requires us to assess. We suffer from "false-consensus bias," overestimating how many other people would agree with us in our measurements of utility. We underestimate how much people like things that we don't. We are prey to "inaction bias," the tendency to underestimate the harm of doing nothing about a problem. And we rarely think clearly about the two-by-two grid of potential outcomes of doing or not doing something, as in: (1) I meddle in something and a friend avoids a harm; (2) I meddle and the harm occurs anyway; (3) I don't meddle and the harm occurs; and (4) I don't meddle and the harm doesn't occur. We tend to focus only on cell #1 in the grid. That makes it very hard to calculate utilities properly. Things are far easier for a Kantian (just do the right thing, and to heck with the consequences) or for a Humean (just do what feels right).

We have all seen movies vividly depicting the "butterfly effect": a man lies about some small matter to his girlfriend, or opens a letter addressed to his neighbor and then ashamedly throws it away, and this small decision sets in motion a devilishly complex cascade of unanticipated effects that ruins many lives. These plots are seductive because, each day, we make many small decisions and recognize that we can't foresee all the downstream effects.

Further complicating matters, you must add to any utilitarian calculus not just the direct impacts of moral decisions, but the impact of sustaining or gradually eroding a rule that has good utilitarian effects. So, for example, even if a given white lie has a good effect in one instance, we should also weigh the ill effects of gradually causing people to stop trusting anything other people say. Once you add that factor, assessing the utilitarian effects of any action becomes truly daunting.

Aren't Some Things Just Plain Wrong?

Many moralists argue that some things can never be justified by utilitarian measurements, and they devise extreme examples to illustrate this. Can it ever be justified to torture a terrorist's daughter to force him to reveal a planned attack? Can it ever be moral to execute a crippling cyberattack to awaken the world to the dangers of complex data systems? Can it ever be okay for a couple to agree that the wife will sleep with a billionaire, who will then give them $1 million and make their lives easier? (See the movie *Indecent Proposal.*) Doesn't morality have to draw the line somewhere and just say No?

Scientific studies yield interesting evidence about this. Research using fMRI imaging has shown that those whose brains have suffered damage to the ventro-medial prefrontal cortex (vmPFC) tend to be more instrumental and utilitarian in their moral judgments than the rest of us. They are more likely to say okay to morally repugnant actions so long as they have practical good effects overall. Apparently, neurologically normal people have an empathy/revulsion module that otherwise pushes the "No–Never!" button. But an injured vmPFC breaks that. Another study found that people who endorse an *extreme* utilitarian approach tend to have a number of antisocial traits.

Such data are suggestive, though far from conclusive. They seem to imply that utilitarianism can be a good moral tool—but only up to a point. Then it needs to be limited by some fixed "Thou shalt nots" regardless of claimed social good.

What of inner morality?

Finally, a major limitation of utilitarian morality is that it addresses primarily social relations. Utilitarian theory doesn't say much about what you might call private or inner morals—questions such as whether I have a duty to believe in God, whether I should strive to achieve fame or inner peace, whether I should be humble, and whether it matters if I do good deeds from kindness or a desire for public praise. Many feel that the utilitarian approach is useful but loses sight of such key aspects of morality.

I'll end this section with a nod to one of those delightful historical moments, a conversation where you wish you had been a fly on the wall. Apparently, Charles Darwin was eager to know what his eminent contemporary, the utilitarian Mill, thought about whether morality in humans was an inborn and innate feeling, or learned social thinking. Darwin had his adult son visit Mill and ask. His son reported that Mill candidly confessed that "he was rather in a muddle on the whole subject." Even geniuses often lack final answers.

Joshua Greene quipped that "Utilitarianism is a great idea with an awful name . . . It is the most underrated and misunderstood idea in all of moral and political philosophy." The esteemed philosopher Bernard Williams said there are at least four "attractions of the utilitarian outlook": (1) It doesn't require a particular religious outlook; (2) happiness seems a universal goal; (3) it posits that "moral issues can, in principle, be determined by empirical calculation of consequences"; and (4) it provides "a common currency of moral thought." In fact, when we have time to consider a moral dilemma, we usually employ utilitarian principles, at least in part. But when we are under time pressure or depleted by stress, we grab onto moral judgments based on gut instincts.

Without doubt, the values behind utilitarianism underlie much of our commonsense morality. Bertrand Russell said Mill's theory was "theoretically somewhat incoherent" but still "practically beneficent." Another scholar says it is a "complex attitude but not necessarily an inconsistent or inconclusive one." The eminent moralist Philippa Foot, who opposed utilitarianism, still pondered the "bewitchment" of the idea, admitting that "it is remarkable how utilitarianism tends to haunt even those of us who will not believe in it." And philosopher Thomas Scanlon says utilitarianism "represents a position one must struggle against if one wants to avoid [its power.]"

As we've seen, both Humean empiricism and utilitarianism offer some useful tools for thinking about moral dilemmas and for reaching decisions in the real world. Both frameworks also have definite limitations and weaknesses. In the next chapter, we'll turn to other approaches to moral thinking that have proven to be popular in the twentieth century and down to our day. You can then consider how much progress has or has not been made in the march toward wisdom.

4

Moral Justice, Virtue Ethics, Stoicism, and Practical Morals

T HE GENERATIONS SINCE THE START of the twentieth century have seen the emergence—or resurgence—of several additional systems for thinking about moral issues. In this chapter, we'll examine them and try to tease out what's most significant about each. But first, I want to briefly discuss three movements that have been provocative and interesting, but that in my view are *moral dead ends.* They hold interest for philosophers but provide little practical guidance for the ordinary citizen seeking to become a more effective judge of moral issues.

Dead End One: Obsession With Words

DURING MUCH OF THE TWENTIETH CENTURY, the ascendant philosophical theory (at least in Britain and the United States) was the *analytic school,* also called *logical positivism* or *Oxford Philosophy.* This approach, championed by Bertrand Russell, G. E. Moore, Ludwig Wittgenstein, A. J. Ayer, J. L. Austin, W.V.O. Quine, and others, asserted that most problems of philosophy and

88

morals are artificial ones created by imprecise use of language. They mocked the "verbal inflation" of the "Continental philosophy" of Baruch Spinoza, Kant, G.W.F. Hegel, Friedrich Nietzsche, and others who talked of transcendent, all-powerful ideas like "Reason," "Spirit," "Unity ," and "Will." They accused these philosophers of building intellectual "castles in the sky," without a strong foundation in any practical meaning.

Some analytic thinkers, like Russell and Wittgenstein, came to the field from mathematics and logic. Charging that philosophy lacked mathematical certainty, they (along with those in the so-called Vienna Circle) tried to give it the rigor of science and logic. They lamented philosophy's "indeterminacy," which to a scientist is akin to uncertainty. Ayer wrote that "a sentence is factually significant to a given person if and only if he knows how to verify the proposition." This became celebrated as the "verification theory of meaning." And verification was highly dependent on the exact words of the claim.

The important corollary is that if a moral statement, such as "Breaking a promise is bad," is not factually "verifiable" (what is "bad"?), then it is not true, false, or even debatable. Factual statements are on one side of a chasm, and morals/values on another. Thus, saying "Breaking a promise is bad" is no different from saying "This movie is bad"—both are simply statements of non-approval. A. C. Grayling summarizes the argument thus: "When people make moral judgments . . . [all they are doing is] manifesting an attitude or an emotional response. . . . [M]oral utterances are [just] expressions of psychological states such as approval or disapproval . . . preferences or desires, not judgments of right and wrong or good and bad." According to Ayer, moral statements are mere "ejaculations or commands" that have "no objective validity whatsoever." But then he went further, declaring that since a claim, such as "It is bad to lie," is not subject to "some sense experience [that is] . . . relevant to its truth or falsity . . . then I hold that it is metaphysical and that *it is not true or false but literally meaningless.*"

But is that true? Couldn't plenty of "sense experiences" be relevant to the morality of lying? Maybe you watch a loved one cry when they learn you deceived them. Maybe a friend refuses to help you out of a bad spot because you previously lied to him. Maybe your daughter learns you lie, and she begins to lie, and then she experiences harm as a result. Aren't these sense experiences relevant to whether it is bad to lie? So Ayer was being provocative; his real contention was that the "badness" of something like lying can't be logically proven *inherently or in all situations.* (Ayer liked being provocative: he even argued that powerful moral statements like "Killing is wrong" or "War is wrong" are literally meaningless!)

A less extreme expression is G. E. Moore's famous "open question," which boils down to the fair observation that you can't claim that doing something is morally good unless you go on to specify *why* it is good and what good means in that context (a good treaty versus a good wine). Moore said this was impossible "not because good is some mysterious, occult [concept] . . . but because *the idea of good is a single notion like that of yellow,*" and there is no way to penetrate it further.

This analogy seems puzzling, since yellow is really not a "single notion"—you can distinguish pale yellow from sun yellow. And you can describe what yellow is supposed to look like in a traffic light versus in a cake. Likewise, you can usually show what "good" means. A good car doesn't break down; a good drug cures the disease; a good friend is reliable. "Good" carries the meaning of doing well what the thing was intended to do. In the moral realm, philosopher R. M. Hare asks what it means to say, "Don't hit a man when he's down." Is it really any different from expressing the preference, "Don't turn up the volume on the music"? Yes, it is. The latter just means I like soft music; you might like it a bit louder. But no one likes to be hit when they are down, and we generally don't respect someone who keeps hitting a downed man. So, the statement Hare objected to actually does have an agreed social and moral meaning.

Philosopher Bernard Williams mocked the analytic school's sterile word-based approach, saying, "Contemporary moral philosophy has found an original way of being boring, which is by not discussing moral issues at all." And A. C. Grayling says, "Analytic philosophy is not a body of doctrine [at all]; it is a style of philosophizing."

In addition to being boring, logical positivism did not connect with real-life experience. In fact, people *do* believe that their moral statements carry special meaning, and the way others react to them confirms this. Think of how differently we all react to being told that "I do not like the way you make chili" versus "I do not like the way you always lie." The average person hardly views as meaningless the remark, that "You are a nasty bastard."

As a result of these limitations, logical positivism turned out to be irrelevant to almost everyone except philosophers.

And here I'll share what surely must be one of the strangest encounters in the history of philosophizing. Let's imagine what would happen if a reflective philosopher had a disagreement with a rather pugilistic man of a different temperament. Well, Ayer happened to be a rascal who partied a lot, married four times, and had many affairs. As the story goes, on one occasion, he was entertaining a number of fashion models at a New York apartment party, and there was a loud commotion in an adjacent bedroom. The famous model Naomi Campbell was screaming that her boyfriend was assaulting her. Ayer went into the room to stop him. Her boyfriend happened to be one Mike Tyson.

"Do you know who I am? I am the heavyweight boxing champion of the world!" Tyson declared. To which Ayer, undaunted, replied, "And I am the former Wykeham Professor of Logic at Oxford. We are both preeminent in our field. I suggest we talk about this as rational men."

Now *that* shows belief in the power of rational moral argument.

Postscript: I am not a famous philosopher, but I too had a run-in with Mike Tyson. He used to live down the street from our house. One time, I was driving nearby and came to an intersection with four stop signs. I inched forward, the convertible to my right inched up too, and I jockeyed further, and he did the same without yielding, turning the encounter into one of those "Oh come on, you @#$%& jerk!" moments. Finally, the driver of the convertible leaned out, shook his fist and swore at me. It was Mike Tyson.

I graciously let him pass.

Dead End Two: Relativism

ANOTHER MAJOR STRAND of twentieth-century moral thinking was the movement called *relativism*. This is the doctrine that morals are just the preferences chosen by different societies in light of their unique customs, economies, and social arrangements. An intellectual sibling—subjectivism—goes further and argues that there can't even be agreed moral judgments in *one* society, because moral judgments are nothing more than expressions of the speaker's own feelings or attitudes. Thus, they hold no meaning beyond each individual.

The notion that moral judgments have a subjective element is not new. Long ago, Hobbes wrote, "Whatsoever is the object of a man's Appetite and Desire, that is . . . which he calleth Good." Likewise, Hume said " The vice [of an action] entirely...escapes you...'til you turn your reflection into your own breast." But modern relativists go farther. Philosopher J. J. Mackie confidently declares that "there are no objective values" or "substantive moral conclusions," and "no definitive facts," either. Richard Rorty sniffs that anyone who thinks there are solid ideas of right and wrong is simply "an old-fashioned prig."

Under this relativist theory, examining morality is not a philosophical endeavor; it's more like anthropology or sociology. Morals are just like quaint customs. In comparing societies, you can't say that one has good and the other has bad morality any more than you can say objectively that one has good hairstyles and the other bad ones. And the proponents of subjectivism argue not that people have subjective moral biases, but that they have *nothing else.*

The relativist/subjectivist perspectives were buttressed by many trends in mid-twentieth-century thinking, including:

- Shock at the rationalizations of brutality by Nazis and Communists.

- The leftist critique of capitalism, in which "bourgeois morality" was simply another tool of the capitalist class used to repress the proletariat.

- The civil rights and feminist movements, which showed that conventional morality had long ignored inequality and disempowerment.

- A sort of Nietzschean romantic critique of rationality by thinkers such as Michel Foucault, Jean Francis Lyotard, Richard Rorty, and Jacques Derrida, who said there are no realities but only descriptive "texts."

- The emphasis by existentialists (such as Henri Bergson, Martin Heidegger, and Jean-Paul Sartre) on the need for individuals to "create" their own moral code through choice and simply "being."

- The writings of ethnographers like Margaret Mead and Bronislaw Malinowski ostensibly depicting a wide range of ethical beliefs that all worked equally well in precapitalist societies.

All these trends left a simplified lesson, a public impression that the really smart people had figured out that morality is subjective, relative bunk, without any rational basis. But as critic Steven Pinker notes, many of these relativist luminaries "are morose cultural pessimists who declare that modernity is odious;

all statements are paradoxical; all works of art are tools of oppression; liberal democracy is the same as fascism," and so on. Consider this bold declaration:

> Everything I have said and done in these last years is relativism by intuition. . . . [R]elativism signifies contempt for fixed categories and men who claim to be the bearers of an objective, immortal truth. From the fact that all ideologies are of equal value, and all ideologies are mere functions, the modern relativist infers that everybody has the right to create for himself his own ideology and to attempt to enforce it with all the energy of which he is capable.

That was Benito Mussolini—hardly an avatar of enlightenment and wisdom. Yet the relativistic approach became *de rigueur* among generations of college sophomores. It became their portal, a rite of passage to a broad, progressive worldview—not just that some judgments are relative, but that all judgments are relative and contestable. It made them feel skeptical, smart, and worldly. As one philosopher observed, "Moral relativism is clearly an attempt to pay intellectual reparations for the crimes of Western colonialism." And many people who are bewildered by moral complexity find refuge in the view that "it's all relative."

A major study of values in 2000 found that moral "relativists" and "absolutists" were about evenly divided in the United States. But elsewhere, "when asked to make a choice between two opposing positions about good and evil, most people around the world choose a relativistic position. This is especially true for the people of the rich and historically Protestant societies." In contrast, Americans have been more likely than their European or Japanese peers to believe that there are "absolutely clear guidelines for what is good and evil." There is some evidence that women and poor people tend more to embrace absolutist morality and reject relativism.

Relativism may lead us to a useful insight. Bernard Gert says that moral relativism is extreme and flawed, but *moral humility* is wise. Thus, you should believe that you are a moral agent, you can make meaningful choices, your choices are justified, and the opposite views probably are wrong. But you should also have the humility to realize that you still might be mistaken and others might be right instead. Nevertheless, your choices remain significant expressions of your moral values and identity.

WHAT DOES RELATIVISM REALLY MEAN?

A core problem of relativism is that it's hard to pin down what it actually means. Even a defender admits, "The term 'moral relativism' is notoriously ambiguous." Many of its proponents' writings are convoluted and hard to decipher. As Foucault once confided to philosopher John Searle, "In France, you gotta have ten percent incomprehensible [in your writings]; otherwise, people won't think it's deep—they won't think you're a profound thinker." So what does relativism actually mean?

- Relativism might mean that, as Hamlet says, "nothing is good or bad but thinking makes it so." This form of relativism contends that there are no objective moral judgments. As Nietzsche said, "There are no facts, only interpretations." Really? Can rape, or abandoning a child to die in the wild, or mass genocide, ever *not be* evil?

- Relativism might mean that people are wired by genes and upbringing to be what they are, so we can't judge them. But why not? Maybe a saintly doctor ministering to those in Africa with dread diseases was wired by genes and parenting to be so good; but can't I admire her anyway? And as to those who commit horrible acts, how do I know who truly "couldn't help themselves" and who just chose evil? Why can't I regard a repeat murderer as evil regardless?

- Relativism might mean that moral judgments are meaningful, but mainly as statements about what a given society accepts. So, "while moral truths hold objectively, they do not hold universally, only locally."

- Relativism might be understood to mean that a person can be confident in their moral beliefs without condemning those who differ. But this wrongly confuses relativism with tolerance. Tolerance says, "People have the right to be wrong, up to a point." But relativism says, "There is no right or wrong to begin with."

- Relativism might mean that moral judgments are just meaningless statements of taste, not even worth arguing over. As Rorty said, "Anything can be made to look good or bad by being redescribed." Except that 99 percent of your fellow humans don't feel or act that way in daily life. They think many aspects of good and evil are real, not just word labels.

- Relativism might mean that moral choice is merely a feature of action, and true meaning is simply the act. The existentialist Sartre asserted that "feeling is formed by the deeds one does; therefore, I cannot consult it as a guide to action. Instead, you are free; therefore choose [whatever you will]." But if there is no prior identity that is you, how do you know that you are acting "authentically," which is the existential ideal?

For a brief period in the late twentieth century, a brand of ethics called *situation ethics* gained public fame. Joseph Fletcher's 1966 book, *Situation Ethics*, came from an avowedly Christian perspective, in which the overriding principle was love. However, situation ethics was really a form of relativism. As Fletcher said, "If a lie is told not lovingly, it is wrong, evil; if it is told in love, it is good, right." He noted that four things matter: ends, means, motives, and consequences, but he provided no guidance as to how these are to be weighed or reconciled. Fletcher also argued strenuously that morals are just a matter of opinion: "Cicero . . . said . . . , 'Only a madman could maintain that the distinction between . . . virtue and vice is a matter of opinion, not nature.' *That is nevertheless precisely and exactly what situation ethics maintains.*" Accordingly, critics have dismissed situation ethics as being, paradoxically, "a Christian system *of non-ethics.*"

SOCIAL VARIATIONS AS EVIDENCE FOR RELATIVISM

As noted earlier, relativism got a boost from twentieth-century ethnographic studies of far-flung societies. Intellectuals were super-impressed that some folks in Papua New Guinea differed from, say, Germans in their sexual promiscuity or methods of child discipline. They were not as impressed that both groups, and virtually all other societies, prized stable marriage, family devotion, care of the elderly, keeping promises, sacrifice for the group, and myriad other moral values. The ethnologists focused on the differences, finding the similarities of lesser interest.

But research across more than 100 countries has revealed a far greater degree of commonality in moral judgments than is asserted by the relativists. If one steps back and looks at the forest rather than the trees, what is remarkable is that twenty-first-century urban Japanese or Peruvians should find anything at all instructive in the ethical musings of a fourth century BCE thinker from provincial Macedonia (Aristotle). Or that American college students should be inspired by the wisdom of an ancient prince from Nepal (the Buddha). Or that modern Nigerians find interesting the moral dilemmas probed by a White sixteenth-century Englishman making a living as a playwright (Shakespeare). If all morals are relative and subjective, why do these thinkers from far different times and cultures still cut to the quick of our moral sense? Answer: because they were all humans, and humans share a lot of internal moral architecture. Should we be more impressed by some superficially different furnishings or by the common architecture of the moral edifice?

OTHER FLAWS IN RELATIVISM

Even taken on its own terms, it's not clear what relativism achieves. Its proponents seem to feel that it's a final *coup de grâce* to say that morality is "merely socially constructed." There's some truth to that. But why does it invalidate morality? Analogously, everything about our lives may derive from the fact that we humans give birth to live offspring—we must nurture them until they are self-sufficient, and so we live in protective social groups. Had we been egg-laying reptiles, everything would be different. But the human world is our world, and we must live in it and judge it as it is.

As Joshua Greene says, "The problem with the moral relativist's answer is that . . . it's not really an answer. . . . Maybe, as the relativist says, there is no ultimate moral truth. . . . [But] people must nevertheless live one way or another. . . . And if the relativist refuses to choose, that, too, is a choice. . . . [T]here is no escape from moral choice." Karl Popper noted that the relativists "define philosophy so that it becomes by definition . . . incapable of making contributions to our knowledge of the world."

A particular irony of relativism is that many proponents invoke it to oppose intolerance or disrespect for alternative lifestyles or disparate cultures. But if you deeply inhale the relativist doctrine, you actually relinquish your moral ability to oppose even extreme evil. In the relativist universe, since cultures and values vary, we have no moral standing to condemn honor killing, incest, bribery and corruption, torture, ethnic cleansing, or aggressive territorial wars.

Relativism also precludes demanding that people treat their children kindly, respect the needs of the elderly, help neighbors, perform their jobs honorably, and not commit treason against their nation. How is this a more enlightened viewpoint? Defenders of relativism say that it doesn't require tolerance of evil, but their doctrine provides no basis for condemning it.

Moreover, relativism is logically self-defeating. As Sam Harris observes, "Moral relativism . . . tends to be self-contradictory. Relativists may say that moral truths exist only relative to a specific cultural framework—but this claim . . . purports to be true across all possible frameworks." Where is the justification for that judgment? Likewise, Thomas Nagel says: "The claim 'everything is subjective' must be wrong, for it would have to be either subjective or objective. But it can't be objective since in that case it would be false if true. And it can't be subjective because then it would rule out any objective claim, including the claim that it is objectively false." Have you got that?

Nagel is using the classic *peritrope,* or table-turning argument that Socrates sometimes used. As applied to relativism, it might run thus:

Relativist: Nothing, moral or otherwise, can be known objectively and with certainty.

Response: Then how are you sure what you just said is true, rather than nonsense?

More recently, this problem has been dubbed the "bias paradox." If you argue that all views are biased, then bias should be measured by the distance from its opposite, objectivity—so objectivity must exist to some degree. Analogously, it would make no sense to say that everything is dark—unless somewhere, some light existed, from which dark can be distinguished. But if you claim that some degree of objectivity exists, the relativist derides you as biased! Their rationally arguing that rational, unbiased views are impossible "is like someone insisting there is no such thing as poetry—and making their case in the form of a poem."

The relativist doctrine is echoed in the currently ubiquitous refrain, "Don't judge me!" The claim is that if a person's values differ from yours, you can't judge them. This is supposed to respect individuality and autonomy. Yet in effect, such a relativist says, "Everybody's beliefs have equal truth and dignity—except all those who disagree with my statement."

Such relativism is also widely impractical. If you are a hermit, you may be able to avoid being judged. But as soon as you choose to live in society, you're going to be judged every day, for good reasons and bad. Some scholars see in relativism a broader rejection of any distinction between fact and fiction, truth and falsity. "Its characteristic feature is . . . indifference to 'truth' or 'bullshit'"—while in reality "intellectual honesty is [itself] a moral virtue." Given all these flaws, they hope that "relativism . . . can subside into the shadows."

To be clear, rejecting relativism doesn't require you to turn into a moral martinet. You can accept your duty as a moral person to judge as best you can, while acknowledging that others live under different conditions. If I lived in a Communist country, would I report my dissident friends in order to avoid official sanctions on myself and my family? I can't be sure.

You can make moral judgments without also believing that you have the right to impose your beliefs on others. I believe in religious toleration, but I'm not at all sure that America should intervene in every interethnic dispute to force other nations to respect this principle.

In the end, we return to the basic problem: pure relativism is not really a moral framework. It is a non-framework, a way of avoiding moral judgments entirely—which ultimately is not possible.

Dead End Three: Pragmatism

THE LATE NINETEENTH-/EARLY TWENTIETH-CENTURY PERIOD saw the birth of another, distinctly American, approach to ethics, the *pragmatism* of Charles Sanders Peirce, William James, and John Dewey.

In contrast to the abstruse style of European philosophy, one has to applaud Peirce for naming an early essay "How to Make Our Ideas Clear." His writing *wasn't* especially clear, but the nub of his approach was to use the scientific method to derive meaning from facts, not Kantian *a priori* ideas. As he said, "There is . . . no difference between a hard and a soft thing as long as they are not brought to the test." So empirical experience proves the value of an idea. Following this, James said, "There is no such thing possible as an ethical philosophy dogmatically made up in advance. . . . There can be no final truth in ethics . . . until the last man has had his experience and had his say. . . . Everywhere the ethical philosopher must wait on facts."

James, a psychologist as well as philosopher, had earlier described two basic kinds of psychological dispositions in people—the tough-minded and the tender-minded. Tough-minded people are skeptical, materialistic, pessimistic, and empirical (fact-focused). Tender-minded people are spiritual, idealistic, optimistic, and rationalistic (idea-focused). James hoped that pragmatism could prove to be "a philosophy that can satisfy both kinds of demands."

James focused on *usefulness* as the test of truth. The truth of an idea is not a stagnant property inherent in it. Instead, "truth *happens* to an idea. It . . . is made true by events." Thus, pragmatism would have us ask what difference it would make in actual life if one regarded a given act—such as a certain kind of lie—as moral versus immoral. James said, "There can be no difference . . . in abstract truth that does not express itself in a difference in concrete facts and conduct." According to James, a statement's truth depends on what difference it would make in the real world to believe it or disbelieve it. Truth is a marriage of prior belief and new information. So, "if you want to know whether any kind of theory is true, try believing it and see if any [good] results ensue."

This thinking appeals to many people. When all sorts of moral claims fly back and forth, they like to ask, "Yeah, but what difference does it make in the end?"

In a phrase only an American philosopher of a certain era would employ, James wanted to assess a claim's "cash value"—what it produces in terms of results. He often used the money metaphor—that it pays for our ideas to be evaluated pragmatically, and that we should "do what pays" in terms of reliable outcomes. An example: It makes a lot of difference, verifiable in an instant, if I say that a knife won't cut your finger and you say it will. The cash value of believing one view or the other is incurring or avoiding injury. But if I say that invisible ghosts can pass through walls without detection and you deny my claim, there is no truth value either way, because we'll never see any different results.

Now turn to a moral statement: If you declare that a store owner has a moral right to shoot a thief and I say the contrary, then who is correct makes a lot of pragmatic difference—to the store owner, the thief, the legal system, and the rest of us in the town.

But such a pragmatic assessment has pretty modest limits. After you count the cash value of a belief, you still have to decide whether the cash value is good, whether the side effects outweigh it, and whether there is greater cash value to other beliefs. How do you do that? Pragmatism offers little help. James was both religious and a humanist, and believed that moral action could improve the world. But he seemed to see morality as largely a matter of "sentiment." He ventured the rather weak principle that our moral duty is "to satisfy . . . as many demands as we can."

Thus, many critics say that pragmatism is at best one handy tool, but hardly a robust system of values or morals. Richard Rorty, with his usual sarcasm, declared that "pragmatism is a vague analysis and overworked term. Nevertheless, it is the crowning glory of our country's intellectual tradition." It leaves us asking, Where do we go from here?

Now we'll turn to some possible answers to that question.

Rawls and Moral Justice

IN THE WAKE OF RELATIVISM and logical positivism, philosopher John Rawls undertook a major effort to restore reasoned rules as the basis of morals, fairness, and justice. He was enormously successful: "Rawls's theory has received, and deserved, more attention than any other work of ethics in [the twentieth century and since]." One major treatise declares that "in philosophy, there was nothing to match it in the previous 100 years," while another says, "political philosophy since [Rawls's theory] . . . might be said to be shaped almost exclusively by it."

Rawls provided a potent antidote to strict utilitarianism, which, as we saw, can be faulted for not addressing the fair distribution of happiness among people, only its total sum. In contrast, Rawls wanted to provide a rationale for "justice as fairness," a criterion that speaks to both people's rights and the fair distribution of resources. As he said, "Justice is the first virtue of public institutions, as truth is in a system of thought." And while Rawls's epic 1971 work, *A Theory of Justice*, focuses on rights, fairness, and justice in society writ large, it also has been influential in discussions of private morals.

What exactly did Rawls argue?

Rawls began by updating the classic Enlightenment concept of the social contract developed by John Locke, Jean Jacques Rousseau, and others. Rawls asks: What social rules would people agree to as being fair, just, and moral if they lived in an ancient "ideal state" before society was formed? His key insight is that we should now apply rules of justice that *we would have agreed to adopt* before we knew what social status or role we would happen to have—rich or poor, female or male, Black or White, brilliant or challenged. This is called the "original position," based on a "veil of ignorance" as to one's future fate.

This leads to Rawls's core concept of justice as the fairness of rules formulated under these conditions, with the rules then applied universally. In this respect, Rawls is largely a Kantian rationalist; in fact, he called his approach "Kantian contractualism." He would have us reason toward ideal rules, get used to how they work, and then apply them evenhandedly, whether or not we like the result in a given situation. He believes that some principles would be so universally accepted as to be recognized as rights, which can't be abrogated by later decisions about distributive justice (i.e., the allocation of social resources). Thus, a rich man has a right not to have any of his five cars stolen, even though he might not miss one and a poor family really needs a car. And even an obviously guilty criminal has the right to command the state's resources for a fair trial, even if others in the community might like to avoid the effort and expense.

Rawls's two basic principles of justice are these: "First, each person is to have an equal right to the most extensive liberty compatible with a similar liberty for others; Second, social and economic inequalities are to be arranged so that they are both (a) reasonably expected to be to everyone's advantage, and (b) attached to positions and offices open to all." One might assume that Rawls favors fixed rules regardless of social impacts. But he disavows that, saying that when tradeoffs must be made, the claims of the poor and needy should bear special weight (the "difference principle"). Thus, we should distribute "primary goods" like food so as to reduce differences in what people have. Why this is mandated by Rawls's imaginary original position is not so well-proven. Rawls doesn't endorse operating purely on principle. Here, he seems to say we must toggle back and forth between principles and new circumstances, and so reach "reflective equilibrium."

In later writings, Rawls argues for two modified principles: "1. Each person has an equal right to a . . . scheme of basic liberties which is compatible with a similar scheme of liberties for all; 2. Social and economic inequalities [should] . . . be attached to . . . [social] positions open to all under conditions of fair equality of opportunity; and . . . *they must be to the greatest benefit of the least advantaged members of society* [emphasis added]." As we will see, this last criterion complicates things a good bit, and many have puzzled over how to implement it.

Rawls's approach has been widely admired, often criticized, and universally viewed as important. Most later books about justice in public policy address his ideas. Rawls's framework has proven adaptable to many fields and approaches. Liberals generally see Rawls as providing a moral foundation for egalitarian social policies. A leading rights theorist, Ronald Dworkin, seems to see Rawls's approach as like a simple "rule of thumb" for what is fair but still may fail to "take rights [sufficiently] seriously." And even the libertarian Friedrich Hayek and the relativist J. J. Mackie acknowledged Rawls's approach as powerful.

Some psychologists believe that Rawls's principles capture the innate sense of fairness that prevails in many societies. Mathematician/economist/ Ken Binmore sees Rawls's rules as a clever effort to simulate the so-called Nash equilibrium, which game theory says will lead to the most stable maximization of group benefits. "The common deep structure of human fairness norms is captured in [Rawls's] . . . device of the original position. . . . [This] principle . . . matches up with the fairness norms that [people] . . . actually use every day."

So Rawls has enjoyed a broad range of acclaim. Yet, like any major theorist, he has also been subject to many criticisms. Here are a few.

THE ORIGINAL POSITION IS A FAIRY TALE

Critics point out that in reality, there never was a town hall meeting among tribes in the state of nature at which they adopted rules like those Rawls proposes. (This argument echoes Hume's criticism that John Locke's theory of a social contract was "a philosophical fiction which never had and never could have any reality.") One answer is that the "original position" was never meant to be a historical fact. It is, as Rawls said, "purely hypothetical," a "device of representation," and a lens through which to see clearly what you would have regarded and should now regard as fair. It clarifies thinking about fair rules by removing the distortions due to what you now know are your social roles and selfish interests.

Rawls believed his metaphor helped to identify the rules we would choose in setting up society. Given the opportunity to create a fair system, people would not gamble by launching a feudal system with big born winners and losers locked in a fixed hierarchy. Yet exactly that kind of social system did prevail for millennia. So what gives? Is Rawls arguing for what did occur, or what *rationally should have* occurred in the original position? Evidently the latter is correct. As Michael Sandel says, "Underlying the device of the veil of ignorance is a moral judgment . . . that the distribution of income and opportunity *should not be* based on factors that are arbitrary from a moral point of view." Rawls has been widely faulted for using an intellectual "skyhook" to pull his metaphor out of the practical ditch and into the aspirational clouds.

WHY SHOULD WE BE BOUND BY ANCIENT RULES?

Suppose we accept the validity of the original position idea. Societies evolve and change. Why should we be chained to rules hypothetically agreed to in the original position? Maybe life was different then, and we would reject those rules today. Also, often in life we believe something, but we are misled or misinformed, or we learn from later experience. Why is there a moral obligation never to change one's mind about social rules?

A conservative might cite the example of welfare. Perhaps in some small, ancient society comprised of related kin, where everyone worked hard and the only people needing aid were those family members unexpectedly disabled by injury or disease, we might all have agreed to bear the cost of their care. But why, it is asked, does that require us today to maintain public welfare programs for large numbers of people who haven't even tried to find work, or those who arrive here from distant nations? Why are rules of justice good only if we would have agreed to them eons ago, with no changes due to new conditions?

RAWLS IS INCONSISTENT

Other critics fault Rawls for violating his own rules. He first erects a lovely system of principles of fairness and justice supposedly derived from reason. But then, to avoid the realities that permit poverty and inequality, Rawls arbitrarily puts a thumb on the scale by saying that in close cases, where the original-position rule isn't clear, we have a moral duty to give special help to the poor or needy. Critics demand to know why—after all, many ancient societies didn't agree with that principle.

An example of Rawls's response is, "Since everyone's well being depends upon a scheme of cooperation without which none could have a satisfactory life, the division of advantages should be such as to draw forth the willing cooperation of everyone . . . including those less well situated." But that has been criticized as just an idealistic declaration. What really is "willing cooperation"?

WHO SHOULD BE HELPED?

Rawls's approach also poses practical difficulties. If you especially wanted to help all of the worst off in society, who would that include? The frail elderly, the poor, and the handicapped, sure. But what of lonely people living in isolated areas, or urban dwellers terrified of neighborhood crime, or those who are chronically obese, or addicted to drugs? Dworkin proposes a distinction between social needs that are "ambition sensitive" (a person is lazy) versus those that are "endowment sensitive" (a person is of limited ability). The former are seen as less deserving of help. But others look at people who suffer from low social success and believe "their ultimate causes are to be found in factors outside the control of the individual. Hence, one cannot hold individuals responsible for being lazy, . . . extremely risk-loving, or for having whatever other character traits keep them at low levels of welfare." Many would disagree with this on moral grounds. How do you measure what is truly outside a person's control and distinguish it from what they could have but just did not control?

Another challenge: What of people who are disadvantaged in one realm but favored in another? Men have long benefited from gender bias against women in the workplace and in allocating social "power." But in the United States today, men die much younger than women. So, should our health resources be focused more on men than on women ("We have a crisis—men are dying young!"), or are men privileged and should they therefore be left to their own devices? The answer depends on which metrics we choose to use—which means that the answer is a far from obvious moral choice.

RAWLS IGNORES PROPERTY RIGHTS

Critics such as Robert Nozick (in his widely admired book *Anarchy, State and Utopia)* take Rawls to task for ignoring the property holdings that people inherit or earn. Maybe a person has more stuff today because they invented, saved, or worked especially hard for what they have. In the original position, wouldn't we all have voted to keep most of the product of our hard work? If so, why is it moral to transfer special resources to the least advantaged?

Nozick was a libertarian who seemed to venerate private property. But in a later book (*The Examined Life)* he acknowledged that his prior work "went wrong" and took "an unduly narrow view" of society by not truly addressing "social solidarity and humane concern for others." Still, his position in defense of property rights is one that advocates of Rawlsian justice must address.

WHY REWARD MERIT?

Rawls argued that neither pure liberty nor pure reward for merit will result in ideal social relations: "From a moral viewpoint, the two seem equally arbitrary." Yet to many people, rewarding hard work and skill is fair. The historic movements to overcome racial, ethnic, and gender discrimination were powered by the idea that merit alone—not these extraneous factors—should determine opportunity and advancement. This was a core tenet of the "American creed." And most economists buttressed it, arguing that nondiscrimination better incentivizes talented people and leads to a more productive economy for all.

But what if a merit system results in massive income inequalities? It's no secret that, since the 1970s, the growth of the knowledge economy has widened the earnings gap between those who are skilled at manipulating information and those who are not. The working class has fallen farther behind the truly rich. Conservatives who defend the market economy say that people will inevitably be paid what they are worth; those with low pay just need to become more skilled.

Interestingly, a new critique of merit as the basis for reward has now emerged on the progressive side of the political spectrum. Merit is viewed as creating what has been dubbed the Meritocracy Trap. The essential claim is that, because wealthier people tend to be both better connected and more able to spend resources to create opportunities for their children, they win out generation after generation, blocking access to talented others. (Think of the admissions process to elite colleges and the factors that benefit the well-off, from test prep tutoring to access to prestigious private schools.) This critique supports a call to change meritocratic systems. Rawls's "difference principle" might be seen as supporting that.

IS RAWLSIAN JUSTICE REALLY A "MORAL" FRAMEWORK AT ALL?

In later works such as *Justice as Fairness,* Rawls tried to answer his critics and fine-tune his theory. He acknowledged that his theory was "not intended as a comprehensive moral doctrine." He noted, for example, that "utilitarianism is a teleological [ends-focused] theory whereas justice as fairness [Rawls's idea] is not. . . . [Still,] all ethical doctrines worthy of our attention take consequences into account in judging rightness. One that did not would simply be irrational, crazy."

Rawls's theory may strike some as overly "legalistic" for something as "emotional" as morals. But then reflect on the fact that most of the key words we use in discussing morals—duty, obligation, right, justify, and even "moral law"—embody the concept of moral principles being binding and following the "laws" of reason.

In sum, then, Rawls's moral justice theory, while not seeking to offer a complete framework for moral thinking, has been highly influential in debates over moral decision-making and social policies. It occupies a unique place in the realm of moral frameworks. Rawls is neither a pure Kantian, nor a utilitarian, but rather, offers a hybrid approach with elements of both.

Returning to Ancient Roots: Virtue Ethics

ANOTHER MAJOR MORAL FRAMEWORK is called *virtue ethics*. It has deep roots in Western philosophy and continues to be a significant source of insights to this day.

Instead of having us decide what is the right moral decision in a given situation, virtue ethics starts with a more fundamental question: What does it mean to act like a moral person? The main goal of ethics, then, is to describe what a virtuous person would do. As the Greek Epictetus said, "First say to yourself what you would be; and then do what you have to do."

There is an aspirational element to virtue ethics that many people find appealing. Lon Fuller observed that while "the morality of duty starts at the bottom" or minimum of what is expected of people, "the morality of aspiration starts at the top of human achievement." Perhaps for this reason, "in the second half of the twentieth century, the 'ethics of virtue' became an increasingly popular alternative to the Kantian and utilitarian theories that had for some time dominated."

In his influential book *After Virtue*, philosopher Alasdair MacIntyre argues that the preceding centuries failed to produce an adequate philosophy of morals—either through "reason" or "feelings." Virtue ethics does not focus primarily on rules, rights, feelings, or consequences, but on achieving good character. Thus, an action is good if it is what a virtuous person would usually do in the circumstances.

Virtue ethics has a history longer than any other approach to moral philosophy. It traces its roots to the Greek Stoics, Sophists, and Plato. But while they explored abstractly what "good" means and what a good person is, their successor Aristotle took a more pragmatic approach. In response to abstract Platonic theorizing, he observed, "A carpenter and a [mathematician] investigate the right angle in different ways; the former does so in so far as the right angle is useful for his work, while the latter inquires what . . . sort of thing it is." Aristotle recommended the former, practical approach: "[We] become builders by building and we become harpists by playing the harp. Similarly, we become just by doing just actions."

Aristotle emphasized moderation and balance in ethical thinking. Thus, "the mark of virtue" for Aristotle is to practice having moral feelings "not too much or too little" and "to have these feelings at the right times on the right grounds toward the right persons for the right motives and in the right way."

Aristotle's ethics revolved around three concepts: excellence of character (in Greek, *arete*), practical wisdom (*phronesis*), and flourishing or using one's given talents (*eudaemonia*). Virtue is "concerned with . . . what the man of practical wisdom would determine"—what would be done by a person wise enough to know how right conduct advances a good life. Using Aristotle's metaphor, you build your virtuous character by adding more and more bricks to your edifice of moral habits. Then you can step back and say, "Indeed, that is who I am."

This practical attitude toward ethical thinking continues to have appeal. The advocate of virtues William Bennett wrote that living a moral life requires "developing good habits which come about only through repeated practice." It has been reported that the Dalai Lama, though coming from a very different tradition, prefers this approach to a fixed set of moral rules.

To some modern ears, referring to someone as "virtuous" sounds prissy. To such people, virtue ethics has "acquired a quaint veneer of antiquarian fretting over how an improper act tarnishes one's soul." People don't use the word "virtue" as much today as in the past. But the substance of virtue ethics has both logical and practical appeal. If we want to know how to act in a good way, isn't it logical to look at what people who are widely regarded as good customarily do? Thus, "what sets virtue ethics apart is that it treats ethics as concerned with one's whole life—and not just those occasions when something with a distinctly 'moral' quality is at stake." Perhaps for this reason, virtue ethics has been an especially useful approach in practical fields such as medicine, business, and law.

As philosopher Mary Warnock writes, "Ethics is a complicated matter. It is partly a matter of general principles . . . but largely a matter of judgment and decision, of reasoning and sentiment, of having the right feeling at the right time, and every time is different." Thus, being "honest" doesn't mean following a single moral rule; it is a way of approaching myriad situations and weighing what should be expected of you in each.

And as a practical matter, doesn't virtue ethics capture how we teach children to be good people? We don't recite lots of complicated rules defining a concept like kindness; instead, we hope that kids watch their parents as they act kindly to others. It's hard to teach complex rule-lessons, such as "Remember, child, it is right to do x in this situation and y in that situation, but z in another situation, unless p or q." It's far more practical to tell children, "Try to act the way you see kind people acting. Watch Grandma and Grandpa." That is virtue ethics.

Reportedly, when eBay went international, it needed to devise some acceptable cross-cultural principle for what, ethically, could be sold on the site. After a lot of brainstorming, the principle they adopted was: "Would you be comfortable telling your mother you were doing this?" That rule worked well across all cultures, illustrating the ongoing value of the core concept of virtue ethics.

Nonetheless, like any single moral system, virtue ethics presents challenges.

WHICH VIRTUES?

First of all, how do we know what primary virtues we should practice? Moral leaders throughout history have offered lists of crucial virtues—but those lists differ.

Confucius regarded the "Five Constant Virtues" as benevolence, righteousness, propriety, wisdom. and trustworthiness.

The Chinese sage Mencius cited benevolence, righteousness, wisdom, and piety.

The Jains cited as core virtues nonviolence, not lying, not stealing, chastity, and non-possessiveness.

The Buddha said the key virtues are lovingkindness, compassion, joy, and equanimity.

The Biblical Book of Solomon says, "[Wisdom] teaches temperance, and prudence, and justice, and fortitude, which are such things as men can have nothing more profitable in life."

Plato lauded wisdom, courage, moderation, and justice.

Aristotle cited prudence, temperance, courage, and justice, but at times added magnanimity, liberality, and gentleness.

The Roman Cicero cited prudence, temperance, courage, and justice.

Drawing on the Old Testament, the Christian tradition (through Ambrose and Augustine), usually cited four cardinal virtues (prudence, fortitude, temperance, and justice), and added three religious virtues (faith, hope, and charity) (1 Corinthians 13:13).

The modern Jesuit scholars Daniel Harrington and James Keenan update the phrasing of the virtues as "be humble, be hospitable, be merciful, be faithful, reconcile, be vigilant, and be reliable."

Some would add the social virtues, including such things as respect for authority, loyalty, civic mindedness, and discharge of duties. Winston Churchill declared that "courage is rightly esteemed the first of human qualities because it is the quality that guarantees all others." But some lament that "civic virtue is a fading trait, our political sphere now understood as merely a contest of group interests. Patriotism and the common good are quaint notions."

A modern philosopher warns that "the list of mandatory virtues is notoriously subject to change." But in fairness, the above lists show considerable durability across time and cultures, and at least provide a place to start.

The leading modern proponents of virtue ethics include philosophers such as Martha Nussbaum, Philippa Foot, Michael Slote, Alasdair MacIntyre, Elizabeth Anscombe, Rosalind Hursthouse, and Mary Warnock. To an extent, they laud the core virtues, including those listed above. But virtue ethics also highlights character traits that transcend particular virtues. As leading bioethics experts write, "What often matters most in health care interactions . . . is not adherence to moral rules but having a reliable character, good moral sense, and appropriate emotional responsiveness."

Hursthouse defends virtue ethics against the charge that it leads to inconsistent, ad hoc morality. Instead, she says, "Virtue ethics provides a specification of 'right actions'—as 'what a virtuous agent would, characteristically, do in the circumstances'—and [this helps in] generating a number of moral rules or principles." So, then, the ultimate virtue is a form of ethical wisdom.

IS VIRTUE ETHICS JUST "CIRCULAR REASONING"?

"Circular reasoning" is a logical flaw that occurs when you reach a conclusion that is really just the same as the premise you started with.

Critics argue that virtue ethics is largely circular: It tells us to learn good conduct by acting like good people. But how would you know which people to emulate unless you already had a firm idea of what constitutes good conduct?

Some people clearly are good in most regards and are widely recognized as such. You might feel secure in emulating the conduct of the rare ethical saint or hero. But they are icons we don't spend time with regularly, which limits their use as exemplars for how to deal with one's children or noisy neighbors. However, in every neighborhood there may be people who are good to their families, neighbors, coworkers, and others, and who thus are worthy of imitation.

Still, there are challenges in emulating good people. Many are good in some realms, but less so in others. Or they do good things on some occasions, but not always. And some of their well-intentioned acts go awry or may even cause harm. When the hardworking immigrant owner of a restaurant generously lends money to his shiftless brother who never repays it, causing the man to lose his restaurant, should we emulate him as a good person? If a female executive gives a coveted promotion to a woman rather than a more able man because she wants to help women "break the glass ceiling," should we emulate her "virtue"? When a man reluctantly beats his beloved son with a belt, believing that in the long run the boy will benefit by learning discipline, should we imitate him? In such situations, we are left to wonder whether the act is good, the person is good, or neither.

Virtue ethics does seem somewhat circular, in that it judges people as virtuous by their conduct, and then judges conduct based on who routinely acts in that way. This may be a flaw, but not necessarily a fatal one. It might be analogized to the circularity of facts and theory in science: The theory helps flag what facts may be relevant, and the facts then inform the theory. Likewise, one toggles between virtuous acts and virtuous people, with each gradually shaping our concept of the other.

DON'T PEOPLE'S VIRTUES VARY BY SITUATION?

Virtue ethics treats virtues as relatively fixed features of a person, but even good people are inconsistently virtuous. They are truthful in a dozen situations and then tell a lie in the next one. This human tendency has been called *situationism*, and it has been confirmed by many researchers in psychology and ethics. Proponents of situationism cite famous experiments such as Stanley Milgram's study in which he induced subjects to administer what they thought were painful electric shocks to subjects. Or they cite real-world examples of large populations being culturally or politically induced to engage in massive evil. Some go so far as to infer that stable character traits don't really exist.

However, it's well established that individuals do exhibit stable and reliable patterns of behavior that differ from those of others. Research shows remarkably stable core personality traits across an individual's lifespan. Our common experience confirms this. We are more apt to say, "Gosh, that just doesn't sound like something John would do," than "Who can really guess what anybody will ever do?" So, the situationist crtitique is probably overstated. Our virtue may be malleable to circumstances to an extent, but people will still reliably differ from one another, with some being predictably more virtuous than others (see Chapter 9).

A remaining problem is that what constitutes a virtue varies according to circumstances. For example, it is virtuous for a police officer to bravely confront drug dealers on his beat but perhaps not so if he is off duty and taking his young children to dinner at McDonald's. Patience is a virtue in a mother, but perhaps not when she sees her son buying guns online and writing screeds about wanting to kill his classmates. And as Tolstoy's Prince Andrei says in *War and Peace,* military exploits may require an *absence* of virtue: "A good commander not only does not need genius or any special qualities, but, on the contrary, he needs the absence of the best and highest human qualities—love, poetry, tenderness, a searching philosophical doubt."

Considering all these nuances, we see that people don't simply belong to the tribes of the Virtuous or the Not Virtuous. They are virtuous in some respects and some situations, and less so in others. It is a common trope that "the hero of a tragedy is a strong man with one weakness, a good man with one fault . . . [so that] a whole ethics of tragedy has grown up around the significance of that single flaw." But if we acknowledge that, aren't we back in the business of needing reliable moral rules for judging such people? Virtue ethics can carry us only so far in that regard.

TOLERANCE

An especially knotty question: When is tolerance of others a moral virtue, and when is tolerance of immorality itself immoral? As political theorist Michael Sandel notes, "One of the great questions of political philosophy is: Does a just society seek to promote the virtue of its citizens? Or should law be neutral toward competing conceptions of virtue so that citizens can be free to choose for themselves the best way to live?"

Many people believe that moral virtue requires us to be tolerant and non-judgmental regarding those who differ. They say we shouldn't criticize people whose lifestyles involve recreational drugs, myriad sexual partners, open marriage, or mocking religion and patriotism. But many of those same people strongly urge *not* tolerating speech that they judge to be racist, sexist, or ethnically insensitive. Conversely, many people want to sanction behavior they regard as depraved, aberrant, sacrilegious, or un-American, while simultaneously demanding that society tolerate their beliefs and conduct if they choose to carry guns in restaurants, refuse to hire foreigners or gay people, and evade legally required child vaccinations. The problem for a person seeking to practice virtue ethics is: When is it virtuous to be tolerant, and when is tolerance merely acceding to (and thus encouraging) bad conduct? Virtue ethics raises this question but provides no reliable answer.

HOW FAR MUST WE GO IN BEING VIRTUOUS?

There is a new doctrine called *effective altruism* (EA) that has gained great popularity among not only some philosophers but also the superwealthy, and many others as well. EA isn't an overall moral theory but a set of principles that could be grafted onto various moral frameworks, though it fits most naturally with virtue ethics.

EA asserts that a truly moral person must go beyond just being nice and avoiding bad acts. They must *actively work* to relieve pain, suffering, and evil in the world, and focus their efforts where they can make the greatest difference. That means, for example, that if they are affluent Americans, they should give away a substantial part of their total annual income—and specifically to world famine relief rather than to an art museum—because doing so would have such a disproportionately powerful impact on human lives. Funding an African farmer to buy a cow, a water purification device, or a bicycle to get to market will have a lot more impact on human welfare than contributing $500 to an American art museum or even to an inner-city homeless shelter. EA urges us not just to be altruistic, but to think about what is the most effective altruistic action.

SUMMING UP

As noted earlier, some critics regard the inward focus of virtue ethics as quaint or prissy. Others see it as tending toward being sanctimonious. This recalls Molière's barb: "I prefer an accommodating vice to an obstinate virtue." But proponents say that virtue ethics comes close to depicting the way most people actually think about moral issues. We ask ourselves, "What would a good person do in this situation?" Thinkers since Aristotle have noted that virtue requires more than just doing the right thing; it requires having the right heart. Virtue ethics also adds that dimension.

The Revival of Stoicism

SUPPOSE THERE WERE A STOCK MARKET with prices reflecting the popularity of our different schools of morality. As of this writing, Kantian rules might be down a bit. Humean sentiments are up significantly. Utilitarianism is holding steady. But the blockbuster going through the roof is Stoicism, which has lately been embraced as the hot new philosophy of the Silicon Valley tech crowd.

You might think that this current market darling must be some fancy new-age, AI-type invention. But in fact, Stoicism is one of the older moral frameworks, dating to the fifth-century BCE Greek Zeno and his followers. Its name derives from the Stoa of Atalos, a long covered walkway or porch attached to a merchant building in the Athenian *agora,* the central plaza. Philosophers, political agitators, and others seeking a public audience would hold forth there. (It has been restored, and you can walk in their footsteps today.) Stoicism "received widespread recognition, including among its followers [several kings]."

Stoicism flowered in the Roman empire. Its main theorists were Romans, including the exiled former slave Epictetus, the dramatist and stateman Seneca, and the emperor Marcus Aurelius. (Now that is some mixed bag of adherents!) In time, Stoicism was almost entirely eclipsed by the rise of Christianity. It was never a mass movement in Rome. "In ancient times, Stoicism had a kind of public relations problem. It was widely seen by the masses as a cold, stern, demanding and rather gloomy creed for the strong and the few. Christianity, by contrast, seemed to offer a 'ray of sunshine.'" While some strains of Stoicism ran through later moral theory, for many centuries it largely fell into desuetude as an alternative moral framework.

Given this history, it's surprising that American bookstores and the internet today are chockful of Stoic offerings. There are myriad books on Stoicism focused on business, self-help, relationships, mindfulness, ethics, and community. There is a *Handbook for New Stoics*, a fine book called *Stoicism for Dummies*, and hundreds of podcasts and online media presentations. The prolific author Ryan Holiday has written a series of books on Stoicism, which have sold some six million copies, and a blog called "The Daily Stoic." There are online Stoic communities, Stoic Week events, and the annual convention Stoicon.

Why all this popularity? Perhaps it's because Stoicism is such an open-ended, fluid set of philosophical principles. It is open to varied interpretations, adaptable to many situations, and seemingly nondidactic and nonjudgmental. These qualities appeal to modern minds. It includes an approach to ethics, but it is really a larger viewpoint on life.

Contrary to common parlance, being a Stoic doesn't mean just "sucking it up" and suffering misfortune or pain in silence. More broadly, "Stoicism is about personal freedom, individual excellence, inner power, human equality, . . . vibrant societies, and a radical recipe for inner tranquility."

That's a lot to promise. Here are some of Stoicism's core principles:

- A person should conquer their emotions rather than allowing emotions to control them. As Marcus Aurelius said, "The agitations that beset you are superfluous and depend wholly on judgments of your own. You can get rid of them."

- Find inner peace by accepting the reality of the world. That doesn't mean not caring (what the Greeks called *apathos*, the root of "apathetic"). It means recognizing the limited effect of our personal actions on the ongoing nature of life.

- Be realistic about personal responsibility. Do your duty, but cease trying to fix what is broken and beyond your control.

- Practice *oikeiosis*, whose root is the Greek word for "home." It means taking on, as if they were part of your own home, the needs and feelings of others.

- Live in the moment. "Keep in mind how fast things pass by and are gone. . . . Existence flows past like a river." Strive to be in harmony with nature.

- Let reason guide ethics. Strive to be a virtuous person; that alone will bring you happiness. One book sums up the Stoic creed as "to cope and conquer with character."

The ancient Stoics thought many other schools just philosophized endlessly without practical results. As Seneca said, "We are taught how to debate, not how to live." In contrast, the Stoics aimed to be down-to-earth and practical. Marcus advised: "No situation is better suited for the practice of philosophy than the one you are in right now." In contrast to turgid tomes of epistemology and moral theory, Stoic advice could often be expressed in epigrams.

The Stoics believed that character determines conduct, that in the words of Heraclitus, "Character is destiny." The goal of life is to achieve good character or virtue. Following Socrates, the Stoics believed that only by living a life of reason and virtue could one achieve happiness (or *eudaimonia,* often translated as "flourishing"). We must free ourselves from pointless, selfish, and impossible desires, and instead follow virtue. More specifically, the Stoics identified four cardinal virtues: self-control/acceptance, courage, justice, and wisdom.

What else do the Stoics proclaim? We can start with the Stoic embrace of Socrates's idea that virtue is a type of knowledge or wisdom about what truly matters in life. Thus, Marcus said, "Begin each day reminding yourself: Today I'll be meeting with interference, ingratitude, disrespect, disloyalty, ill-will and selfishness, all of these things being done due to the offenders' ignorance of what is good or evil." In response, the Stoic should always focus on truth and virtue. As Marcus said: "The best revenge is not to be like your enemy."

Then the Stoics emphasized what is called the "dichotomy of control," which is "the central concept in Stoicism." As Epictetus said, "Of all existing things, some are in our power, and others are not. . . . In our power are [our own] thought, impulse, will to get and will to avoid. . . . Things not in our power include the body, property, reputation, office." Focusing on what we can impact rather than what we can't is a key element of Stoic wisdom.

Stoicism has many other useful things to say about how to live the good life. Do not chase wealth and possessions. Avoid unkindness and gossip (social media!). Expect the world to be imperfect; don't grind your gut over its lack of fairness. Enter each day anticipating that life will throw up obstacles, and be joyed by how many times people act well. Deal generously with difficult people. Seek inner acceptance. As Marcus said, "How much more unconscionable are our anger and vexation than are the acts that made us angry and vexed." Acceptance leads to more charitable views of others: "When you want to cheer your spirits, consider the excellence of those around you." Moreover, "If you discover in human life something better than justice, truth, self-control, courage . . . then turn to it with all your heart and enjoy this prime good you have found."

Sayings like these seem to fall somewhere between superficial bromides and wisdom for the ages. There are surely kernels of wisdom here. But Stoicism also presents contradictions and problems.

First, Stoics believed that everything was fated in advance. That presents obvious problems for those who believe in free will, personal choice, and moral responsibility. The venerable doctrine often used to reconcile this tension is called *compatibilism*—the idea that fate and causal determinism can coexist with free will. Thus, you can work to make free moral choices and they do matter, even though, unbeknownst to you, your choices are predetermined. But many philosophers, and many of us regular folk, still find that paradoxical. For example, if God knows in advance that I am about to tell a lie, how could I decide at the last minute to tell the truth?

Another problem with Stoicism is that its stress on the dichotomy of control seems to verge on touting passivity and accepting social suffering or evil, since they are out of our control. Thus, "it is senseless to nurture aversion of poverty, illness, or death because these things are outside our control." The Stoic creed was capsulized by Epictetus: "Do not wish for everything that happens to go as you wish, but to go as everything does happen, and your life will be serene." Fine, but if war, famine, disease, and drug cartels afflict my fellow humans, should serenity really be my main moral goal? Is throwing up our hands in the face of those painful realities besetting others really moral?

Furthermore, we face situations every day in which we aren't sure whether our actions can or cannot change the outcome. If I defend a coworker to a boss who is considering firing her or I urge a relative to patch up their marriage, I can't know whether these actions will work or prove pointless. I can't know until I try—and even then, the outcome may not be clear. So, then, is it morally just as good for me to do nothing? How can Stoicism accept such passivity while touting the virtue of courage? Doesn't courage often require doing the hard and right thing even though you can't be sure it will change the outcome?

And what of the Stoic commitment to justice, which they defined as "giving each person their due" or what they deserve? The Roman Cicero called this "the brightest adornment of virtue." But remember that the Stoics preceded the Christian turn-the-other-cheek era; they began in the eye-for-an-eye age. Does giving each person their due mean lying to the liar or swindling the cheat? That may be only fair, but how does it embody virtue? Besides, do we always know enough to decide what another person we encounter truly deserves? And what is the criterion for deservingness? Stoicism urges us to be fair, but doesn't seem to offer much guidance about what fairness means.

The Stoic answer to such conundrums seems to be "Do the right thing and try to be virtuous, even if it makes no difference." That is noble, but hardly a realistic guide for mortal humans. We act honorably in part because we believe that *it does* make some difference to others, not just to the purity of our character. Soldiers in war don't jump into firefights so that they will feel good about themselves afterward; they do it to try to save their buddies. One Stoic guidebook even goes so far as to advise that "You should not desire to be loved by your partner, but only to be the most lovable person you can be." Be kind and lovable, but if your partner doesn't see it—hey, what can you do? So be it! That is not a maxim likely to take hold in the world as we know it.

What of one's ethical duty to society? Here, the Stoics take a broad view. Ahead of his time, the Stoic Hierocles posited circles of community—the idea that we should broaden our circle of caring, beyond our own friends, family, and neighborhood, to the larger world. Seneca said, "The first thing which philosophy undertakes is to give fellow-feeling with all men, in other words, sympathy and sociability." And Marcus Aurelius said, "Whether in a city or the wilderness, you are a citizen of the world," so that "in whatever I do, my one objective will be this and only this: to benefit and live in harmony with the community."

At this point it is only fair to note that as Roman emperor, Marcus waged lethal wars against the Parthians (Iranians), the Armenians, and various

Germanic and Gothic peoples along the Danube, who did not celebrate Marcus's sense of harmony and community.

Modern Stoic writers range from the scholarly to the pop psychological. One leading modern Stoic philosopher, Massimo Pigliucci, sees Stoicism as "a rational, science-friendly philosophy that includes a metaphysics with a spiritual dimension, is explicitly open to revision, and most importantly is eminently practical." In explaining Stoicism, Ryan Holiday says, "While we will describe the profound moral dilemmas of life, the purpose will be to cut through them, . . . not bog you down with hopeless abstractions." That leads to guidance such as "What is right is what works."

Stoicism's tendency toward simplification leads some to criticize it as a collection of ill-fitting pieces. Professor Nancy Sherman laments that "Today Stoicism is not so much a philosophy as a collection of life-hacks for overcoming anxiety . . . and exercises for finding stillness and calm."

That said, the strengths and weaknesses of Stoicism may be two sides of the same coin. Stoicism is a set of very general life principles. It is open and non-dogmatic. It suggests a path to both inner peace and external moral decency. That is all to the good. But as a result of this vagueness, it is hard to know what a Stoic moral stance guides us to do in the tough ethical situations we all face— when loyalty and fairness conflict, or when telling the truth hurts those we love.

However, the next framework—the final major one we'll discuss in this book—at least attempts to provide tools to formulate moral answers.

Practical Morality: Casuistry

A FINAL MAJOR APPROACH TO MORALITY is *casuistry*, which has been called a process for "the practical resolution of particular moral perplexities or cases of conscience," especially those "in which there appears to be a conflict of duties." Casuistry recognizes that being moral isn't just a matter of having the right spirit or values. Because even good values can conflict, being moral also requires skill in ethical problem solving. Casuistry provides hope of reconciling Kantian fixed rules, Humean sentiments, and utilitarian weighing of good and bad effects. It replaces fixed rules with imaginative problem solving—a set of skills for wise moral judgment. But it also upholds the concept of duty and tries to discern what truly is right, beyond what feels right, in a given situation.

Casuistry is consistent with the well-documented "dual process" theory of mind, in which we try to reconcile our quick intuitive instincts with our more deliberate, reasoned judgments. "As the mind oscillates between alternatives, it successfully champions the case for one or another decision—changing its justifications and criticisms." Casuistry may also offer a concrete way to arrive at Rawls's goal of "reflective equilibrium." It's not just after-the-fact justification. Casuistry is what good people do when they work their way through a tough moral choice. It involves thinking and struggling with both facts and feelings. We may wind up being right at times and wrong at others, but casuistry itself is a moral process. This is because "moral values and moral principles . . . arise from our ongoing communal experience of moral disagreement, . . . argument and experimentation."

Casuistry has a long history in several intellectual traditions, including Talmudic Judaism, where one "wrestles with God," and wisdom lies in the questions as well as the answers. Casuistry also lived deep within ancient Greek philosophy (especially in the works of Aristotle), canonical Catholicism, and the Jesuit tradition. In the Greek tradition, casuistry sought to unite theoretical moral knowledge (*episteme*) with practical judgments about right conduct (*phronesis*). Thus, "theoretical arguments are chains of proof, whereas practical arguments are methods of solving problems."

Originally, Roman law gave public officials wide decision-making authority, and they were not generally required to explain or justify their decisions. The College of Pontiffs (judges) could simply declare their rulings without explaining them—i.e., they could "pontificate." Only as the empire grew and it became important to reconcile decisions across many cultures did Roman law begin to require officials to state rationales and develop reliable precedents. They decided and reconciled "cases"—thus giving rise to "casuistry."

Like every moral method, casuistry has its critics. Some charge that "casuistry destroys [morality] by distinctions and exceptions . . . and effaces the essential difference between right and wrong." Hence the term *casuistry* is often used in a mocking way, to describe pointless "dancing on the head of a pin" or merely "quibbling with God." Jonathan Haidt says that when people face a moral choice, they "have strong gut feelings about what is right and wrong, and they struggle to construct post-hoc justifications," which may not have real moral quality. At its worst, casuistry can be nothing more than such after-the-fact rationalizations.

On the other hand, proponents of casuistry say it reflects the reality of life—that we engage in "imaginative moral deliberations" in the process of making a moral self. This is necessary because morality has a radial structure, with a basic rule ("Don't steal") and archetypal cases at the core ("Don't steal from a bank"), and then rings of cases of decreasing similarity located farther from the archetype ("Don't take towels home from a hotel," or "Don't 'forget' to tell the waiter that he failed to charge for the bottle of wine"). The boundaries are often fuzzy. So, naturally, we argue with one another about where the boundaries should be drawn, asking just how similar to stealing a given action really is.

Casuistry is in many ways analogous to the Anglo-American legal process, which involves interpreting laws, weighing the equity (fairness) of various options, and allowing space for wise judicial decisions. As Justice Oliver Wendell Holmes famously acknowledged, "General propositions do not decide concrete cases"—which means that lawyers and judges must reason their way to a legal decision in each case by comparison of many factors. In American law, first there is Constitutional or statutory law that sets general rules. Then the so-called common law applies the rules in specific cases and refines them through judicial decisions. And finally, courts sometimes apply what are called "equitable" principles to craft exceptions based on overriding fairness.

The last element of equity strikes many nonlawyers as arbitrary. After going to all the trouble of enacting laws and adopting precedent rules, why would society allow a judge *not* to follow them? Yet this equity power of courts has a long judicial history. A few examples will show its moral basis.

Suppose an important legal rule is "Contracts shall be enforced." A man buys a million-dollar life insurance policy and names his only son as the beneficiary. The son then kills the father and demands the insurance proceeds. The legal principle says, "Enforce the contract, make the payment." But the court likely will refuse based on the "equitable" principle that society doesn't want to reward people for their own criminal acts, and doing so would be "unconscionable."

Likewise, a contract stating that "I'll pay you $100,000 to cut off your arm" won't be enforced because it is against public policy to use the law to support such bad behavior. The law says that enforcing contracts is a good rule, but there are exceptions in the service of morality. Casuistry is like that.

Casuistry also has been analogized to the decision-making process used by physicians. Doctors have scientific knowledge about the usual causes of diseases, and clinical practice guidelines embody what generally have proven to be the best treatments, so these are rules to guide medical professionals. But each patient is different. Medical education in recent decades stresses listening to the patient, being alert to unique differences, and using judgment to discern when *not* to follow the textbook treatment. The physician is supposed to weigh what is deemed right by and for this particular patient, not just follow a rule book.

Many experts believe that bioethics—the application of moral thinking to medical issues—*requires* casuistry. This is in part because our goals and values often conflict. We want the autonomy to decide what medical procedures to undertake, yet we demand reliably good results. We want innovation, but not errors. We want freedom of choice, but not grossly unequal health disparities. We want proven, evidence-based medicine, but also patient-sensitive flexibility. Accordingly, a leading treatise on biomedical ethics concludes, "It is a mistake in biomedical ethics to assign priority to any basic principle over other basic principles—as if morality is hierarchically structured . . . without consideration of particular circumstances. The best strategy is to appreciate the contributions and limits of various principles, virtues and rights." Philosopher Janet Radcliffe Richards agrees: "There is nothing so useless as telling a doctor that if you're a Kantian you do this and if you're a utilitarian you do that, because what the doctor wants to know is what to do [now]. . . . So, the challenge is to see how many practical moral conclusions can be reached without settling the fundamentals of ethical theory." This approach is similar to Aristotle's. As Jonsen and Toulmin note: "Far from being based on general abstract principles that can at the same time be universal, invariable, and known with certainty, [Aristotle argued that] . . . ethics deals with a multitude of particular concrete situations, which . . . resist all attempts to generalize about them in universal terms." On this view, moral principles are starting points, but not end points.

Importantly, casuists believe their approach embodies what good people actually do (and should do) in everyday life as they wrestle with moral issues, trying to find the right solution. One analyst of ethics sees four basic steps. We ask ourselves: (1) What are our guiding principles? (2) Do we have the right information? (3) Who are the stakeholders? and (4) What are the consequences to them? In the process, we start with moral instincts; we try to see what moral rules apply; we think of what a good person would do; we struggle with our conscience; and we muddle through to some conclusion.

Steps like these are needed because we are all conflicted as we face moral dilemmas. Psychologist Marc Hauser explains it this way:

> The [psychological] systems that generate intuitive moral judgments are often in conflict with the systems that generate principled reasons for our actions because the landscape of today only dimly resembles our original [human] state. The Rawlsean creature will, therefore, fire off its intuitions about moral rights and wrongs, the Kantian will fire back principled arguments against those intuitions, and sometimes caught in the middle will be the Humean, generating angst, attempting to tilt the evidence toward one of the moral poles.

In fact, imaging studies reveal how this battle rages between different parts of the brain.

So, in the broadest terms, morality is a suite of "moral habits, wisdom and skills consist[ing] largely of know-how" in resolving these conflicts. Casuistry provides a process for dealing with moral dilemmas. It encourages us to use judgment, discernment, compassion, and fairness. Rather than giving us fish (moral rules), casuistry teaches us how to fish for ourselves.

Getting Specific: Moral Particularism

MORAL PARTICULARISM IS A COUSIN OF CASUISTRY, but differs in important respects.

Casuistry recognizes that moral principles, however wise, must be adjusted to specific problems, and may not fit them all. Particularism goes farther and questions whether a moral principle can ever solve any particular problem. Thus, "moral particularism, at its most trenchant, is the claim that there is no defensible moral principle," and hence, "the morally perfect person should not be conceived as the person of principle." Some prominent proponents of particularism, such as John Dancy and John McDowell, argue that trying to be consistent by articulating moral principles actually does more harm than good.

Many critics find this puzzling, since "it is hard to deny that morality has something to do with rules." Some of the particularists' examples seem a bit too cute. For example, they point out that even a seemingly good rule, such as "You should return what you borrow," may have exceptions—for example, if you discover that the person you borrowed an object from actually stole it from someone else. But that doesn't vitiate all general rules; it just means this rule should have been stated more precisely: "You should generally return what you borrow—unless the person doesn't actually own it, or they plan to use it to hurt others."

I faced that issue myself once, while working as a bartender. One night, a frequent customer—a decent guy who often drank too much and was now sloshed—pulled out a gun and woozily said, "Cliff, I should just shoot all those loud bastards over there. . . ." I sweet-talked him into giving me the gun, which I stowed under the bar, with the promise that I'd give it back when he was through with his fifth scotch. I lied, and didn't give the gun back. He stumbled out, but came by to get it when he was sober the next day.

Martha Nussbaum notes that since antiquity, moral thinking has recognized three levels: theories, rules, and concrete judgments. But how do we connect these levels? Moral particularism says it doesn't deny the importance of moral judgments, just principles. But if we simply decide what we think is right in each situation, pretty soon wouldn't we begin to think inductively and derive some patterns . . . what might be called principles? Even those who espouse moral particularism usually find themselves applying moral principles from time to time, perhaps without acknowledging it.

HAVING TAKEN A WHIRLWIND TOUR through the most influential frameworks for moral thinking that have evolved over the millennia, we're now in a position to examine how these frameworks might help us tackle the moral dilemmas we face in everyday life.

5

Moral Frameworks and Solving Daily Dilemmas

L ET'S LOOK AT HOW THE THEORIES WE'VE EXPLORED might play out in a few moral situations. I've intentionally avoided extreme and rare examples, such as risking one's life to save another, and instead focused on the kinds of smaller moral challenges we encounter more often in everyday life.

"Nobody Likes You"

OUR FIRST EXAMPLE INVOLVES a group conversation at the office during a morning of turmoil.

It all starts during the team meeting held every Monday, when two coworkers, Jim and Amy, drift into an argument about whether Amy was responsible for a significant mistake the week before. One thing leads to another, and Amy appeals to her colleagues to defend her from Jim's criticisms. Jim then cuttingly declares, "Don't ask them to get involved. Let's face it, *nobody in this office really respects or likes you!*" Close to tears, Amy leaves the meeting room and retreats to her office.

This results in a heated debate among Jim and his colleagues about the moral rights and wrongs of this situation:

- Jim says he didn't mean to hurt Amy's feelings, but he believes in telling the truth. (Jim is a Kantian: Intent, not effect, is the measure or rightness.)

- Mary says truth isn't the point. We all want to be liked by others. Jim should have been more restrained, and his remark to Amy was cruel—even if it was mostly true. (Mary is a Humean: If something just feels mean, it's morally wrong.)

- Tom argues that we need to respect the general value of candor, because even if Amy's feelings were hurt in this instance, she's better off knowing that her coworkers will be straight with her. We shouldn't treat her as an object and decide what's best for her. She deserves true information that she can use to alter her behavior if she wants to. (Back to another Kantian principle.)

- Rosa says we need to consider not just the impact on Amy, but the effect on her coworkers, too. Are they relieved that someone finally told Amy that her screw-ups are problematic, or are they ashamed that Jim's crack was over the top and may lead to further backbiting at work? (Rosa takes the utilitarian approach.)

- Stan says Jim is known to be a decent guy, so when he told Amy she was disliked, it probably was a good call. Maybe it will help her improve her behavior in the future. (Stan appeals to virtue ethics.)

- Jamal says the whole debate seems pointless. Jim values candor over kindness. Others may disagree, but it's a personal judgment call, and there's no way to say who is definitely wrong. (Jamal is a relativist.)

- Ariel accepts Jamal's point that there aren't hard and fast rules about conduct. But she says Jim should have thoughtfully weighed the pros and cons of so openly criticizing Amy. He should have considered Amy's personality and the political dynamics of the office to determine whether snapping at her would make things better or worse. (Ariel is acting as a casuist).

- Finally, David declares that while the group might talk all day about rules of behavior and the pros and cons of various choices, in the end, he feels that Jim's remark was just plain nasty. (Back to Hume).

My main point here is not that these people have different approaches to moral conduct—it's that you probably have a degree of sympathy with almost all of them! You might imagine yourself making any of these arguments in a given situation.

That doesn't mean that you're confused or morally wishy-washy—not at all. As we'll see in the next chapter, the reason is that each of the main moral frameworks appeals to and activates an important part of our shared human psychology. Then there begins a tussle for hegemony in our minds and hearts. Mature thinking about morality requires the ability to apply several frameworks, each of which places primary stress on certain factors, and to discern which factors should matter most in a particular situation.

Equally important, almost no one embraces a single moral framework and applies it logically and consistently. In fact, the way we reason and argue about morality is almost always a mosaic of reason, emotion, analogies, excuses, exceptions, special relationships, and personal experiences.

Now let's look at a second example that illustrates how this works.

"We Ate the Loser for Lunch!"

EIGHT-YEAR-OLD BILLY COMES HOME one evening after spending the weekend at a friend's house and excitedly tells his mom, Debby, "It was so cool! Jimmy's dad raises chickens and trains them to fight. We each got to pick one that looked strongest, and my chicken beat up the other one and then we ate the loser for lunch. It was awesome!"

Debby just about faints. She is horrified. Later that evening, she calls Jimmy's mother Rhonda, and the ensuing argument goes like this:

DEBBY: I can't believe what you and your husband did—teaching kids to enjoy cruelty. Don't you have any moral sense?

RHONDA: Do you take your kids to McDonald's for chicken nuggets? Well, somebody had to kill the chicken first.

DEBBY: That's totally different—my children aren't watching the chicken being killed!

RHONDA: So in your mind, something isn't evil as long as you don't need to see it? You're just teaching your kids to be hypocrites!

DEBBY: No, the point is that watching chickens maim each other and cheering them on will make kids cruel in other ways.

RHONDA: You say that, but my son Jimmy is actually very kind—ask anyone in town about that. If your son turns out different, that's on you!

DEBBY: But who does things like chicken fighting anyway—what is it with you people?

RHONDA: "You people"? Are you saying you're better than us? Why does everybody need to act the same as you?

DEBBY: Well, we need some basic moral rules. One of those is that you don't have the right to expose other people's children to weirdness without asking them first.

RHONDA: You just moved here from Ohio, and suddenly you tell everyone how to live?

DEBBY: Well, if everybody just does whatever they like, we'll have a lot of really bad behavior.

RHONDA: So now our chickens are responsible for murders and bank robbery?

DEBBY: Don't you feel at least a little guilty? This is not what nice people do!

RHONDA: You don't even know me, do you? What right do you have to say I'm not a nice person?

You can see in this little capsule every moral approach we have analyzed. As the debate unfolds, Debby and Rhonda each reach into the grab bag of moral tools for whatever seems to counter what the other argues. At times, they appeal to principle (Kant), gut instinct (Hume), consequences (utilitarianism), what good people do (virtue ethics), and "decency" (custom).

As psychologist Paul Bloom has observed:

> Few adults are [always] Kantians or utilitarians or virtue ethicists; we don't
> normally think about morality as philosophers do. Rather, we possess what
> the psychologist David Pizarro has dubbed "a hodgepodge morality"—"a
> fairly loose collection of intuitions, rules of thumb, and emotional re-
> sponses." But . . . adult morality is influenced by rational deliberation . . .
> [W]e have sentiments plus reason.

"We Have to Take Away Pops's Car Keys!"

HERE IS A PAINFUL MORAL CHOICE faced by lots of families. Pops is 85, has
poor eyesight and hearing, but insists that "I can still drive the car just fine." You
are his son or daughter, and how you handle this challenge reveals a lot about
your moral framework.

If you're a Kantian, you might just feel that your father has the right to autonomy. You'll try to convince him to stop driving, but you would generally want
the universal rule to be that each person decides for themselves.

If you're a utilitarian, you'll likely come out the other way. Sure, Pops values
still having the freedom to drive—but there is no way his happiness ("utility")
from driving can outweigh the total misery created if he ever runs over and in-
jures or kills some poor kid he couldn't see crossing the street or riding their
bike.

If you believe in virtue ethics, you ask, "What would a good person do?" We
might like to think that if we were Pops, we would know that stopping driving
is the "right thing to do." But would we? Or would we, like many people, engage in denial, motivated thinking, and excuses: "Oh, I know I'm old, but I pay
real close attention when I'm driving, and I haven't had any serious accidents
yet . . ."). But surely that is not virtuous.

And if you're a Humean, you are really stuck. Taking Pops's car keys away
feels terrible; you're robbing him of dignity and freedom, and he may see it as
an unloving, even cruel, action. But it also feels terrible to think of a neighbor
coming to you and crying, "How could you let your Dad keep driving at his age
and run over my child?"

This situation is a good example where many people would, knowingly or
not, engage in casuistry. You might say to yourself: "Pop's had some recent
fender-benders—he's not seeing as well as he used to, but he seems okay most
of the time. I can't just impose this on him; maybe if I ask him what he thinks,

and then if all three of us kids say we wouldn't worry all the time if he just stops driving, and we can shuttle him where he needs to go, he might find it easier to accept. But still, he won't take it well, so if he refuses . . . " That is good moral puzzling-through of a tough problem. It may lead you to a morally "good" answer, though not an easy one.

"Should I Take the Job?"

NOW LET'S LISTEN TO A STRESSFUL CONVERSATION between a marketing executive named Justin and his wife, Antonia. Justin works for an apparel company, but he's been offered a bigger position with a major tobacco company.

JUSTIN: It's a real step up, with a higher salary. I should take the job, but I don't know how I feel about marketing cigarettes and chew that cause cancer.

ANTONIA: You *do* know how you feel—it's terrible.

JUSTIN: But if I don't take the job, somebody else will—and so it all winds up the same anyway.

ANTONIA: Yeah, but it won't be *you* that causes the deaths.

JUSTIN: If I do take the job, I won't be "causing" anything. It's a free country, and people can choose whether or not to smoke. I'm not doing anything intentionally bad.

ANTONIA: Okay, but there are lots of other jobs you could try for that don't involve you in something that kills. I read that tobacco kills about half a million people in America each year!

JUSTIN: Look, cars kill, and alcohol kills, and falling off ladders kills—so am I supposed to refuse to work for half the businesses in the country? I can't cure the problems of the world. This is a great job, and my first duty is to our family.

ANTONIA: Family? How are you going to feel looking our kids in the eye and telling them not to smoke or chew or vape—while you go to work every day trying to convince people to do it? Don't you want to set an example of what a good person decides to do?

JUSTIN: I'm not sure. I agree it doesn't feel great, but my head says that taking the job is the smart thing to do.

Once again, we see two decent people trying to figure out what decent means. They juggle intent, effects, competing duties, what good people do, and whether the mind or gut should prevail.

"It's Not Really Stealing!"

STEALING IS MORALLY BAD. Almost everyone agrees with this principle—but applying it to specific cases is not always easy. So which of these would you personally regard as stealing?

1. Bob is at a friend's barbecue and likes the brownies so much, he puts two extra ones in a plastic bag and brings them home.

2. Bob is at a dinner party and likes the wineglasses so much, he grabs two and asks his wife to take them home, hidden in her handbag.

3. Bob is staying at a hotel and likes the coffee mugs so much, he takes two home in his suitcase.

4. Bob is working late at the office on Friday and realizes he may need to print many hundreds of pages for a work project over the weekend, so he grabs several reams of printer paper to take home.

5. Bob gets the check at a restaurant and realizes the waiter forgot to charge him $20 for the desserts; he quietly pays the mistaken check and leaves.

6. Bob gets really bad service at a restaurant; when he sees the waiter drop a $20 bill on the floor, he pockets it.

7. Bob steals $500 from the petty cash drawer at work after his employer stiffed him by not paying a promised bonus after a huge year-long project.

8. Bob is closing on the sale of his house when he notices that the statement allocating closing costs between him and the buyer has mistakenly shifted $2,000 in taxes to the buyer. Neither party's broker notices the error. Bob says nothing and finalizes the closing.

Which of these eight behaviors would you call stealing? Make your own judgments, then compare them with my personal responses below. Your yes-or-no verdicts are significant, but so are the the thoughts and feelings that underlie them.

For me, case #1 (brownies) is definitely not stealing; it's just being rude. Bob's friend probably doesn't care whether Bob eats three brownies at the barbecue, saves one for later, or brings a couple back for the kids—unless the plate obviously only has enough for one brownie per guest (so Bob's behavior now means there aren't enough for everyone). Even in the latter case, "stealing" seems too strong a word. "Selfishness" might be more apt.

Case #2 (the wineglasses) is clearly a case of stealing. Even if the wineglasses aren't too expensive, it doesn't change the equation. Unlike brownies at a barbecue, wineglasses at a dinner party are not offered for the guests to make their own.

Case #3 (mugs) offers an interesting comparison to #2. I might be inclined to say that it isn't stealing, because people take hotel souvenirs all the time. But wait—why is it okay to take the mugs but not the wineglasses? Is stealing from a family bad, but stealing from a business is acceptable? Maybe the hotel budgets for people taking mugs—or even considers mugs that are taken a useful way of promoting their brand to potential customers? We can kid ourselves, but I would still call this stealing.

I find case #4 (printer paper) a closer call. If Bob routinely takes office supplies—especially for his personal use—it's probably stealing. But I wouldn't expect Bob to pay for several reams of paper for big copy jobs for work, so taking the paper home, instead of printing copies at the office, is okay with me.

Case #5 (restaurant check) is another interesting one. I suspect most people don't regard overlooking a favorable billing error as stealing. But why is ignoring the duty to pay for desserts less bad than taking money from the restaurant's cash register? Maybe the notions that Bob didn't "do" anything, and that "lots of people" ignore errors on checks, anesthetize our moral sense. But rationally, you can't defend it (unless, of course, the desserts were small and lousy, so not paying seems only fair!).

Case #6 (the $20 bill) seems clear to me—it's stealing money from the waiter. The fact that he dropped the $20 bill doesn't change that, nor does the fact that the waiter was rude and Bob got bad service. As your parents told you, "Two wrongs don't make a right!"

Case #7 (taking $500 from the cash drawer) is another clear case of stealing. Maybe it "feels" less immoral because the employer treated Bob badly, but consider the broader social implications. We don't want to let people steal whenever they feel unfairly treated.

The final case, #8 (the real estate closing), is just one more example of stealing. In a house sale, each side is normally represented by a broker who is supposed to read the settlement sheet and make sure it's correct. So, some people might think, "It's not my job to do their work," and that silently accepting the windfall is simply smart dealing. But I'd call that morally obtuse. Bob has intentionally deprived someone of $2,000 that was rightfully theirs—that's stealing.

Once again, in these examples, we see ourselves bouncing from one criterion of morality to another—a rule, a feeling, a custom, action/inaction, the amount, fairness, and so on. It is hard to see rhyme or reason in the pattern of choices we make.

Life presents endless challenges with moral dimensions. You can think of many in your own life. But in case you want further exercise, here are a few more examples. These questions may help you consider how you deploy your personal moral framework.

- As a hiring manager, can you intentionally deny a job to an applicant who is so good, she might be a threat to your position some day?

- Should you report the misbehavior of a friend who is engaged in really bad conduct at work?

- Is it okay to "forget" to tell a friend about the tryouts for a traveling sports team that both your child and hers would want to compete for?

- When, if at all, should you tell a child that they were adopted?

- When should you tell a child that a bad disease runs in your family?

- Should you tell a friend their spouse is cheating on them?

- Is it right to keep moving cities so you get promotions at work, even though your spouse keeps suffering career setbacks? Does it affect your answer if you earn more than your spouse, or does that miss the point?

- Is it okay to cheat on your taxes "a little," because "everyone does it"?

- Is it moral for a doctor to lie on a patient's medical record so their insurance company will cover a needed treatment?

- When should you overrule your frail mom's desire to continue to live alone and instead place her in an assisted living or nursing home?

- Is it okay to stop all contact with your brother because he's so difficult to deal with, or do you have a duty to just keep trying?

- Is it moral to look the other way if your teenager is into violent stuff online and then buys a gun, because you know he is basically a good kid?

- You're a decent person and don't do really bad things. But what else could you do to make the world a little better place morally? Does your answer to this question create any moral obligations on your part?

As we've seen, when you wrestle with such questions, no one answer may feel totally right. Each of the moral frameworks we've explored has strengths and weaknesses. That's one reason why we tend to slip from one to another when we confront a tough moral choice.

Since we are emotional as well as rational creatures, it's not enough for us to *think* that our moral framework makes sense; we also crave the sense of inner peace that comes with *feeling good* about it.

The chart that follows summarizes some of reasons why a person may feel good or feel bad while relying on each framework.

Pros and Cons of Each Moral Framework		
Framework	**You may feel good because:**	**You may feel bad because:**
Clear Rules (Kant)	You can state clear moral rules	Sometimes, your good intent has bad consequences
	People can rely on you following principles, not making convenient exceptions	Your "pure" rules can lead you to ignore special relationships or factors
	You don't feel guilty over uncontrollable consequences	At times, you seem like an egghead, not a practical person
What Feels Right (Hume)	You follow what feels right and moral (based on God or conscience)	It's hard to state your moral principles
	Your guidance can be flexible, based on individuals and situations	Others may think you act inconsistently based on convenience, not morality
	You probably won't be racked by guilt	Some of your intuitions are a poor guide to good outcomes
Utilitarianism	What's best for the most people overall seems like a solid moral ground	Sometimes it seems to trample the rights of minority groups who are outweighed
	The standard of judgment is not selfish or parochial	It makes you ignore your special caring for family and friends; they count no more than others
	The framework allows you to make moral judgments about public justice as well as private morality	Often you can't know or compute all the plus and minus effects or each action; then what do you do?

Framework	You may feel good because:	You may feel bad because:
Fairness (Rawls)	Obeying principles that would be fair regardless of our position in society seems a strong moral ground	This framework has little to say about simple two-person morality
	This framework adapts well to judging social justice as well as morals	The stress on the original position doesn't let us change our morals based on changed social conditions or our experience
	The preference for helping the least-well-off is consistent with Christian and other moral views	This framework provides few quick, easy solutions; it seems to involve a lot of abstract ruminating
Relativism	This framework seems tolerant; you aren't judging others	This framework requires that you accept bad things like oppression of women or honor killings
	The framework embraces different cultures	It does not inspire others' confidence in your moral behavior
	You avoid the need to struggle over hard moral choices when you and others disagree; just say "to each his own"	It still leaves you having to decide what courage, honesty, or fairness mean
Stoicism	This framework urges one always to seek virtuous conduct	It doesn't tell you what kindness, honor, or justice mean
	It allows you to accept what you cannot control	It may leave you confused: Why be courageous if you shouldn't be concerned with fights you can't win?
	It speaks both to inner morality and outer conduct, but allows a lot of flexibility	It seems to make you a person who just accepts evil "out there"

Framework	You may feel good because:	You may feel bad because:
Virtue Ethics	This framework captures the basic human desire to be a good person	It may seem circular: "follow good people"—but how do I know who to follow?
	It gives you a way to teach children morality: watch good people and imitate them	In hard cases, do I follow a rule or good people? What if they are ignorant of what I know—does that affect their virtue?
	It allows flexible working-through of touchy issues and close calls; doesn't require rigid rules	It's pretty vague; allows convenient inferences about what others would do

Framework	You may feel good because:	You may feel bad because:
Casuistry	This framework realistically captures what most of us do when we struggle with a moral problem	You may still be confused whether to follow a principle or make an exception
	You can keep your core principles, but still adapt to unique situations	Others may feel that you are just making it up as you go
	To others, you seem to have good, sensible judgment	It requires a lot of time, thought, struggle, and may still leave you in a quandary

6

The Psychology of Morals

A S WE'VE SEEN, MORAL JUDGMENT isn't just a cerebral activity. Emotions, relationships, social conditions, customs, and other things all intertwine as we judge people's conduct. Human psychology is the machine that assesses and reconciles these inputs. So now we'll turn from philosophies about how people *ought to decide* moral issues to psychological research about how they *do decide* them.

Aristotle was ahead of his time in concluding that "neither by nature then, nor contrary to nature, do the virtues arise in us; rather we are adapted by nature to receive them, and are made perfect by habit." So, the moral sense is derived from nature—and nurture—and practice! All three elements operate together in a complex system that shapes our sense of what is right and wrong.

In recent years, morality has been cast in a new light by a raft of innovative scholars, including Richard Shweder, Paul Rozin, Jonathan Haidt, Paul Bloom, Joshua Greene, Steven Pinker, Mark Gazzaniga, Michael Tomasello, Marc Hauser, and others. What then are the psychological mechanisms that shape our moral choices?

While experts differ on some important points, a general picture of moral psychology has emerged from this research, with the following elements.

Both Instinct and Reason

IT IS NOW CLEAR that we are not born as blank slates, entirely free to choose our moral framework. Instead, the human mind is wired to attach significance to certain things more than others. We have strong moral instincts or sentiments like empathy and a desire to avoid harming others. Reason also plays a role in our moral lives; when faced with a difficult moral choice, we try to find principles or rules to guide us. But recent research confirms the superior power of Humean moral instincts at the expense of Kantian rational rulemaking.

In his famous dialogue *Phaedrus,* Plato analogized the soul as a chariot, with a charioteer of reason straining to reconcile the stallions of virtue and base passions. As I mentioned earlier, psychologist Jonathan Haidt enlarges the metaphor, describing the tiny rider of reason atop an elephant of emotions. And many other psychologists agree. They have confirmed that we draw on two systems to resolve moral questions—a system of fast, instinctive feelings, and a system of slower, more effortful rational judgments. They disagree primarily about the balance between them, but the clear recent trend has been to deem emotions or cognitive/emotional biases as more dominant than reason. Some believe we should not see an instinct like repugnance as opposed to reason but as an element of reason. For example, Leon Kass says that in cases such as the taboo on incest, "repugnance is the essential expression of deep wisdom, beyond reason's power . . . to articulate it." And psychological researchers find that "disgust sensitivity can positively predict the severity of moral judgments." This is said to "provide convincing evidence for the model that moral judgment is primarily driven by emotion."

It seems that our instinctive emotions are often the engine, with reason trying hard to pull up in the rear. In a vivid example, researchers have found that if you ask people what's wrong with consensual incest between a loving brother and sister, they immediately concoct a bunch of reasons having to do with avoiding birth defects, or ruining relations with future spouses who learn of it, or disgracing the family. But then the researchers neutralize all these risks by building precautions into their hypotheticals. They tell the test subjects that there can't be future children because the siblings use multiple forms of contraception. Both siblings have decided never to marry, so there will be no future spouses to be grossed out. They agree never to tell anyone, so the family can't be disgraced. Yet studies show that all these precautions don't matter to most people in the end. They just say, "Yuck—it's still disgusting and morally wrong!"

Likewise, if you ask people how they would feel about eating a beloved dog who just died, or urinating on a tombstone while alone in a cemetery at night, most people have trouble articulating reasons to refuse, when the real reason is that is just *feels* horribly wrong. We shouldn't automatically devalue instinctive, emotional reasons as "lower" than rational explanations. When you ague moral issues with people, you should expect to encounter those kinds of reasons. At some level, we are all Humeans with strong moral sentiments that arise from deep inner psychology. They are tied to our sense of identity, community, and humanity.

And yet . . . we don't judge morally based *only* on emotion. The "dual process" model of mind remains at work. As we will see, we also reason, justify, excuse, explain, recharacterize, fudge, bargain, rationalize, and engage in a raft of other mental gymnastics in an effort to devise a means to reconcile our principles and emotions.

Other Psychological Dynamics Affecting Moral Thinking

WHETHER ONE DENOTES THEM as "cognitive" or "emotional" or "habits" or "biases," a common set of psychological dynamics strongly influence our moral thinking. The fact that these forces are at work doesn't destroy the moral value of our judgments. Many of these dynamics arise from a good instinct, like trying to avoid harm to others. But then they acquire momentum and perhaps overshoot the mark. The key point here is to be aware of these forces within you so that you can modulate or reconcile them as you puzzle through moral challenges. Here are some of the major ones.

METAPHORICAL THINKING

In assessing how rational your moral thinking is, reflect on how often key moral concepts aren't logical and literal but wildly metaphorical, drawing a figurative comparison or analogy between one situation and another. When facing a moral dilemma, rather than invoking a rule, we say something metaphorical, like "He's being a turd," "You can't let yourself be bullied," "She shouldn't have stabbed me in the back at the meeting," or "Don't act like a baby—man up!"

In many cases, the metaphor takes charge of the argument and imports into the situation covert features that may not really be present. That leads us to judge actors and actions based on the metaphor rather than the actual facts. For example, stabbing someone with a knife in the back is almost always covert and evil, so using this metaphor practically forces the listener to accept a prepackaged moral judgment. Yet the underlying facts may tell a different story; what people call "being stabbed in the back" may be nothing more than not being supported in a conflict by a friend—who has the right to disagree and does so openly.

Affect Bias

As we saw in Chapter 3, we all have a tendency to confuse how disgusted an action makes us feel with how morally bad it actually is. If you've ever been jilted by a person you were dating, then when that happens to a friend, you think it's truly awful. But really, in the scope of moral conduct, how bad is it? Paul Slovic and colleagues believe we use our emotions as a *heuristic* or rule of thumb for making judgments; it is more easily accessible to our minds than a complex ethical rationale.

Action/inaction bias

Humans have been wired by evolution to pay attention to actions, because they pose risks and opportunities. And a concrete physical action can usually be seen. By contrast, just doing nothing is more abstract (it might be "not doing" a variety of possible acts), and its effects often lie in the unknowable future. Hence, people have a tendency to assess the morality of conduct differently depending on whether it involves action or inaction, even if these ultimately have the same effects.

For example, it is viewed as far worse morally to slam a door in someone's face than just to let them walk into the door while they're distractedly looking elsewhere. In the words of one analyst, "We are more likely to judge an action with negative consequences as forbidden whereas we judge the omission of an action with the same consequences . . . as permissible." If a government social worker were to beat a child, the government would be liable (legally and morally). But if the social worker just looks the other way at parental abuse, there might not be liability—despite there being, at least arguably, an equivalent moral failure.

Unfortunately, the action/inaction bias underlying moral judgments can cause major damage. Social scientists have argued that it tends to make us too cautious in adopting social policies that could prevent harm. Thus, delaying stricter new regulations on auto safety, drugs, food additives, water quality, or mine safety could cost thousands of lives. If government approval of a new drug is too lax and 100 die because of dangerous side effects, there is general moral outrage. But if government withholds approval and 1,000 die before a life-saving new drug is approved for sale, there is little reaction—it's just "the way government works." Similarly, if gun dealers don't enforce background checks on criminal buyers who then kill people, few would say they "caused" the deaths.

Logically, the cost of acting and not acting should be considered equally when making moral judgments—but this isn't the way our minds and emotions are wired.

No-harm bias

Normal people have an aversion to seeing others hurt. Our first reaction is usually to help. But as the research by Nobel laureate Daniel Kahneman and Amos Tversky shows, this bias may lead to decisions that are rationally questionable. For example, if given the choice of (a) taking action that will save 200 out of 600 people *for sure,* or (b) taking a different action that has a one-third chance of saving all 600 and a two-thirds chance of saving none, people overwhelmingly choose the first option. Statistically, in terms of likely lives saved, these options are the same. But psychologically, we frame the first option as a good action in which we save people, while the second action leaves us anxious that we may have done something bad that turns out to "cause" 600 deaths.

This psychological glitch might actually impair the effort to save lives. What if the first option was would surely save only 150 lives? We might well still favor it—and, in effect, statistically sacrifice 50 more lives—just because we feel it is more moral to try to save everyone. Yikes!

Loss-aversion bias

Research has shown that humans tend to rate the loss of something they value as far more significant than an equivalent gain. As Kahneman said in an interview, "There is a powerful rule of fairness that people identify with, not to cause losses. You have to have a very good reason to inflict a loss on someone. The injunction to share your gains is much weaker." For example, it has been shown that people rate a \$1 loss of what they have as being about twice as painful as not getting a \$1 gain. Accordingly, we view people as much worse morally if they cause us a loss than if they decline to help us achieve an equivalent gain.

This may be illogical, but it's still emotionally powerful. If your boss says, "You'll do well in the company if you move to our Houston office," do you assume he can predict the future with certainty and thus you can rely on his promise? Probably not; and if you make the move and fail to earn a giant promotion in two years, you probably won't blame him. But if you turn out to be *worse off* after the move, you're likely to really hate him. Losing what you already had feels much worse than not getting something you never possessed.

Another example: Suppose an avid golfer undergoes surgery on a painful shoulder because his doctor predicts a 75 percent improvement in motion. A year after surgery, the improvement is only 50 percent. Does the patient have the right to be morally outraged? He is 50 percent better off than before—but 25 percent worse than the doctor predicted. His moral judgment of the doctor will probably depend on the reference point against which he measures the outcome. Does he focus on how much he gained compared to before or on how much he fell short compared to his expectations or hopes?

IMMEDIACY BIAS

Causing harm in the future is usually felt to be less bad than causing harm now. For example, we regard it as really bad for a drug dealer to sell someone powerful LSD that causes a psychotic event the next day. But we don't generally condemn the owner of a convenience store for selling cigarettes that may well cause a death from cancer in ten years. A restaurant knowingly serving tainted fish today seems morally very bad, but a company slightly polluting a river continually over decades may draw little criticism. It's just "the way business works."

PROXIMITY OR KNOWN-VICTIM BIAS

People more harshly condemn harm caused to identifiable people than harm to unknown victims—even when the unknown victims are more numerous. For example, if an assembly line worker is killed by a machine that was badly maintained by the employer, people usually see it, know about it, and talk about it—events like these tend to draw media coverage and generate public outrage. But if the same company markets a defective product that leads to multiple customer injuries, we may never hear about those disparate, far-flung victims.

Similarly, we care more about harm to people who live near us, and we will give more to charitable relief efforts if we live near the disaster. Paul Bloom has argued that this is one reason that empathy alone is a poor guide to morality.

CONFIRMATION BIAS

This has been called "the mother of all misconceptions, the father of all fallacies." It's the strong tendency we all have to seek out and accept information that confirms our prior beliefs but avoid or disbelieve equally credible contrary information. Extensive psychological research confirms this dynamic in varied situations—and we see it all the time in everyday life. It is one reason people say, "Don't bring the boss bad news." Rarely will the boss thank you; he'll say you must be wrong.

Confirmation bias is also powerful when we make moral judgments. For example, in a classic study, pro- and anti-death penalty advocates were given summaries of *made-up* scientific studies, some showing that capital punishment deterred violent crime and others showing that it failed to do so. Almost all the test subjects found more convincing the studies that supported the opinion they held before reading them. People are just better at absorbing information that reinforces their prior beliefs; contrary information has a harder time getting through. This is also called "motivated reasoning."

Think of excuse-making. Suppose you really let down a friend named Tim. You're talking about it with two other friends, and one says, "Oh, no big deal, Tim won't really care," while the other says, "No, you're wrong, that was important to him, and it really stings." You're far more likely to believe the first one. As a famous economist said, "Faced with the choice of changing one's mind, and proving that there is no need to do so, almost everyone gets busy on the proof."

Even worse, there is at times a "backfire effect," where being confronted with information showing that we are wrong actually *strengthens* our belief instead of weakening it (though the prevalence of this is disputed). And a classic psychological test—the Wason card game—shows that people actively search out information to confirm their belief, rather than disconfirming information, even when asked to do the latter!

INTENTION BIAS

Unintended harms usually are seen as less blameworthy than intended ones (unless the unintended harms were obviously predictable). You aren't blamed for firing Tom from his job, which directly led to his divorce, because you didn't *intend* the divorce. But you can be blamed for spreading false rumors about his work performance, because you *knew* those rumors would impede his new job search.

A related dynamic is known as *fundamental attribution bias*. This is the tendency to infer that people's actions are due to their inherent "character" rather than to different beliefs or circumstances. Importantly, when assessing other people's actions that cause harm, we are inclined to hold them accountable regardless of intent ("Whether you meant it or not, what you said ruined the whole dinner party"). By contrast, when explaining our own similar actions that cause harm, we usually exculpate ourselves by denying any bad intent ("I didn't mean to hurt her feelings").

SIDE-EFFECT BIAS

People usually get more blame for the bad side effects of their actions than praise for the good side effects. For example, if you promise to pick up pills for Grandma at the pharmacy, but you forget, and her stomach problem continues—that's "on you." But if you leave your antacid pills at her house by mistake, and she takes them and feels better, you get no credit for your act, because it wasn't intended. Neuroscientist Robert Sapolsky says this is wired into our brains. Because evolution conditioned us to focus on danger and risk, "we're better at detecting violations of social contracts that have malevolent rather than benevolent consequences (e.g., giving less rather than more than promised). We also search [our minds] harder for causality for malevolent than benevolent causes."

This asymmetry has come to be known as the Knobe Effect, due to research by Joshua Knobe. In one experiment, subjects were asked whether they morally faulted a corporate CEO for adopting a program he was told would increase profits but harm the environment. About 82 percent said he was morally responsible for the environmental harm. Then another sample was asked about a CEO adopting a program that would increase profits and also help the environment. Again, the CEO's goal was just profit, and here, only 23 percent of subjects said he should be morally credited with protecting the environment.

So Knobe's experiments suggest that, to most people, the CEO should be faulted for an unintended bad effect but not credited with an unintended good effect. Why the morally different treatment? It's another example of how psychological biases shape our moral judgments, regardless of what logic might dictate.

SELF-INTEREST BIAS

Research demonstrates that most of us believe we are more moral than in fact we are, as well as more moral than most other people. Just like the children in Garrison Keillor's mythical Lake Wobegon, we like to think that we are all "above average." One of the ways we preserve this self-flattering belief is by remaining oblivious to the almost universal bias created by self-interest.

Even honest people are susceptible to this bias. The honest dentist may tend to see the need for more crowns for teeth than are strictly necessary. The professor may tell a graduate student that she really ought to do her doctoral dissertation on a subject that will just happen to produce data the professor needs for her own research. A father who believes "boys will be boys" tells his wife that like him, "lots of parents" aren't offended by certain behavior, conveniently ignoring that plenty of *other* parents would fervently disagree. In such situations, even honest people tend to overweigh information that supports their doing what they wanted to do in the first place.

RECIPROCITY BIAS

As we saw earlier, reciprocity is at the core of morality as it evolved in humans. If I lend you my car, I expect you to do a similar favor for me. But because reciprocity is such a key principle in human relations, we often overapply it. Reciprocity means doing a *similar* good act, not necessarily the *same* act—and surely not the same act in different circumstances, which may change the act's moral meaning. For example, if you lend me your car to take my mother to the hospital, that doesn't mean that I must later lend you my car so that you can go on vacation—or, still worse, rob a bank. The demand, "You owe me . . ." is not morally unanswerable—though sometimes if feels that way.

ESSENTIALIZING BIAS

We tend to judge others' morality based not just on their specific actions, but how we see their moral "essence." If they seem committed to the morals of the community, then we overlook occasional moral lapses ("He's basically a decent guy"). But if the person seems to have antisocial attitudes, then we judge them harshly even for the same conduct.

FAIRNESS AND RESPECT

Fairness is a key moral factor. People want it and expect it. When asked to define fairness, most people cite something like the fair distribution of goods or results. But research shows that people actually experience fairness less in terms of stuff received and more as respect for them as persons. When people are treated unfairly, they feel they are being regarded as a thing, with less dignity than other people—and that really hurts. Conversely, we will often accept even an unpleasant result, if we feel the process was fair and we got as much respect as others. Injustice stings far more than misfortune.

Most people try to act in ways they see as fair. But a key qualification is the idea of deservingness. When people evaluate the moral quality of an action, they customarily assess whether the affected person really deserves equal moral treatment. Maybe it's okay that Ralph is the only one who didn't get a bonus, because, after all, it's his first year with the company. Maybe it's fine not to invite Sally to the class party, because everyone knows she's a terrible gossip. Maybe we tolerate substandard housing for welfare recipients, because if they want to deserve better, they should find work.

People often think this way. But on what basis do they judge who is deserving? In Chapter 10, we'll explore many of the factors that shape our understanding of fairness in a variety of circumstances.

Punishing Moral Violations

HUMANS EVOLVED WITH A STRONG URGE to uphold behaviors that we see as prosocial and moral. That's why we devote time and energy to arguing our personal moral judgments. We care about right and wrong, and we're usually willing to speak up when we see our values being disregarded.

But most people are far more reluctant to be involved in *enforcing* ethical rules. We want to be surrounded by moral behavior—no stealing, no fraud, no cruelty, no discrimination—but we want somebody else to do the enforcing. Few people relish being the person who must fire an employee for misconduct, or serve on a jury, or even confront a friend who has committed a serious moral lapse. We tend to forget that sustaining a moral society requires not just public policing but private sanctioning of bad behavior.

People generally understand pretty well the gradations of badness within a given category of conduct: stealing a watch is bad, stealing a car is worse, and stealing a child is far, far worse. But comparing badness *across* categories of conduct can be challenging, and of course people's views may differ. Sure, a mugger violently attacking a person to steal their wallet is worse than, say, a cashier lifting a couple of twenty-dollar bills out of the register at the end of their shift. The former is a crime of violence, the latter "merely" a financial crime. But what if the stealing is by Bernie Madoff, who bilked a large number of people out of their life savings? And what if Madoff's theft led some people to commit suicide? Is his crime still "merely" a financial one?

Even the "same" crime may seem very different when some of the circumstances differ. Have you ever thought of what factors would cause you, if you were a judge, to be tougher or more lenient in sentencing? Would you punish based mostly on evil intent, the repellent nature of the crime, its painful effects on the victim, its impact on society's morals generally, the offender's remorse, his potential to be rehabilitated, the need to deter others, or some other factor?

Consider the following crime scenarios. In each case, *Steve killed Brad*. How bad is each crime?

- Steve killed Brad from ambition; Brad was blocking his career at work.

- Steve killed Brad, who was sleeping with Steve's wife.

- Steve killed Brad, whom he had never met, in a bar fight over a pretty girl.

- Steve killed Brad, who welched on a gambling debt for $5,000.

- Steve killed Brad, who was an enforcer for a bookie and threatened to kill Steve if he didn't repay a gambling debt right away.

- Steve killed Brad, who was a clergyman.

- Steve killed Brad, who was a single guy and a drug dealer.

- Steve killed Brad, who had a wife and six kids.

- Steve has a wife and six kids, and Brad was single.

- Steve is Black, and Brad was White and called him the N-word.

- Steve is Black and Brad was Black, and Brad called Steve an "oreo."

- Steve is 18 years old, and Brad was 82.

- Steve is 45 and Brad was 22.

- Steve was high on marijuana when he killed Brad.

- Steve is a NFL star, and Brad was a rapper.

Now let me suggest that you write in the margin how long a sentence you would impose if Steve is convicted in each case. Just go with your "gut." You probably won't be consistent. Then go back and try to figure out which factors swayed you to be harsher or more lenient in particular examples—and why. If you're like most people, you were likely influenced in your sentencing decisions by how you weigh degrees of harm, sympathy, feelings of outrage, justifications, what should be expected of certain people, stereotypes, and other factors, too.

One surprising factor in punitiveness is a person's tendency toward intense rumination versus instinctive judgment. Research reveals that people who tend toward recursive, detailed cognition are less punitive, even when factors like age, education, gender, and political orientation are eliminated as variables. Of course, what people say and what they do may differ. In one study, people were asked whether the most important thing to them in imposing a criminal sentence was retribution or deterrence, and there were plenty of people in each camp. But in the end, their stated views didn't matter: almost everyone in both groups—97 percent—sought out more information relevant to retribution, and they didn't care to know about deterrence!

One benefit of our little experiment above is that it may reveal what factors influence you most and cause you to be "inconsistent." Many believe that "consistency always has a particular kind of normative [moral] force" because it implies lack of self-interest or bias. But consistency is not a self-defining concept. You have to ask, consistency with respect to which factors? There can be justifiable inconsistency and indefensible inconsistency. It isn't in-consistent to sentence a five-time repeat felon more harshly than a first-time offender.

It should upset us to know that in the real world, criminal sentences, parole decisions, and similar judgments are often quite inconsistent, affected by unfair, irrelevant factors. Yet there is massive evidence of this. Racial bias is one important factor. But studies show that sentences also vary depending on factors like the time of day when the decision is made, and even whether the decision-maker is hungry at the time! As Kahneman, Sibony, and Sunstein explore in their 2021 book *Noise,* criminal sentences are often inconsistent when measured by criteria for the same or similar crimes.

Excuses and Rationalization

As we all know, excuses are the most common response to any accusation of wrongdoing in everyday life. People almost reflexively make excuses for why they didn't or couldn't act ethically. One interesting thing about excuses is that, to work, they must tap into the same kind of moral principles that created the duty to act in the first place. If you don't repay money you borrowed from a friend, you can't say, "I decided I don't like you"—that's not a moral excuse. You have to say something like "I'm sorry I forgot," or "I'm tapped out, but I promise to pay you back next month." Those acknowledge the duty and thus sound morally acceptable.

Rationalization goes way beyond excuses. As the word implies, it is an effort to make rational what is essentially irrational. It's often described as a psychological defense mechanism that uses self-serving but false reasons to explain away painful facts and preserve one's self-image. Suppose that Jane confronts her sister Ann and accuses her of flirting too intimately with Jane's husband, Bill. It's likely that Ann will say things like "You're crazy; we were just talking," "I didn't do anything; Bill came on to me," "Who are you to criticize? You flirt with every guy in the room," "You make stuff up because you've been jealous of me since I was more popular in high school," or a dozen other equally predictable things. Like most people, Ann will seize on anything to rationalize her actions. She does so both to protect her self-identity, and to get off the hook for her bad behavior. Like most people, she has what experts call *bounded ethicality*—she is ethical, except when she's not.

Moral Foundations Theory

AN ESPECIALLY INFLUENTIAL STRAIN of recent psychological research on morals is the Moral Foundations Theory (MFT) developed by Jonathan Haidt, Craig Joseph, and Jesse Graham, and since expanded by others. They conclude that a person's moral orientation can best be explained by how much relative significance they attach to each of six core values:

- Caring and avoiding harm to others
- Fairness and penalizing cheating
- Loyalty to others and penalizing betrayal
- Respect for authority and penalizing subversion
- Sanctity and not degrading what is sacred (God, family, nation)
- Liberty and avoiding oppression

Haidt argues strongly that these values and intuitions drive our moral decisions: "The first principle . . . [is] that intuitions come first; strategic reasoning second." Researchers administering diagnostic questionnaires to tens of thousands of people have found that the MFT framework powerfully predicts people's responses to a range of issues in the moral and political spheres. MFT slices across the moral frameworks we have explored and helps reveal what is most important to a user of any of them. And on a personal level, MFT allows you to construct a vision of your own values—what you might call a *moral matrix*.

For example, as you consider an issue such as illegal immigrants massing at the U.S. border, do you tend to focus on the human needs of asylum seekers (caring), their jumping the line ahead of other immigrants (fairness), or their violation of legally established borders (disrespect for authority)? What matters most in your thinking?

Or suppose that a friend at work tells you that he used someone else's urine to fake a required drug screening test. Is your reaction driven mostly by loyalty to your friend, anger at the breach of fairness, a feeling that drug tests infringe liberty, or a concern that maybe someone will be harmed if your friend is high on drugs and operates large machinery?

Moral Foundations Theory can help you understand what forces are working as you try to decide where you stand on moral issues. (More on MFT later.)

The Big Five Model

THE MOST WIDELY RESEARCHED and accepted model for people's personality traits—which affect not only our response to moral issues but how we interact with the world in general—is what is variously called the Big Five, Five Factor, or OCEAN model. It measures one's personality on the key gradients of Openness, Conscientiousness, Extraversion, Agreeableness, and Neuroticism. Generally, these terms mean what you would think, though there are nuances in different studies. In essence:

OPENNESS = Being curious, imaginative, thinking abstractly, seeking and accepting new experiences

CONSCIENTIOUSNESS = Tending to be organized, responsible, diligent, obedient to norms

EXTRAVERSION = Having interests and energies oriented to the outside world rather than internally, being outgoing, talkative, sociable, assertive, ambitious

AGREEABLENESS = Being cooperative, empathic, kind, seeking connection/agreement, goal-oriented, resilient

NEUROTICISM = Being emotionally unstable, prone to anxiety, moodiness, self-doubt

This model has been experimentally validated in a large number of studies and has proven its predictive value across many cultures. (I discuss its impact on the broader domain of values in Chapter 9.)

Moreover, these personality dispositions are genetically influenced, heritable to a significant degree, and durable over a person's life span. There is "robust evidence that genetic factors substantially influence personality traits." As leading researcher Robert Plonim summarizes: "Inherited DNA differences account for 30 to 60 percent of the variance for most psychological traits. Few other findings in psychology account for [even] 5 percent of the variance." Moreover, the average heritability of openness is about 57 percent and that of conscientious-ness is about 59 percent.

For our purposes here, the most relevant finding is that people's personality dispositions on the Big Five scales significantly impact their values, and specifically how they perceive, assess, and judge moral issues. Just for example, those high in Conscientiousness tend to expect strict adherence to rules and norms, and to be more comfortable punishing violators. In contrast, those high in Openness tend to be more forgiving of divergent behavior. People who score high in Agreeableness are less likely to be "reactive" and hostile to those with different behaviors or moral views, while those high in Neuroticism tend to be more so.

Researchers have also examined the interaction of these personality traits with the so-called CNI model of moral judgment, which focuses on sensitivity to *consequences* (C), focus on moral *norms* (N), and general preference for *inaction* over action (I). People with certain personality traits display clear patterns on these scales as well. So, when you argue ethical issues with others, just bear in mind that you aren't just engaging with "opinions" they happen to have formed last week. You are engaging (messing?) with their embedded personality traits and inborn genetic nature. No wonder the stakes often seem so high!

Liberals and Conservatives: Different Moral Tribes?

PERHAPS IT SEEMS ODD to see political labels in a chapter on the psychology of morals. But one important reason that political liberals and conservatives disagree so bitterly these days is that political issues are increasingly refracted through a moral lens. What's more, liberals and conservatives tend to differ somewhat in their genetic profiles and biology, and in their tendencies to have certain of the major "personality dispositions." That in turn affects how they sort out on the Moral Foundations Theory values. It means these two groups tend to (not always, but usually) approach moral issues with a different blend of inclinations. John Hibbing and colleagues conclude: "Though moral foundations theory starts from a different place than trait-based personality research, . . . it ends up in pretty much in the same place, at least in terms of politics. That is because the moral foundations you use to decide what's wrong and what is right are fairly accurate predictors of your political beliefs."

It may surprise you, but differences in liberal and conservative biology have been confirmed by a range of research methods. They include studies of twins reared together or apart, research on differences in enzymes and taste receptors, analysis of neurotransmitter levels under variable conditions, genome-wide association studies, studies of political extremists, and more. One large study of identical and fraternal twins concluded that "there is not just a genetic component to [political orientation] but a large genetic component, more than half the observed variation." Indeed, "other studies, employing different designs, samples and statistical techniques, arrive at essentially the same conclusion."

Here are some examples of the biologically linked differences between people who identify as liberal or conservative. (For sources, see the Notes.)

- Liberals and conservatives tend to have different thresholds for disgust at repulsive things and behavior, and for the physical startle and gag reflexes.

- They usually have different levels of anxiety vigilance, response to negative stimuli, and tolerance for risk to themselves and others.

- Liberals and conservatives tend to differ on the Big Five personality dispositions.

- They have different dopamine neurotransmitter reactions to being taxed in experimental financial games.

- Conservatives tend to want to identify good or bad quickly in situations. Liberals are more prone to probe causes and accept uncertainty, which may lead to moral ambiguity. Accordingly, when we are under stress and feel a need to cut to the bottom line, our judgments tend to become less liberal and more conservative.

- Liberals and conservatives tend to differ in their reflexive response to whether someone is an in-group or out-group member.

- Young political liberals are more likely to possess the DRD47R dopamine receptor gene and to be more "risk-taking" and "novelty-seeking" than others.

- Cognitively, "liberals are more likely to be soft categorizers and conservatives hard categorizers."

- Liberals are more likely to believe that people are inherently good; conservatives worry that most people are capable of evil. In general, "political liberals . . . tend to take a rosier view of human nature."

- Conservatives and liberals tend to seek and process information in somewhat different styles.

- Liberal and conservative brains may develop and reinforce certain structures differently. Indeed, "[fMRI] brain images cluster according to whether you are strongly conservative or strongly liberal. Moderates are in between."

These and other differences are not trivial. Biology and life experience of course interweave. Scholar George Lakoff explains that as they develop in life, "liberals and conservatives have very different moral systems and . . . much of [their] . . . political discourse . . . derives from their moral systems"—which he argues are drawn from their internalized "different models of the family." Conservatism is based on the Strict Parent model, which stresses "moral strength, self-control and self-discipline, . . . respect for obedience, . . . strict guidelines and behavioral norms [to advance] . . . the overall self-interests of all." It sees that "life is a struggle for survival . . . a matter of competing successfully," which "requires . . . self-discipline . . . and a form of ascetism." Hence, the world is seen as in tension between self-disciplined good and self-indulgent evil, between order and disorder. Finally, "the metaphor of moral strength rules out any explanation [of bad conduct] in terms of social forces or social class." It's up to each individual to do right and make a success of themselves regardless.

This is in marked contrast to liberalism, which Lakoff says is based on the Nurturant Parent model of the family. Here, "Moral nurturance requires empathy and helping those who need it. This model does not see children primarily learning through "reward and punishment [but] through their attachments to their parents." They try to meet "their parents' expectations, . . . become nurturing, . . . [and] develop a social conscience." As adults, their duty is not just to compete with others but to try to help them make a better society. Competition yielding "winners and losers" must be tempered by a "safety net" of support to help raise up everyone.

These two internalized models of the family and society naturally affect how liberals and conservatives tend to assess many issues that have a moral dimension. John Hibbing and colleagues summarize the research findings in this way:

> One of the important implications of moral foundations theory is that liberals and conservatives disagree not because they have rationally analyzed their way to different issue positions but rather because they have different reflexive responses to what is going on in their . . . environments. These responses are emotionally rooted cues to what is right and wrong, . . . [what we call] predispositions.

Such predispositions cause these two groups to react differently to many of the recurring challenges of social life. For that reason, the moral foundations you use to decide what is right or wrong are fairly accurate predictors of your political beliefs. The stereotype that conservatives are morally strong while liberals are morally lax is not accurate. They each elevate certain moral values to paramount importance and fight hard for them, but they differ in how they rank those values. Both types are moral people; they just tend to affix their primary moral concern to different things. For example, in the public sphere, liberals don't want to live in an immoral society that accepts discrimination, poverty, rigid gender roles, and destruction of the environment. Conservatives don't want to live in an immoral society that accepts promiscuity, obscenity, and crime, and disrespects patriotism and religion.

However, it is *not* true that liberals usually embrace one moral framework (say, flexible utilitarian weighing of factors) while conservatives opt for another (say, strict Kantian rules). In fact, both liberals and conservatives rely on all of the main moral frameworks, but they tend to switch from one to another depending on the issue and the argument.

Let's look at some examples of how they do that. (Disclaimer: These shorthand renderings of each group's usual posture don't do justice to the deep reasons behind them or to the range of views within any large group of people such as liberals or conservatives. But I think you will still recognize the general alignment.)

Liberals are usually Kantians (principle-and-rule-based) about:

- Whether torture can be used to get information from terrorists. (No, because torture is always morally wrong, even if it might save lives in a given case.)

- Global warming and environmental protection. (We have a high moral duty not to destroy nature and burden future generations, even if we must incur some economic costs now.)

- Foreign aid. (We have a moral duty to help poor nations, even when they don't prove to be friends to America.)

- The death penalty. (It's morally repugnant, even if the defendant was 100 percent guilty, and even if it deters other crimes. Also, it has been used in a racially skewed way, so that makes it just plain wrong.)

- Welfare. (We have a moral duty to fulfill basic human needs even if some recipients, like criminals or drug addicts, may not seem deserving.)

- Child discipline. (It's always wrong to physically discipline children, even when it might improve their behavior.)

But liberals then turn into flexible utilitarians about:

- Abortion. (It may be morally disturbing, but the social harms of outlawing it entirely are seen as worse.)

- Prayer in school. (Many liberals are religious, but in a pluralistic society, it's worse to put pressure to conform on those from other traditions.)

- Affirmative action. (Disregarding a person's greater merit may be unfair, but it's more important to overcome the effects of prior discrimination.)

- Criminal rights. (It's unfortunate to release an obviously guilty criminal because of police or prosecutor misconduct, but protecting the rights of all is more important.)

- Vaccinations and health quarantines. (One's right to personal liberty and choice is important, but it's outweighed by the moral duty not to endanger fellow citizens.)

- Tolerance of groups that are themselves intolerant. (Islamic screeds about Jews are ignored, but fundamentalist Christian denunciations of gays are abhorred).

On the other side of the aisle, *conservatives tend to be Kantians (principle-and-rule-based) about:*

- Abortion. (It's always immoral to terminate an innocent human life; we should deal with related social harms like teen pregnancy in some other way.)

- Prayer in school. (Religion is an essential part of educating youth. If others disagree, they can sit quietly and not pray.)

- The death penalty. (The Biblical rule of an eye for an eye is morally justified in extreme cases; problems like inconsistent sentencing or uncertain deterrence can be fixed without abandoning the principle.)

- Vaccination and COVID quarantines. (Liberty is a fixed moral value; the government should inform but not compel me. If others get sick, that's not my responsibility.)

- Affirmative action. (People should be evaluated based solely on ability; we shouldn't penalize an individual to try to fix some societal issue.)

But then conservatives turn into flexible utilitarians about other issues:

- Torture. (If it works to prevent loss of life to patriotic soldiers or innocent citizens, it's worth compromising the principle of no-cruelty.)

- Criminal search and seizures. (If crimes are solved and prevented, then it's less important that police violated idealized rules protecting privacy.)

- Global warming and environmental protection. (Protecting our environment matters, but we must weigh the economic impact of tight emission controls on jobs for people today.)

- Immigration. (There is no right to immigrate even by people in great need; the criterion for immigration to the United States should be whether a person brings needed skills or will be a burden. It's all a matter of balance in light of national interests.)

- Bullying, and verbal sexual harassment. (These may be morally bad, but you can't totally prevent them, and by setting rigid government rules, you'd do more harm.)

In sum, both liberals and conservatives draw their arguments from several moral frameworks, depending on the particular issue and circumstances. Still, there is some evidence that conservatives tend to align more with the absolutist (Kantian) moral approach while liberals tend to align more with the utilitarian or relativist approaches. Haidt and some other MFT advocates believe that liberals and conservatives have "different moralities" mainly in the sense that they weigh values differently. Others offer the analogy that these two groups have different "taste receptors" for moral issues. Importantly, according to Haidt, liberals tend to frame most moral issues in terms of the single, transcendent value of empathy or avoiding harm, while conservatives appeal more broadly based on the values of sanctity, loyalty, cheating, and duty.

Haidt has proposed a chart to depict how much of their total caring about issues liberals and conservatives invest in each of the major values within MFT, such as care/harm or sanctity/degradation. As you might guess, liberals invest more in the former and conservatives in the latter, and they differ in how much they invest in other values as well.

In many situations, liberals tend to focus on the fact of pain or harm, while conservatives tend to focus on justifications. As John Hibbing and colleagues summarize: "A liberal likely sees a moral wrong when an individual is being, say, socially ostracized. A conservative is more likely to take into account communal considerations in formulating a moral judgment. Is that guy being ostracized because he is not one of us? Because he was disloyal? . . . [If] yes, maybe he had it coming." Sam Harris concludes that "conservatives have the same morality as liberals do; they just have different ideas about how harm [usually] accrues in the universe." And philosopher Bernard Gert offers that "liberals tend to emphasize moral *ideals*; conservatives generally place more emphasis on the moral *rules*."

Are Men From Mars and Women From Venus?

ON AVERAGE, DO WOMEN AND MEN tend to differ in their approach to moral issues? Some people may dislike even having the question posed. But why? We know that men and women generally differ in numerous ways, though many individuals diverge from the pattern. There is lots of research showing female/male differences in the distribution of personality traits, patterns of social interaction, political opinions and so on. So why not morals as well?

Still, this is a sensitive subject, and I am not an expert psychologist. So, in this section, I'll just present the question and point you toward some of the scholarship.

One approach to female/male moral behavior emerged in the 1980s. It took the form of a feminist critique of mainstream psychology. Scholars such as Carole Gilligan, in her pathbreaking book *In a Different Voice*, and Nel Noddings, in *Caring: A Feminine Approach to Ethics and Moral Education,* asserted that much of classic moral theory (such as Kant) was distorted and wrong from a genderized perspective.

Gilligan criticized the biased approach she saw in the work of moral philosophers and psychologists, saying that "they studied men—and then described [all] humans." In particular, she criticized her former professor Lawrence Kohlberg as having suggested that as girls develop, they rise less than boys to the challenge of formulating moral rules and principles. The basic critique was that "a very masculine sense of 'reason' and 'rationality' has dominated ethical evaluation, at the expense and even denigration of emotion." In contrast, "the female experience was said to be more particularistic, caring and nurturing."

Gilligan and others also said that women focus more on moral/interpersonal responsibilities rather than rights. Thus, "some researchers have proposed that women prefer care reasoning, which considers issues of need and sacrifice, and men prefer justice reasoning, which considers issues of fairness and rights." The new feminist "ethics of care" or "relational ethics" bore some kinship to virtue ethics, which has been a focus of many female ethical philosophers, though of course others remain in the Kantian or other camps. Noddings said that ethical caring derives from normal human caring, but goes further, emphasizing that being a caring person is an aspirational goal.

After a period of ascendency, this view was itself strongly challenged, including by women, such as Alison Jaggar, Jaclyn Friedman, Christina Hoff

Sommers, Elizabeth Spelman, and Sarah Lucia Hoagland. They felt that the "ethics of care" theory reinforced the stereotype that women ought to be the nurturing ones, or that they didn't normally embrace rational moral deliberation. Later research also asked whether any apparent differences in moral thinking between women and men may arise not from innate tendencies but from differences in the social interactions, and hence moral dilemmas, that members of the two sexes routinely encounter.

Whether or not there is any general difference in how men and women think of moral issues, some particular tendencies have been identified. For example, populations of women and men differ on moral foundations theory gradients. In a major survey across 67 nations, women generally scored higher on the care, fairness, and purity scales. However, there were no meaningful differences on the loyalty and authority scales. The differences were greatest in Western, individualistic, and more gender-equal societies.

Some studies have reported that women tend to have a stronger internalized sense of their "moral identity." Reportedly, this leads to specific attitudinal changes, such as a greater resistance to unethical business practices. A meta-analysis conducted on 470 experimental studies indicated that cheating and dishonest behavior are more prevalent in men than in women. We also know that across many different cultures, women and men tend to array somewhat differently on the political liberal/conservative scale, and that liberals and conservatives differ in how they weigh factors bearing on ethical judgments. As just one example, research suggests that in assessing fairness, most women incline toward equal distribution of benefits, while men incline toward distribution proportional to some criterion of desert. Some studies, but not others, suggest that women and men tend to react differently to Trolley Problem dilemmas (discussed below).

Does all this add up to a significant difference in moral thinking between females and males? You can be the judge of that.

Trolley Morality: What Would You Do?

PHILOSOPHERS ARE OFTEN PRESUMPTUOUS in describing what "most people" naturally or instinctively perceive as moral or immoral. But how would they really know?

In pursuit of the answer to this question, we encounter one of the stranger features of modern moral philosophy: An entire bookcase could be filled with books discussing the moral decisions made by people faced with runaway trolley cars. This literature was spawned by an elegant ethical mind game conceived by philosopher Philippa Foot. (Incidentally, she was a granddaughter of President Grover Cleveland. How often do presidents spawn philosophers? Plato, who thought philosophers should govern, would at least be amused.) Widely known as the Trolley Problem, its initial form was essentially this:

> A trolley (or train) is barreling down a track, and the engineer has fallen asleep. Five workmen are unaware and on the track, and the track is bounded by steep banks, so they can't escape. There is a side track with one workman sitting on it. You are a bystander who happens to be near a switch that can divert the trolley onto the siding, thereby saving five people, but killing the one sitting on the side track. Would you pull the switch?

How you answer this question reveals a lot about your intuitive moral leanings.

If you're a Kantian, you focus on good intent and fixed rules—never kill, and never use a person as a mere "means" to an end. So, you can't pull the switch, because that would make you responsible for the death of the one workman on the side track. Maybe you feel bad that five people will die, but you have your principle, and you believe the world is better if people stick to their principles.

But if you're a utilitarian, you do the math: Saving five people is worthwhile, even if you can't avoid killing one, and reluctantly you pull the switch. It's a terrible choice, but you know it's the right thing to do based on the greatest good.

If you're highly religious, you might feel that what happens is God's decision, and you don't have the right to decide who lives and dies, so you are saddened, but you do nothing, allowing five people to die. On the other hand, you might feel that God would want you to save as many innocent people as possible, leading you to pull the switch. Your decision would depend on how you interpret God's will in this situation.

If you are a Humean, you may feel it is repugnant to pull a switch that kills another person as you watch, regardless of the arithmetic of lives saved versus lives lost. "It feels awful, and I just couldn't live with myself" is the impulse that will probably drive your action.

If you believe in virtue ethics or casuistry, you might struggle to think of what a good person would do, weighing all the pros and cons—but where you finally land is hard to predict.

As we saw earlier, because none of us is 100 percent Kantian or Humean or utilitarian, you may flip-flop and change your thinking from one second to the next. For example, even if you're a Kantian and feel you shouldn't kill anyone, would you feel the same way if instead of doing so to save five lives, it would save five hundred lives?

This basic version of the Trolley Problem is just the start. Over the years, scholars have devised many variations of the Trolley Problem, testing nuances in our moral thinking. For example, would it matter whether to save the five people (1) you have to *pull a switch* that diverts the train that kills a man, or (2) you *pull a switch* that opens a trap door on a footbridge over the tracks so that *a large man falls* onto the tracks and his body stops the train, or (3) you personally *push the large man* onto the tracks, or (4) you *use a long pole* to push the large man?

These mechanical differences may seem like dancing on the head of a pin morally, since the point is to save lives by whatever method—right? And yet we are dealing with human beings, and we aren't necessarily rational. These and related scenarios have now been presented to *hundreds of thousands of people across dozens of cultures*, and researchers have found that these mechanical details actually do matter to people. Specifically:

- More than 80 percent of people say they would pull the switch to divert the train.

- But only about 63 percent would pull a switch to open the trap door, dropping the large man onto the tracks.

- Just 21 percent would physically push the man off the footbridge to stop the train.

- But 33 percent would push the man off the footbridge, as long as they could push him with a long pole instead of their hands.

Why do so many people attach different moral significance to only slightly different actions that have identical results as to life and death? The start of an answer emerges from a key 2001 research study. Joshua Greene and colleagues hooked people up to fMRI brain imaging and recorded what happened when they thought about the Trolley Problem. It turns out that people are conflicted because different parts of the brain—an emotional response part (the amygdala) and a rational decision part (the ventromedial prefrontal cortex or vmPFC)—fight with one another. As Paul Bloom summarized the results: "It turns out that all neurologically normal people, not just trained philosophers, draw a moral distinction between the switch case and the [foot]bridge case. . . . Laying your hands on [the man] . . . and *shoving* [him] gives rise to a powerful emotional response, much more than the thought of just throwing a switch, and this is why most people see this [shoving] act as morally wrong."

This clearly suggests that people's moral judgment—at least in this kind of scenario—is Humean. It's a matter of instinctive feeling, not utilitarian thinking or rational rules. Pushing another human to their death just feels wrong, no matter what else is involved. The utilitarian calculus of lives saved versus killed matters to us—but we are still reluctant if we must get our hands dirty.

Greene finds that three factors influence how we are willing to act here: whether it requires significant physical action, how far we are from the affected person, and how direct or indirect the action is. Let's look at how these factors affect people's decisions in still other variations of the Trolley Problem.

THE ROCK

In another scenario, instead of pulling the switch, derailing the train, and killing a person by your decision, you derail the train so that it will be stopped by a large rock—but just as you are about to pull the switch, a person steps in front of the rock. You didn't intend to cause the death, but you caused it anyway. Here, most people say they don't feel responsible for the death, so there's no moral guilt. This is the moral "doctrine of double effect" we saw earlier.

THE WORKMAN

In this scenario, you can save the five people by pulling a switch, but to get to it, you must run along a footbridge, and unavoidably knock a workman off of it, who will then die. Some 80 percent of people approve of this (compared to just 21 percent who approve of pushing the large man off the bridge). Apparently here, the guilt at using physical force is neutralized by the lack of intent; the death was "unavoidable." But it's only physically unavoidable given your choice; morally, you could have chosen not to do anything.

RACE AND OTHER FACTORS

In saving human lives, why should race matter? One study found that liberals tended to be more willing to sacrifice one person to save 100 if the sacrificed person was White rather than Black. But other studies find most people believe race is irrelevant. Interestingly, in one research report, when subjects were asked abstractly what personal characteristics might affect their willingness to "sacrifice" a person to save others, the most common features cited included the victim's age (62%), health (49%), gender (20%), and nationality (13%).

YOUR SPOUSE OR CHILD

In the trolley scenario, would you kill your spouse or child to save five strangers? If you believe that all human lives are equally valuable, you need to say Yes. But if you do, you aren't normal. As Sapolsky says, "Somebody with damage to . . . part of the brain will give the same answer [as if the person sacrificed were a stranger]. . . . It doesn't register; they don't process relatedness the same way. And every primate on Earth would look at that and say there is something desperately wrong with this person's brain."

THE TROLLEY PROBLEM is a vivid illustration of how we struggle with moral decisions. No moral framework seems to yield great answers in all circumstances. Instead, depending on subtle differences in situations, people jump from one criterion to another to find what is morally right: What's the good result here? Should I take action or do nothing? Do I need to get physically involved? Who are the victims? Does the action feel right? Can I live with myself? No wonder people get confused.

As Greene's research suggested, the moral tension we experience in such situations has its origin in conflicts between parts of the brain. Different parts activate in response to various perceptions and then struggle with one another. It seems that the instinctive brain ("Oh my gosh, I can't just push this guy onto the tracks and kill him—that's horrible!") is fighting with the reasoning part

("Yeah, I know it feels awful, but it's right to save those five people. Do the math and just do it!"). This explains why people who have a damaged vmPFC in the brain are less troubled by pushing the guy onto the tracks. "These patients were about five times as likely to give utilitarian answers in response to 'personal' moral dilemmas."

WHO CARES ABOUT SILLY TROLLEYS ANYWAY?

Some have criticized the Trolley Problem as artificial, questioning whether people would actually act as they say they would. Analogously, most people say they would come to the aid of the victim of a criminal attack, but in many real situations, bystanders look the other way. However, this doesn't happen as often as sometimes believed; often bystanders do help, and there are many situations where people act far more heroically than we might expect.

In fact, the kind of thinking revealed by the Trolley Problem is far from irrelevant to our real lives. In one study, researchers found that "public health officials, compared with [treating] doctors, gave more utilitarian answers to both the trolley-type dilemmas and to our more realistic healthcare dilemmas. . . . [They] were also more utilitarian than ordinary people, whose judgments resembled those of the [treating] doctors." One reason for this difference might be that a treating physician is supposed to focus solely on the welfare of each single patient. That encourages Kantian absolute thinking: Just do what's best for this person. But public health officials (like those worrying about COVID response or a natural disaster) can't succumb to that tunnel vision. In setting priorities and allocating limited resources, they can't avoid making utilitarian tradeoffs in trying to maximize the overall health of the population. When limited resources are directed to one location or group of people, it unavoidably means that less is available to some others.

Philosopher Gilbert Harman posed two examples that vividly show our conflicting impulses. In the first, six accident victims arrive at the emergency room. The doctor faces the choice of focusing all his energy on saving the one who is most severely injured and risking the other five, or allocating time to the other five, in which case the one most injured will die. Most people seem to feel that saving five at the cost of one is justifiable.

But in the second invented scenario, there are five patients in the hospital and each will die without the transplant of a different organ. So, the doctor decides to save the five by sacrificing another healthy patient in the hospital and harvesting his organs. That strikes us as evil and criminal—as it should. But why the difference? It has something to do with the moral difference between "letting die" and "killing," and the social acceptability of misfortune versus assault, but there is probably more, too.

Hypothetical scenarios can reveal surprising things about real-life thinking. Recall the example I noted earlier that was conjured by Tversky and Kahneman. They asked people how they would resolve the problem of an unknown "Asian disease." They said: Imagine that the United States is preparing for the outbreak of an unusual disease that is expected to kill 600 people. Two alternative public health programs to combat the disease have been proposed (assume science makes these predictions reliable):

- If program A is adopted, then 200 people will be saved.

- If program B is adopted, there is a one-third probability that 600 people will be saved and a two-thirds probability that no people will be saved.

Which of the two programs would you favor?

It turned out that the vast majority of people—72 percent—favored program A. They were attracted by the certainty that 200 people would be saved, making them feel heroic. The alternative program B was disfavored because it pointed out the chance that no one would be saved. The fact that program A didn't mention the other 400 who will surely die diverted attention from that consequence. People didn't notice that from a mathematical perspective, the projected value of lives saved—and also the probability of any single person's life being saved— is exactly the same in both scenarios. That is true mathematically, but apparently not psychologically.

Then it gets even more interesting. Tversky and Kahneman gave a second group of interviewees essentially the same choice, but with one subtle change in how they framed the problem:

- If program C is adopted, then 400 people will die.

- If program D is adopted, there is a one-third probability that nobody will die and a two-thirds probability that 600 people will die.

Once again a strong majority—78 percent—agreed on one moral choice. But they chose Program D, not Program C! All the programs are mathematically identical. So why did three quarters of people choose program D? Again, it's because the wording focused only on *saving lives* ("nobody will die") makes us favor an option even if it doesn't actually produce a better outcome.

This is experimental confirmation of a kind of moral affect bias: We have a desire to do good even if imperfectly, but we really can't accept doing ill, even for a good reason.

Now think about a real-world analogue to the Trolley Problem. If you were in charge, would you order the military to shoot down a plane hijacked by terrorists that was aiming to crash into a city? If you do, many will die, but many more will likely be saved. On September 11, 2001, apparently Vice President Dick Cheney approved such action if it became necessary. And in an online survey in Germany, about 87 percent of people said that in such a scenario, it would be moral to shoot down the plane.

Take a step further. Suppose that *you were on the plane* that terrorists planned to crash into a city. Would you hope against hope to survive the crash, knowing it's almost certain you would die, along with thousands in the city? Or would you decide to sacrifice your life to save many others by rushing the terrorists and trying to crash the plane in a deserted area? Heroic passengers on United Flight 93 on 9/11 made the latter choice.

In wrestling with such moral choices, we draw on each of the philosophical frameworks I've outlined, because each embodies real wisdom. A person may rely heavily on one but hear the others echoing in their mind:

- We are all Kantians; we want rules that are clear, reliable, and right. We don't respect waffling.

- But we are all Humeans; some actions just feel right or wrong regardless of the rule.

- We are all utilitarians; we try to weigh the good against the bad effects of an action—for the people involved.

- We all hear virtue ethics in the back of our heads ("What would a good person do?").

- We all engage in casuistry to some degree ("Option A is better than B, but I need to think more about C . . .").

Thus, different parts of our minds engage in a moral struggle. A leading researcher explains that when we think about the effects of actions, and then about moral rules in trolley-type scenarios, "the former is about intuitions rooted in the vmPFC, amygdala and insula, while the latter is the domain of the dlPFC [dorsolateral prefrontal cortex] and moral reasoning." Our instinctive, automatic judgments tend to be Humean, while our slower, later judgments tend to be utilitarian. And the prefrontal cortex reasons about whether this particular person deserves help. Our biology and morality thus are intertwined in complex ways.

As Hauser vividly says:

> The systems that generate intuitive moral judgments are often in conflict with the systems that generate principled reasons for our actions, because the landscape of today only dimly resembles our original [evolutionary] state. The Rawlsian creature will, therefore, fire off its intuitions about moral rights and wrongs, the Kantian will fire back principled arguments . . . ; and sometimes caught in the middle will be the Humean, generating angst, attempting to tilt the evidence toward one of the moral poles.

We may be troubled and inconsistent, but the struggle to be moral, in deeds as well as words, is still a noble project. In the end, the best way to see what moral principles a person holds may be to watch closely what they actually do.

7

Arguing Morals Well:
The Roles of Facts,
Logic, and Words

W E HAVE SEEN THAT IT TAKES A LOT to try to be a moral person and do the right thing. One needs to think about moral principles, which can be complex and even contradictory. You need to know what features of a situation to pay attention to. You need to understand the psychological dynamics that can influence and distort moral judgments. Having weighed relevant factors, you must actually do what you believe is right—which may be difficult, costly, or painful.

Finally, having done all this—and depending on circumstances—you may need to explain your choices and persuade others. Several additional domains become especially important: They are *facts*, *logic*, and *word choice*.

It may seem surprising to see facts and logic being linked to morals. Often one hears "cold" logic and facts being portrayed as the antipode of "warm" emotions and morals. But I will argue that such a view is deceptive and wrong.

To begin, the actual facts of the situation matter greatly, whether your moral judgment depends primarily on duty, rights, intent, consequences, feelings, or any other factor. Without facts, all we bring to judgments are biases and predilections, and we may wander far astray from our real target.

Likewise, logic isn't alien to morals. Logic just means good thinking, the kind that reliably connects premises (information) with conclusions. Illogical thinking can ruin moral judgments just as it can wreck legal, scientific, or business judgments.

And word choice matters greatly to moral arguments. Too often the ill-chosen or inflammatory word can derail a promising exchange about a sensitive moral issue. So now let's examine the roles of facts, logic, and words in moral discussions.

Facts: Basing Your Moral Arguments on Reality

SOMETIMES, TALKING ABOUT MORALS can be pretty abstract and up in the clouds. It feels good to say, "I have strong morals; I stick to my principles." But as soon as we start to apply nice principles to the messy realities of everyday life, things get harder. As a result, we may begin to hedge. We find ourselves saying things like "Well, it's not really lying in this situation if . . ." or "I don't feel it's my duty here because . . ." or "I know I said I could never do that, but what changed was . . ." This doesn't necessarily mean we are hypocrites or that our moral beliefs were wrong. It may just reflect the recognition that the actual facts of each situation matter to the moral conclusions. As Aristotle said, "We must know . . . the facts about the subject on which we are to speak and argue. Otherwise, we can have no material out of which to construct arguments."

If you think about the typical argument in daily life, this seems pretty obvious. Why argue about whether a coworker is a bad person for tearing people down behind their back, sexually harassing underlings, or embezzling funds—until you confirm that those things actually, or at least very probably, happened? Truth matters, and so facts must matter.

Unfortunately, in some spheres of modern life—especially where social media have powerful influence—the bedrock assumption that facts must justify our moral judgments has been eroded. Many people now live psychologically in what has been called a post-truth world. In a historic break from the pursuit of objective reason in Western intellectual life, thinkers now observe that "we don't live in an age of reason; we live in an age of empathy." Thus, "feelings [are now] exalted above everything, from reason to law to facts." In this world, "there are no universal truths, only smaller personal truths, perceptions shaped by the cultural and social forces of one's day." You can hear this subjectivism in the now common refrain "You can't judge me; you don't know how it feels. . . ."

Of course, there's a role for subjective feelings in moral discussions. Our perceptions are colored by our interests and experiences, and there is value in trying to see the different truths perceived by others.

But feelings alone are not reliable guides to reality. (Hence the title of Robert Leahy's book *Don't Believe Everything You Feel*.) What's more, the idea of never judging others is fundamentally at odds with any meaningful concept of morality. Your knowing how I feel or why I feel that way may be one relevant datum that goes into your moral judgment of me. But you retain the right to exercise moral judgment even if you don't fully get, share, or understand my motivations or feelings. I may never understand how an unrepentant serial killer feels, but that doesn't bar my rightly declaring that his behavior is evil.

Now consider a more ordinary example. Suppose Diane, the boss in your company, calls an employee (Jane) into her office and says, "I've got to tell you that you just aren't cutting it. You're too quiet and don't assert yourself; your sales numbers are pitiful; and frankly, you dress like a homeless lady and that turns off our customers. You better shape up, or you'll be looking for another job."

As you can imagine, Jane is devastated. Later that morning, she pulls you aside, repeats Diane's words, and exclaims: "What a nasty bitch! She's just a queen bee who tears down other women. She went out of her way to hurt me. And saying I look homeless? Diane knows I'm overweight, so I wear loose dresses. I know in my heart I'm a good employee."

Your immediate reaction is likely to be sympathy for Jane. No one likes to be harshly criticized, and Jane's encounter with Diane was undoubtedly painful. But painful and immoral are two different things. Would it make any difference to your moral judgment of Diane if you know that Jane's sales numbers *actually were the worst* in the whole department by a lot, and had been that way for three years running—despite Diane's sending her to several sales training sessions to help improve her performance? Would it matter if, during that time, Diane had promoted four other women who all described Diane as a supportive and helpful boss? What if a bunch of customers actually had complained about Jane's shoddy appearance? Does it matter if Diane herself is also overweight?

In short, when making a moral judgment about Diane's behavior, do the facts count, or is the only thing that matters Jane's own "truth"? You can empathize with Jane's pain without endorsing her moral condemnation of Diane.

In many situations today, people say, "Whether you know it or not, that [action/comment] hurt me—that was wrong, and so you owe me an apology." This claim implies that subjective feelings are morally conclusive, even apart from intent, factual accuracy, duty, or any other factor we've seen embedded in moral frameworks. But that's an unpersuasive notion. Of course, people should be kind, avoid hurtful remarks, be sensitive to cultural differences, avoid using demeaning dog-whistle epithets, and so forth. But social life isn't simple. Sometimes we need to say painful things. Maybe a professor has a duty to tell a student why their work is way below par; a manager has an obligation to fire a worker who is driving away customers; a restaurant owner has a right to tell a waiter that his body odor is a real problem and his herbal deodorant just isn't working. The recipients of all these messages will all be pained—but the facts also matter.

Distinguishing between actions that are needlessly offensive, bigoted, or cruel, and others that may be hurtful but justified by the facts, isn't always easy— and it can't be done simply by referring to personal feelings.

Now let's consider the interplay of feelings and facts in the context of some public policy issues with a moral dimension. To have legitimacy, and to have any hope of persuading others, our moral judgments must reflect the actual facts. Consider examples such as these.

"IT'S IMMORAL THAT THEY DENIED THAT POOR PERSON JOHN SMITH AN ORGAN TRANSPLANT OPERATION."

Note the subtle word "denied," which subliminally starts us off feeling that something is morally wrong here. Usually when you are denied something, you have a *right* to it. Is that assumption valid in this case? To answer that, we need to know the facts about how available organs are allocated among needy recipients, including the workings of the national nonprofit UNOS (United Network for Organ Sharing), which sets standards for rating eligible candidates. Were UNOS standards applied correctly in John Smith's case? Other facts may also be relevant. Was Mr. Smith covered by Medicaid, and if not, why? Did he need a kidney, liver, or heart? What percentage of needy recipients can actually find a donor, given the limited availability of each organ? Did Mr. Smith have an ethnicity or genetic profile that made it especially hard to match compatible organs? If we care deeply about Mr. Smith and all the folks who need organs, we ought to care about facts such as these.

"WE'RE STANDING UP FOR MORALITY AND PROTECTING KIDS BY REMOVING ALL THOSE DISGRACEFUL BOOKS FROM THE LIBRARY."

Children are the most precious things to us, so our desire to protect them has almost no limit. But is removing books from libraries really doing that? Who decides which books to remove, and what is guiding them when they do? Recently, two of the main factors provoking local governments and school boards to remove books have been concern over transgender issues and so-called "critical race theory." Many parents worry about books that are said to promote the ideas of gender fluidity or change, and the belief that America is an inherently racist nation. But is the local library removing only these kinds of books? In 2023 and 2024, both the American Library Association and PEN America reported local bans involving many thousands of books, even without all states reporting. They did not all involve transgender or critical race issues, by any means.

Would you care if some of the banned books were great classic literature, or written by Nobel Prize winners, or had been read in schools for many decades? What if they included classic books like *Harry Potter, To Kill a Mockingbird, Brave New World, Of Mice and Men, Animal Farm, Catcher in the Rye, Rabbit Redux, Forrest Gump, Dune, Invisible Man, Anna Karenina,* and *As I Lay Dying*? In fact, many of those titles have been removed in various places. Are there less restrictive ways of protecting kids than community-wide bans, like requiring parental consent to borrow certain books? These and related facts are relevant to our moral judgment about the book-banning issue. Engaging with others about real facts and tough issues is a lot harder than just intoning "Ban the Bad Books!"

"IT WAS COURAGEOUS OF MS. JONES TO BLOW THE WHISTLE ON WHAT HER EMPLOYER, THE CIA, IS SECRETLY DOING IN FAROFFISTAN."

In a democracy, we feel we ought to know what the government is doing, and none of us like being misled. So, it's easy to feel that anyone who feeds the public new, secret information about government activities is doing a moral act. Some whistleblowers have exposed bad conduct that harmed the public interest. But before drawing general conclusions, let's look at the relevant facts. Does the whole public really need to know in detail everything the CIA is engaged in, or is it enough if Congressional leaders have been briefed? Suppose that, to gather information in Faroffistan, the CIA cultivates allies and sources of information who can help protect the world from terrorists. Those locals take big risks. Do we really want to "out" them? When Ms. Jones blows the whistle, will those valued allies of the U.S. be endangered? Will her revelations damage local ethnic and political alliances? Will people in other countries be reluctant to cooperate if they believe that American whistleblowers may make their activities public? Before you make a moral judgment about a whistleblower, facts like these should be taken into account.

"I HAVE A MORAL RIGHT NOT TO VACCINATE MY KIDS AGAINST MEASLES BEFORE THEY ATTEND SCHOOL."

Of course, health is very personal, and our children are precious. Most states accept religious or conscience-based refusals to vaccinate kids. But before a person decides about the morality of vaccine refusal, they should want to consider facts about the disease involved and the safety and side effects of the vaccine. In the case of measles, how infectious is the virus? Are vaccination rates declining and disease rates rising? How many kids get infected with the disease, how many kids die, and how many suffer serious effects of measles like pneumonia, encephalitis, deafness, and immune disorders? How many unvaccinated babies or children will an infected kid typically transmit the disease to?

Broader questions of fact may also be involved. Should the right to opt out of vaccinations be absolute? Would we apply the same principle to the polio vaccine if polio began to take hold again? The Americas were declared polio-free decades go; now rare cases are being reported due to pockets of unvaccinated people. Should one person have the right to create that risk for large numbers of others in their community? Before making a moral judgment with such a serious potential impact, facts like these should be closely examined.

MY POINT HERE IS SIMPLE: Learning the facts that could justify—or under-mine—your moral judgments takes more effort than just spouting off, but it's essential to the integrity of those judgments. It doesn't make one a moral person to post comments on social media signaling righteous indignation on some is-sue, based on little more than gut feelings. Taking the facts seriously and using them to shape one's judgments is a better path. You might even call it a moral obligation.

Unfortunately, the polarization of opinion in our society has led many people to resist facts they don't like, and some come close to rejecting the whole idea of verifiable facts. As Simon Blackburn notes: "Today's relativists, persuading them-selves that all opinions enjoy the same standing in the light of reason, take it as a green light to believe what they like with as much conviction as they like." This is the opposite of the classic wisdom, stated pithily by David Hume: "A wise man proportions his belief to the evidence."

Making matters worse, the evidence shows that most of us know a lot less than we think about major public policy issues. Many of our most popular sources of information—especially social media—are peppered with bunk, mis-information, and even carefully crafted disinformation from motivated people and groups. We are subject to both organized and implicit manipulation. The algorithms that control the content of our social media feeds exacerbate the problem. In an effort to keep us engaged online—which drives advertising reve-nues—the algorithms are designed to continually expose people to content that will excite and reinforce the opinions they already hold. That can include con-tent that is unreliable, distorted, biased, or completely fake.

Today, when asked how they "know" something, people often say, "I've heard it from a lot of people"—meaning a cousin, a bartender, a Facebook post, and a tweet on X. Unfortunately, as the leading researcher on expert forecasting has noted, "Aggregating the judgments of many people who know nothing produces a lot of nothing."

In time, the well-documented *Dunning-Kruger effect* takes hold. This is the finding that the *less* people know about a subject, paradoxically, the *more* con-fident they tend to be in their judgments about it. Confirmation bias sets in, leading us to seek out and embrace confirmatory information and slough off contrary information. As a result, we are all far from accurate about a lot of things we think we know. In the words of the old saying, "It ain't what you don't know that gets you into trouble. It's what you know for sure that just ain't so."

Here are just a few examples of the kinds of misconceptions that beset us all, based on Paul Duffy's provocative book *Why We're Wrong About Nearly Everything*. Duffy surveyed Americans and compared what they believed to be facts, with the actual reality. (He did the same for many other nations, but that is beside our point here.) Many of us were *wrong on almost every issue—and not by a little*. Then consider how such big gaps between perception and reality could influence you in making sound moral or fairness judgments.

- Suppose you're trying to decide whether it's fair or right to raise the eligibility age for Social Security from the current age of 65. People have long relied on the current system, but it's also true that people are living longer, and the Social Security trust fund may need increased tax support soon. In deciding what is fair or right, one relevant fact would be the percentage of Americans who are 65 or over (which impacts how many people will be affected by raising the age and how many non-elderly people there are contributing to the trust fund.) When people were invited to guess what percentage of Americans are over 65, the average response was 36 percent. The fact is 14 percent. Not even close.

- What if you're trying to decide whether the United States has a moral duty to admit immigrants or we already have so many that it threatens American culture. Facts might be relevant. The average American believes that first-generation immigrants constitute 28 percent of the population; the real number is 14 percent. This may not change your opinion about immigration and policing effective borders, but it is at least relevant to the question of immigration's cultural impact.

- Suppose that you're arguing with someone about what is fair in our tax system. Are average Americans paying too much while the rich can easily pay more? Most people do not know that 40 percent of American households actually pay *no* federal income tax at all. Or that the top 10 percent of income earners have 49 percent of all income—but pay 72 percent of all federal income tax. On the other hand, state sales taxes are highly regressive, meaning that the poor and lower income folks pay a much higher percentage of their total income than the well-off. Shouldn't these and lots of other facts affect your judgment of overall fairness?

- Many people have debated whether providing welfare for the poor is
  a moral duty or an excessive burden on others. In evaluating this,
  wouldn't you want to know how much of the national budget goes to
  welfare payments? On average, people estimate 20 percent. The actual
  number is around 1 percent. Again, maybe that doesn't change your
  final answer, but it should matter when forming a moral judgment
  about the issue.

Too often, we resist hearing facts that might cause us to consider morally
painful ideas. For, example, liberals or progressives tend to resist information
that might suggest that some people are genetically born as psychopaths and are
impossible to rehabilitate, or that females and males differ in any realm of ability. Conservatives tend to resist evidence that *in vitro* gene therapy can correct
certain defects and prevent disease, or that communities with comprehensive
school sex education programs have fewer unwanted pregnancies and sexually
transmitted diseases. The facts on these issues are complex and in dispute. But
it's not morally sound to simply turn away from facts whenever you don't like
where you think they might lead. As Aldous Huxley said, "Facts don't cease to
exist because they are ignored."

Determining the facts can be difficult. There is a profound body of literature
about what it takes to establish something as a fact, though that is beyond my
scope here. But as a working concept, let's say that a statement is factual to the
extent that it is in accord with other facts of the world as we know it, is verifiable
(and potentially falsifiable) by others, and is objective, credible, and internally
consistent. The phrase "to the extent" acknowledges that factualness can range
from the indisputable (2 + 2 = 4; Rome is the capital of Italy), to the convincing
but still open to elaboration (fevers are caused by viruses; most violent crime is
committed by younger males); to what may ultimately be proven but is currently open to debate (higher taxes always deter entrepreneurship; ingested
cholesterol is the main risk factor for coronary disease). Since factual claims
range from pseudo-factual nonsense to massively documented reality, learning
how to assess such claims is an important element in reaching sound moral conclusions.

When you make moral judgments—or you try to persuade others to share
them—it is essential to be honest about the relevant facts, both pro and con. As
Boghossian and Lindsay conclude, in today's world, "moral conversations take

place in an environment where people know far less about topics than they think they do, [and yet] intensely feel the truth of their beliefs, hold those beliefs with self-righteous tenacity, [and] have a sense that their beliefs should be obvious to everyone." In such an environment, we all have much to guard against.

Logic: Sound Connections Among Ideas

WE TEND TO THINK OF MORALS as composed of emotions, values, and abstract beliefs, all of which are far afield from the rigid formality of logic. But that just isn't so. What we call logic is an important inherent feature of the way the human mind functions. Logic has been described as a system "of standards of reasoning" to "distinguish good reasoning from bad." Indeed, its "rational force is . . . psychological; it is something we experience in the mind." This is true in moral arguments, like any others.

Imagine arguing with a friend who says, "I never lied to you. And if I did, I didn't mean to. But anyway, what I said was true, or even if it wasn't, you deserved it." Your head is spinning because of all the logical contradictions. Did he say something that wasn't true? Did he intend to? If he didn't intend it, then it wasn't a lie to begin with. And if what he said was true, it wasn't a lie. Saying that you deserved it undercuts his denying ever saying it. So what's the truth?

No one wants to waste time arguing with a person who flies on despite such contradictions. As Bertrand Russell said, "If the law of contradiction were . . . false, nothing will any longer be incoherent with anything else." We would then be entirely adrift in all our arguments—moral or otherwise.

There is no need to succumb to such irrationality. Sure, when people argue moral issues, they tend to get emotional. But one can frame a moral argument logically, just like any other argument. The basic requirements for an effective argument still apply: You state a claim; you offer reasons that make your claim more likely to be true; you provide facts or other support for the reasons; and, when needed, you rebut contrary claims. Any good argument—one with a chance of persuading others—is supported by this sort of logical structure.

In the next few pages, we'll look at how logic works—or can go astray.

As relevant here, there are two principal types of logic. (See the Notes for others.) The first is *formal deductive logic* (FDL). This includes *categorical logic* and *propositional logic*. One simple example is the logic of the syllogism, where if each of two premises is true, the conclusion *must be true*. In Aristotle's words, a syllogism is a "discourse in which, certain things being stated, something other than what is [already] stated follows *of necessity* from their being so." Think of a claim like this:

Torture is always immoral.
Waterboarding constitutes torture.
Therefore, waterboarding is always immoral.

One might challenge either of the two premises stated, but if both are true, then the conclusion surely is. (This points up a key feature of logic: It is a relationship of propositions, not of facts themselves.)

Another common form of FDL is the *conditional syllogism*, "If *a* is true, then *b* must be true; *a* is true; therefore, *b* must be true, too." (If you want to impress friends, tell them this is known as *modus ponens*.) Thus the moral argument: "If the NATO treaty promises mutual defense from of an attack on any NATO country, then if Poland—a NATO nation—is attacked, the United States *must* defend Poland. Article 5 of the NATO treaty does make that promise; and so, we have *a duty* to defend Poland when it is attacked."

FDL has been called "container logic." It works because humans are classifiers; we naturally place things in categories, which are inside other categories. Shoplifting is within the category of stealing, which is within the category of crimes, so shoplifting is a crime. This kind of FDL logic is useful because it's simple and conclusive.

However, in life, the categories are often fuzzy-edged or their boundaries are disputed, so the argument shifts to whether one thing really does fit in a given category or a different one. Is a white lie still in the category of immoral lie? Is a man "cheating" on his wife if he goes on secret dinners with another woman but never has sex? If you feel that running a business has taught you that lots of Irish American guys are gregarious and make good salesmen, but that's less so of Asian Americans, does that make you a "racist"? What is inside and what is outside that word category?

When applying FDL to real-world thinking, accurate categorization is often the thorniest challenge. You need to decide what criteria really place an example within or outside of a word category—especially if it is a morally and emotionally potent one.

Another whole realm is *propositional logic*. It is too technical for me to lay out here. But it involves, for example, a series of propositions for which one may learn enough to assign them "truth values." Then logic helps you determine the effect of related True and False statements, as well as those that are "contrary" or "contradictory" to them, and so on.

Then there is the problem of *fallacies*. These are arguments that appear valid but are not. They represent forms of broken thinking that seem okay and are hard to spot, so we often fall into using them. (More on fallacies below.)

A classic example of the irresistible syllogism is: "All men are mortal; Socrates is a man; therefore, Socrates is mortal." (The mortality of the historical Socrates was, of course, confirmed when he was convicted of the crime of corrupting youths in Athens; as required by law, he drank hemlock and died.) But what do you think of this only slightly different syllogism: "All men are mortal; Socrates is not a man; therefore, Socrates is not mortal."

It kind of sounds right, until you think for a minute. Being a man is a *sufficient* condition to being mortal, but it isn't *necessary*—that is, men are not the only mortal beings. So the fact that Socrates is not a man does not prove that he is not mortal. "Socrates" could be my very old and mortal cat. So, this logic is flawed, i.e., fallacious.

Moral arguments are often made in the form of a conditional syllogism. For example:

If capital punishment deters major crimes, then it is moral.
Capital punishment has not been shown to deter major crimes.
Therefore, capital punishment is not moral.

But this isn't persuasive, because a person might well have reasons other than deterrence for believing that capital punishment is justified and moral. These might include retribution, justice, and catharsis for the victim's family, or the permanent removal an incurably evil person from society. The syllogism would have been logically valid if it had begun "*If and only if* capital punishment deters crime can it be moral."

Of course, in daily conversation, people don't usually say things in a tight conditional syllogistic form. But you can still deconstruct what they say and realize that at times, a syllogism is in play. Then you can decide if it is logically persuasive. (For example: "You said that if I told Maria what people were saying behind her back, she would be grateful to me. I told her, but today she is mad at me. So, you were wrong." Hint: Maria might be mad at you for totally separate reasons!)

The second main type of logic is *informal* or *inductive logic*. It is often said that deductive logic works from the top down, while inductive logic works from the bottom up. In deductive logic, we start with known premises that point down to a conclusion. In inductive logic, we start with known facts; then we try to fit them together with other facts we learn; we make a guess about what it all means; we test that guess against any new facts, and finally we build up to a conclusion. There is a variant with a good name: "inference to the best explanation"—which conveys pretty well what occurs.

Inductive logic is the basic approach of doctors, scientists, historians, police detectives, and many others. Bertrand Russell said that without induction, all science would be impossible, because "every attempt to arrive at general scientific laws from particular observations [would be] . . . fallacious." As a more down-to-earth example, you use inductive logic every time you take a pill from a bottle of medicine. You infer that all the pills in the bottle are supposed to have the same composition, and this pill looks normal, and usually the pill helps get rid of your headache, so . . . you'll trust this pill.

In daily life, we use inductive logic far more than deduction, but its versatile value comes at a price. Unlike syllogistic deduction, induction isn't 100 percent reliable or compelling in its conclusions. Layers and layers of induction can at best lead to greater degrees of probability—but never to complete certainty.

Many inductive arguments are based on generalizations from experience. For example, we know that people don't often "accidentally" run over their spouse with the car—backwards and forwards, five times. So we inductively assemble the known facts; we look for alternative explanations; we exclude possibilities; and we arrive at the conclusion: "She murdered him." On the other hand, we have all seen TV crime dramas in which an innocent person is framed, and the evidence of guilt all falls neatly into place, until a final revelation breaks the mold, and the suspect is shown to be innocent. So, induction yields degrees of confidence, but not 100 percent certainty or logical compulsion.

Many moral judgments are made by induction. If we know that Tom lied to his boss about a subordinate being in his hotel room while on a business trip, and that he inflated travel expenses submitted for reimbursement, and that he falsely called in sick on Monday so that he could go fishing, then we can make an inductive judgment that when his claimed new customer list proves illusory, that is probably because Tom is kind of a liar. We might still be wrong, but the layers of evidence make the inference about Tom more likely.

But we must bear in mind the defects that can beset this kind of thinking. We may have gotten some facts wrong. We may have succumbed to "patterning," the tendency to connect the dots even if they don't really fit in a line. We may have fallen prey to "fundamental attribution error," erroneously ascribing people's acts to firm intention or character rather than just circumstances. In our example of Tom the liar, might it change our conclusion to hear Tom admit he's been totally distracted and confused lately, because his doctor just told him he has cancer?

Another reason we make mistakes in moral reasoning is that we succumb to fallacies—errors in logic that seriously weaken sound judgments. These are not simple, stupid mistakes that people should be ashamed of. On the contrary, many of these thinking errors have been known since antiquity and even recur in the writings of geniuses. They continue to be common because they tap into ways that all of our minds work. Often, fallacious thinking is valid up to a point, and then it's not. It takes conscious effort to avoid fallacies.

In the pages that follow, I'll explain some common fallacies that can invade thinking about moral issues. Each has a traditional name attached to it by generations of thinkers. Bear in mind that logic arose in ancient Greece as an element of persuasion, in an argumentative context. So many of these venerable fallacies relate to deceptive or flawed techniques of persuasion.

APPEAL TO AUTHORITY

This fallacy arises when an argument relies on the judgment of an expert, leader, or another authority figure. For example, "My pastor says we have a moral duty to let people seeking asylum come to America." That is a useful thing to know, but it hardly settles the debate about national immigration policy. Other pastors, priests, rabbis, and imams may disagree. How much does your pastor actually know about what's happening at the border? If you rely solely on his judgment, and he changes his mind, has your moral duty also changed? Appeals to authority are seductive because we respect wise people, and such appeals offer a quick way to make up our minds without further analysis. But even morally wise people don't know every issue or have every right answer.

APPEAL TO POPULAR OPINION

"Most people agree with me that secretly checking your teenager's emails and texts is immoral." The first question to ask about this kind of argument is, "How sure are you that your premise is true?" People tend to associate with people who share their values; as a result, we routinely overestimate the proportion of people who "agree with me." So, this argument is weak. Common sense tells you that parents differ a lot about when they exercise authority versus defer to their kids' autonomy, and various approaches may have merit. This argument also fails to show why such an opinion—even if it were widespread—would be wise. It's good to consider what most of your neighbors think. But majority opinion can be seriously flawed. Generally, an appeal to popular opinion is not strong enough to settle a moral debate.

BEGGING THE QUESTION

This common fallacy involves assuming the very thing that is in dispute. An example: "Whistleblowing is morally wrong because it violates your duty to keep a secret." It kind of sounds right, but wait a moment. Here the underlying question might be: "Is it really part of the duty of a physician employed by a drug company to go along with concealing from the FDA the adverse reactions in patients? Or instead, is it his duty to become a whistleblower?" A duty could be interpersonal, professional, contractual, moral, or all of them, and often such duties conflict. Depending on circumstances, the physician's duty might or might not require going public with the facts. But simply saying "It's your duty" without explaining why, doesn't resolve the argument. It's just circular, inviting the natural response: But *why* is it my duty?

RED HERRING

This fallacy involves throwing into an argument something inflammatory that diverts attention from the real issue. It happens often in arguments about what is right or moral. You might hear someone say, "Why should I care if the Pope says we need to give more foreign aid to relieve world hunger? Didn't the Catholic Church cover up child abuse among its clergy?" The latter statement is true, but it isn't really relevant to judging the morals of foreign aid. It's just a distraction from the issue being debated.

REDUCTIO AD ABSURDUM

This is an argument that a principle is bad because it would be indefensible if taken to its ultimate extreme. For example, "You say that government should never meddle in family business, like how to raise and discipline children. So then, should the state just stand by if you horsewhip your eight-year-old and deprive him of food for a week?" The real challenge in such *reductio* arguments is assessing whether there is any realistic risk of the end point occurring. If so, the argument may have force; if not, it's just a distraction from the real dispute, which is usually about the morality of far more common acts that are way, way back on the severity continuum (like whether parents should be able to spank their kids without fear of state intervention).

AD HOMINEM

This fallacy occurs when an argument relies on a personal attack against someone with a contrary opinion. For example, "Who are you to complain about cruelty to animals? You eat steak and bacon every chance you get!" The person's meat-eating habit might affect how we judge their personal sincerity about animal welfare. But it has no relevance to the broader question whether animal cruelty, in slaughtering hogs, hunting deer, or caging gorillas, is or is not morally acceptable.

A version of *ad hominem* that often occurs in moral arguments is the charge that "you shouldn't get so emotional about this!" People feel strongly about moral issues, and so the emotional stakes may be high all around. But making the issue whether the other person's emotional tone is "right" (i.e., the same as yours) or "excessive" is an unfair distraction. The issue being argued is what matters. And rather than hurling the demeaning epithet "You're so emotional," it would be better to say, "Let's both take a deep breath and just talk this through."

SPECIAL PLEADING

This occurs when someone asks to be excused from the usual requirements of proving what they argue. For example: "Trust me, I'm a very kind person. I wouldn't have done [x] without a very good reason." This tries to divert attention from the real issue, which is whether the action was right or wrong, by invoking the speaker's own general virtue. But "I must be right because I am a nice person" is not a potent argument.

THE "NOT-AS-BAD-AS" FALLACY

Often people say something like this: "How can you say that sexual harassment is a serious offense? It's not nearly as bad as being mugged or kidnapped." Perhaps—but so what? Something bad doesn't get sanitized just because we can think of something worse. We are not limited to condemning only the very worst crimes; we can sanction lesser ones as well. Arguing "not as bad as" is a common way of avoiding a moral judgment, but it's a cop-out.

DROP IN THE BUCKET

People often seek to avoid their moral duty by saying that doing the right thing would make little difference anyway: "After all, it would only be a drop in the bucket." This argument can be used to justify a range of behaviors, like withholding charitable giving, not cleaning up your trash from the beach, and refusing to vote. It's true that as individuals we can only do what we can do, and our acts usually won't change the world. But this fact doesn't render individual good acts meaningless. We are still defined by our moral choices.

HEDGING, OR MOVING THE GOAL POSTS

This occurs when someone makes a bold claim, but then shifts to defending only a smaller or weaker claim when the original one proves indefensible. Here's an example:

> AARON: Your candidate is the most corrupt politician in the country! He's made millions by promising favors to the rich and powerful.
>
> FRED: Actually, when a top journalist investigated those charges, he found that they were completely false.
>
> AARON: Yeah, but your guy agreed to appear at a business convention and got paid $50,000 for a one-hour speech. How is that ethical?

Notice how the claim of being "the most corrupt politician" has suddenly been watered down a lot. Sometimes people move the goal posts so frequently in an argument that you don't know what they are really claiming—or what could possibly refute it.

AMBIGUITY OR EQUIVOCATION

Another common problem in moral arguments is ambiguity (not being clear about what is claimed) or equivocation (claiming two inconsistent things at the same time). Suppose someone says, "No one should be forced to go to church." It's ambiguous whether they mean "forced" by the government, their priest, their spouse, or their own sense of guilt—and these are very different "forces." An example of equivocation would be: "You shouldn't have to go to church if you don't want to, but you should do what your family does." Which is it?

FALSE DICHOTOMY

This fallacy treats a complex or nuanced issue as a simple, black-and-white question. Moral arguments often call forth this fallacy. People say things like "Look, either you believe in God or you don't"; "Either you told him the whole story or you lied"; "Either you're loyal to your friends no matter what or you're just a creep." Experience teaches that such blanket statements are usually false. Some people have a general sense of faith in God while also harboring doubts; an abbreviated story isn't necessarily a lie; and in friendships, the bounds of loyalty can often be difficult to define. In moral arguments, false dichotomies should be resisted.

Recognizing fallacies when other people use them is an essential tool for effective arguing. But recognizing them in your own arguments—and avoiding them—is even more important. Don't be ashamed when you occasionally slip into fallacies during moral arguments. Just be alert to them, and get your thinking back on track.

Words to Clarify Rather Than Confuse or Inflame

"WORDS MATTER. When we think we are using language, language is using us." That captures the power of words to guide, distort, or inflame our response—it all depends on the words we choose. Words matter in part because they reveal *thinking* and *attitudes.*

We are often contradictory about the use of words. In arguing, we often protest when people scrutinize our words too closely. We say, "Don't mince words—focus on what I'm really saying." But then we turn around and get righteous about one offensive word used by someone else. Many arguments pivot on whether someone committed a "lie" or just an "omission" or an "honest mistake"; whether they "knew" or just "should have known" that an action would hurt someone; whether a comment was "nasty" or just "oblivious"; or whether a remark qualifies as "sexist," "racist," or another "-ist."

All of these are "power words" that have consequences. As one commentator says, "Language is like fire. Depending on how you use it, it can either heat your house or burn it to the ground."

So one basic rule is: When you use power words in arguments with people who matter in your life, be restrained and thoughtful. Saying that someone is "assertive" usually is fine; calling them "a bully" may have long-term consequences.

When you ponder how to express yourself in a moral argument, bear in mind some basic features of language. For example, words usually fit well in their home domain and less well in others. Morality is one such linguistic domain; others are business, law, friendship, and civic life. Words may have different meanings when ported from one domain to another. (As the experts say, most words are not *field invariant*). For example, what constitutes "abuse" is very different when the word is applied to child rearing, legal contractual relations, or the pool privileges extended to you by your neighbor. What is improper "meddling" in your private life will differ depending on whether it is done by your friends, relatives, and neighbors, or by the government. So don't assume that a concept has the same meaning in customary social relations, in morality, and in law.

Remember, too, that words come in families of graded tones, like notes on a musical scale or sounds that can get softer or louder. As a moral discussion progresses, people tend to keep turning up the implicit pitch or volume of their words. A person may begin by complaining that she was "surprised" by what her friend did, then progress to being "shocked," "outraged," and finally "disgusted." Those really are different, and when emotions run hot, escalating language can drive us to levels of intensity we don't completely intend and may later regret.

Often in moral arguments, key concepts aren't prepackaged and self-defining. Slapping a child hard doesn't come with a socially agreed label "child abuse." The argument likely will be about whether or not that label *should be* applied. Arguers often try to get the moral upper hand by using an emotionally evocative word, without necessarily defining or defending its meaning. Is assisted suicide actually "murder," or is it something else? Is there a "right" to decent housing for those who can't pay—or are you just arguing that there *should be* such a right? Is it "unethical" for a high school soccer coach to take money from the wealthier kids' parents to pay for extra sessions with those players? In such situations, one must be able to explain and justify the label, not just affix it.

Over time, moral concepts are often argumentatively expanded. This can be a reasonable evolution of language. Thirty years ago, "bullying" at school meant getting punched in the nose. Now it includes the perhaps even more painful practice of public shaming and ridicule on social media.

But in other cases, concept categories are expanded in questionable ways: what has been called "concept creep" or "verbal gerrymandering." Consider the actions now called "microaggressions"—conscious or unconscious negative references to a person or group. (For example, asking a person of color, "What do *you people* think about this issue?" which tends to dissolve individuality into group-ness.) Sometimes, such microaggressions have been grouped together with "violence," a questionable category extension. Or look at the promiscuous way that the distinct concepts of "inequality" and "inequity" are now often used interchangeably. Inequality means that two quantities are different; inequity means that the difference is unfair or unjust. Not every inequality is inequitable—a moral distinction that too often is overlooked.

And then there are words that we all use but don't truly understand. My favorite example is "cause," as in "cause and effect." This word is one of the most important in our language and in our lives. A great part of existence depends on being able to understand what actually leads to or causes an effect. Causation words often recur in arguments, and they imply moral responsibility for the results. People say things like: "The boss's personality caused him to quit" or "You made me look incompetent"—or even "By just standing there and saying nothing, you caused him to conclude . . . " But what exactly does it mean to "cause" something?

There are fine books on this subject (see the Notes). But Aristotle devised an early typology that has rarely been improved on. Let's say I bought an expensive new desk chair and it turned out to be uncomfortable. What is the "cause" of my disappointment? In Aristotle's thinking, there are four possible causes, each reflecting a different facet of the concept. The first is the *formal cause*—the chair may not have been designed correctly by its manufacturer. Second, is the *material cause*—what the chair is made of; perhaps the fabric is stiff plastic, making it unpleasant to sit on. Third, is the *efficient cause*—the work of those who assembled the chair, who may have been unskilled or uncaring. And fourth, is the *final cause*—the purpose of the chair; maybe the chair is well made but not really intended for daylong sitting.

Aristotle's distinctions are very useful and underline many of our intuitions about causes. But when people talk about personal or social problems, you'll hear them advert to all sorts of "causes." These include main causes, contributing causes, indirect causes, second-order causes, minor causes that still were the "straw that broke the camel's back," social-condition causes, psychological causes, statistical-correlation causes—and even doing nothing as a cause!

In moral arguments, this multifarious ambiguity creates real problems. Suppose I say that when Tony slept with Carolyn, the wife of his friend Norm, Tony "caused" their divorce. Does that mean that without that tryst, they wouldn't have divorced? Isn't that what "cause" means? But what if Carolyn had three prior affairs, too? And how can anyone know the counterfactual of what would have occurred if the affair with Tony had never happened?

What's more, is there any way to measure the inevitability of the divorce in the aftermath of the Tony affair? Could Carolyn and Norm have averted divorce through marital counseling? If they refused even to try that, does Tony still bear the blame?

And if we probe still deeper, we can look at Carolyn's troubled childhood (from which she emerged insecure and in constant need of affirmation), Norm's grinding job (which kept him on the road three weeks out of four, leaving Carolyn feeling lonesome), and the economic recession that hit their state especially hard (which forced Norm into a job he never really wanted).

The more we look at the realities of the situation, the less convincing it is to say that "Tony caused the divorce."

"Cause" is a key word in moral arguments because it ties in to other potent psychological concepts: responsibility, blame, shame, guilt, and apology. So be thoughtful before flinging the *cause* word at people and actions. Sometimes alternative words like *contributed to, influenced,* or *was a factor in* fit the situation better.

You might think that these kinds of word distinctions are just nitpicking. But words matter. They carry interpersonal power and can affect relationships for a long time. When deployed hastily or carelessly, they also can throw moral arguments into confusion, making it more difficult for people to understand one another or reach agreement. So think about the words you use, and choose them with care.

8

Overlapping Mandates:
Customs, Morals, and Law

MANY ARGUMENTS BEGIN WITH AN EXCLAMATION like, "That's just gross—who does that in public?" or "That's immoral," or "You can't do that—it's probably illegal." All three remarks express strong condemnation. But what is repulsive, immoral, or illegal can get intertwined, sometimes rightly and sometimes not. Listen to this argument:

SHE: I can't believe what just happened—I saw Professor Humbug and his student Sarah together at a romantic restaurant. He's old enough to be her father, but he leaned over and kissed her on the lips. He should go to jail for sexual harassment!

HE: Unless you know more about the situation, it's not illegal.

SHE: Well, it should be illegal. It's immoral for sure. He has the power to grade her. She's a vulnerable college student, and she probably worries what happens if she says No. So he's taking advantage.

HE: But you know Sarah—she's dated professors before, and she's a pretty smart cookie.

SHE: That's not the point. It's immoral of him to prey on her even if she accepts it.

HE: Are you sure it's "preying"?

SHE: Well, whatever you call it, it's disgusting and wrong.

HE: I think the worst part is that the other students probably all know about it. Think about how that affects the other women in the class.

SHE: I don't care about that—they can deal with it however they want. I'm just mad that he's getting away with being a creep.

Note how morality, custom, and legality all get rolled up together here. Aren't those three things rather different?

You may feel that drawing this distinction is splitting hairs—that a far older professor having an intimate relationship with a college student is just plain wrong, and how you label it doesn't much matter. But in real life, it does matter whether an action simply offends customs or is deemed immoral—or is even illegal. In this case, if you were a friend of Professor Humbug, you would want to be sure about which domain applies to his behavior. If his conduct is *illegal* (as is true in some states) or if it violates the university's faculty code and thus is a basis to fire him—you'd surely tell him he must stop. If you felt it was *immoral,* you'd argue hard that he should stop. But if it just *isn't customary,* then you'd feel on weaker ground, since people are allowed to break customs all the time.

Specific facts might play a role in your judgment. Would it matter if Sarah is a divorced woman attending college at age 35? Would it matter if she completed Professor Humbug's class last year and is no longer his student? Would the professor's marital status make a difference? Does it affect your judgment if Sarah has had intimate relations with other professors? What bothers you most about this situation?

Moral judgments often get confused with what we feel is normal, customary, or expected. And some conduct so strongly violates social norms that it has become illegal. We tend to think that law controls everything, and that moral and social norms are relatively weak by comparison. But actually, it's the reverse. As Mark Twain said,

Laws are sand; customs are rock. Laws can be evaded and punishment escaped; but an openly transgressed custom brings sure punishment [by one's neighbors]. The penalty may be unfair, unrighteous, illogical and [cruel]. . . . [N]o matter, it will be inflicted just the same.

Twain's statement captures a deep truth about social sanctions: There is a pyramid of enforcement. Within the broad base of everyday behavior, custom reigns supreme, and it is enforced by family, neighbors, and coworkers. A narrower layer of conduct is deemed immoral and can lead to more formal sanctions, like losing a job. Only a still narrower layer of bad conduct rises to the top level of being penalized as a civil or criminal wrong.

The interactions among customs, morals, and law are complex. In many traditional societies, violating custom was also seen as transgressing moral duty and could lead to a collective sanction. Most traditional societies had strong religious or tribal customs and rituals about food, dress, agriculture, birth, marriage, death, authority, appeasing nature or the gods, and many other things. Violating any of them was viewed as harmful. It risked the wrath of the gods and harm to the whole community. So, in such societies, breaking custom was usually equivalent to acting immorally.

The ancient Roman religion that prevailed in the empire for centuries was based on *orthopraxis* (doing rightly), not *orthodoxy* (believing rightly). The Romans didn't much care if conquered peoples believed in a bunch of their own gods, as long as they also respected the prerogatives of the Roman gods and offered appropriate rituals and tribute. But it was uniquely offensive to the Romans when those vexatious Judeans declared there was but one God, which meant that the Roman deities couldn't be worshiped, too. Later, when a Jewish apocalyptic prophet named Jesus proclaimed the good news of the one God's plan for man, the Romans cared less what he believed than that his followers would no longer participate in the Roman gods' rituals. This emphasis on outward behavior is in marked contrast to the significance of correct belief—even apart from action—that would later animate the Catholic Church.

Today, we tend to sort things more distinctly into three different buckets—what is required by custom, morality, or law. As one scholar puts it, "The moral domain varies by culture. It is unusually narrow in Western, educated, and individualistic cultures. Sociocentric [community-focused] cultures broaden the moral domain to encompass and regulate more aspects of life." Fortunately, extensive research confirms that we have an innate capacity to learn to distinguish what is merely custom from what is a moral obligation.

When engaging in moral arguments, it's important to grasp how a given society regards the sacred and its relation to the immoral. In Hindu society, the world is seen as suffused with a great many sacred things. A wide range of acts or omissions are seen as affronts to sacredness. But in modern, secularized Western societies, the range of sacred things has been greatly narrowed—essentially to God, family, and life itself. People differ on whether the nation is within that group. Hence, in Western societies, we see less equivalency between what is demanded by custom and by morality.

The Venn diagram below depicts the separate but overlapping realms of custom, morality, and law. Each defines proper conduct and imposes sanctions in its domain.

The Separate but Overlapping Domains of Custom, Morality, and Law

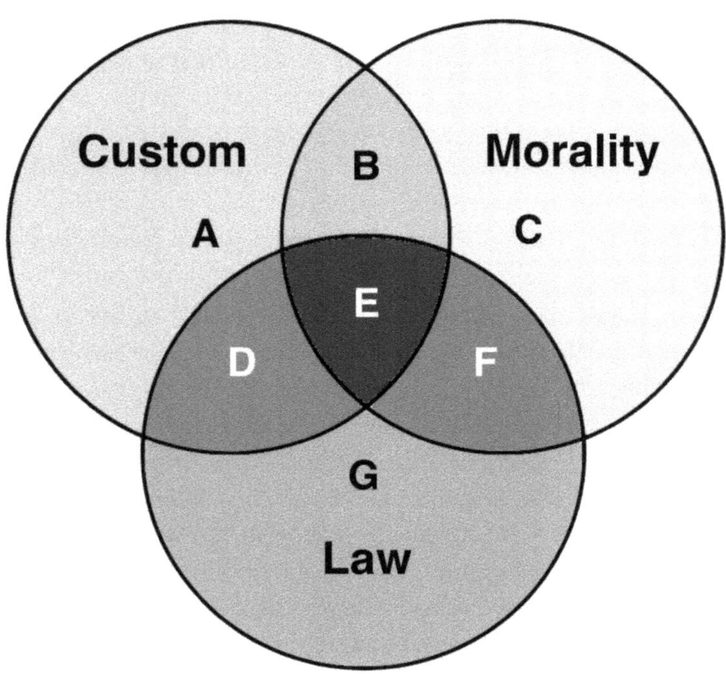

Here are some examples of the sanctions imposed by each domain (at least in the United States).

A. ACTIONS THAT VIOLATE CUSTOM, BUT NOT MORALITY OR LAW (letting weeds grow high in the front yard; wearing flip-flops and a halter top to a parent–teacher meeting).

B. ACTIONS THAT VIOLATE CUSTOM AND MORALITY, BUT NOT LAW (spending freely on oneself but being cheap with your children; trying to get ahead by spreading gossip about rivals at work).

C. ACTIONS THAT VIOLATE MORALITY, BUT NOT CUSTOM OR LAW (a politician or corporate leader refusing to admit a harmful mistake; a man not telling his wife he's having an affair).

D. ACTIONS THAT VIOLATE CUSTOM AND LAW, BUT NOT MORALITY (not renewing your car registration; screaming "Repent, God is angry and you shall die" all day outside a high school).

E. ACTIONS THAT VIOLATE CUSTOM, MORALITY, AND LAW (robbery; child abuse; stock fraud).

F. ACTIONS THAT VIOLATE MORALITY AND LAW, BUT NOT CUSTOM ("forgetting" to report small amounts of income on your taxes; repeatedly spitting on the sidewalk).

G. ACTIONS THAT VIOLATE LAW, BUT NOT CUSTOMS OR MORALITY (ignoring a parking ticket because you were only two minutes late; paying only part of a painter's bill under a contract because he didn't finish on time).

You may not agree with all of these categorizations, and of course, special circumstances could vary them. But however you would sort the specific behaviors, this typology is inherent in our everyday life. We are often unmindful of the boundaries between these categories. For example—as we saw in Chapter 6, on the psychology of morals—if we have a visceral reaction of disgust (or "ick") at something that violates customs, we tend instinctively to decide that it's also immoral.

As social values change over time, certain conduct can become more regulated, migrating from being just customary to having an obligatory moral quality or even being legally required. For example, for much of American history, children worked on farms and in factories, and it wasn't expected that they would receive much book learning. In time, it became more of a moral duty for parents to educate their children, if they could afford it. Later, educating children became a legal duty. Likewise, racial discrimination was once the accepted custom, but later was seen as immoral, and finally became illegal.

Conversely, some conduct can become less regulated. Same-gender sexual relations were long condemned by custom, morality, and law. But now they are lawful and seen by most Americans as not immoral but a matter of personal nature and choice. Marijuana use and pornography, formerly illegal, are now seen by many people, and by the law in some states, as "no big deal."

One subject on which, surprisingly, we have become more rather than less socially censorious is disfavored speech. Today, you can be ostracized, financially penalized, fired, canceled, and doxed for saying certain things that are socially disfavored—such as using gender or ethnic characterizations seen as demeaning. Lack of bad intent will not exculpate you. So, amid all the talk of our becoming a more tolerant and permissive society, in this respect we have become more punitive.

As to patriotism, we have moved in the other direction. Patriotism used to be viewed as a universal civic duty and a badge of morality. Now it seems to be regarded by many as an elective choice ("Why should I be patriotic? That's just not me"). Marriage before having children was always a strong rule of morality; now it is seen by many (though not all) as just a lifestyle choice. So over time, specific conduct can escalate up the chain of social sanctions and become regarded as immoral or illegal, or move down and become legal, morally permissible, and just a matter of choice.

Of course, and this hardly needs to be said, you don't need to go along with these trends (except for obeying the law). As an autonomous person, you can decide when conforming to customs just isn't right for you, or when conventional morality is mistaken in your view. And conversely, you can choose to uphold a much higher standard of courtesy, neighborliness, and morals than is customary.

Professional Ethics Codes

SOME PEOPLE ACQUIRE ADDED MORAL OBLIGATIONS because of special social roles they assume—such as priests, doctors, psychotherapists, accountants, lawyers, and civil engineers. Many of these professions have developed specialized codes of ethics, which are largely intended to protect the public from shady or dangerous practices. Some of these practices would be profitable for the profession, but they are prohibited anyway. Law firms turn away millions in business every day to avoid conflicts of interest that many similar professions (like consultants and investment bankers) see no problems with. Doctors used to make a lot of money directly selling patients medical devices, or doing itinerant surgery from town to town without arranging follow-up care. But these practices now are largely barred by the medical profession's ethics code. Businesspeople can have sexual relations with their customers, but psychologists cannot, or they violate their profession's ethics code and can lose their licenses.

Some cynics charge that professional ethics codes serve mainly to defend an in-group's monopoly against less expensive competitors, rather than to protect the public. Historically, there were examples of this, but many have been over-turned by legislation or antitrust challenges in the courts. Most professional ethics codes serve a genuine purpose by supplementing the moral rules of society at large and making practitioners more responsible.

In fact, the adoption of a true code of conduct is a key way to distinguish a profession from a trade. What's the ethical difference between a trade (house painter, grocer, or car salesman) and a profession (architect, accountant, or electrician)? The word "trade" is derived from the Middle English words for "course" or "track," so a "tradesman" literally *trod* the ground, hawking his wares from village to village. The ethics of *caveat emptor*—buyer beware—ruled when dealing with a tradesman. But the word "professional" derives from the Latin word for "to profess," meaning "to accept a vow." A professional must *profess* belief in a clear set of values, and those values are often embodied in the given profession's ethics code.

So, when an argument involves the moral conduct of these kinds of professionals, it's not just a matter of personal belief. An argument in this arena also must take into account their profession's ethics code, which they are bound to obey.

Business Ethics

LET'S BE HONEST: Many people think the title of this section is an oxymoron. Business ethics? Businesspeople just try to seduce customers and crush the competition, right? Well, not exactly.

Start with the fact that in modern society, businesses operate under many kinds of legal regulation. In the United States, manufacturers of drugs and medical devices must prove to the Food and Drug Administration (FDA) that they are safe. A company can't sell toys that are dangerous or cribs that collapse. Restaurants must pass sanitation inspections. Banks are required to tell you their fees. Businesses aren't supposed to collude with competitors or engage in obviously false advertising. And so on. Of course, these laws are imperfectly written and enforced, and some companies consciously plan how to skirt them. But most businesspeople will tell you that their company spends a lot of time and money working to comply with complex laws. And in most cases, they don't do it just to avoid getting caught. They comply because obeying the law is the right thing to do.

In fact, most successful companies spend large amounts of money and effort building their reputation for practicing good business ethics—far above mere compliance with law. They are convinced that the economic value of the company is enhanced by ethical behavior. Consultants advise that being known as an ethical business helps companies win customer loyalty, attract and retain top employees, secure better vendor contracts through trust, minimize lawsuits and government investigations, avoid bad publicity, and maximize the number of large pension funds and other institutional investors who will buy the stock and support its price. So companies go out of their way to commit themselves publicly to ethical behavior. For example, Google's Code of Conduct at one time stated bluntly, "Don't be evil," which is an appropriate but low standard. But then it also said that everything the company does "should be measured against the highest possible standards of ethical business conduct." Whether or not it's always met, that's a high bar to set. When they fail, it's hard to deny failure.

Business ethics are taken seriously. Almost every industry has a company or two that everyone lauds for taking the high road, while others are less respected. There is a surprising degree of agreement on who those companies are, because people share some sense of what business ethics ought to mean. That is why the annual lists of "most admired companies" include many of the same ones year after year. Companies like Target, Publix, Microsoft, Whirlpool, Procter & Gamble, Coca-Cola, Johnson & Johnson, Costco, Berkshire Hathaway, Eli Lilly, and Apple keep being listed. People differ on the weighting of criteria and whether some of these companies deserve to be included; few if any are wonderful in every respect. But their strong reputations don't just happen without massive effort.

Companies today feel pressure to use an avowedly moralistic vocabulary to convey their culture. They don't just tout profit; they speak of having a "mission," a "North Star," a "public trust," and committing to an "ethical company culture." One overarching value that covers a lot is "integrity."

But what exactly are the principles of business ethics? One treatise says, "Business ethics is about how you make your money. Do you make money in an honest, fair and open way, free of coercion and exploitation? Does your product or service create value for your customers, without forcing third parties to bear your cost?" One author asks her Stanford students each year to name the most important ethics principles. The top ones listed in 2019 were honesty, integrity, kindness, compassion, loyalty, empathy, authenticity, respect, and responsibility. It's interesting that this list emphasizes "touchy-feely" values; only farther down on the list were such concrete deliverables as reliability, consistency, or fair pricing.

Here are some commonly cited principles embodied in corporate ethics statements:

1. Provide high-quality goods and services that improve people's lives.
2. Be truthful to the customer.
3. Treat the customer right, and stand behind our products.
4. Don't make products that are obviously bad for society.
5. Value employees. Pay them fairly, respect their knowledge of the business, and give them the chance to advance.
6. Treat vendors fairly. Chose vendors who treat their own employees well.
7. Don't skirt the law.
8. Admit when the company has made a big mistake. Fix it fast and do it right.

9. Support competition; don't try to crush the little guy.

10. Bring fair return to shareholders, but don't put earning an extra dollar above all other goals.

Right there you have ten good principles. But some are not exactly unarguable. For example, take #4: Do you believe that it violates basic business ethics to manufacture cigarettes, assault rifles, or movies about violent predators? Or would you say, "If it's not illegal, and customers want it, who am I to tell people what business to be in?" One answer is that a company can choose its lines of business—but I also have the right to judge a company and its executives who choose to make products that contribute to needless deaths. Rather than hiding behind the everybody-has-a-right-to-make-a-buck trope, leaders should own up to their choices and their effects on society.

And what of principle #2—being truthful to the customer? In fields where customer disclosures are regulated by law—like auto sales, pharmaceuticals, or bank loans—some executives believe that following the law is sufficient, while others strive to practice a much higher degree of transparency. But how high is high enough? Suppose that our company makes really good, reliable washing machines. But when they break, the circuit board will cost a lot—$250—to replace. Must we disclose that up front? If so, we'll surely lose customers, and they'll just buy from our competitor, whose machines actually break a lot more often. You can see that kind of argument going round and round. Or what about "dynamic pricing"? Should online sellers inform customers that they use complex algorithms to determine in advance, and then offer, only *the highest price* that customers like you will pay, while offering lower prices to other kinds of folks?

Principle #10—how to balance profit with social good—is the pivot point around which most arguments about corporate ethics revolve. The principles listed above focus mostly on just the company and its customers. But over the past decades, two major movements have developed, demanding that corporations, especially large public ones, pay attention to a broader set of social concerns. These are the Corporate Social Responsibility (CSR) and Environmental, Social, Government (ESG) movements, both of which include the potent Diversity, Equity, and Inclusion (DEI) imperative. These movements challenge corporations to consider their impact on the big problems facing society. Is earning profit for shareholders the only duty of management, is it the most important duty among others, or should it fall somewhere lower in the rank of corporate obligations?

Given the stakes, you would think that all the corporate lawyers and judges must have settled this question, but they haven't. One can find a host of broad but contrary statements. Some experts believe that company directors must make stockholder welfare their sole end. Others disagree, and the U.S. Supreme Court has said, "Modern corporate law does not require for-profit corporations to pursue profit at the expense of everything else, and many do not."

Some try to square the circle, reconciling the duty to maximize profit with the duty to serve society by focusing not on short-term profit but on long-term company value. They believe that the fiduciary duty of directors is to promote the total value of the corporation for the benefit of its stockholders. They argue that if a company pollutes the environment, underpays its workers, and doesn't contribute to local charities, then even if it's profitable now, over the long term, it will lose brand value, customers, and profits. That justifies being a good citizen even at greater cost and reduced profit now. That is the thesis. Yet legal commentators continue to express the concern that "if directors were allowed to deviate from shareholder wealth maximization, they could turn to indeterminate balancing standards [for various social goals], which provide no accountability."

In 2019, about 200 CEOs of large companies, organized by the Business Roundtable, adopted a new, ideal statement of corporate purpose. It moved beyond the corporation serving only shareholders and emphasized duties to employees, customers, suppliers, and communities. But companies still would face myriad challenges in deciding how to trade off costs and social good. Just for example:

- Should the company pay the average wage in the industry, or a bit more, in order to foster worker loyalty and dedication?

- Should it provide health benefits to all workers, or try to shift some workers to being mere "contractors" so as to avoid paying benefits?

- Should the company just obey environmental laws, or go beyond in abating its carbon emissions to help reduce the impact on climate change?

- Should the company avoid sourcing products from factories in nations with very poor worker conditions? Or should they source there and help create jobs, but insist on increased pay for workers and accept the cost?

- Should the company implement a major program to use minority and women-owned vendors?

- Should the company use its balance sheet to invest in local businesses, or environmentally responsible businesses, and should it withdraw investments from socially questionable companies?

A lot of analysis attempts to determine just how much profit a company might need to sacrifice to pursue these social goods. For example, there is research on the stock performance of "green" or ESG-driven mutual funds, compared to those that just seek the most profitable investments. The record seems to be mixed. So, the ethical question still remains: Just how much should a company be willing to sacrifice in profit, to achieve how much perceived social good?

We might also ask, which social goods should we rank highest? Should our company put an extra $10 million into raising workers' wages, *or* improving the safety of our products, *or* preventing possible cyber-hacking of customers' data, *or* giving to the United Way in the community where we operate a large factory? In deciding that, what is our ethical standard? What if we manufacture clothes in Bangladesh and sell them in stores in Ohio, and the $10 million would have a much bigger impact on improving workers' lives in Bangladesh than in Ohio? Does that settle the question of where to put our extra $10 million, or do we start with the idea that "we're an American company"? Suppose that a company operating mainly in California and Vermont has goals for diversity among middle managers. It's easy to meet the diversity goals given the ethnic mix of California, but harder in Vermont. Should the company say, "So what, our numbers look good overall," and not worry about the managers in Vermont?

Of course, some supposed corporate ethical dilemmas aren't really dilemmas at all. Sometimes, when a big corporate error harms people, the moral action is to jump on it and fix it almost regardless of cost. When Boeing discovers that its 737 Max aircraft has major flaws that cause crashes, or British Petroleum faces the Deep Horizon oil disaster in the Gulf of Mexico, or Wells Fargo engages in a massive scam to set up phony accounts—the issue is pretty clear. They need to use resources to fix the problem in the fastest and smartest way.

Even more, these kinds of disasters teach us to plan for moral excellence in advance. As one expert says, "Ethics are an early-stage endeavor, not an eraser or a cleanup act after harm is done." But many business experts take a less idealistic tack. One says, "When ethical dilemmas heat up, quiet business leaders often look for ways to buy time." He recommends "strategic stalling," carefully "picking battles," "bend the rules, don't break them," and "find a compromise" that is "good enough." That sounds like a pretty weak approach to ethics. Another scholar says that corporate morality shouldn't be likened to the high morals of a good person, but rather to the rather rudimentary level of a good puppy: "We do not need to identify the puppy's intentions . . . [but just] agree that its 'ethical' fulfillment of the social contract consists of not soiling the carpet or biting the baby."

In my view, this is a very impoverished idea of ethics. It also runs up against another often noted business reality: "The way the chief executive exercises moral judgment is universally acknowledged to be more influential than written policy." Both ethical and "unethical business practice reflects the values, attitudes, beliefs, language and behavioral patterns that define an organization's operating culture." To be meaningful, business ethics must go beyond just following the law or written policies; they must inspire the daily actions of everyone in the business, starting with its leaders.

Finally, note that being a good corporation is unavoidably different from being a good person. For example, as an individual, you can decide what kind of moral person you want to be. But a corporation is a complex collectivity, in which no single will can always hold sway. A single board member might get outvoted, the CEO can be told No, or the board might be overruled by a shareholder vote. If you believe a company is acting unethically, even selling the shares you personally own doesn't fix the problem. Business ethics demand collective action by a large group of people who share a set of common values and the determination to practice them.

Another practical difference is that individuals can try to be saints; companies can't. A few rare people are exemplary in every domain; they seek out noble, dangerous jobs, take in foster children, staff the church food kitchen for the homeless, and *also* contribute more than their share to local charities. But all businesses operate in a competitive economic environment, so a corporation finds it very hard to be morally "superior" across all domains. Most companies strive to be about as ethical as their industry peers, or maybe a bit better. But practically, they can't be saints who pay workers more than average, spend more on product safety, are environmentally better, and also give lavishly to local communities. So, the broader notion of corporate ethics has finite limits. Ultimately, corporations will be as moral as we are willing to require or pay for them to be.

The challenge of business ethics illustrates the broader theme of this chapter: that morality is not a system with clear, fixed rules for right and wrong. Instead, it's a complex way of viewing the challenges human beings face, which calls for different responses depending on the situation.

9

The Broader Domain of Values

DOING THE RIGHT THING IN LIFE involves far more than just acting morally. The range of situations with a moral dimension is broad—but those that touch on some core values span an even broader range.

Both morals and values are key elements of how we construct our identities and want to live our lives. Acting morally is important to most of us. But we hold other values that might sometimes weigh even more. As just one example, many people would be willing to act dishonestly when necessary to protect a loved one from harm—maybe even from a penalty they deserved. Love of family is, for many, the very highest value. So, in a broader sense, doing the right thing means doing what protects and preserves their values. Now let's explore in some detail what that entails.

To start: What exactly are values? Basically, values are described by psychologists as "a person's beliefs about ideal modes of conduct and ideal terminal goals [of life]." They are abstract "concepts of the desirable" or "preferences and principles" about what should be sought in life. (I'll elaborate on that later.)

Most people can describe their core values. They may include things like family, faith, freedom, decency, loyalty, morality, community, respect, status, security, income, fairness, reason, making a better life for one's children, and building a better society. And as we'll see, one's values aren't a chaotic or random list. They exhibit an organized structure that allows many predictions about individual behavior. Because values run so deep within us, they're implicated in almost any personal or political disagreement you have with others—not just those carrying labels saying "moral dilemma" or "value question."

You can't avoid arguing with people about values. And we can't solve the major problems facing society unless we're willing to engage productively with others in arguments about values.

Yet often, people reflexively say, "There's no point in arguing; we just have different values!" My guess is that they mean they can't see an argument ever getting them to *give up their core values*. Fair enough—but that misconceives how values work in practice. Our values aren't usually clear and consistent, enabling us to see easily in every situation how to uphold or forsake them. Instead, our values are abstract, fuzzy-edged, and often in conflict with one another. Daily life is full of conundrums about how to reconcile competing values: candor versus kindness, ambition versus collegiality, inner peace versus outward striving, honesty versus self-interest, loyalty to some versus fairness to all. Deciding a value-laden issue involves discerning which of your values really are in play, how to weigh them, and how they can best be reconciled in the given situation. A good argument can help.

To start, how your values fit into a situation often isn't obvious. Suppose you value kindness to friends. But kindness isn't like a thermostat that you just set higher or lower. It's more subtle. Is it kinder to tell a friend about some feature of their personality that's causing problems with others, or is the kind choice to say nothing to avoid upsetting them? Is it kind to tell a friend that your spouse treats you far better than theirs does and they shouldn't accept being dominated? Is it kind to keep paying for dinners together with a friend who's less well off—or will that make them feel demeaned? These problems are worth struggling with, in part because you probably value things like honesty and autonomy as well as kindness. The way you act will "develop into a values structure, through experiences in which two values are placed in conflict, forcing the individual to choose one over the other."

Abstract values can be challenging to define. Why is loving one's siblings and children touted as a "family value," but to some, loving their gay or gender-different family members . . . not so much? About half of America's children receive health care only by being enrolled in the Medicaid or CHIP programs. How can people demand cuts to those programs at the same time they tout "family values"? If teaching about faith is a family value, why isn't also teaching about science, since the truths of both faith and science will be important to your children's future lives? Liberals see lauding the importance of two-parent families as moralizing; but there is probably nothing that would reduce poverty and improve children's welfare more than having more two-parent households. Family values, then, is a pretty protean concept.

Or take the value of freedom. Many would say that freedom means being able to do what I want, unless it really hurts somebody else. But assessing the importance of a freedom and the associated harm isn't always easy. Is it really an important freedom to be able to spit on the sidewalk, be bare-chested in a restaurant, smoke in a theater, not wear a motorcycle helmet or seatbelts, or refuse to wear a mask in a store during COVID? I'm not asking you to give final answers. I'm just trying to show that it takes some reflection to decide when a value like freedom is really threatened. Why is prohibiting riding a bicycle on the shoulder of the highway generally not seen as infringing freedom, but requiring a motorcycle helmet is? Is having to drive on the right side of the road a blow to freedom?

Conflicts between values are also commonplace. Let's assume that, like most people, you value both individual freedom and being a good neighbor. But what actions make you a bad neighbor instead of just someone who is properly exercising their freedom? Holding a loud wine party on your patio every Saturday? Using a wood-fired stove that often sends smoke into your neighbor's house? Using binoculars to peer through your neighbor's windows? Not vaccinating your kids even though they play with everyone in the neighborhood? Engaging in archery or pistol practice on your own property? When are these things freedoms, and when are they just wrong?

As all these examples show, it isn't impertinent for a person to say, "Actually, I do want to argue with you about values!" Values are an important part of relationships—among family members, friends, business colleagues, and fellow citizens. As one expert says, "When values are activated, they become infused with feeling." Far from being pointless, arguments about values can be among the most valuable arguments we have.

What Are Values?

LET'S DIG A LITTLE DEEPER into what values are. The leading scholar Shalom Schwartz explains that "values (1) are concepts or beliefs, (2) pertain to desirable end states or behaviors, (3) transcend specific situations, (4) guide selection or evaluation of behavior or events, and (5) are ordered by relative importance. Values . . . differ from attitudes primarily in their generality or abstractness . . . and in their hierarchical ordering by importance." So, the takeaways are:

- Values are broad and abstract. Wanting the Pittsburgh Steelers to win on Sunday is not a value. But general camaraderie with friends or community spirit may be.

- Values are about what is valuable and right to seek in life. Pleasure, achievement, social respect, power, safety, new experiences, doing good—all these are generalized values.

- Values can be compared and then ranked in relative importance—but only in normal circumstances. For you, leisure time may be a higher value than money; but if you lose your job and can't pay family expenses, suddenly earning money may become your top value.

- Values are arrayed across several domains, such as values relating to yourself (like self-reliance); to family/friends (love, loyalty); to work (diligence, reliability); to the social group (prestige, duty); or to the civic polity (patriotism, equality).

- One's actions are influenced by the relative importance of various values in a given situation.

Schwartz studied values across many nations and cultures. He identified ten core values that recur across all of them, revealing a deep common core of human nature. The Schwartz Value Scale (SVS) includes Benevolence, Universalism, Self-Direction, Stimulation, Hedonism, Achievement, Power, Security, Conformity, and Tradition. Values give rise to more specific norms of behavior. For example, the value of Benevolence can be supported by norms like helping new employees at work, being a good neighbor, and giving to charities. (More on the SVS later.)

Note that values aren't just things that a person happens to like, such as travel or sports. Values imply beliefs about what is worth striving for in life. In that sense, values are inherently argumentative. That doesn't mean believing that everyone ought to agree with your values. You can say, for example, "I greatly value marriage and children—but I can also see they may not be right for Steve and Anna." But holding a strong value does entail believing that it matters, that it is right or good, and that others should try to see that. So, if you deeply value family, it means you believe people should at least consider marriage and children, that duty to family usually outweighs other desires, and that others should respect your family obligations.

If you value faith, it entails belief that everyone should at least wrestle with faith and seek to know the spirit of God. If you deeply value loyalty, it means you think ill of those who violate it. Saying "I really value patriotism" implies the argument, "and I feel that you should care about it, too."

To be clear, this doesn't mean imposing your values on others. There is a big difference between believing something deeply and wanting to force others to act likewise. (More on that in Chapter 11.) But when we believe in deep-seated values, it's natural to want to explain and defend them to others.

Values Versus Interests

EXPERIENCE SHOWS US that people tend to argue that something is moral, true, or wise when it happens to align with their own selfish interests. We all suffer from bounded (i.e., limited or biased) rationality and bounded ethicality. Our minds work overtime to figure out in each situation why "it's only fair" that we get what we really want.

But as we've seen throughout this book, that's not the only thing people think about. We struggle with our morals and values, and often act contrary to our immediate, selfish interests. People give money to distant relatives (even those who never reciprocate), trust new acquaintances (who sometimes prove unworthy), lend a helping hand to coworkers (who may soon leave the company anyway), avoid firing a weak employee (who then screws up again), and act honorably (to their detriment) in myriad situations. They do so in service to their values.

Note just one large-scale example: About 65 percent of all the firefighters in the United States are volunteers. It's hard and dangerous service, yet many folks in our communities do it, simply because they value helping.

In the realm of public policy, many so-called realists say that values are airy-fairy nonsense, that people always act based on hard calculations of self-interest defined mainly in economic terms. The long-dominant *rational choice theory* depicted humans as cool computers of how choices will bring them personal benefit and avoid risk or harm, again in economic terms. This is captured by hoary aphorisms like "Where you stand is where you sit" or "Whose food you eat, whose song you sing." But research in behavioral economics, psychology, and political science has now shown that to be a severely flawed description. It's wrong so often that the "realists" turn out not to be so realistic!

For example, voting patterns don't support the simple prediction that people just vote according to their economic self-interest. In the United States, most highly educated, affluent professionals now tend to vote liberal—which tends to result in higher taxes on them, with tax revenues then used to support transfer payments and social programs that don't benefit them economically. This goes against their economic self-interest.

Conversely, many middle-class whites vote conservative, which means elect-ing candidates who generally don't support expanding health care services, college loan programs, day care, and other social goods that those voters could benefit from. True, they don't want to be taxed for those services. But since about 40 percent of American families (including lots of those in the lower middle class) wind up paying no federal income tax, higher tax rates wouldn't hit them much.

What's more, every "National Election Study has shown that [even] the poor are no more likely than the rich to vote in favor of redistributive economic poli-cies that would clearly serve their financial interests." Across the presidential elections spanning 1996–2004, "there was no significant relationship between family income and voting for the Democratic or the Republican candidate." A 2024 Pew Research Center study found that Democrats had a numerical ad-vantage among only the richest and the poorest tiers—which makes no sense in terms of their shared economic interests. A leading expert says that while excep-tions exist, "the conclusion is quite clear: self-interest ordinarily does not have much effect on the ordinary citizen's sociopolitical attitudes."

When groups vote against their economic interests, they do so because of *other values* that are important to them. "Lots of evidence indicates that people do not simply vote their economic self-interest. Political behavior in general is determined more by ideological commitments or by moral intuitions." As Joan Williams wrote in 2025, "sharp increases in inequality have been accompanied by decreasing rates of support for Democrats among . . . noncollege voters—despite the fact that far right policies exacerbate inequality." What is going on is a sea change in the cultural and class affinities of people toward the two political parties. Thus "class identity is expressed not only through economics but also through cultural differences"—primarily resentment at "elites." Leading scholars find that "compared to self-interest, people's *values* and their [social] . . . evaluations are better predictors of their views [on issues like] . . . spending, law and order, race and gender issues, social welfare policies and foreign affairs."

This is no secret to political campaign experts; they know that voters act on many values other than economic self-interest. The polarization of politics in recent decades has been driven by this reality. Political appeals are now dominated by value-laden "wedge" issues like diversity, transgender issues, immigration, books in schools, critical race theory, abortion, and global warming. People are being appealed to via the ongoing culture wars over their vision of what kind of America they want to live in.

This voting behavior is often described as emotional and not rational. On this thinking, anytime a person is motivated by values other than economics, they're being irrational. That makes no sense. People naturally desire to have society embody the values they hold dear. In a diverse and pluralistic democracy, they shouldn't always expect to get their way. And importantly, the separation between public and private spheres remains fundamental to our democracy. But people will continue—rationally—to care about the values the government supports as well as the dollars it spends.

Of course, this doesn't mean self-interest plays no role in politics. As complex creatures, we humans also are capable at times of turning on a dime, casting aside our values and landing back on self-interest. This is illustrated by the NIMBY (not-in-my-backyard) syndrome, in which many people support building low-income housing or group homes for the mentally disabled—but only if it isn't in their neighborhood. They want to allow asylum to lots of immigrants—as long as they stay in far-off states. Values are most tested when they hit close to home—when they clash directly with self-interest.

How Do Values Change?

WE TEND TO THINK OF VALUES as like morals: Ours are good, sturdy and permanent, so that change is probably bad. But in reality, value change happens often during a person's life. Here is how.

BASELINE SALIENCE

All our values aren't equally important to us, so the starting point for measuring any change is a value's *baseline salience.* That is how much you care about that value, relative to others. Salience is on display when someone says to a spouse, "All you ever care about is money," or "Whatever it takes, we'll do it for the kids."

VALUE REWEIGHTING

Some values are reweighted over time. Young adults tend to value excitement and new experiences. But having a child usually alters how they weigh stable income and a family support system, while lowering the value they attach to foreign travel or risky behaviors.

VALUE RESCALING

This occurs when how much it takes to fulfill a value changes. For example, a college student might say that what's really important to him is future "financial success," by which he means making $100,000 per year by the time he is age 30. But by age 50, he may define it as requiring $250,000 per year. And to some people, no amount of money is ever enough.

VALUE REDEPLOYMENT

This important dynamic involves applying an existing value to a new issue or domain. Suppose a man has always felt that he was an empathic person, supporting things like the local food bank and foreign disaster relief. But after talking with his friend Meaghan, who is a vegan, he develops a concern for slaughtered animals—a domain where he never before focused his sympathy—and he decides to stop eating meat. Or let's say that an economist has always looked at issues first in terms of jobs and growing the economy. She favored the oil and mining industries. She is also religious. Then she takes a trip through the

American West and is struck by the tremendous loss of open land and habitat since she visited it in her youth. She becomes interested in environmentalism, suddenly feeling how important it is that future generations continue to share and be inspired by God's natural works. Her religious values become redeployed to the environmental issue, where previously they weren't. Values are often redeployed in this way.

New Value Acquisition

We don't acquire new values very often, but sometimes life throws us a curve. Suppose a young man named Bill is generally nonpolitical and says he never really "got" the whole idea of patriotism. Then his cousin joins the Marines and is stationed in a war zone. Suddenly the whole question of what America gives to us all, and what we owe America, becomes a real issue for Bill.

Despite these drivers of change, most people feel that their own values are good and durable—but those of society are somehow fragile. Each generation laments the "loss" of values. And it is true to a degree: One main driver of value change is *generational substitution*. "The experience of members of a generation in adolescence and early adulthood forges a common outlook and collective identity that persists throughout the life cycle." But then the next generation has very different values. Thus, the free-thinking, countercultural baby boomers replaced the more authority-respecting Greatest Generation.

But there are other drivers of value change as well. Common ones include a person's change of jobs, partners, or living situations, aging, negative reactions from people they care about, and traumatic events. Economic change is an important factor. The generation that lived through the Great Depression never stopped being anxious about economic security. Millennials are often described as concerned with their economic prospects, having come of age around the scary 2008 financial crisis.

Major technology change can also alter values. The adults of the 1950s first experienced affordable cars and an expanded national highway system: mobility became a more realizable value. Gen Z were the first to grow up with ubiquitous social media. Being "followed" and "liked" online became a key value—and a cause of much misery, too.

Sociologists say that maintaining a given value depends on the costs and benefits it brings us over time. A person may value "fostering freedom" and "supporting America's allies," but if a war drags on, casualties mount, and the outcome seems unknowable, they may reconsider. When children become adults, parents often face the question of how much they are willing to "pay" in friction in order to tell them candidly what they think about sensitive issues like the proper rearing of grandchildren. As the cost of being candid rises, candor as a value may get downgraded from a "must-have" to a "can live without." Moreover, "people are reluctant decision-makers who do their damnedest to minimize cognitive effort, emotional dissonance and moral angst by denying that important values conflict."

Studies in some 80 nations have yielded statistical benchmarks to compare values and value change across societies. Most Americans feel that our values have changed markedly, and there is surely evidence of that. A *Wall Street Journal*/NORC poll compared people's responses in 1998 to the question "What values are very important to you?" with responses in 2023. The percentage who cited patriotism dropped from about 70 percent to 30 percent; religion dropped from about 60 percent to about 30 percent; having children dropped from about 60 percent to 20 percent; and community involvement dropped from 40 percent to less than 20 percent. One value rose dramatically: making money.

Still, a major survey surprisingly finds that "American values are more traditional than any other wealthy country except Ireland, as well as more traditional than almost all other societies. . . . Americans have some of the highest levels of religious belief, conservative family values, absolute moral standards, national pride and other traditional beliefs." From apocalyptic media reports, you wouldn't know this. But what key values will the next generation of Americans propagate?

Personality Traits and Values

EXTENSIVE RESEARCH HAS SHOWN that a person's values are the result—to varying degrees in different people—of factors such as their genes, parenting, personality and cognitive style, society, ethnic/cultural group, childhood experiences, education, job, relationships, gender, and age. (That won't have surprised you.) Your values then become bound up in your identity, the kind of a person you are or want to be. And you display your values through your words, your behavior, and the moral choices you make. People who know you well can describe your values fairly accurately. Others trust that you'll continue to exhibit the values they see in you. So, not surprisingly, our values tend to be quite durable:

> Our attitudes [on a specific issue] are not based on a rational, detached evaluation of the evidence. . . . [B]eliefs are deeply intertwined with other beliefs, shared cultural values, and our identities. To discard a belief often means discarding a whole host of other beliefs, forsaking our community, going against those we trust and love, and changing our identities.

I hate to impair your sense of free will and choice. But there is strong evidence of an inborn inclination toward certain values. People are born with personality dispositions or traits that remain relatively stable throughout life. (Recall our discussion, in Chapter 6, of the Big Five or OCEAN framework of traits.) There is a complex relationship between these personality traits and values, but the former strongly influence the latter.

What is critical to our discussion here is that people with a given pattern of these personality traits tend to weigh certain values more heavily than people with alternative dispositions. For example, people who are low on openness and extraversion tend not to value jobs that constantly involve new challenges and meeting others. What may be less obvious is that such people also are more likely to be negative about ethnic diversity, immigration, and raunchy media—yet this is so.

Of course, some of our value patterns are not innate, but instead are shaped by life events. Inborn personality simply provides a disposition to weigh some values more heavily than others. Through our lives, each of us develops self-narratives that can embody and then further shape our pattern of values. Still, research shows that "the basic values of individuals tend to become fixed by the time they reach adulthood and remain fairly stable throughout the life course." Not only that, but "intergenerational differences persist as cohorts age." Thus—in general—the members of the so-called Greatest Generation, raised during the 1920s and '30s, were obedient and hard-working until the end, and the baby boom hippies of the 1970s are still challenging and "seeking" at ages 70–80, at least more so than most generations.

The Key: Your Value Matrix

NOW HERE IS A KEY to understanding values: Each person's values cohere into a discernible pattern, or what I'll call a Value Matrix. One's values aren't a random hodgepodge with no rhyme or reason. There are deep and predictable psychological connections among a person's values. Some of these may seem obvious (like the nexus between religiosity and altruism), but many others are surprising.

Let's approach this phenomenon by imagining that you're a time traveler who has zipped through a wormhole in time from America in 1800 to America in 2026. A new friend engages you in a challenging game:

- She tells you that here in 2026, some people love to eat red meat while others are vegetarians.

- Some feel that it's proper to strike or spank their children when called for, while others think that's never acceptable.

- Some go to church often, while others are atheists.

- Some tend to dislike other ethnicities and immigrants, while others welcome them.

- Some believe in trusting scientists to answer most technical questions, while others distrust the experts.

- Some believe in tougher law enforcement and longer sentences, while others think that social and economic help for the poor does more to reduce crime.

- Some believe that teachers should have authority to make poor students repeat the grade, while others say that a teacher's job is to ensure that all succeed.

Your friend then challenges you to sort these attitudes into Tribe A and Tribe B—for example, are the tough-on-crime people generally meat or plant eaters? Do the churchgoers or the atheists want longer prison sentences?

Now, if you really were a time traveler from 1800, I bet that you would be completely puzzled. Why in the world would people's views on eating meat, punishing crime, or spanking kids have anything to do with whether they go to church, like immigrants, or tend to believe scientists?

Yet living in 2026, we know from a welter of psychological studies, opinion surveys, and voting patterns that people generally sort themselves into Tribe A and Tribe B. Let's call them conservatives and liberals. And logically or not, all the characteristics mentioned above line up predictably with membership in one of these tribes.

While individuals vary, in general, the politically conservative tribe are in fact *more likely* to eat red meat often, attend church, disapprove of interethnic dating, accept spanking kids, distrust scientists, respect authority, be worried about immigration, and favor strong crime enforcement.

And in general, the politically liberal tribe are *less likely* to eat a lot of red meat, attend church, disapprove of interethnic dating, engage in physical discipline, disregard scientific expertise, accept all authority, oppose immigration or new ethnic groups, and be hard-edged about enforcing law and punishing crime.

This kind of pattern wouldn't emerge if people made a totally fresh assessment of each issue. It exists because seemingly unrelated issues are in fact connected within each person's underlying Value Matrix. We tend to associate with others who share our Value Matrix, and that in turn reinforces our values. The Value Matrix helps us understand other people's concerns, predict what they will value and why, and appeal to and persuade them.

Some scholars depict values as falling into "radial categories, with central cases and variations on them, [which] are normal in the human mind." A radial category is organized around a core value like respect for authority. The central case for respecting authority is the respect for parents that we learned as children. Later in life, this serves as the model for how we view other authorities. Radial values around respect for authority might include politeness, deference to customs, fulfilling one's duty, belief in experts, complying with institutional rules, and support for law and order.

Note how these seemingly disparate values are tethered to the same core value—respect for authority. This framework helps explain why apparently unrelated beliefs cluster together in a certain kind of person.

Importantly, Shalom Schwartz's research found that people's values can be depicted in a graphic way. The Schwartz Value Scale (SVS) uses a segmented circle with pairs of values occupying opposite poles—for example, Universalism versus Power over others. In the SVS system, people who hold a given value highly (like Universalism) will typically be low on its polar opposite (Power). Likewise, people who are high on Self-direction tend to be low on its antipode, Conformity. The SVS also helps us understand how values that are adjacent to one another, such as Security and Conformity, sometimes fuse. Thus, people who worry a lot about external threats also tend to want a high level of internal conformity to rules. Likewise, the adjacent values of Benevolence and Universalism often fuse: Kind people tend to want to extend kindness to everyone, and assume they deserve it. As we will see, the SVS even helps predict political orientations.

This SVS value structure has been shown to be largely consistent with the Big Five model of personality dispositions. For example:

- People high on Openness and Extraversion attach higher value to new experiences, people, ideas, and cultures.

- People low on Openness and Extraversion place less value on new things and greater value on tradition, close community, social order, and protection.

- People high on Conscientiousness and low on Neuroticism have a stronger impulse to fulfill duty, get a job done, respect established rules and authorities, and not let one's personal desires overcome doing what's right.

- People low on Conscientiousness and high on Neuroticism place higher value on "being who I am" and fulfilling their own desires. They feel less need to fulfill others' expectations or go along just for the good of society.

The SVS also ties into the moral foundations theory (MFT) we discussed in Chapter 6, as developed by Jonathan Haidt and others. MFT focuses on the key subset of values relating to morality: caring and avoiding harm to others; fairness and penalizing cheating; loyalty to others and penalizing betrayal; respecting authority and penalizing subversion; sanctity (not degrading God, family, and nation); and a sixth dimension later added by Haidt—liberty and avoiding oppression.

As with the SVS, values on the MFT scales aren't randomly distributed. People who rank high on avoiding harm to others but low on obeying authority tend to believe certain things. To them, breaking rules doesn't demand harsh sanctions if there was a good reason; disloyalty is sometimes justified by a higher good; subversion may be warranted to oppose an unjust system; and institutional authority shouldn't be a shield for unfair conduct.

Conversely, people who rank high on respect for authority, loyalty, and obedience to rules, and lower on avoiding harm, tend to believe differently. To them, society can never be perfectly fair or prevent all harm; institutions must be obeyed anyway; loyalty to one's group or nation is critical; and the sanctity of institutions must be protected from threats by outsiders. We can recognize these contrasting patterns in people we know.

Another fruitful and widely used framework was developed by Stanley Feldman. Beginning in 1992, he worked to include in the American National Election Studies (ANES) survey questions about what people thought were the most critical qualities for children to have. People were asked to rank the relative importance of (1) independence versus respect for elders; (2) obedience versus self-reliance; (3) curiosity versus good manners; and (4) being considerate versus being well-behaved.

Because we all want to convey good values to our children, these few questions efficiently reveal people's worldview. Some people see it as critical that children behave, have good manners, and obey elders. Others see it as more important that children be curious, independent, and self-reliant. Marc Hetherington and Jonathan Weiler see people with these respective views as settling into *fixed* versus *fluid* worldviews. Those with a fixed view see a dangerous world; they want rules that provide security; and they tend to believe that hierarchy and authority will sustain order and protect us. In contrast, those with the fluid view see the world as more benevolent and intriguing, and believe that letting people make their way as they think best will enhance society.

Scholars have administered the Feldman questions to a huge number of people over many years. They report that on average, about 16 percent of Americans are purely fixed; 26 percent are mostly fixed; 19 percent are mostly fluid; 13 percent are purely fluid—and the remaining 25 percent of us are sort of in the middle.

Here it gets even more interesting. The ANES survey has asked these questions since 1992, and two massive online surveys have followed up. What they find when correlated with people's political stance is almost exactly what you might expect. Those with the fixed worldview tilt strongly—over 70 percent—

conservative/Republican on almost all key issues: race, immigration, gay marriage, warrantless wiretapping by police, and so on. And those with the fluid worldview tilt in exactly the opposite direction—liberal/Democrat—to a similar extent.

Another effort to organize value orientations into a predictive model was developed by George Lakoff. As we saw in Chapter 6, Lakoff depicted people's dominant orientations as cohering into two paradigms. One is the Strict Father paradigm, stressing values like authority, discipline, and obedience. The other is the Nurturing Mother model, stressing empathy, caring, and self-fulfillment. (I think it is better to degenderize them and refer to the Strict Parent versus the Nurturing Parent models. Nothing in the model depends on whether a given child's father or mother was the stricter one; what matters is just the dominant parenting style that the child experienced.) The model doesn't say that parenting style alone dictates one's future values as adults. But Lakoff argues that people generally wind up with different dispositions on the Strict Parent/Nurturing Parent gradient. This is not just abstract theorizing. Researchers David Barker and James Tinnick found that people's attitudes toward parenting and child rearing strongly correlated with their political views and "these relationships were consistent with Lakoff's model."

The broader values associated with Lakoff's two paradigms are listed in the following table. I think you'll be able to see many people you know as falling into each category.

Strict Parent Beliefs/Values	Nurturing Parent Beliefs/Values
Materialistic	Idealistic
Pessimistic about the future	Optimistic about the future
People are selfish by nature	People are good by nature
Hierarchy is legitimate	Egalitarianism is legitimate
Skeptical of experts	Respect experts
Authority is usually legitimate	Authority is often abused
Strong discipline is legitimate	Discipline should be a last resort
Individualistic	Communitarian

Strict Parent Beliefs/Values	Nurturing Parent Beliefs/Values
Focused on in-group	Open to other groups
People respond to sanctions	People respond to encouragement
Importance of doing	Importance of being
Importance of order and obedience	Importance of self-fulfillment
Preserve traditions	Innovate, try new things
Help those who strive and work	Help those who are in need
Use natural resources	Respect and conserve nature
Strongly patriotic	Universalist

Framing Issues to Activate Values

THUS, EACH OF US HAS a personal Value Matrix—a pattern of values that cohere into a more or less stable, consistent framework that guides us in responding to many kinds of life decisions and issues.

It turns out that the key is how a given issue *activates* particular values you hold dear. That activation may at times feel like a lightbulb going on, or instead, just a slower, gradual dawning of realization. And importantly, the *framing* of the issue is critical in drawing forth and activating certain values we may care about.

Let me begin with a simple example. Recently, while biking through nearby neighborhoods, I saw three signs with the same purpose:

One said: "Slow Down."

The second said: "Slow Down—Children."

The third said: "Drive Like Your Children Lived Here."

These signs are all making the same argument: Drivers should slow down! But which one is most effective? To assess that, let's see what values each sign activates in you, and your reaction.

I would guess that the first sign triggers a negative reaction in many people based on the value of freedom/autonomy. They think, "Why should I have to slow down in your neighborhood—are you special?" or "I'm a safe driver, so why is this sign barking at me?"

The second sign may be more effective because it doesn't just command, but gives a reason to slow down. It triggers values many people hold strongly—love and protection of children.

But to me, the third sign seems most effective. It invokes the protect-children value, but then adds the potent values of self-interest and reciprocity. It makes us think, "How would I feel if my children were playing here and some guy went speeding by?" And it also defuses any tendency toward macho resistance ("Who are you to tell me what to do?") by conveying, "Hey, I'm just asking you to consider how you'd feel if you lived here."

This example illustrates how *framing* even a simple argument in everyday life implicates, draws onto the field, and activates particular values—with varying degrees of effectiveness.

Framing shapes what you pay attention to, what is felt to be at stake in an argument. Thus, in many arguments, framing is the whole ball game. Framing an issue in a certain way triggers the deployment of specific values, delimits the ideas and facts that seem relevant, and affects the weight you accord various reasons. As one expert notes, "We tend to value things as a function of how we frame them," and so "it makes sense to move away from simply talking about values to talking about frame-relevant values."

Before you can decide what you think about an issue, you need a sense of which of your values actually are in play. In some cases, this may seem simple. When your young child asks for a third cupcake, you feel the tension between valuing her happiness and teaching her good eating habits. But in more complex situations, it can be hard to see exactly which values are at stake. Our values influence how we frame an issue for decision. But how the issue is framed also affects which values are called into action. So, there is a dialectical interplay between values and issue framing.

You've experienced this interplay many times. Consider the question of what to do about homeless people sleeping outside shops and restaurants in your city. If you're devoutly religious, you may see this problem through the lens of charity and kindness to the poor. Then someone tells you that many homeless are drug abusers and petty criminals. Maybe that makes you see them as morally astray rather than unfortunate and activates the value you place on uprightness. As a result, you may feel that the police should get them off the streets.

But the dialectic doesn't end there. Next, you learn that the city has built more than enough homeless shelters, but many homeless refuse to sleep there because they fear others or prefer the street. Having empty shelter beds makes you mad since it wastes taxpayer money, and you value financial prudence. You learn that many homeless suffer from mental illness; that makes you both sad and fearful. But then a friend points out that some homeless are veterans who can't find jobs or afford the rising cost of rent. That activates your strong sense of patriotism; you feel that there is something wrong with a person loyally protecting America yet coming back to poverty and the feeling of being abandoned by an ungrateful nation.

As this interplay of facts and values evolves, your picture of the typical homeless person changes several times. Importantly, so does your *framing* of the issue of homelessness, and hence the values the issue activates in you. You're not sure whether homelessness is mainly a matter of housing, policing, mental health services, jobs, or welfare. As you consider these alternate frames for the problem, different values come to the forefront or recede into the background of your thinking.

For a complex issue like homelessness, no single "frame" is probably sufficient. But by being aware of how facts, frames, and values interact, you can better assess why you feel as you do, and how others might be persuaded to address the issue effectively.

Or consider a typical family argument. A teenager comes home at two a.m. from a party after not answering his phone for three hours. Mom and Dad are apoplectic. They frame the issue as one of love, caring, fear, and safety. They say, "Don't you care that we were worried sick about what might have happened to you?" But the son frames the issue differently—as one of freedom and autonomy. He says, "Stop already. I'm seventeen, I can take care of myself. My phone just died. Stop treating me like a little kid."

How will the parents and child ever resolve the argument if their framing walls off the other side's values? Clearly, this argument is about both caring and autonomy/responsibility. So the parents need to say something that taps into the son's autonomy values—for example, "Okay, you're old enough to go out on your own—but you're also old enough to be responsible to charge your phone, or borrow one and call us if you're going to be hours late. If you couldn't find us for hours at night—you'd be worried, too." This validates the son as an almost-adult who should bear the reciprocal obligations of one.

Conversely, the son needs to say something that at least acknowledges the parents' caring: "I'm sorry if I scared you. You know parties sometimes go late, and you know I don't drink, but I should have called, so I mean it when I say it won't happen again."

Since framing determines which values are deployed, it strongly influences how an issue will be resolved. And here is an important point: It's much easier to change the frame than to get people to change their values. For this reason, interest groups and political parties work hard to win the contest to "name and frame" key issues. It is well documented that "in politics, changes in the labeling of alternatives can have marked effects on public opinion." Some examples:

- Are we arguing about "illegal immigrants flooding across the border" or "asylum seekers" and "dreamers" pursuing a better life in a land of opportunity?

- Are we arguing over "efficient economic globalization" or "exploitation of workers"?

- Are we arguing over "gay people's rights" or "the homosexual lifestyle"?

- Are we arguing over "the right to life" or "a woman's right to choose"?

- Are we arguing over "big government regulation" or "protecting people from harm"?

- Are we arguing over "protecting our children from violence" or "the right to bear arms"?

These aren't just verbal games. The values brought to bear in resolving each issue will differ depending on which frame is adopted. In a famous study, people were asked whether a political extremist group should be allowed to hold a rally. The respondents' opinions changed significantly if they were asked about the group's First Amendment right to speak, or about the risks of violence at the rally, even though both factors—freedom and keeping the peace—were inherent in the situation.

Consider the highly emotional issue of diversity and affirmative action in hiring. The values that come into play depend importantly on how you frame what affirmative action actually does. Is it "fixing prior injustice," "leveling the playing field," and "breaking the glass ceiling," or is it "reverse discrimination" and "hiring less-qualified people"?

Once you decide on the main way you frame the issue, different facts and different values will swing into action. If the issue is framed as the unfairness of hiring less-competent person X rather than more-competent person Y, then the facts regarding prior injustice are seen as irrelevant and don't need to be discussed. Empathy for prior victims of discrimination and the value of a diverse workforce aren't even part of the equation.

Conversely, if the issue is framed in terms of the injustice of bad social conditions and discrimination affecting some minorities, then those facts do become relevant. The values of "righting wrongs" and "opening opportunity to all" come into play. But conversely, the resulting unfairness of penalizing people who never even participated in the prior injustices is ignored.

Obviously, affirmative action involves all these values and facts. Logically, we can't wall off what matters to the other side by preemptively declaring it irrelevant. But that's exactly what often happens in both private and public arguments. Always be alert when someone declares, "Fundamentally, this is just about x" or "All we need to decide is y," or "Look, we have a clear choice, either it's z or it's not." They are trying to control the conversation via framing. You are allowed to reframe the question as you see it. You can say, "Yes, that's part of the problem, but we also need to consider . . ."

Framing plays a crucial role whenever a new issue arises. Consider some recent examples: artificial intelligence, cryptocurrency, internet neutrality, and fetal gene therapy. I don't know about you, but I have a hard time figuring out exactly what the single "core issue" is with such new phenomena. Without some sensible framing—and a real understanding of relevant facts—deploying one's values and forming an opinion on such issues isn't easy. Sometimes, your emotions give you a start, but then mislead you. Thoughtful reflection is required to decide which values actually are in play.

The Values Matrix and Political Affiliation

OUR POLITICAL LEANINGS are significantly genetically and biologically influenced. This an uncomfortable thing to hear. It impairs one's sense of self-direction and rationality. But the body of research supporting it is large and growing.

Here is one example: fMRI studies show that liberals tend to have a larger, more well-developed part of the brain called the anterior cingulate cortex (ACC), while conservatives tend to have a larger part called the right amygdala. While each brain region performs multiple functions, the amygdala plays a major role in regulating the intensity of emotional responses, both positive (appetite and reward) and negative (fear and anger). The ACC plays an important role in connecting the emotional (limbic) system and the rational (prefrontal cortex) system, such as when evoking empathy or self/other judgments. Thus, the documented "tendencies for liberals to engage more with uncertain or unfamiliar stimuli and for conservatives to be more sensitive to threatening stimuli may be reflected in brain anatomy." In a repeat study, the authors "were able to correctly classify 72 percent of their subjects in ideological terms [by measuring] . . . gray matter volume in the ACC alone."

Now let's look more broadly at the interaction of genes, biology, personality, and politics. One clear pattern shown by research is this: Liberals tend to be less alert to and anxious about risk, and more comfortable with uncertainty, while conservatives are more alert to risk, and quicker to seek closure and certainty. Conservatives' genetic makeup leads them to respond more to danger, threats, and discomfort with unfamiliar groups. Liberals' genetic makeup leads them to be less attentive to danger signals and more open to new (and possibly risky or unwise) interactions. Conservatives more strongly seek the familiar and orderly; liberals seek the new and will tolerate some associated disorder. As one scholar summarized, "These relationships hold up across time; across societies; and in studies using a variety of conceptual and methodological approaches."

Here are just a few further examples of the surprising findings connecting genes, biology, personality, and political viewpoint (for more, see the Notes).

- As shown in the massive "Minnesota Twins" study by Block and Block, identical twins who are separated at birth and raised by different families still tend to wind up with similar political viewpoints as adults. This correlation is consistently shown to be about .40 to .60. The correlation is somewhat less in fraternal twins, which also supports the genetic vector. Genes seem to outweigh the influence of parental environment.

- In a later study, Alford asked some 9,000 twins to react to various questions on the Wilson-Patterson Conservatism Scale. Impressively, "for every single item, the identical twins' political orientation is correlated more strongly than for the fraternal twins, and in every single case, the correlation was significant."

- Differences on Chromosome 4 and a gene called NARG1 are believed to affect neurotransmitter processing related to risk, fear, and anti-social behaviors. In a large study of 13,000 people, differences in this and related genes were associated with a 13 percent difference in political orientation.

- Teenagers and young adults who possess the DRD47R variant of the dopamine receptor gene tend to be more "risk taking" and "novelty seeking." They are also more extroverted—and more likely than peers to be politically liberal.

- After exposing subjects to even a single "disgusting" image (like a person eating worms), brain imaging proved "about 85 percent [accurate] in predicting whether subjects scored as conservative, moderate or liberal on the Wilson-Patterson inventory." Conservatives had a stronger disgust response.

- In studies of the brain's ACC, when subjects handled complex patterns, researchers found that liberals had weaker attachment to prior patterns and were less aroused by departing from them.

- As shown in many studies, liberals tend to be more open, trusting, and tolerant of others; conservatives are less so. But you can manipulate people's degree of trust/openness to caring by exposing them (via nasal spray or other vectors) to the hormone/neurotransmitter oxytocin. As previously mentioned, researchers say, "We found we could turn the behavioral response on and off like a garden hose."

Overall, a large body of research now shows that "genes likely set the potential for inclinations that under given conditions may turn into values, social attitudes and political preferences." More directly: "Research to date shows a substantial genetic component in the transmission of value orientations, particularly liberal or conservative ideology." The genetic contribution to one's political orientation seems to be about 40 percent, though some studies suggest it is closer to 60 percent.

In addition, strong liberals and strong conservatives differ in how they routinely seek out and process information and think through issues. This is crucial because it can affect all the issues they encounter. "There is a relationship between conservatism and cognitive rigidity or high levels of cognitive structure as well as decisiveness. . . . The implication is that quick decisions, seizing on what is most salient, most apparent, or most concretely understood, and a tendency to avoid overthinking, describe an information processing style characteristic of people on the political right." A "substantial body of research" confirms extreme conservatives' "intolerance for ambiguity," and "need to reduce fear and uncertainty" through "epistemic closure" (i.e., deciding what is in fact so).

As one scholar finds, "Conservatives acquire the information they believe necessary to draw adequate conclusions, then call it a day. Liberals go on acquiring new information even if . . . they might not be able fully to absorb [it]". Recall the research on "fixed" versus "fluid" personalities, the former tending to be conservative and the latter liberal. Liberals may at times keep endlessly "noodling" an issue, trying out various answers, and having trouble "landing" on a conclusion.

This cognitive difference is especially important to public debate over *scientific* values and issues. Just starting out, you might assume that conservatives more than liberals should venerate science. Science is hard facts—not just emotions, opinions, and pie-in-the-sky social schemes. But a key feature of science is its open-endedness, its commitment to remaining open to revision by new findings. That is a problem for the conservative cognitive style. Over the decades of "science wars," conservatives have fought battles to deny the carcinogenic impact of smoking, the truth of evolution through natural selection, the innateness of being gay in some people, global warming, and many other things. When scientists reveal new research, conservatives often decry it, complaining that "science keeps changing; the experts don't all agree." But the "change" may be further refinement of well-known truths, and there may be a high degree of consensus, even if not unanimity. But as top COVID adviser Anthony Fauci later noted, "One lesson learned from this is that we must make it very clear when we're speaking to the public that we are dealing with evolving information . . . and that is because the virus and the outbreak are changing—not because the scientists are flip-flopping."

But before liberals get too inflated with their superior scientific sophistication, note that at times they, too, have been "science deniers"—about the safety of genetically modified foods, the reliability of new-generation nuclear plants, certain gender differences, the psychological risks of marijuana use, and other topics. Science denial seems to be a prime example of "motivated reasoning" on both sides of the political spectrum.

Conservatives often have a faster and stronger tendency to categorize or stereotype. They favor clear and rigid categories ("You're either a friend, or an enemy"). Liberals tend to be softer categorizers. Interestingly, research reveals this difference not just when the categories are socially potent ones like "criminal" or "foreigner" but even abstract ones like groups of animals or geometric shapes. Conservatives also tend to prefer simpler, more direct explanations ("Joe is just out to get me") rather than vague, more complex ones ("Maybe he's under pressure from the boss, or he's just insecure, or . . .")

People on the left tend to exhibit greater openness to revising views; a reluctance to commit to fixed principles; a feeling that opinions are relative, so "Who's to say who is right?"; and difficulty in accepting hard-and-fast rules. This can be seen as leading to wise nuances, or to being wishy-washy. Keith Stanovich and colleagues describe the difference between an "algorithmic mind" (seeking simple, quick, and useful answers) and the "reflective mind" (seeking more depth and reasons). Some researchers report lower levels of cognitive "integrative complexity" among believers at either end of the political spectrum. But even moderate conservatives tend to seek more certainty, less complexity, and less nitpicking debate than do liberals. A major review by John Jost and colleagues, assessing 88 studies across 12 countries and involving 23,000 individuals, found that liberals and conservatives differed markedly in their tolerance for ambiguity and integrative complexity.

Liberals tout their openness to multiple viewpoints, but that strikes conservatives as unprincipled waffling. Consider a typical grenade lobbed by conservative personality Ann Counter: "Whenever you have backed a liberal into a corner—if he doesn't start crying—he says 'It's a complicated issue.' Loving America is too simple an emotion. To be nuanced, you have to hate it a little. Conservatives may not grasp 'nuance,' but we're pretty good at grasping treason." A liberal might reply in the famous words of a judge propitiously named Learned Hand: "The spirit of liberty is the spirit that is not too sure it is right."

Mapping the Value Matrix Onto Policy Issues

AS WE HAVE SEEN, LIBERALS AND CONSERVATIVES each tend to bring to any issue their vision the world, which embodies certain critical values.

The conservative worldview tends to see people as self-directed, and navigating through a difficult, competitive world with other largely self-interested people. This has both aspirational and pessimistic strains. People should work hard, aspire to get ahead, and be left free to compete and achieve. On the other hand, you can't expect society to be totally "fair"; the world is tough, and there will be winners and losers. Out task is to struggle as individuals, do the best we can, build a community, and obey social rules whether we like them or not. The core conservative economic argument is that society will be more prosperous if everyone is incentivized to strive and people are not "leveled." And freedom is seen primarily as restraint on government intrusion, not freedom from prevailing social norms.

The liberal worldview, in contrast, is that of a community organized to be fair, to meet people's needs, and help everyone meet their potential. Competition yielding "winners and losers" must be tempered by a "safety net" of support to help "raise up" everyone. Authority is seen as legitimate only when it is exercised to advance right principles. We should not accept gross inequality or social ills as inevitable; we should fix them. Here, freedom is seen less as relief from government restraints and more as freedom to "be oneself" and depart from majority social norms or practices.

In simplified terms, the general pattern of leading liberal and conservative values lines up as shown in the table that follows.

Salient Liberal Values	Salient Conservative Values
Help those in need	Reward those who work
Greater equality	Greater opportunity
Respect/tolerate diverse values	Respect good values, social norms
Fairness in punishment; second chances	Firmness in punishment; deterrence
Free choice unless it harms others	Free choice unless it harms others, or decency

Salient Liberal Values	Salient Conservative Values
Social rights	Social duties
Openness to experimenting	Concern that the new will be worse
Personal freedom from majority coercion	Personal freedom from government

Accordingly, conservatives and liberals generally argue for public policies in different ways:

- Conservative arguments often *laud* values like hard work, striving to succeed, opportunity, earning reward, self-discipline, self-reliance, obeying rules, being strong, protecting property, preventing crime, moral uprightness, and patriotism.

- Conservative arguments often *condemn* by using words like lazy, free-loading, coddling, cheating, meddling, self-indulgent, degenerate, and special treatment.

- Liberal arguments often *laud* values like helping, fairness, empathy, equality, health, caring, individuality, diversity, dignity, dreaming, and fulfillment.

- Liberal arguments often *condemn* by using words such as harsh, punitive, deprive, discriminate, oppress, social forces, rigid rules, unfairness, inequality, and greed.

An important and provocative thesis advanced by Johathan Haidt is that conservatives are increasingly successful in political and policy debates *because they appeal to a broader range of values than liberals*. For example, Lakoff had proudly proclaimed that "behind every progressive policy lies a simple moral value: empathy." But Haidt doubts that empathy alone is a sufficient guide to every wise social choice. Haidt and other critics believe that liberals lose the chance to persuade many people because they keep harping only on empathy— while being tone deaf to why people feel that other values matter so much.

In fairness, may liberals would disagree with Haidt, believing that they do appeal to a broader set of prominent values. For example, liberals invoke *fairness* in urging changes to the tax system. They deploy *dignity* in arguing for public school funding and that the rich shouldn't be able to ignore such needs while their kids attend pricey private schools. Liberals invoke *autonomy* in urging limits on how tech companies can retain and use private data. And they appeal to *sanctity* in protecting the environment and slowing global warming.

But these alignments are ever evolving. For a well- documented exploration of this, read Joan Williams's 2025 book *Outclassed*. Among many interesting phenomena, she charts voting pattens that show the dramatic rise of "Scaffles"—working-class people who are "socially conservative and fiscally liberal." These are people who dislike, for example, liberals' championing of diversity, immigration, and transgender issues, but support their demand for affordable health care coverage and their attacks on the wealthy who "screw over the little guy." Thus, potent "populist" values are now in ascent on *both* the left and the right.

When a new issue comes to the fore in public policy, people naturally want to figure out what the "essence" of the issue really is, and hence, which of their values are in play. After mapping our values onto several issues, we instinctively fall into a pattern of framing analogous issues similarly. So, after people came to see race discrimination in employment as unacceptable, that paved the way for also barring job discrimination based on gender and sexual orientation.

Thus, when a new issue arises, we sort it into one of the available categories. But it's not always intuitive which box it best fits into. Is a new economic proposal mainly a "stimulus to the economy"? Or is it really a "tax loophole," "pork barrel spending," or an "investment in a strategic industry"? Are tariffs, taxes, user fees, and surcharges kind of similar because they all hit your pocketbook—or are they conceptually different?

After sorting an issue into a category—and here is the critical, often unconscious step—people assess the new issue based less on its unique features than on the typical or archetypal features of the category to which they assign it. It's as if, having decided that a parakeet and an eagle are both "birds," you then conclude that they must both be good house pets.

A silly example? Yes—but note how categorizing anything as a form of discrimination automatically equates it to a venal practice. Is discriminating against people below a certain height in eligibility to be police officers really the same as racial discrimination? What about barring biological boys who identify as girls from a girl's sports team?

Consider the category of freedoms. For most Americans, it's clear that some big-picture freedoms like freedom of religion should be sacred. But American legislatures have agreed that government can rightly limit my freedom to sell pornography, drive without insurance, beat my dogs, own a machine gun, marry my sister, travel to North Korea, declare that I want to kill the president, falsely say that my stockbroker is a thief, truthfully reveal that my employer is working on a trade-secret microchip, refuse to have my children educated, work as an electrician without a license—and a zillion other things. All these rules restrict my freedoms. The question in each instance is whether society has good enough reasons why my freedom should bow to other values. Just labeling something as a "freedom" or a "right" shouldn't persuade us about a tough policy choice.

Sometimes, issues with similar features nevertheless get sorted into different categories, so they are perceived differently than sibling issues. Then they activate different parts of the Value Matrix, and both liberals and conservatives twist themselves into pretzel shapes to rationalize their inconsistencies.

Deafness to others' values

Another problem in political debate today is that both liberals and conservatives not only weigh values differently but are willing to remain *totally deaf* to values the other tribe cares deeply about. A few examples:

- Punishing rule violations. Liberals are reluctant to see that providing a community service also requires effective sanctions for violators. If you want nice public parks, you need to bar people from permanently camping there. If you want investment and jobs in revitalized urban centers, you need to deter and punish crime. If you want unemployment insurance, you can't just let people abuse it and avoid work. Liberals usually want to provide more social goods—but they often resist the corresponding need to police their proper use. They just don't hear those who are troubled by free-riders or cheaters.

- Line-drawing. Providing social benefits also requires that "lines be drawn" on eligibility. You are eligible for Medicaid only if your income is below a certain level. Liberals usually focus on what they see as underinclusion of worthy people, like the family that misses eligibility by just $1,000, while conservatives are troubled by overinclusion, such

as a drug dealer who hides his illegal income so he can get welfare or
Medicaid. Hence, many public policy arguments pit liberals who
say, "Look at the remaining unmet need!" against conservatives who say,
"Look at those unworthy cheaters!" Each tries to ignore the other
problem.

- SACREDNESS AND DIGNITY. To many conservatives, it matters that
  people stand and salute the flag, respect religion, acknowledge the
  morality of our Founding Fathers (and Mothers!), and dress appro-
  priately in school. They want to live in a society that respects such
  things. To many liberals, the issue is the freedom to feel differently
  and not be forced to conform. They don't see how it hurts anyone if
  a football player kneels in protest during the national anthem, or
  denounces America as "founded on racism." Conversely, many
  conservatives insist that a Confederate general's statue or a Christmas
  manger displayed in front of a public building doesn't hurt anybody
  and that removing them would degrade their values. However such
  issues get resolved, it's just obtuse to pretend that affronting the other
  person's sacred values is somehow "harmless."

- INJUSTICE AND INTENT. Conservatives tend to see injustice only
  when they can pinpoint a bad actor with ill intent. Decent conservatives,
  like decent liberals, wouldn't engage in intentional racial discrimination—but they see life as a welter of largely competitive activities and
  resist liberal assertions that systemic racism produces injustice even
  when it's difficult or impossible to pinpoint a specific bad actor.
  Liberals often cite "systems" while conservatives cite "individuals" as
  causes of injustice.

Values and Political Extremism

OVER MANY PRIOR DECADES, enormous scholarly attention was focused on
people at the extreme ends of the political scale. After World War II, analysts
struggled to explain the psychological appeals of Nazi ideology on the right and
Communist ideology on the left. Theodor Adorno described the "authoritarian
personality" as measured on his so-called F Scale. Robert Altemeyer later described the "authoritarian attitude syndrome" as measured on his right-wing

authoritarianism (RWA) scale, whose key feature was what Milton Rokeach called the "closed mind." There have been dozens of studies of the RWA scale in countries as varied as America, Russia, Spain, Israel, South Africa, and Australia, and key patterns hold. For example, "When RWA scores (i.e., conservativeness) rise, [Big Five] Conscientiousness goes up and Openness goes down."

Then in the 1960s, Glenn Wilson and William Patterson developed their W-P Conservatism Scale, which was generally viewed as more reliable. It added measures such as a person's recourse to metabeliefs to deny facts ("The government always lies to us anyway"), and a strong focus on protection of in-groups. Later, Rokeach found that those high on the authoritarian scale "are more rigid in their problem solving behavior, more concrete in their thinking, and more narrow in their grasp of a particular subject; they also have a tendency to premature closure and . . . an intolerance of ambiguity." They suffer from what Russell Hardin called the "crippled epistemology of extremism." Altemeyer found that authoritarians share several cognitive tendencies, including (1) compartmentalized thinking, (2) contradictoriness, (3) confirmation bias in absorbing new information, and (4) fundamental attribution error (usually ascribing conduct to a person's "nature" rather than the specific situation).

More recently, John Jost and colleagues conducted major reviews of all the outstanding studies and concluded that those drawn to strong conservative positions tend to value certainty and seek to avoid disruption, disorder, or change. Hence, they oppose diverse moral lifestyles, changes in status hierarchy, and lax law enforcement. Those high on the social dominance orientation (SDO) scale tend toward a competitive or law-of-the-jungle worldview, driven by low agreeableness, low openness, and high conscientiousness. They tend to see the world in Manichean terms—it has good and bad people.

Especially illuminating is the extensive research by Janet Stenner on extremists—not conservatives or liberals within the normal range of American opinion, but people at the far ends of the political spectrum—those who display the authoritarian dynamic or disposition. "This basically measures how much a person values group authority and uniformity versus tolerance for individual autonomy and differences. This disposition can affect everything from how to raise one's children to which political party to support." Our desire to instill in our children the strong values we hold dear helps to explain the finding that "fundamental . . . preferences on whether children should be obedient, neat, and well-mannered, account for almost a third of the variance in contemporary opinion on such issues as interracial marriage and residential segregation; civil rights; censorship and freedom of speech . . . pornography, homosexuality and compulsory school prayer, gun ownership, aggressive policing, and capital punishment."

As Stenner concludes, this disposition "leads to the "familiar triad of racial, political and moral intolerance," the "tendency to glorify 'in groups' and to denigrate 'out groups.' This disposition also generates a strong effort to protect the 'common good' by 'stamping out' offensive ideas and 'cracking down' on misbehavior."

Stenner debunks the idea that an authoritarian disposition is simply "learned prejudice" or "national character." Instead, it has deep genetic and biological roots in the individual. Among other data, she cites a "natural experiment" comparing the level of authoritarianism in West and East Germans compared to their similar neighbor nations—"something roughly analogous to identical twins reared apart." The data show that in 1990—even after decades of divergent (Democratic versus Communist) societies—Germans resembled one another on the authoritarianism scales far more than they resembled their Western or Eastern nation neighbors. A series of later German studies of twin pairs found that environment influenced personality traits by about 25 percent—while genetics accounted for more—about 40 percent.

Importantly, "authoritarian" does not mean "conservative." Research shows that American conservatism has a number of strains, including status quo conservatism, which is not generally authoritarian, and libertarianism, which is strongly anti-authoritarian. Libertarians reject many obligations to "groupness," but they don't object to what others do unless it impairs their own liberty. Conservatives want to conserve the good from the past and thus limit change, while authoritarians want to limit differences from the dominant norm. These concepts can overlap, but they differ.

Often overlooked is the strong strain of progressive or liberal authoritarianism. There is a popular narrative that only conservatives are authoritarian and want to "tell people how to run their lives" according to old-fashioned norms. But there also is a potent authoritarian element in the progressive demand for "political correctness" in private speech, and "wokeness" in behavior. In this sense, progressives, too, are "telling people how to live their lives." Some within the politically correct tribe demand that all schools teach the new orthodoxy about race, gender, history, and oppression. They demand that everyone adopt language conventions approved by the progressive political agenda ("non-binary," "gender-affirming," "white privilege," and "inequity"). And they would engage in "canceling," "doxing," or shaming of anyone who publicly differs. The more extreme instances of this echo the mandatory confessions and required re-education of bourgeois people by the Chinese Red Guard Communists during their Cultural Revolution in the late 1960s. It would be a sad irony if the American progressive movement—which long fought for tolerance—instead left a legacy of draconian intolerance.

Most progressives would be shocked to learn, as Stenner's data showed, that "a greater proportion of Democrats than Republicans prove to be authoritarian [on the survey scales], and authoritarians are more likely to call themselves Democrats than Republicans." Political scientists Marietta and Barker's data lead them to conclude that "in recent years, Democrats appear to have moved rapidly to the Left and now resemble Republicans when it comes to ideological extremism and constraint."

On the other hand, Jost and colleagues reviewed 13 published studies of people with extreme political views, and found none showing greater left-wing than right-wing rigidity. Most showed the opposite and some were ambiguous. When all factors are considered, there appears to be at least some correlation between authoritarianism and conservatism. These dispositions are "mutually reinforcing to some degree, presumably by virtue of sharing some aversion to novelty, unfamiliarity and uncertainty." Stenner concludes: "Authoritarianism can provide the most complete account of intolerance, explaining about 32 percent of the variance in intolerance." And its impact on multiple kinds of intolerance all grew markedly between 1972 and 2000. The pattern since 2000 is more complicated, as I noted.

One can only wonder what the numbers will look like in the years to come.

A Note on Political Philosophy

SOME READERS MAY FEEL that this whole discussion of how biology and psychology influence one's political viewpoint ignores how people develop and follow their rationally chosen political philosophy. Perhaps that's so for some highly politically engaged people. Political philosophy is important; it helps elites and political parties establish principles for governing and appealing to voters. But the evidence shows that as human beings develop, their psychological dispositions well precede their development of a political philosophy, and continue to influence them throughout life.

No ten-year-olds and few fifteen-year-olds have a political philosophy—but they all have personality dispositions and values that will affect them throughout their lives. Even the average adult doesn't wake up in the morning with a strong sense of their political philosophy. They have a range of views, and if pressed, they might say, "Overall, I tend to be liberal," or "In general, I'm for smaller government." But they haven't worked through exactly why they adhere to Rousseau or Hobbes, Jefferson or Madison, Rawls or Hayek, and why that warrants a certain position. In fact, many defy political theory by holding a mix-and-match array of views that don't fall neatly on the liberal or conservative side. The psychological factors we have surveyed help explain why.

Why Arguing Is So Hard: Sorting Ourselves Into Tribes

I'VE SUMMARIZED RESEARCH SHOWING that people's genes and personality dispositions influence their political views. But *influence* doesn't mean *determine*. Many other factors affect one's political posture. They include gender, age, ethnicity, occupation, educational level, home location, marital status, religion, and so on. Nevertheless, one striking reality is that increasingly, Americans are sorting themselves into different ideological tribes. This is driven by many factors.

For example, consider religion. It has been found that in the U.S., non-Hispanic Catholics are generally somewhat more conservative than non-Catholics. That isn't because Catholics share the same profile on the Big Five or OCEAN personality gradients. Other social and historical factors are at work. These include the Catholic tradition of church hierarchy and belief in doctrine, and the potent polarizing impact of the abortion issue. (The Supreme Court that reversed the *Roe v. Wade* decision in 2023 consisted of six Catholics, one Protestant, and two Jews.) Conversely, Protestants and Jews tend to be somewhat more liberal, influenced in part by their less authoritative religious structures, and cultures of individual questioning and judgment. On world values surveys, eight of the top ten most individualistic nations are historically Protestant.

Or consider how people sort themselves across industries or professions. People in the following four industries are on average the most liberal:

academia, entertainment, mass media, and online technology. The most Republican job categories include trucker, mason, police officer, and bond trader. The most Democratic include social worker, OB/GYN physician, artist, and scientist. Did those lineups shock you? Probably not: your intuition is based on "just looking around" as you go through daily life. But the fact that you can predict a lot of these patterns is itself remarkable.

Then consider geography. A state like Alabama isn't politically conservative because the people who originally happened to settle there or be enslaved there, or whose employers recently moved there, all rated similarly on the Big Five/OCEAN personality gradients. Massachusetts isn't highly liberal because all its people were born opposite of Alabamians on those gradients. Instead, social, ethnic, economic, and other factors are at play. But personality factors aren't totally unrelated either. Here is why.

Over time, it makes sense that the folks who yearn for a larger social circle (extraversion), who are comfortable with new experiences (openness), and who are less offended by frictions from new social interactions (agreeableness) are more likely than others to leave small towns and rural areas and move to large metropolitan areas. Conversely, their neighbors who are lower on these scales, or perhaps higher on the need to fulfill duties to the family business or relatives (conscientiousness), might decide to stay in those smaller communities. Over time, as people with these divergent personality profiles cluster together, more of the folks who respect traditional "duty" values will be living in small towns and rural areas, and more folks who value new experiences and multiculturalism will wind up living in big urban areas. This phenomenon has been called the Big Sort: Americans are now "sorting" ourselves into psychological tribes by our choices of where to live.

The gap between the self-sorting tribal groups is widening. We see growing polarization in politics, incendiary media that feed the flames, and the collapse of intergroup civility. The political parties likewise have sorted themselves into more homogeneous groupings—for many reasons apart from people moving their homes. In 1960, there were plenty of conservative Southern Democrats and lots of liberal Northern Republicans. Today that isn't so. Political polarization between people, and between political parties, has dramatically widened.

Recent research shows that the actual policy positions held by most Americans aren't nearly as extreme as their perceptions of the political tribes' views. What's more, "the increase in partisan ideological *identity differences* is more than twice as large as the increase in *policy differences.*" Political argument has been transformed from the expression of specific policy views to a battle of overall tribal cultures.

Political parties have become symbols not of policy opinions but cultural identities. When liberal Democrats refer to "redneck racists," "Joe six-pack," "deplorables," "gun-toting hicks," or "extreme Evangelicals," those are not critiques of policy positions. They are tribal slurs. Conservatives, and many others, recognize that these terms insult and degrade people in the guise of some higher virtue.

Likewise, when conservative Republicans lambaste "Ivy league elitists," "abortion lovers," "people who hate America," "man haters," "welfare queens," "sexual weirdos," and "ghetto dwellers waiting for a handout," the human beings who are the objects of those barbs know they've been disrespected and threatened.

This verbal warfare is dangerous because identity is even more powerful than ideology. People who feel their identity threatened will fight without compromise.

We need better thinking and better arguing—not tribalizing. The other side has reasons for what they argue for. And those reasons arise from wellsprings of values that most of us hold, to varying degrees. You can use what we have learned about the Value Matrix to discern what the person you argue with is likely to care about most. And then see whether you can persuade them that their values can be accommodated in a different way. Neither you nor they need to abandon your values or betray your tribe.

Of course, arguments about values aren't restricted to the public spheres of policy and politics. They affect our personal lives as well.

Arguments About Values in Private Life

THERE ARE MYRIAD BOOKS ABOUT how to improve one's relationships, care for loved ones, and cultivate good values. Those books focus on significant themes: listening, empathy, getting outside yourself, appreciating what matters to others, being candid, and showing care. Here, I'll focus on just a few dynamics that are important to value-laden discussions in private life.

FRAME TO THE DOMAIN

If you want to persuade someone, you must frame your argument in a way that activates the dominant values of the domain where the argument occurs. That may seem obvious, but all domains are not the same. At home, the prime values include things like love, unselfishness, support, security, and fulfillment. But at work, different values dominate, such as efficiency, competition, cooperation, and creativity. Arguing based on caring and unselfishness is less effective at work; arguing for efficiency at home is usually beside the point. It's useful to write down what values the main participants in your life care about most—and bear them in mind when you argue.

That's not to say that other values are irrelevant. Sometimes even at home you argue about finances or legal obligations. And many employees today care whether the company expresses their values through its mission. But still, you'll be more successful if you argue based on the key values of the applicable domain of life.

FRAME TO THE PERSON

To be effective, you need to address the values held high by the person you're arguing with. As every parent knows, you can't persuade a nine-year-old child to eat vegetables by saying it will help them to "stay healthy to a ripe old age." That's not a value they care about yet. You have to appeal to what the other person does care about. If you don't know—ask.

Suppose your teenager is thinking of quitting the hockey team at midseason after having beaten out two dozen other kids to make the team. You might ask him, "Why do you think it's okay to quit? What do you think a friend on the team who disagreed with you would say?" Then you'll hear the values your son brings to bear. Possibly you can get him to consider other values, too.

DRAW OUT WHAT'S REALLY AT STAKE

You have to understand *why* the other person sees particular values as being in play. Even in spousal arguments, people often misread this.

Suppose that a husband forgets that he promised to stop by the pharmacy and pick up his wife's prescription on his way home from work. She says, "How could you be so thoughtless and selfish, after everything I do for this family?" In her mind, this event symbolizes big issues and values.

Suppose that the husband then says, "Don't make such a fuss about it—I just forgot because I'm so busy with a big project at work. If it's so darn important to you, I can go back and get it tonight."

Oh boy, is that the wrong response! The wife may have been wrong in reading selfishness into forgetfulness, and linking this to an overall "balancing of accounts" of everything the spouses do. But the guy is being obtuse and tone deaf. You can easily see that the wife is seeking acknowledgment that her needs count, too; that she is not just a caregiver, but she, too, is owed caring and respect. That's what the argument is really about.

ACKNOWLEDGE THE OTHER'S VALUES

Acknowledge the significance of what the other person values in the situation. It does no good to tell a spouse, "Your cousin won't even care if we miss her party"—if your spouse feels that attending is a duty that should be met even if the cousin won't care.

ADMIT THE TRADEOFFS

Be honest and admit that when values conflict, often there aren't right and wrong answers. To argue effectively, you need to explain why your proposed solution to the clash of values makes the most sense, while admitting that it does downplay some other values.

LISTEN ACTIVELY

When faced with an argument we disagree with, we often stop listening and immediately start crafting our zinger riposte. Don't do that. Really listen. Don't get hung up on one word that you feel is unfair; you might be right, but still focus on the real issue. Try to understand not just what your argument partner wants but *why* they feel as they do.

LISTEN FOR WHAT'S NOT BEING SAID

Frequently in personal disputes, people argue by indirection. They don't want to come out and say what's really troubling them, so they seize on a trivial example. Spouses aren't *really* arguing about being late or leaving the window open to the rain or not taking out the trash; they're arguing about caring, sharing responsibility, and appreciation. Parents and teenagers aren't *really* arguing about particular clothes or a social media post; almost always the teenager sees the issue as control versus freedom, while the parent sees it as decency or safety. So, it will be better if the participants cut through the surface and frankly admit what really concerns them.

ASK "WHY" QUESTIONS

Too often we adopt a simplistic, binary view of arguments: "You say x is true, but I say it's false." And then we repeat our positions. That gains little. One should always ask the other person *why* they believe x. They may offer facts, reasons, or just feelings to support their belief. You can then reciprocate—and be far more trenchant, because you know the real drivers of their viewpoint.

ASK CALIBRATED QUESTIONS

These are open-ended rather than Yes or No questions. Suppose your argument partner asserts that having an armed guard at your neighborhood school won't make the kids safer. You might ask questions like these: How do you know that? How sure are you? How could we measure whether guards help or not? If they helped, why might that be? Are there other steps that might work better?

ASK FOR EVIDENCE

This shouldn't be a challenging demand, but a sincere request for information. Facts do matter and might change your view. And it can help to admit when *neither* of you actually knows the answer (like what the research says about the effects of permissive parenting, or iron in your tap water, or vouchers versus tax credits). Even apart from facts, good reasons for believing something matter (such as common sense, logic, probabilities, and so on). One of the most powerful things you can ever ask is "Okay, let's assume for today that you're right. What could you learn in the future that, if it were true, might lead you to change your mind?"

AVOID FALLACIES AND GAMES

Don't tell your argument partner that "it's just either/or." Don't hedge or weasel out of claims you've asserted. Don't drag in a red herring. Don't invoke the *reductio ad absurdum* ("The way you're talking, we'll have to lock up every second person.") These are all fallacious arguments. Don't do that to your argument partner—especially one who matters in your life.

BE CAREFUL WITH WORDS

Be careful before you hurl loaded words like "bully," "dishonest," or "cruel." Don't hide behind jargon words ("that's just mansplaining"); say what you think is really happening. Don't get stuck fighting over a scientific-sounding word when neither of you probably knows the technical definition anyway. (What really makes someone a "psychotic"?)

DON'T BE DECEPTIVE

If your wife asks you straight out if you have had an affair with that young intern named Monica, don't say, "I did not have sexual relations with that woman"—with the hidden proviso that you do not consider oral sex "sexual relations." There is no point in arguing if you are just going to be deceptive.

SHOW SIMILARITIES

People are more likely to be persuaded if you can show them similarities in values between the issue at hand and one they already care about. Many of us didn't grow up feeling that chugging a soda from a bottle and throwing it in the trash had any moral meaning. But today, we might see the idea of millions of plastic bottles filling landfills and being dumped in the ocean as a moral issue—sort of like dumping trash in the empty yard at the end of the street. If online jokes are seen as like just having fun at a party, they invoke one set of values; if they are more like mean bullying in the schoolyard, we respond differently. Perceptions of similarity guide us in deploying values and arguing over them.

OFFER EXAMPLES

To most people, talking about values is pretty abstract; giving examples works better. Almost everyone agrees we should try to be good citizens. But what does that require? Being sure to vote? Staying informed on the major issues? Not criticizing America to foreigners? Speaking English? Giving to charities? Not cheating on your taxes? Not building a 20,000-square-foot mansion? Recycling trash? Attending public rather than private schools? You could give a hundred examples. But offering some and debunking others will help you and your argument partner see what values you embed in the idea of good citizenship—and perhaps reach consensus on some of them.

ADDRESS CONTRADICTIONS

We are all inconsistent at times, but we try to avoid rank contradictions. So let's ask: Why do we have laws against animal cruelty but not against hunting? Why do many liberals venerate tolerance, but not for intolerant groups (antigay, sexist, or racist groups)? We all struggle with such things. It can be effective to point out that a person's values in one situation contradict what they value in another. They may reflexively say, "The situations are different." And of course, no two situations are exactly alike. But the real question is whether they differ in ways essential to the issue at hand. That is a worthy subject of discussion.

DON'T DEMEAN EMOTION, AND DON'T USE IT AS A WEAPON

When arguing, people often say things like "Don't get so steamed up about this," or "Gosh, you seem awfully emotional." The person you are addressing may have every right to be upset about the issue, and even if their emotional reaction seems excessive to you, that's not your call. Don't try to change the debate by making it about whether their level of emotion is the "right" level. Go back to the real issue and explain why you think they *shouldn't be* so upset by your viewpoint. Psychological research has shown that people confuse how strongly they feel about an issue with how certain they are that they got the facts right. You should address those separately; they are different. And people should avoid browbeating their argument partner by saying things like "I just can't get over that you said *x*. It's just outrageous; you should be ashamed just to sit there . . . "

AVOID NEEDLESS ESCALATION

This is one of the most corrosive features of value-laden arguments: People can't resist upping the stakes with each verbal exchange. A justified complaint, "You forgot the PTA meeting," escalates into "You never think about the family" and then, "You are just a selfish brute." And then the receiver of these epithets will respond in kind, on the principle that the best defense is a good offense. Don't do that if you care about maintaining the relationship.

MAKE PARTIAL CONCESSIONS IN THE QUEST FOR COMMON GROUND

One of the most powerful moves in any argument is to sincerely admit that the other person has persuaded you on some point, or at least made you unsure whether you were entirely right. This can be an effective step toward discovering some common ground.

INCISIVE SUMMING UP

It can help bring an argument to an amicable close if one person says, "Okay, let me see if I got this about right. You feel x, primarily because y. And I worry more about z, because of q. Is that mainly where we differ?" The key here is to be scrupulously fair, to give your argument partner the benefit of the doubt, and to state their view in the strongest, not weakest, way it could be expressed. And then ask them to respond. This often leaves both people feeling that at least they've been heard. This may narrow the gap between them and open the way to a deeper resolution in days to come.

KNOW WHEN TO STOP

Arguments—even ones involving important values-- don't need to end by declaring a winner and a loser—and they almost never do anyway. Arguments don't even need to lead to an agreed conclusion, though it's terrific if they can. Often in value-laden arguments between people who have a relationship, it is best to say at some point, "Okay, we've argued enough. Let's go get some coffee."

10

The Morality of Fairness

I N OUR JOURNEY THROUGH MORALITY thus far, we've spoken a lot about empathy, avoiding harm, and altruism. But you could start with a different core value. Thus, "many modern accounts [focus on] contrasting a morality of sympathy with a morality of fairness." The latter kind of morality stresses not empathy or avoidance of harm, but what people "deserve." Recall that much Old Testament morality, endlessly repeated, involves "just desert," kindness to friends, but vengeful death blows to enemies, and even to apostates, who *deserve* it. This is one way to define fairness. But it's certainly not the only way. So what exactly is fairness?

Fairness—or its related concept, justice—is one of the most strongly felt human values. People yearn for it and will fight to get it. It is closely connected with reciprocity, which, as we saw, is one of the core ideas from which morality evolved. But there is much more to fairness than just two-person reciprocity. Fairness embodies the concepts of desert and just process. These lead to three main questions: (1) Who should establish the criteria for being deserving? (2) What criteria should be used? and (3) What is a fair or just process for applying those criteria?

On the first question, fairness expectations are created in two ways: informally by common opinion, and formally by social institutions.

In many daily situations, there is no formal enforcement mechanism for fairness, but social patterns define and enforce expectations. If you're standing in the middle of the line for seats at a movie, being ahead of another person means you get in before them, and everyone else in line will support that. It's only fair. But if you're pregnant or on crutches, then most people will let you go to the head of the line.

In other contexts, fairness rules are set by an institution. At a sales-driven company, people are paid very different salaries based on their results. At a summer camp, all the counselors might be paid the same, with perhaps a small increase for more experienced counselors. And at a volunteer church food kitchen, people aren't paid at all. An institution adopts rules intended to be fair in its own world.

The second question is often the hardest—deciding what criteria are fairest in allocating resources or benefits in a given domain. I'll elaborate on that later in this chapter. Here I'll just state the key principle: Fairness usually means that benefits are allocated based on the criteria that best advance the core purpose of the given activity. This may sound like a platitude, but it is not, and as we will see, this principle is often violated in practice.

The core purpose offers a basic starting point for fairness. Consider: What rule is fairest in choosing players for a high-school soccer team? The core purposes of the team are to help players compete to improve their skills and to put a high-quality team on the field—so it's fairest to let the coach choose the most dedicated and talented players. But in other realms, random selection may be a fairer selection tool—for example, in choosing which kids will be given spots in a county summer camp where places are in short supply. In still other cases, wealth is accepted as a fair winnowing tool. At some fancy golf clubs, the core purpose is to let well-heeled individuals network with one another privately while enjoying a sport—so they ration membership by admitting only those who can afford to pay a fortune. Each criterion is generally seen as fair for that particular enterprise.

The third question is: What makes a *process* fair? This has many elements, but we start with the idea that the process rules ought to be reasonably clear. When the rules are fuzzy, people get skeptical about fairness. For example, is it fair for you and your kids to move up to more expensive seats during the fifth inning at the baseball stadium, after it becomes obvious that whoever bought those tickets isn't coming? Nobody gets hurt—but you paid less and would get something you didn't deserve (based on the ticket price you paid), which is likely to generate looks of annoyance from some other fans. Here, the rules are unclear, leading to a moral quandary and perhaps conflict.

Not putting enough money in the parking meter at a busy beach location breaks the rules, but it hardly seems unfair as long as you ultimately pay the $50 if you get ticketed. But what about a rich person who decides to hog the only handicapped space, saying, "What do I care? A $50 fine means nothing to me." That feels unfair and immoral—after all, that spot was set aside specifically for the use of someone for whom a long trek to the beach is onerous. It seems that there are rules and then there are *real fairness* rules.

Sometimes we turn around and call conduct unfair even if it doesn't break any rules. Our free-market economy is based on supply-and-demand pricing. If more people want a certain handbag, concert ticket, or car, the price goes up. That's just the nature of the market, and not generally considered unfair. But studies show that people believe it's morally wrong for a store to jack up the price of snow shovels after a big storm, or the price of water bottles when a hurricane interrupts the water supply. Aren't those stores also just responding to the market? Yes, but many states prohibit this under the name of price gouging. Uber, Amazon, and many other companies use so-called dynamic pricing—which is a fancy name for jacking up prices when demand increases, and yet it's legal. Why is that different? (It may have something to do with "normal" versus "abnormal" situations, but the distinction is vague.)

Beyond clear rules, procedural fairness entails a bunch of other concepts. We have developed expectations in various contexts. For example, if you are threatened with sanctions after being accused of serious errors or misdeeds, you might expect "process protections" like notice if something can be corrected; a chance to explain yourself to a fair-minded decider; some level of consistency in decisions; proportionality between the penalty and the nature of the error or bad conduct; the opportunity to appeal a decision; and so on.

As I noted earlier, a central concept embedded in fairness is *outcomes based on desert* (i.e., a person's deservingness). An achievement test is fair if the most competent test-takers actually score higher. A lottery is fair if every ticket has an equal chance to win. A restaurant is fair if it charges more to the people who actually order more food. These are easy examples, because they present clear correlations between outcome and desert. But what defines a fair taxation system for poor, middle-class, and rich people? We sure don't all agree on what they deserve to pay.

And that brings us to the additional concept of *justice*. Justice often refers to official, legal processes like those we lump together under the blanket term "the criminal justice system." The law has codified procedures that are intended to achieve, or at least approximate, fairness at every stage of the legal process. This extends from how criminal charges can be brought to how jury members are selected and instructed, the kinds of evidence allowed at trial, and the range of possible punishments. The system is far from perfect; in fact, it has been documented as biased, flawed, and in some respects broken. Reforms are tried from time to time. But nobody has yet devised any overall better system for addressing the painful realities of crime. Bad people do bad things; often they get away with them; and sometimes innocent people are convicted. But I think we understand most of what people mean when they say they want a fairer criminal justice system.

By contrast, when people use a vaguer term such as "social justice" or "environmental justice," they are trying to expand the concept to many things that do not yet have established meanings. They're often motivated by a belief that social rules are the result of a callous, biased, or even rigged economic and social system. But what measures would be needed to yield "just" solutions in those realms? That remains to be determined in our society.

Conflicting Ideas of Fairness

AND SO, WE RETURN to the core challenge: There are many different meanings to being deserving, which lead to disparate notions of fairness.

Consider, as a test case, the problem facing executives of a company that has had a bad year financially, leaving a very limited pool of dollars available for bonuses. How should they distribute them?

For some, the concept of fairness begins with merit. An executive may think, "I worked my tail off this year; I really increased our profits. I deserve a bonus even if others don't." But to other people, fairness begins with a recognition of the utilitarian "declining marginal utility" of income, a fancy way of saying that a bonus will mean a lot less to those higher up on the economic scale. On that basis, since even hard-working executives don't *need* a bonus nearly as much as workers on the factory floor, maybe it's fair to give bonuses only to those front-line workers.

Other people may think, "Look, in tough times, we all should hang together. We should all get the same bonus." Indeed, much research shows that people's satisfaction with a division of resources depends less on the absolute value of what they receive and more on a comparison to what other people receive. It turns out that many people would be happier if they get a $5,000 bonus and the person in the next office gets $4,000, than they would be if they got $10,000—but the person next door got $12,000. If we focus on fairness in this sense, then equal bonuses for all may be the best choice. Do we care that some employees gave 110 percent while others dogged it all year?

What criterion for bonuses do you think is fairest? Hard work? Actual achievement? Relative need? Equality? Contribution to profit? Seniority? Some other factor? Or overall deservingness—meaning what? One could craft an argument for any of these.

The conclusion here is that invoking "fairness" in a moral argument isn't really meaningful unless you are willing to define, first, what your criterion for fairness is, and second, why that criterion is justified as best in the particular context. People laud fairness, but they ignore that lots of different fairness principles are embedded in various social practices and laws. Each of them is regarded as fairest—sometimes. These principles include:

- Fair intentions
- Fairness as transparency, not being deceived
- Fairness (accuracy) in judging people
- Fairness as reciprocity (tit-for-tat)
- Fairness as neutrality between people's interests (lack of bias)
- Fairness as holding people to their promises and contracts
- Fair individual chance to get ahead (equal opportunity)
- Fair outcomes based on talent and effort
- Fairness by correcting for chance or bad luck (insurance)
- Fairness between individuals

- Fairness between groups (e.g., ethnicities, genders, generations, communities)
- Fairness in meeting all basic needs
- Fairness by limiting inequality, regardless of ability or luck
- Fairness of procedures
- Fairness as economic rationality ("let the market work")
- Fair rewards based on investment or work effort
- Fair protection of owned property
- Fair and assured penalties for misconduct
- Fair allocation of burdens and duties
- Fair allocation of decision authority (i.e., power)
- Fairness in balancing individual rights and community interests
- Fairness in requiring individual sacrifice for the common good
- Fair allocation of risks to those who can best bear them
- Fairness as not creating bad spillover effects or unintended consequences
- Fairness toward those with no voice (animals, future generations, the Earth)

There you have 25 good—but different—meanings of "fair." Each is supported by a sensible rationale. Each has been adopted as the prevailing standard for some important functions. No wonder people aren't sure exactly what fairness requires! And no wonder we argue so often about whether what you want or what I want is fairer. Fairness is not one thing but many.

Self-interest leads us to call fair whatever algorithm rewards the thing that happens to be our strongest feature of deservingness (need or excellence or seniority). Yet we would stress a different feature if it favored us in another situation. Kenneth Binmore, author of two volumes titled *Playing Fair: Game Theory and the Social Contract*, had "come close to despair . . . as attempt after attempt to create adequate foundations for a scientific theory of fairness norms simply revealed loose ends."

When Americans are asked what they mean by fairness, most give a single answer. They say (drum roll): "Equal opportunity." This is a noble principle that yields good results in many ways, though we have fallen short in others. But equalizing all the inputs that affect everyone's chances in every domain is obviously fanciful. We can seek but not achieve that goal.

Then consider a political fairness principle like "one person, one vote." Who can argue with that? But in a condominium building, the occupants of each condo get one collective vote regardless of whether they are one person or six. The reason is that here we are pivoting off property rights, not political rights. But then, if you paid twice as much for your huge condo as I did for my small one, shouldn't your property rights warrant two votes to my one? Yet that doesn't occur. But if I buy two small units costing less than your one huge one, then I do get two votes. The rationales are hard to pin down, even though they are apparently adopted as being "fair."

What Is the Right Fairness Principle?

WHEN ARGUING, PEOPLE OFTEN DECLARE, "That's not fair!" as if fairness were a binary value, either present or absent. But as we've seen, any judgment about fairness requires weighing different interests and thus different elements of fairness. The closer we look at fairness, the more it appears to be a mishmash. Sometimes, we identify a desired outcome and then mix and match rationales to arrive at that outcome—which we then denote as obviously fair.

Since maximizing one feature of fairness usually requires impairing another, you have to explain which aspect of fairness you think is paramount in the situation, and thus which aspect of fairness you're willing to downplay or even sacrifice. Usually there is no free lunch, where everyone is better off and no one less so—although we typically avoid acknowledging that.

Now let's look at a range of situations, how a person might justify what is fair, and the challenges each example presents.

"WHEN YOU NEED TO FIRE SOME PEOPLE, THE CHOICE SHOULD BE BASED ON FAIR CRITERIA."

Sounds good. But what criteria are fair? Solely merit, you say? What about seniority—doesn't that count for something? Or what if an employee just moved her family across the country when you offered her the job—is it fair to fire her just three months later? Or what if you know that a longtime but weak performer has cancer? Maybe based on merit, he ought to be fired—but then he'll lose his health insurance just when he needs it most. Is that fair?

"WHEN RESOURCES ARE LIMITED, EVERYONE SHOULD HAVE THE SAME CHANCE TO GET THEM."

That sounds fair. But wait, didn't we give priority in receiving the COVID vaccine to the elderly and those with compromised immune systems because the virus could be especially lethal to them? If a hurricane damages an agricultural area, should disaster relief be paid out the same to family farmers who are barely making ends meet and to industrial farming firms that make millions in profits? Is the "same chance to get resources" always best?

"IN CASE OF HARDSHIP, BURDENS SHOULD BE SHARED EQUALLY."

Suppose that six people agree to go on a week-long camping trip together. Unfortunately, on the first day down a raging river, one canoe capsizes, and they lose half the food and tents. What is the fairest way to handle this tough situation?

- They draw straws, and the half who pick the short straws go back home.
- The ones who signed up last for the trip go home.
- The ones in the canoe that capsized go home.
- Everyone stays but eats half rations.
- Everyone eats half rations except for Gino, who has diabetes.
- Each person sleeps outside with no tent on alternate nights.

Can you explain why your chosen principle is fairer than the other alternatives?

"WHEN RULES ARE SET UP TO ACHIEVE A GIVEN PURPOSE, THAT PURPOSE SHOULD GOVERN."

Government agencies usually buy stuff through a sealed-bid "procurement" process. Vendors submit proposals, and the government is supposed to choose the one with the best quality at the lowest price. But in many cases, small or woman-owned businesses get a special bump up in the scoring because social value is accorded to having a diverse entrepreneurial base. Fostering diversity isn't what the sealed-bid system was set up to accomplish, but a broader base of business suppliers might improve quality and pricing in the long run. So is this system fair or unfair? What about giving a preference to companies that are located in-state or owned by veterans or other "deserving" people?

"WHEN PRIVILEGES ARE ALLOCATED, THE DECIDERS SHOULD BE UNBIASED AND ALL APPLICANTS SHOULD BE TREATED EQUALLY."

Maria is trying out for a highly selective traveling soccer team that has 18 roster spots. The coaches all rate her as very good, but not in the top 18. But she makes the team because her dad is the head coach. Is this unfair? Or is it only fair to allow a hardworking dad who puts in lots of hours coaching kids to have a chance to spend time with his own daughter?

Suppose that the manager of a large consulting firm has a dozen new graduates to choose from for a coveted entry-level job. All have similar credentials and apparent ability. The manager hires Sukan because she feels that "Asian Americans tend to be hard workers who want to get ahead." Is that fair? What if she *doesn't* hire Sukan because she feels that "Asian Americans usually aren't outgoing; they're not 'people people.'" Is positive bias fair, but negative bias unfair? What if she hires a state university grad because, as she says, "I've found that the top grads of big state universities are just as smart, but work harder and do better with clients, than snooty Ivy League grads." Does extensive personal experience convert unfair bias into fair wisdom?

"FAIRNESS MEANS TREATING PEOPLE THE WAY THEY TREAT YOU."

The idea of reciprocity—tit-for-tat—certainly seems right. So, it's only fair for a small business owner to send customers to another who, in turn, sends business his way. But if he knows the other business produces mediocre products, is that fair to his customers? What if a doctor has a loud and insulting patient. Is it fair for the doctor to play tit-for-tat and become loud and insulting to the patient? Obviously not.

"FAIRNESS IS EQUAL PAY FOR EQUAL WORK."

Suppose that you happily take a job for $110,000 per year—a significant boost from your previous salary. Soon you learn that someone else started in the firm just a month before you in the same position and got $120,000, apparently to match the offer from a competing company. Should you demand $120,000 or quit because you weren't treated fairly? What about those who started the year before you and got only $90,000 to start and now make $100,000 compared to your $110,000? Do they also have the right to demand a raise up to $110,000 or even $120,000? Is it fair for factors other than equal work to affect your salary—like "the free market"?

"FAIRNESS IS BEING CONSISTENT."

Suppose your boss tells you that your four-person team needs to supervise critical projects by having somebody in the office working weekends for the next three months. The team gets to decide who. Should they be consistent—for example, by requiring each team member to work every fourth weekend? Or should Sam be assigned every second weekend because he has no social life anyway, while Tim is allowed to work only every sixth weekend, because he's a single dad with young kids at home?

Consistency isn't really a moral quality on its own, but we sometimes treat it as such because it feels like a proxy for fairness. Demanding consistency tamps down the impact of some bad things that can taint fairness, like prejudice, being bribed, personal animus, or simple irrationality. But that doesn't guarantee that consistent results are fair ones. For example, a judge might be consistent—but aberrantly harsh—in imposing sentences on convicted offenders. Even young children understand that consistency isn't always right. In experiments, they will share a reward (like candy) more generously with peers who did real work to get the reward; they share less if the peers just pulled a lever; and they share still less if the peers just arrived on the scene. Children above a certain age know that fairness doesn't always mean treating everyone the same.

Consistency is not a reliable test of fairness; it's just one of many possible diagnostics.

"Fairness means keeping your promises."

Certainly, one rule of fairness is keeping promises—but there are exceptions based on other fairness principles. Suppose a neighbor promises to sell you his fishing boat in two months, at the end of the season. You save your money and wait. But when Labor Day rolls around, your neighbor tells you he already sold the boat—sorry! That sounds unfair. But what if the other buyer was his brother; should an exception be made for family? What if a stranger suddenly arrived and gave him an amazingly high offer? What if your neighbor suddenly needs the money for a medical operation? What if he heard that you were also negotiating with someone else to buy a different boat—and he worried that you'd welch on your deal with him? Which of these excuses for breaking a promise would you accept as fair?

"Fairness means enforcing the rules."

We tend to fall into the habit of seeing fairness only in its uplifting, positive sense, of rewarding those who deserve it. But fairness also means penalizing those who violate the rules. Fairness doesn't come without a cost. If an exam has a one-hour time limit, is it fair to let somebody turn in their exam 15 minutes late ("Gosh, I got confused about the time")? If a job posting for an accountant says it requires a CPA, is it fair to make an exception for your cousin? And sometimes fairness even involves punishing those who break laws or other-wise damage the community. If looters ravage the only big food or retail store in a community and then it closes, reducing jobs and hollowing out the neighborhood, is it fair to be lenient on the looters?

These examples may be frustrating, because we all yearn for a simple rule of fairness that is morally and practically satisfying. But it can't be devised. Fairness is a general goal; in striving for it, we can learn what might be called criteria of fairness, and tools of fairness.

Mental Glitches in Judging Fairness

UNFORTUNATELY, THERE IS ANOTHER major kind of problem in achieving fairness—the prevalence of *cognitive biases,* the selfish, blinded, or illogical ways of thinking and feeling that beset us all.

Here's an example: The overwhelming majority of Americans profess belief in a free market economy, which should mean among other things that prices are set by the market, based on supply and demand. But research shows that most people believe (1) it's unfair for a store to raise prices for batteries after a storm increases demand, but (2) it's okay for a store to stop giving discounts on the same batteries. Of course, ending a $3 discount and raising the price by $3 both mean that you pay $3 more. Yet people evidently judge fairness compared to the reference price they have come to regard as normal.

In other cases, the reference price itself may be perceived as unfair. Consider this example: Imagine you and some friends are on a beach, with both a convenience store and a fancy hotel bar nearby, and you want some beer. Apparently, most people think that it's fair for the hotel to charge $6, while the convenience store should only charge $2—but it would be unfair for the convenience store to raise its price to $4 a beer on a hot holiday weekend. Somehow, the fair price of a beer is locked into our expectations of each vendor—even though the beer itself is the same.

For a more consequential example, consider how people judge as "outrageous" and "unfair" the prices charged for things like pharmaceuticals or a university education. But what is a fair price? An economist might start by asking what it actually costs to produce the products delivered, plus a typical profit margin. A smart consumer might look at the prices of alternative products (comparing generics to patented drugs, and comparing community colleges to universities). An expert analyst might also try to assess whether drug companies or universities deliver their services "efficiently."

But let's be honest—almost no one who objects to drug costs or college tuition has done this kind of homework, or has a clue about how to build a financial model that would justify a certain level of prices. People are offended by drug and college costs because they've gotten locked into ideas of what they *should* cost. Most drug companies make healthy profits, but they also risk billions funding research over many years, hoping that it will yield a drug that gets to market. Most universities lose money on operations year after year and survive only due to charitable gifts and earnings on endowment funds. How should these factors influence our judgments of whether the prices they charge are fair? Also, both pharma companies and universities derive substantial funds from government sources, in different ways. Should that have any impact on our assessment of fair fees?

Those who complain about increases in college tuition often ignore that the services demanded of universities have multiplied and become more complicated over time. Today many people expect universities to provide financial aid for large numbers of needy students, serious safety/security services, state-of-the-art technologies, robust student support services, dozens of athletic programs, expensive gyms, high-quality cafeteria food, and much more. Some also demand that universities should avoid endowment investments in profitable but "bad" industries, like those that contribute to global warming. Where is the money supposed to come from to pay for all that is expected?

After examining all these factors, you might still conclude that drug companies and colleges have set their prices far too high. But your idea of what *seems* unfair and what *is* unfair might differ.

As we deal with "fairness," we are also affected by most of the psychological dynamics I outlined in Chapter 6, such as no-harm bias, affect bias, loss aversion bias, inaction bias, side-effect bias, reciprocity bias, and fundamental attribution error.

Fairness as Equality Before the Law

ANOTHER OFT-CITED ASPECT OF FAIRNESS is equality before the law. This surely is not the prevailing rule in many nations. And even in America, people are not equal before the law in all respects. This isn't just because they don't have equal access to lawyers and resources—though that's so. Even aside from that, the law generally treats people equally only if: (1) they have relevantly similar characteristics; (2) they are in relevantly similar circumstances; (3) they are mentally competent adults; (4) the situation doesn't involve certain legal matters where equality has been limited for other reasons; (5) the people involved are not within a group that has been granted special benefits for a social purpose; and (6) one accepts that equal final outcomes are not in any way assured. Let's look at each of these factors that can complicate our understanding of what legal equality entails.

RELEVANTLY SIMILAR CHARACTERISTICS

In a courtroom, equality before the law means that what matters is the merits of the case, not whether the plaintiff of the defendant happens to be Black or White, male or female, rich or poor, and so on. We say those factors just shouldn't matter. But if people are *relevantly* different, they can be treated differently. For example, the Americans With Disabilities Act gives a handicapped person the right to insist on a "reasonable accommodation" from their employer, such as a special desk—but others can't demand the same. If two people each place an order for 1,000 pounds of ammonium nitrate, and one operates a family farm in Iowa that uses the product as fertilizer, while the other leads a terrorist group that wants to prepare explosives, the seller and the police can treat them differently. They are relevantly different.

When differences in treatment are based on certain factors—such as race, gender, sexual orientation, ethnicity, religion, or age—the law requires especially strong justifications. Often such discrimination is unlawful, but not always. Hence, it can at times be legal to discriminate based on age (the minimum age for driver's licenses and for consensual sexual relations); physical ability (required standards of visual acuity for airline pilots and height for police officers); citizenship (granting security clearances); gender (jobs such as acting, where gender is a bona fide job qualification); or even religion (a Lutheran minister can't demand to be hired by a Catholic church).

And let's be honest—personal characteristics are used all the time to discriminate lawfully, such as when a person is offered or denied a job because they are seen as self-confident or insecure, arrogant or likable, attractive or not, articulate or mumbling. Is it fair to make decisions based on these factors that the person may not be able to change? That's just life.

RELEVANTLY SIMILAR CIRCUMSTANCES

The law can and does treat people differently depending on circumstances. A supplier of goods might be legally excused from delivering on time if he was prevented by a hurricane, but another won't be excused just because he took a vacation. A divorced American man might not be awarded custody of his son if he moves to France, but if he remarries and moves back to Ohio, he might. If twin brothers each seek loans to start separate businesses, the bank may grant a loan to one but not the other based on the bank's judgment that one business will succeed and the other fail. But if the brothers were adopted and are of different races, the bank can't make the lending decision simply on that basis. As a society, we've decided that the likely success of the business is a relevant factor, but race is not.

MENTALLY COMPETENT ADULTS

The law treats certain categories of people differently. Children don't have the same rights as adults. Mentally challenged people may have special defenses if they are duped into abusive contracts. Resident aliens may not be able to get a security clearance giving them access to sensitive information or facilities. And when it comes to regulating financial transactions, so-called sophisticated investors (those who meet specific income and net worth requirements) receive less legal protection than the average investor. Most people seem to agree that these reasons for treating people differently are fair and should be legal.

LEGAL MATTERS WHERE EQUALITY IS LIMITED

For certain kinds of decisions, such as child custody or adoption, the law allows "discrimination" (that is, differential treatment) based on a person's age, health, income, or criminal history. This departure from equality is permitted because it has been judged necessary to advance important social goals, like ensuring that a child will have has a safe and stable home.

SPECIAL INTERESTS OF CERTAIN GROUPS

People with disabilities have special rights to reasonable accommodations in employment. Observant people of various religions (e.g., Muslims, Sikhs) may have special rights to be excepted from rules about clothing in school or offices. Police, firefighters, and first responders may be given preference for certain public housing. These are all felt to be fair exceptions to perfect legal equality.

NO PROMISE OF EQUAL OUTCOMES

Equality before the law doesn't mean that people with the same claim are assured of the same outcome. Injured plaintiffs who sue based on suffering the same kind of harm may receive vastly different monetary awards because of their age, appearance, the quality of their lawyer, the biases of jurors, and many other factors. Customs in different industries lead to different results, so if you are injured in one industry, you might receive a lot more compensation than in another.

FINALLY, WHAT ABOUT CONSISTENCY?

Consistency is an oft-touted feature of fairness . . . except when it isn't. As I noted, many people reflexively see any lack of consistency as a sign of bias. But we also create many processes that inevitably lead to inconsistency. For example, in the United States, our federal/state/local system of government is embedded in the Constitution, and most Americans feel it confers unique political benefits. Local government is "closer to the people," and we laud states as laboratories of democracy in which to experiment with social policies that other states can learn from. But the resulting jurisdictional patchwork yields lots of inconsistencies. If you're charged with a crime by federal authorities, you may be treated very differently than under a state justice system. And if you're smoking marijuana in your car, you may be treated very differently if you cross over the state line from Colorado (where it's legal) into Wyoming (where it isn't).

Inconsistency is built into our legal system. For example, most of the law we live under is *not* prescribed by statutes enacted by our legislatures. Instead, it's common law, shaped by the accretion of judicial decisions over many decades. Judges often lament that prior decisions "have not been a model of consistency." That's putting it mildly. Contesting litigants and judges draw upon an array of past court rulings to justify specific outcomes in cases with disparate facts, and that means that inconsistency is inevitable.

What's more, it's pretty clear that public opinion actually *insists on* inconsistency in the law. On the one hand, in criminal sentencing, most people like the idea that judges should follow sentencing guidelines to temper their personal biases and be more consistent. But we also expect them to mete out justice in light of each person's unique situation and special "mitigating factors"—which produces inconsistency.

So, if we don't like rigid rules, and we don't like inconsistent, individualized decisions, what's the fair method? Legal theorist Ronald Dworkin suggests: Follow *principles, not rules,* because principles are more reliable guides to action. That carries its own challenges, but it would allow for consistency at a higher level of generality, and flexibility in specific cases. There is much more to justice than invariable sameness before the law, and perfect justice is an elusive goal to be sought rather than grasped.

Defining Fairness in Public Policy

IF WE MOVE FROM THE LEGAL SYSTEM to the political system and ask what is fair in allocating public resources, once again we find a motley array of rationales.

Jonathan Elster's excellent book *Local Justice* starts by observing that "a classical definition of economics is that it deals with the allocation of scarce resources with alternative uses. An equally well known definition of politics is that it is about 'who gets what, when and how.'" So, we should usually ask: On what principle should society allocate this particular resource? In the United States, many people's first response is "the market." Yet, in practice, we take many choices out of the hands of the market and give them to government instead. In the process, we even declare some market choices illegal.

Let's consider how, as a society, we mix and match fairness criteria. My goal here is not for you to throw up your hands in dismay at human irrationality. It is to encourage us all to tone down our "righteous indignation," and be a little humble about how fair we are. Also, we must shoulder the burden of explaining to others exactly *why* a given criterion, process, or outcome is fair in a given context.

NEED RATHER THAN EQUALITY

Sometimes, need trumps equality as the operative principle. During the COVID crisis, the vaccine was made available first to the elderly and those with compromised immune systems. They were at greatest risk and had the greatest need, and most people accepted this as a fair rule for allocating the then limited resource. Ventilators in short supply were also allocated based mainly on the patient's severity of need. Even apart from crises, hospitals routinely allocate intensive care unit beds based on need.

For a more complex example, consider how Medicaid works. The program pays for medical care only to those in need, defined as those whose family income is below a defined percentage of the federal poverty level (FPL). Let's say that, in a given state, the ceiling on income for Medicaid eligibility is 200 percent of

FPL, or a total of $66,000 for a family of four in 2026. One family just below the threshold might get free health care worth hundreds of thousands of dollars, while a family with income just above the line might actually have greater need due to other factors (like supporting relatives). Yet they aren't eligible for Medicaid, because we must draw a line somewhere. We think we are allocating resources based fairly on need, but we can't be perfect and we fail. Benefits are definitely not made available equally to all those who have a real hard time paying for medical bills.

Relative Benefit

Many believe that resources should be allocated based on relative benefit, not relative need. Those sound the same, but they can differ. For example, when people need an organ transplant, livers and kidneys are allocated based largely on how likely it is that a candidate patient will benefit by actually surviving—not on how desperate they are right now. The usual standard is what are called quality-adjusted life years (QALYs), which measure how much added life you'd get with what degree of functionality. Most clinicians see that as a sensible standard, though it means that those who are old, obese, diabetic, or happen to have an antigen profile that's difficult to match get downgraded on the list of people awaiting organs. But UNOS, the national nonprofit coordinator of transplants, has been urged to modify the scoring system to weigh more heavily how long someone has been waiting on the list, to achieve more geographic balance across the United States, and to ensure better racial balance among recipients. None of these is really a medical criterion, and some oppose such adjustments. Each of the added factors is controversial, illustrating once again that fairness is far from self-defining.

Merit

When it comes to affording access to limited resources, merit is often invoked as a good criterion. But even defining merit isn't always simple.

The most familiar controversy over merit involves affirmative action or diversity, equity, and inclusion (DEI) in college admissions, which is usually thought of as encouraging the acceptance of students of a historically disfavored race or ethnicity, even if they are somewhat less accomplished. Until 2023, Supreme Court decisions essentially said that colleges could not use strict racial quotas in making admissions decisions but could use race as one factor among many in a holistic scoring of applicants. Affirmative action was allowed in order to enable universities to achieve what they argue is the educational value of a diverse class, and to encourage diversity in socially significant professions such as law, medicine, and science.

These court rulings did not settle the issue. Some white applicants to elite universities resented that minority students with lower grades and test scores might get the seats instead. Politically conservative organizations agreed and found effective allies among some Asian Americans, who are statistically over-represented at elite universities, and apparently would be even more so if academic merit were the only standard. They sued Harvard and the University of North Carolina to require that academic merit alone should govern. In a watershed 2023 decision overturning prior precedents, the Supreme Court ruled that most current kinds of race-conscious affirmative action in college admissions are unlawful.

The simplified treatment of this issue in the media tends to ignore some important context. It isn't widely known, but most universities in the U.S. admit more than half of all applicants, and many admit a lot more than half. They beat the bushes to try to fill their classes, so exclusion due to affirmative action isn't really an issue. The ability to afford tuition is the real problem—for families of all races. Furthermore, the most highly selective colleges in the U.S. also allocate lots of slots based on home location, gender balance, athletic ability, influence of donors, and academic majors. Some also consider legacy status, low income, and other things. All these factors—most of them noncontroversial—undermine the idea that admission has been or must be based only on academic merit.

Merit is also defined in specialized ways when certain other public goods are allocated. When a city has a limited supply of good public housing or day-care programs, is it fair to give preference to their police officers, firefighters, teachers, and emergency medical personnel because of their service to the community? Should we continue to give military veterans preference in government hiring? Personally, I can see the moral rationale for such preferences.

But the point is that there are many kinds of merit. And so, we need to consider: Is the patchwork we have for determining special benefits irrational, or does it reflect sensible fairness judgments?

TIME INVESTED OR AGE

Apparently, we think it's fair to allocate certain benefits based on people's willingness to queue up and spend time to get them. For example, it's common for the slots in low-cost county summer camps to go to the first 100 kids whose parents apply online or come to the camp.. Slots in homeless shelters often go to the first 50 people who show up; after that, too bad. But would you apply the same principle to adopting children—whichever adult applies first, regardless of parenting qualities? You probably wouldn't do that, because you think decency and merit really matter when it comes to raising children. My sense is that time standing in line seems like a good principle only to decide things that are minor or transitory. A child's future family is too important to use that criterion.

People often earn higher pay, more vacation time, or a higher pension contribution rate based on their seniority, that is, their time in service with the same employer. This tends to favor older workers. But the Supreme Court has ruled that this practice isn't unlawfully discriminatory, even in situations where it has disproportionate racial impact because it continues to reflect old employment practices under which few minorities were hired.

However, in some other circumstances, you can be disfavored for being older. For instance, in most states, it's very hard for parents to adopt a child after they reach a certain age, such as 40 or 50. This is justified by the best interests of the child, who shouldn't bear the risk of a parent dying. But some younger parents lamentably do die, and most people don't die until after age 70—which would allow them to adopt a child even after 50 and still raise the child for 18 years. And about one quarter of American kids have only one parent; another's adoption by two parents, even older ones, might be better odds. What if both parents are super-healthy vegan runners? Is the prejudice against older adoptive parents fair?

LOCAL RESIDENCE

Almost all state universities charge a lot more to out-of-state students. In one sense, this seems fair: The state's citizens paid for the development of State U. and now support it by their taxes, so they should get a break over out-of-staters. But then if the state starts a big new construction project, should state residents get a preference in hiring for jobs? Does that include people who just moved to the state last month?

Similarly, states give tax exemptions to nonprofit hospitals, because their services are important to local residents (hospitals also get federal exemptions). But if I'm driving cross-country and happen to need the emergency department at a local hospital, should they be able to charge me more because I'm not a resident? When is residence relevant and when irrelevant?

Achieving Fairness: The Big Picture

AS YOU'VE SEEN, what is sometimes called "simple fairness" is far from simple. Fairness can be defined in many ways, depending on the goal to be sought and the factors to be rewarded.

And even if we devise a good fairness rule for a given context, we encounter another important problem. Any rule will likely result in both overinclusion and underinclusion compared to the ideal allocation of benefits. These unavoidable effects are sometimes called "false positives" and "false negatives."

For example, no matter where you set the eligibility level for a social benefit (like welfare or Social Security), some needy and deserving people won't be eligible (false negatives), while some who aren't deserving for other reasons—like being drug dealers on welfare or billionaires on Social Security—will be eligible (false positives). Which of these is a greater concern? The answer depends on your general philosophy about government and fairness. Stated in broad terms, "if you care more about false negatives than false positives, you believe in expanding social services, while if you care more about false positives than false negatives, you believe in reducing social services." However eligibility is set, there will still be over- and underinclusion. This isn't because of incompetent administration but because no rule can capture all the variations in human circumstances—ones that have moral or fairness significance.

Finally, we might ask this question: In fairness, what duties does the individual owe back to society?

We've seen that much about fairness traces back to the instinctive value of reciprocity between individuals. But fairness to my society is more complex. I expect the police to come to my house after a burglary, but I won't be reciprocating any time soon by helping them with night patrols. I expect the hospital to treat my relative, but I won't be helping the hospital with patient care. So, when it comes to our duties to society, instead of such simple reciprocity, we create other social obligations, which include voting, paying taxes, and serving in the military if drafted.

But that list feels inadequate. It doesn't even touch the lives of many Americans. After all, fully one third of adults don't bother to vote even in presidential elections; about 40 percent of Americans pay no federal income taxes; and we have long had an all-volunteer military. And beyond that, far fewer people participate today in local civic associations. So how are many of us giving back our fair share to the nation as citizens? What does our country have the right to expect of us as the fair price for all our benefits? There are deep questions whose answers could fill many other books. But we should at least ponder that civic fairness is not a one-way street.

The examples in this chapter underscore the fact that fairness is not a simple concept. In fact, it isn't even a *single* concept, but rather a domain of related principles that morph as we apply them to varied situations. As Jonathan Baron observes, "People often take some simple principle, such as equality or proportionality, and elevate it to an absolute. . . . Once they have a favored principle, they convince themselves that following it requires no sacrifice. Compromise or discussion becomes difficult." So, when you argue with others about fairness, seek a righteous result—but retain both honesty and humility. Admit that by elevating one criterion of fairness over another, you will likely help some people and appear unfair to others. You should have a good reason why. And remember that you may not even be seeing an aspect of fairness that the other person deeply values.

Binmore provides a useful reminder: "When two people use fairness to resolve an everyday cooperation problem, I believe they are implicitly calculating the agreement they would reach if . . . their identities would be reassigned at random after the negotiation was over." That is at least a good starting point for discussing fairness.

11

Pathways to Effective Moral Thinking and Arguing

DEAR READER, YOU'VE HUNG IN THERE with me as we explored a number of moral frameworks—Kantian, Humean, utilitarian, virtue ethics, casuistry, and more. And you continued the journey as we examined how these frameworks can help us grapple with the wide range of challenges involved in making good moral decisions. Along this path, we considered some of the ways that thinking and talking about moral choices can go astray, and how we can make our moral reasoning more effective. And then we delved into the broader domain of values, and how they become organized in a mental and emotional matrix that often guides—or pushes—us as we face personal or political choices.

Maybe one of the moral frameworks you've learned about seems best suited to your mind and heart. But very few of us other than philosophers consciously choose a single moral framework. Instead, we gravitate toward one or another framework, guided largely by intuition, emotion, and nodal experiences, but then we tilt toward another when it feels better in a given situation.

If you're looking for a way to explain to a friend why one of the moral frameworks seems most compelling to you, ethicists Beauchamp and Childress propose a useful list of qualities that such a framework should have. In their view, a moral system is strong to the extent that it embodies:

- Clarity
- Internal consistency
- Comprehensiveness
- Simplicity
- Explanatory power
- Justificatory power
- Output power (i.e., it can cause you to rethink or change your principles)

I think you'll find that, whichever is your customary approach, it rates higher on some of these criteria than others. We expect a lot of a moral framework. None is simple or perfect. But creative moral thinking, using the strengths of several frameworks, can help you become a better thinker and communicator about moral issues that matter to you.

As we've seen, each moral framework emphasizes certain factors and unavoidably downplays others. Since each framework has particular strengths, we tend to hop around among them, landing on one for a time, then hopping to another in the effort to make and justify a particular decision. (The table on pages 134–136 may help you recall the tradeoffs among the frameworks.) But the key conclusion is that no moral framework or principle is going to align uniformly with your instincts and feelings. Life is just too complex for that.

Our personal identity is strongly bound up in our morals and values, so we don't change them easily. But that doesn't mean that arguing over moral issues is pointless. There are several mechanisms by which you might change your moral views, even on significant issues.

Sometimes, the person you argue with mentions important new facts that change how you see the problem. Maybe you feel that kids with special needs deserve accommodation and should get whatever help they need. But then you hear that a lot of parents let their kids who don't even have ADHD use medications just to try to improve their college test scores. That affects your view.

Or your argument partner may help you rotate the problem in your mind so that you see an entirely new angle. ("Veterans' preferences in government hiring aren't just a bonus for a few—they help encourage people to enlist in the armed forces to protect America.")

Or you may find that people whose morals you respect have altered their views, and that makes you curious about why. (Your minister has always said that we should have compassion for people in need, but now he says that even a compassionate nation must enforce its borders in a crisis.)

Or you may find that the moral issue is a different one than you thought. (You heard that security agencies routinely scrutinize social media posts, which you felt was a terrible incursion on freedom. Then you're told they focus on references to guns and planned violence, which makes the moral issue seem different.)

Or you find that the moral question implicates additional values that you hold dear but didn't realize were involved. (You felt the whole issue of who has a sufficient right to claim Native American ancestry is a bunch of liberal bunk. Then you learn that to many tribes, this is a deep matter of family, clan, honor, and tradition. Those are things you respect, and it affects your thinking.)

Finally, broad social trends can alter our morality or values. People talk with neighbors and observe what they do. They read and watch the media. Research suggests that people change faster when they get inputs from a variety of sources, including media, coworkers, and family.

Shifts in morals and values are happening around us—and inside us—from time to time.

The Continuum of Moral Judgment

THIS BOOK HAS EXPLORED both how to think about issues of morals and values and how to argue respectfully with others about them. But here is a final important point: As you argue, be conscious and deliberate about how far you want to go on the continuum of moral and value judgment.

Let me explain. Suppose that you feel strongly that it's morally wrong to kill animals for food. This might lead you to a number of different points along a continuum of judgments:

STEP 1: "I just prefer not to eat meat." (I prefer to avoid it, but I'll eat meat if a friend serves it for dinner. I don't want to act all high and mighty and make her feel bad.)

STEP 2: "I will never eat meat." (It just disgusts me to think about animals being killed.)

STEP 3: "I believe it's morally wrong to eat meat." (Having read about animal slaughter, I think it's ethically indefensible)

STEP 4: "I feel strongly that no one in our society should eat meat." (If I'm with others, I feel I ought to urge them to rethink what they're doing.)

STEP 5: "I just can't respect anyone who eats meat." (If you just avoid thinking about all the pain and slaughter, how can you call yourself a good person?)

STEP 6: "Our society should make people stop eating meat." (We have alternatives. We shouldn't knowingly tolerate such cruelty.)

As you think about each of these steps from personal preference, to principled disagreement, to coercing others, note that some steps are small and others quite large indeed. Be aware that we often slip unconsciously from Step 1 (personal disgust) to Step 3 (you are immoral if you don't agree with my disgust). But doing so is wrong. A thoughtful person might well say, "Personally, I'd never be able to shoot a deer. But I keep reading about how they're starving due to overpopulation, so I guess it's not really morally bad if others want to hunt them and then at least use the meat." Unfortunately, we often don't take the time to question ourselves in that way.

Then consider the move from Step 3 to Step 4 (since meat eating is wrong, I believe no one else should do it either). Some people feel that is judgmental and aggressive. But that, too, is mistaken. As I've noted, the very nature of a moral judgment (unlike taste) is that if it's wrong for me to do something, it's also wrong for you—assuming we are in the exact same circumstances. (If your health condition requires eating meat, then of course I see the exception.) Take this example: You really cannot say, "I believe it is morally wrong of me to slap my elderly grandmother, but I don't think ill of you for slapping her." Of course, you think so—that's what "morally wrong" means.

The following analogy highlights an important insight. The deeply Christian scholar C. S. Lewis said, "[Arguing morality] means trying to show that the other man is in the wrong. And there would be no sense in trying to do that unless we had some sort of agreement as to what Right and Wrong are; just as there would be no sense to saying that a footballer had committed a foul unless there was some agreement on the rules of football." Of course, we may disagree as to what constitutes a moral foul. But arguing that something is morally right inherently means that you believe others should see that, too.

Note especially that the move from Step 4 (I regard *x* as immoral) to Step 5 (so I must dislike anyone who does *x*) is a perilous one. In today's environment of public debate, almost every issue is moralized and polarized. That poses grave problems for personal relations and civic life. If you are going to dump your family and friends whenever they disagree with you on any of the top dozen issues of moral import in public debate, you may be very lonely. Try not to do that. Good people can disagree with one another.

Finally, moving from Step 5 (I can't respect people who do *x*) to Step 6 (they must be stopped) is fraught. Society does enforce lots of moral rules (against stealing, killing, or committing fraud, for instance), but it refrains from many more. Very few people would seriously propose banning meat-eating. But if you consider examples like abortion, or sexual relations with minors, or assisted suicide, many people feel the stakes are so high that society should indeed step in and prevent such acts. Deciding these issues wisely remains one of the core challenges of democracy.

The key point is that when you argue moral issues, try to be clear about just how far you are going—which steps in the continuum you really mean to take. And be candid about it. Sometimes, people use ambiguity to slough off moral issues. Suppose I tell a friend, "Nobody should ever hit a dog," and he responds, "So now you want to put me in jail because you don't like how I discipline my unruly dog Rex?" That's just a red herring. Deserving moral condemnation and deserving jail are different. We can be moral humans without demanding that society enforce all our morals against everyone else.

Taking Moral Initiative

MORALITY IS OFTEN CARICATURED as just an endless series of "Thou Shalt Nots" running contrary to human nature. I hope this book has shown that morality is a lot more. It's not just rules to prevent bad conduct. It also involves skills at thinking, feeling, and problem solving to promote helping, kindness, honesty, duty, fairness, and other values. Morality has an important aspirational dimension. At its heart, morality involves deciding what kind of person you will commit to being. And what kind of society you want to help—even in small ways—to create now and for future generations.

This latter aspirational goal is sometimes seen as the privilege of the affluent. A single working mom with three children who struggles to pay the bills probably can't take the time to volunteer for community organizations, mentor teens, go on a church mission abroad, and contribute to charities. Yet remarkably, some may! And has long been observed, poor people are often kinder than the rich. They are often more neighborly and help others in their community, because they know that almost everyone needs help at times. Some studies conclude that poor people tend to be more religious.

Even so, relatively affluent people have greater ability to do certain things, and as has been said, "Of those to whom much is given, much is expected." In any event, to the extent they can, people might want to consider aspirational questions such as these:

- Does my job contribute to meeting real human needs in some constructive way?

- Is there something I can do to make the organization where I work more ethical?

- Do I have skills that a charitable organization could use?

- If I'm complaining about problems in my community, what could I do to help?

- Do I know someone who needs help that I could provide?

- What could I do to make society fairer and better?

- What do I do in terms of paying taxes, voting, and supporting our armed forces?

- Can I afford to give more to charities, and which ones would do the most good?

- If I have children or grandchildren, am I teaching them good moral values?

- If I can't do more now, can I see a time in my life when I will?

These are just a few examples of aspirational questions; you'll be able to think of others that may be more relevant to your values and life. But taking moral initiative in some way is an important feature of a moral life, even if we never totally succeed.

Morality and Values: Some Takeaways

IT SHOULD NOW BE OBVIOUS: Doing the right thing is a complicated subject! There can be no cookbook guide to thinking or arguing about morals and values. I hope this book has provided you with some tools to help understand why you handle moral and value-laden questions as you do and what some alternatives might be. When you find yourself arguing with others, here are a few things to recall.

1. Morality is not just one thing. It is a system of emotions, thoughts, and behaviors emanating from a suite of values, such as empathy, altruism, reciprocity, sacredness, fairness, honesty, and loyalty. People weigh these values differently in various situations. Sure, a few people are recurrently selfish, dishonest, and immoral. But most people you disagree with are usually moral—they just weigh values differently in a given situation. So, arguments about morals can be engaged in rationally, even when people's values clash.

2. Each of the main moral frameworks rests on deep insights and fulfills some part of our inner desire that morality make sense:

- Those who draw primarily on religion have deep faith that they act as they do because it fulfills God's plan and will for humans on earth.

- The Kantian approach satisfies our desire for clear, consistent rules based on our urge to do good and a recognition that we often can't control the consequences of our actions.

- The Humean approach realistically employs our strong, instinctive moral feelings. No matter how much we "noodle" an issue, we want to do what ultimately feels right.

- The utilitarian view embodies the insight that at the end of the day, being moral means at least trying to produce the best outcome overall for the affected people.

- Moral relativism is not really a moral system and is hard to pin down. It first denies the value of any moral judgments on the ground that they are merely subjective, which says little. But its stronger core principle is tolerance. It says, "Don't be too sure you're right; others may have good reasons to differ."

- Virtue ethics is the practical approach of watching those you and others believe are good people and generally trying to emulate them.

- Casuistry is a flexible approach to moral thinking that helps us reconcile a range of moral imperatives and creatively solve problems.

3. You can draw useful insights from each of the leading moral frameworks. We often mix and match them as we wrestle with moral issues. That is one reason why we are unavoidably inconsistent in our moral thinking.

4. Bear in mind that whenever you argue moral questions, strong emotions and a sense of personal identity are involved. We all want to be moral, so your argument partner may feel that their identity and dignity are at issue. Be respectful.

5. Ask the other person not just what they think is the right moral answer, but *why* it's right. You will quickly find out whether they are thinking in terms of gut feelings, rules, or consequences. And ask, "What change in the facts might make you change your conclusion?"

6. Acknowledge the tension between several good values or moral factors. In most situations, there isn't just one valid consideration. Moral decisions are hard precisely because they make us balance or trade off one value for another.

7. Having to balance moral values does not mean that you throw up your hands and say, "Who's to judge?" Being a human with moral autonomy means you do judge. Moral people stand for something. Judging for yourself doesn't include the right to force others to comply with your standards. But neither are you required to give up your convictions.

8. Be mindful of the cognitive biases that can beset us all in thinking about moral issues. We evaluate action differently than inaction. We weigh possible losses more heavily than gains. We stress effects that will occur soon and ignore later effects. We assign blame for bad side effects but don't give equal credit for good side effects. And we tend to think that most others agree with us. You

can't eliminate these biases, but you can try to temper them as you weigh moral issues.

9. Politics is an important domain of morality because we all want society to reflect our values—to be a "good" society. Political liberals and conservatives disagree for many good reasons. One of them is that they tend to weigh moral factors differently. For example, liberals tend to stress empathy and avoiding harm to people in need, and tend to have a higher threshold before they're bothered by unusual behavior. Conservatives are more easily offended by socially odd behavior, and they tend to stress respect for social norms, adhering to right conduct, avoiding dangers and not degrading social life. It's not as if one is a good, moral tribe while the other is an immoral tribe. They each need to listen carefully to the valid reasons the other may be troubled by something.

10. Research involving huge numbers of people participating in simulations such as the Ultimatum Game and the Dictator Game has shown that people's natural instincts may be more moral than cynics contend. But as the Trolley Problem research shows, we also are dominated by emotions and have trouble "keeping our eye on the ball" in deciding what's right.

11. To be effectively moral, you must care to learn the key facts about the situations you're called upon to judge and resolve. What actually happened, what science actually knows, what are the real, predictable results of your choices—such factual matters strongly affect the quality of your moral decision-making.

12. To be effectively moral, you also must think logically—at least as much as is realistically feasible. Beware the seductive and common fallacies that often corrupt moral decision-making.

13. In moral arguments, words really matter. Be thoughtful and judicious. Resist the impulse to engage in verbal escalation, and avoid the careless use of intimidating power words.

14. Bear in mind the important differences between conduct that violates customs, morals, or law. Which bucket you believe bad behavior falls into is a key threshold judgment. Some conduct violates only one type of mandate, while other conduct violates all of them. But beware of converting every breach of social custom you don't like into a charge that the offenders are also immoral.

15. Take values seriously. Your sense of identity is bound up with the values you hold dear, and that is true of other people, too. Bear in mind that people's genes, biology, personality disposition, and values are deeply interwoven. That's

one reason political liberals and political conservatives differ; they react viscerally and intensely to different values being at risk. Those are powerful forces to contend with.

16. Your values are not a random assortment; they cohere into a value matrix. It's important to understand how some values in that matrix relate to, reinforce, or undercut others. And when you try to persuade someone else on a moral or value-laden issue, you must frame the question so as to conscript values they really care about.

17. Fairness is one of the most critical concepts in social life. But it doesn't help just to righteously exclaim, "That's so unfair!" Arguments about fairness won't get anywhere unless the arguers recognize that we shuffle our criteria of fairness in various contexts. We demand that decisions be made based on merit, reciprocity, relative benefit, equal outcomes, equal opportunity, recompense for past ills, advancing a social goal, following a process, or in a way that yields consistency. The hard work is in arguing *why* your preferred criterion is fairest in the situation and why other criteria are less fair.

18. Finally, relish your arguments over morals and values! They are an important part of what it means to be human and to live in a community with others you care about.

Acknowledgments

W RITING A BOOK LIKE THIS necessarily draws on what the author has learned, not only from books and journals, but from living one's life. And so, I start by deeply thanking my wife, Ava Feiner, a charismatic, beautiful, funny, and loving person in every way, and one of the most incandescently brilliant minds I've ever encountered. Since marrying quite young, we've puzzled through life together. With her Yale and Harvard degrees and free-roaming mind, she has helped me learn more while exploring issues together than I could from a library of books.

Thanks to our children, Kim Stromberg Waldmann and Eric Stromberg, who seem to have emerged from the womb as skeptical questioners, ever challenging just why their parents perceive so little. They are now accomplished and delightful adults. Bless them and their wonderful spouses, John Waldmann and Jen Stromberg—and their glorious children, Levi Waldmann, and Blake, Jackson, and James Stromberg.

Thanks to my late mother, Greta Stromberg—fashion model, painter, sportswoman, seeker, and polymath, a whirling bundle of creative energy, a great mom who radiated love of life. And thanks to my late father, George Stromberg, who worked his way up from poverty to become a respected lawyer. Dad was an old-school, right-stuff kind of guy. He had a high sense of moral justice and treated everyone with respect. You were supposed to do the right thing because, well, it was only right and fair. And he always had the twinkle of love in his eye.

Thanks to my wonderful sisters, Denise Schwartz and Christine Bakacs. It's great fun to see shared genes and the environment interact in so many surprising ways.

Thanks to my late parents-in-law, Lola and Ignace Feiner, who endured so much and yet retained their warmth and optimism.

Thanks to many friends over the years, who naturally taught me a lot about human nature, right, wrong, and how people see things. I can't name them all, but thanks at least to: Helen Atkeson, Meaghan Atkinson, Susan Blum, Doug Colton, Keith Dunder, Omar (Clark) Fisher, Dave Flitter, Keith Ghezzi, Matt Gutwein, Bill Kauffman, Susan Kratz, Frank Mallon, Phil Moon, Reid Morgan, Joel Perwin, Doug Peterson, Llew Pritchard, Penny Rezet, Jeff Schneider, Howard Silver, Michael Snow, Peter Stokes, Marna Tucker, Bryant Welch, Al Wellner, Michael Williams, and Ron Wisor.

Thanks (mightily) to my two fabulous assistants spanning a period of decades, Melissa Gross, and before her, Karen Nemes. Both are smart, feisty, and yet kind. Their friendship, day after day, has been an invaluable blessing.

Thanks to my teachers and professors, who are so warmly recalled. They planted the seeds in so many people that grew to an immense forest. Among the special ones to me:

- At Eastchester High School: Marie Carrera, John Dougan, Suzanne McGrath, and James Sloan
- At Yale University: Isaac Kramnick, Frederick Oscanyan, and Alfred Stepan
- At Harvard Law School: Archibald Cox, Alan Stone, and James Vorenberg

And finally, massive thanks to my editor, Karl Weber at Rivertowns Books. He combines rare intelligence, diligence, professionalism, and kindness to the fragile authorial ego. He guided me with much wisdom, without which this book would be far poorer.

CLIFF STROMBERG

January, 2026

Notes

Virtually all the sources cited in the following notes are listed fully in the Bibliography, beginning on page 342.

The notes are of three kinds: (1) Source citations for quotations appearing in the text. (2) Explanation or commentary relating to topics in the text, generally citing specific sources. (3) References to books and articles for readers interested in delving more deeply into related topics. Notes that cite a book in its entirety generally fall into category #3.

Introduction

12   A term often used interchangeably with morals is *ethics*: Our word *ethics* has roots in three Greek words meaning roughly habit, custom, and character (what a person habitually does). Hence, ethics came to mean the proper way of acting, or the field of thinking about proper conduct. *Morality* is derived from a Latin word meaning mores, customs or right ways of conducting oneself. Many people today, including scholars, use *morality* and *ethics* interchangeably. See, e.g., B. Williams, *Morality: An Introduction to Ethics*; Harman, *The Nature of Morality* 1 ("This book is a philosophical introduction to ethics"); Geisler 14 ("Ethics deals with what is morally right and wrong"); Grannan, "What's the Difference Between Morality and Ethics?" 1 ("most ethicists... consider the terms interchangeable"); Mosely 17 ("Ethics is defined as a set of moral principles dealing with what is good and bad behavior"); Darwall et al. *Moral Discourse and Practice*, whose back cover says its subject is "What are ethical judgments about?"

Nevertheless, *morality* tends to be used to refer to personal principles and values, while *ethics* refers to more formal, public rules like "medical ethics" or "legal ethics." At times ethics includes vaguer, non-codified concepts such as "journalistic ethics" or "environmental ethics." But "generally, it is said that ethics are societal decisions with rigor and structure. Morals are more self-determined." (Oxford Learning College, "Ethics Versus Morals: What's the Difference?") In reading ancient Greek works, one must bear in mind that the Greek *ethike arete* meant "excellence of character" not "moral virtue." Indeed, "Plato and Aristotle [had] . . . no word for morality" as we know it. (D. Russell 151.)

12   **And there are other fields of ethics—like "Christian Ethics" and "Jewish Ethics":** As to Jewish ethics, see, for example: Claussen; Borowitz & Schwartz; Mittelman; Ariel; *Journal of Jewish Ethics.*

As to Christian ethics, see, for example: Heimbach; Grudem; Niebuhr; Geisler; O'Donovan. Christian ethics (like Jewish ethics) is more like a field than a doctrine. For example, there is the Christian ethics drawn mainly from Augustine and Aquinas, or the Christian humanists like Erasmus, or Luther, or Calvin, or the Jesuits, or Anglican rationalism, or Methodism, or modern Catholicism, or Evangelism, or other movements. Their ethical beliefs can differ in significant ways. (See Heimbach Ch. 5.) But an important common theme is that "whereas Christian ethics starts with revelation, philosophical ethics starts with human experience." (Id. 234.) There is another literature from the less theological perspective of "social ethics" or "practical Christian ethics." (See Heimbach Ch. 8.) Provocatively, the scholar Huston Smith (2001) 248 says, "Ethics is absent from polytheism. It is inseparable from monotheism."

A Note on What's Missing: Morality is so vast a subject that this book cannot possibly address it comprehensively. Just for example, I do not discuss aspects such as these: How do we know what we think we know about right and wrong (epistemology)? Do we possess free will? What are the different roles of guilt, shame, and aspiration? How do we use excuses, rationalizations, denials, and blame-shifting? How could we elevate the level of moral thinking and conduct in society? What dynamics lead to true amorality or evil? When do we "overmoralize" issues? How could our educational system teach moral "competency" without encroaching on parents' values? What should scientists do if a potential discovery might be used for both good or evil purposes? What economic principles would reinforce social morality? How moral should we expect society to be, and what costs are we willing to pay? What moral issues are properly decided by individuals versus by society? Are there "moral" principles in international relations, and what are they?

The biggest limitation of this book is that it addresses almost exclusively the morals and values of people in modern, Western, and wealthy societies, which are quite unusual in worldwide and historical context. For a compendious but lively analysis of this, see Joesph Henrich's *The Weirdest People in the World* (Picador, 2020).

1. Morality and Human Nature

15   **"The need of an external moral order":** William James (1963), Lecture 3.

15   **Research studies confirm the commonsense fact:** Greene (2013) 45, citing Dunbar. Other studies suggest the very high number cited by Dunbar (two-thirds of all conversational time involves morality in some way) is overstated. See, e.g., several studies by Atari et al. (2023) finding people *recalling* that about 20-25% of their talk has some moral element, while on-line content assessment suggests it is more like 2-5%. But such ratings depend on what one calls a "moral element." Saying that "Joe is a back-stabbing liar" surely qualifies. But "Joe is just a jerk" might or might not, depending on what gives rise to that judgment.

15   **A leading theorist says:** Gert 4.

16   **But most share the core concept . . . [of] right and wrong:** *Oxford English Dictionary.* For readers interested in learning more about the related topics of *epistemology* and *metaethics*, see Jackson & Smith (Eds.) 3-152, 681-763; Darwall (1992); Harman; Searle (1964); Mackie; R. Hare (1952); B. Williams (1972). "Moral . . . is an orientation toward understandings about what is right and wrong, just and unjust, that are not established by our own actual desires or preferences but instead are believed to exist apart from them, providing standards by which our desires and preferences can themselves be judged." (C. Smith 8; see also Keller 151-152.) Morality establishes "commitments" and "entitlements" and leads to interpersonal "score-keeping." (See, generally, Brandom.)

16 **"Morality is primarily concerned":** Gert 9, 13.

16 **Psychologist Joshua Greene says, "The essence of morality is altruism":** Greene (2013) 23. See also Warnock; Hamilton; Kitcher: Dugatkin ("Altruism is about incurring some personal cost in order to help others, and that is close to what most of us mean when we speak of doing good").

16 **"the *sine qua non* of all things moral":** Tomasello 1.

16 **Some humanists may say that morality should focus:** Lakoff & Johnson (1999) 290.

16 **As Patricia Churchland says:** Churchland (2019) 169. See also Prinz 180.

16 **Greene offers this nutshell definition:** Greene (2001) 23. See also Gazzaniga 166; Hinde 21; Haidt (2012) xviii. This concept of morality as a system yielding *mutual* benefits is far from Shakespeare's epithet in *Richard III*: "Conscience is but a word that cowards have devised at first to keep the strong in check."

16 **In this sense, morality is seen as a "theory of rational behavior":** Harsanyi 43.

16 **Morality evinces "shared values":** Tomasello 114.

16 **Rabbi Jonathan Sacks goes further:** Sacks (2020) 12.

17 **Usually, you get moral credit only for [acts] . . . beyond the call of duty:** See Svoboda, citing Franco et al.; Duntley & Buss 32; Beauchamp & Childress 47-48; sources cited in Heimbach 245.

17 **"Identity is a tapestry of beliefs":** Boghossian & Lindsay 158. As Hinde states: "Moral development includes the incorporation of precepts into the self-system, so that thinking morally can occur spontaneously, without reflection. Ideally, moral behavior then becomes how individuals *automatically* behave, and how they *want* to behave." 48. See also Stanley et al.; Lefebvre and Krettenauer.

17 **And researchers find that "moral character traits are among the most important determinants":** Atari et al. For further study of the issues around this aspect of morality, see Kenny 62-65 and *passim*.

17 **As psychologist Jonathan Haidt says, "We're born to be righteous":** Haidt (2012) 31.

17 **As we try to get a handle on the idea of morality, we often resort to metaphors:** For an extensive discussion of metaphors, see Lakoff & Johnson (1999 and 2003). See also M. Johnson 179-180. For an interesting cross-cultural perspective, consider the work of linguistics scholar Anna Wierzbicka, who examined how the words used in various cultures to describe our *moral capacity* carry different meanings. The common English term "moral sense" implies a quick, intuitive perception (like a "sense of rhythm" or a "sense of smell"). But Wierzbicka says this intuitive term actually doesn't have a good cognate in most European languages, in Chinese, and in some other languages. For example, in Spanish, the phrase corresponding to "moral sense" is *encuesta de juicio*

moral, which might be translated as "inquiry" or "survey" of "moral judgment," thus implying not an intuitive sense but a more careful, rational process of questioning and judging. Those are quite different concepts of what goes on when one makes a moral decision. Researchers use a "moral sense test" to survey people around the world. See moralsensetest.com, but their responses are likely more than just intuition.

18   **Thus, as Tomasello says, "Human morality is not a monolith":** Tomasello 128.

18   **And yet, when we make moral decisions, we try to do so in a . . . way that can . . . persuade others:** Singer (2011) 109-110 ("In making ethical decisions, I am trying to make decisions that can be defended to others"). See, generally, Uhlman et al.; Mercier & Sperber; Haack; Mikhail (2007); Paxton & Greene.

18   **The Greek philosopher Plato famously depicted the soul as a chariot:** *Phaedrus*, in Cooper (Ed.).

18   **But in the 18th century, the influential philosopher David Hume:** Hume, *Treatise*, Book 2, Part 3. Sec 3.

18   **And in our own day, social scientists have portrayed morality as just a "thin veneer":** This concept was first ascribed to Thomas Henry Huxley, and the metaphor to Frans de Waal. At times, it has been expressed by Robert Wright, George Williams, and others. It has been criticized based on research by de Waal (2006), Trivers (1971), Tomasello, Turiel (2002), Franco & Zimbardo (2016), and others. Philosophers tend to discount it, believing that deep moral reasoning does occur. See, e.g., Korsgaard (2006); Kamm; Rawls.

19   **As Darwin wrote in his notebook:** Darwin, Notebook M (1838).

19   **Yet researchers have observed . . . self-sacrificing behavior in species:** See Kitcher Ch. 1-2; Christakis 207; Shermer 354-361.

19   **The keys to these behaviors seem to be:** de Waal (2006); Tomasello 21; Trivers (1971); Hamilton; Boehm.

19   **As Patricia Churchland concludes: "In the wild as well as captivity":** Churchland (2011) xii, italics added. "At the very least, the data suggest that there are evolutionary precursors to human morality." Id. 166.

20   **And dog trainers reportedly say:** Boehm 22.

20   **Apes seem to make up with one another:** Boehm 118-125.

20   **Hence, most scholars hedge:** Sapolsky 523. See also Prinz 259-260.

20   **In the view of philosopher Thomas Nagel:** Nagel 16. See also Kitcher 19.

20   **Jesse Prinz notes that "reciprocal altruism is actually rare":** Prinz 247. Others interpret the term more broadly, to include many kinds of animal behavior. See *Wikipedia*, Reciprocal Altruism.

20   **Darwin saw this long ago:** *Descent of Man*, Ch. 4. Darwin elaborated, speaking of the "ever-enduring social instinct," man's "deep regard for the good opinion of his fellows," the role of "remorse . . . or shame," and finally the development of "the conscience [that] looks backward and serves as a guide for the future." But he seems to have had some doubt about the selection/survival advantages of altruism, except via kin selection. Later, in his Notebooks, he summed up: "[There are] two classes of moralists; one says our rule of life is what will produce the greatest happiness. The other says we have a moral sense. But my view unites both and shows them to be almost identical." On these themes in Darwin, see S. Uchii.

20   **Indeed, only very limited moral behavior has been observed even in . . . chimpanzees:** Sapolsky 483-487. See also de Waal (2005) Ch. 5. Note the differences, however, between the evolved state of monkeys and of chimps. De Waal says that "all scientists who've set out to find consolation [of stressed group mates] in monkeys have come up empty-handed. . . . Monkeys fail to provide reassurance even if their own offspring has been bitten. They do protect them, but show none of the cuddling and stroking with which an ape mother calms down an upset youngster. This makes ape behavior so much more humanlike." Id. 193.

20   **The leading researcher Frans de Waal has documented "the exchange of food for grooming":** de Waal (2007) 44; de Waal (1996). Apparently, this is more common among bonobos.

20   **But apes don't seem to cooperate much:** Tomasello 24. See also Warneken & Tomasello (2006); Warneken et al. (2007).

21   **Moreover, caged chimps usually *will not* pull a lever:** Tomasello 30.

21   **Some researchers report that monkeys will starve themselves:** Harris 170; Masserman et al.

21   **As de Waal vividly states, "Chimpanzee group life is a [constant] market in power":** de Waal (2007) 2-3; see also de Waal (2005) Ch. 2.

21   **Only occasionally do chimps cooperate:** Tomasello 25, 61; Hatemi (2011) 54; Brosnan & de Waal. But they will help injured troop mates (de Waal (2005) Ch 1). Bonobos may be a bit more cooperative. (See B. Hare.) And one meta-review of studies concluded that "reciprocity in primates is present but underestimated." Schweinfurth & Call.

21   **As Tomasello says, for example, "It is inconceivable":** Tomasello, quoted by Haidt (2012) 217.

21   **Others report that in general, "chimps simply do not seem to care":** Gigerenzer (2007) 66, citing Silk et al.

21   **He interprets such behaviors as demonstrating . . . "the building blocks of morality":** de Waal (2005) 225. They may also help others to avoid a fire (de Waal (1996) 83). See also Christakis 217-227, describing "friendships" among whales and among elephants.

21   **He also sees them as having "primitive social rules":** de Waal (1996) 171-173. See also Hauser 337-339, 373-374, 394-397.

21   **And one widely noted (but also questioned) study reported . . . a rudimentary sense of fairness:** Brosnan & de Waal, cited in Shermer (2015) 360; Hauser 394; Sapolsky 483-487. But demurring to this, see Tomasello 25, 33, 76-77, and Kaiser et al. Some studies suggest that crows and dogs can intuit this sense of fairness (Sapolsky 765).

21   **Others are even more skeptical.** See Jensen & Silk, arguing that chimps lack the cognition needed for truly reciprocal altruism.

21   **Christopher Boehm says that:** Boehm 118.

22   **Many scholars believe that a "great leap forward":** See Trivers (1971); Hamilton; Boehm Ch. 12; Mosely 19-21.

22   **And bonding/empathy/altruism developed a powerful biological reinforcer . . . [that one can turn] "on or off like a garden hose" :** Zak xi. It has been wrongly called the "love molecule" or the "moral molecule." But for a discussion of its effects on attachment, see Churchland (2011) Ch. 2.

22   **Initially, as psychologist Paul Bloom notes:** Bloom (2013) 172.

22   **Thus, "humans are inclined to come up with systems based on indirect reciprocity ":** Boehm 182. See also Alexander; Cosmides & Tooby.

22   **Scholars such as William Hamilton:** See Ale et al.; Trivers (1971); Hamilton; Alexander; Axelrod; Boehm.

22   **James Q. Wilson vividly points out:** Wilson 67.

22   **This gave rise, according to many scholars, to *reciprocal altruism*:** See Trivers (1971); Axelrod; Hamilton; Gazzaniga; Kitcher; Batson; Dugatkin.

22   **As Darwin observed, "Selfish and contentious people will not cohere":** *Descent of Man* 134.

23   **And as Joshua Greene says:** Greene 24.

23   **Reciprocal altruism has been documented:** Boehm 192; Henrich et al. (2004).

23   **The key moral mechanisms that developed . . . were empathy, reciprocity, and fairness:** Thus "empathic concern produces altruistic motivation." (Batson et al. 443; see also Nowak; Hoffman.) Kitcher distinguishes among biological altruism, behavioral altruism, and psychological altruism, the latter adding insight (Kitcher 18-20). Prinz believes guilt is a more powerful motivator than empathy (Prinz 105).

23   **Empathy . . . is not "catching another's emotion":** Batson et al. 444: "Empathy does not refer to 'catching' emotions (emotional contagion) but to responding emotionally to the perceived needs of another." Indeed, "The link between empathy and compassion . . . is far more nuanced than many people believe." (Bloom (2013) 43.) See also Vollhardt.

23   **And then there is fairness.** Tomasello 1-2. See also T. Singer et al. Empathy is strongly affected by judgments of "deservingness," which feed into fairness (Bloom (2013) 44).

23   **Overall, there are dozens of ways:** Tomasello 2, 77.

23   **This [the extension of fairness] represented, according to evolutionary biologist Marc Hauser . . . "a uniquely human cognitive adaptation":** Hauser 82. See also Trivers (1971); Bartels (2008). Churchland (2011) 9 sums up the accumulated adaptations thus: "What we humans call ethics or morality is a four-dimensional scheme for social behavior that is shaped by interlocking brain processes: (1) *caring,* . . . (2) *recognition of others' psychological states,* . . . (3) *problem solving in a social context,* . . . and (4) learning social practices."* (Italics in original.)

23   **Indeed, neuroimaging studies reveal:** Harris (2010) 92.

23   **This sad defect [psychopathy] in normal human capacity:** Churchland (2011) xv, 41, 130; Shermer 345-347; Haidt 73. For a checklist of diagnostic traits, see Bloom (2016) 197-199, citing R. Hare, (2003) *Manual for the Revised Psychopathy Checklist.* Multi-Health Systems.

23   **By the time modern humans emerged as a species:** Tomasello 129.

24   **In a similar vein, human development expert Elliot Turiel:** Turiel (2002) 24.

24   **Cooperation and selfless action for the group only continue to work:** Thus, "punishment allows the evolution of cooperation." Boyd and Richerson 166; see also Kitcher 87-92; Fehr and Gachter ("Fairness and cheater detection are specialized capacities that support reciprocal altruism); Cosmides and Tooby 110 ("The survey results were surprisingly clear cut. They all supported . . . the hypothesis that punitive sentiments evolved to eliminate the fitness advantage that would accrue to a free-rider society.")

24 **He concludes that . . . "everywhere hunter-gatherers do in fact readily punish":** Boehm 15, 196.

24 **Thus, as Paul Zak notes:** Zak 85. Id. 175 also notes the extraordinarily high level or moral "compliance" in close-knit cultural groupings with very clear conduct rules, such as Jewish diamond exchanges and Japanese sushi markets.

24 **Effective punishment for antisocial behavior:** Boehm 84-87, 158-159; Shermer 52, 364; Fehr & Gachter; Greene 41.

24 **Today, game theorists have used computer simulations:** Ale et al. See, generally, Binmore.

24 **When experimenters conduct such games:** Christakis 310-315.

24 **Importantly, in the real world it has been found:** Greene 71-72.

24 **As Churchland says, "Morality in humans . . . is intensely biological":** Churchland (2011) xvii. See also Cosmides & Tooby; Zak. But culture also reinforces and shapes whatever moral impulses biology kindles. (See Richerson and Boyd (2004).

25 **In today's wealthy, industrialized nations:** See, generally, Beauchamp & Childress, Ch. 1; Wilson.

25 **Indeed, "countless ethnographies have [confirmed] that punishment . . . is essential":** Hauser 101. For a summary of how these sanctions apply in premodern societies, see Boehm 195-201.

25 **Nicholas Christakis surveyed a range of cultures:** Christakis 315.

25 **Reciprocity is a core component of the moral systems:** Hauser 99-103, 391-403. See also Gintis et al.; Axelrod; Axelrod & Hamilton; Trivers (1971); Fuller 11 ("The literature of the morality of duty is filled with references to the . . . principle of reciprocity.").

25 **As the ancient Roman leader Cicero said:** *De Officiis* (On Duty), quoted in Ridley 104.

25 **Indeed, when experiments test what happens when subjects engage in bargaining :** Hauser 287. Others see "a signature of a uniquely human cognitive adaptation. Whereas we inherited a largely selfish nature from our ancestors, we evolved a uniquely human psychology that predisposes us toward a different form of altruistic behavior— strong reciprocity." Id. 82.

25 **When researcher Robert Axelrod:** Axelrod. See also Binmore 78.

26 **As mathematician-economist-ethicist Kenneth Binmore concludes:** Binmore 15.

26 **For example, in the "Ultimatum Game":** See Greene 57, 70-73; Bloom (2013) 73-77; Sanfey et al.; Oosterbeck at al.; Henrich; *Wikipedia,* Ultimatum Game.

26 **Paul Bloom reports that "there have been more than a hundred published studies":** Bloom (2013) 73-74. See also Guala & Mittone.

26 **Marc Hauser concludes that:** Hauser 83, 91.

27 **What's more, a massive genetic study found:** B. Wallace.

27 **People will pay for shared public goods:** Greene 70-76; Bloom (2013) 88-92.

27 **Indeed, research confirms the correlation:** Bloom (2013) 90-91; Boehm, Ch. 9; Baker; Sapolsky 497.

27 **As Darwin said, "Ultimately, our moral sense or conscience":** *Descent of Man* 137, quoted by Haidt (2012) 226. See also Hinde Ch. 2; Prinz 270-271. But Thomas Henry Huxley believed that humans are inherently amoral and all morality must be learned. See Huxley.

28 **Many people with deep religious convictions consider the process of evolution:** See F. Collins; Keller; Biologos; Peterson 469-510; Van Biema; Pope Francis ("Evolution is not inconsistent with the notion of creation."). Others, of course, have disagreed, prominently among them Richard Dawkins and Christopher Hitchens.

28 **As Churchland says, "Conscience is a brain construct":** Churchland (2019) 147.

28 **Most people believed that human life:** Leviathan Bk.1, Ch. 13.

29 **Researchers in ethnography and sociology delighted in describing far-off cultures with "totally different" . . . morality:** See Christakis, Ch. 1, referring to Clifford Geertz, Margaret Mead, Ruth Benedict, and Bronislaw Malinowski. See also Mosely 336-348. As seminal anthropologist Frans Boas asserted, "Civilization is not something absolute but . . . is relative . . . and our ideas and conceptions are true only as far as our civilization goes." (Boas 589.) Some scholars like Benedict championed what came to be known as "cultural relativism," which entailed not judging other cultures' morality. She believed that each culture chooses certain qualities from "the great arc of potentialities" and a culture is like an individual personality writ large. (Benedict, *Patterns of Culture* (1934).) Mead's influential book *Coming of Age in Samoa* (1928) was seen as touting something akin to a moral paradise. But Mead's work was later strongly challenged by others such as Derek Freeman, who in turn was critiqued by Eleanor Leacock. A later review by Martin Orans found even further defects in Mead's work. In a 2016 survey of several hundred anthropologists, *two thirds* faulted Mead for "romanticizing" some aspects of Samoan life and morals, and not being scientifically rigorous. See Horowitz et al.; Edgerton. See, generally, Brown, *Human Universals* (1999).

29 **Thus: "our moral faculty is equipped with a *universal moral grammar*":** Hauser xviii. This is a widely used analogy. See, e.g., Dwyer; Mikhail (2007); Bloom (2013) 5. But it has also been criticized. (See Churchland (2011) 111.) Hauser's "Moral Sense Test" has been used by tens of thousands of people across more than 120 countries. See moralsensetest.com.

30 **Many people make the added mistake of inferring that if morality isn't *precisely uniform* [it can't be objective]:** From a philosophical view, see, e.g., Mackie; Rorty (1982 and 1989); Harman; Prinz. Such assertions are beset by many flaws. They often derive ultimately from the sense that finding some historical or cultural exceptions voids the commonality of morality. But deniers of common moral values are vague about whether they deny any general norms or just the uniformity of specifics. Does it really impair the universal moral principle "Don't kill innocent people" if we find that the special rules for exculpation due to "self-defense" vary a bit between two countries?

30 **Instead, "we must look at the deep structure of human social contracts":** Binmore 14.

30 **As philosopher Mary Warnock says, "Radical [moral] relativism denies":** Warnock 179. See also Boehm 185-212; Aknin et al.; Jensen; C. S. Lewis, in Peterson 243; Gert 4. Sacks 259, 299 cites a study across 60 cultures that identified "seven moral rules found all around the world." They are "Help your family; help your group; return favors; be brave; defer to superiors; divide resources fairly; and respect others' property." Brown, in his major work, *Human Universals* 8, identified hundreds of common and recurring features of societies, including many that had a moral quality. Henrich et al. found that in *all* the societies they studied, people "care about fairness and reciprocity, are willing to change the distribution of material outcomes . . . at a personal cost to themselves, and reward those who act in a pro-social manner while punishing those who do not, even when the actions are costly." See also Gintis et al.

30 **In fact, specific differences are noticeable:** See Christakis; Johnson 155-162; Beauchamp and Childress; Gert 4. As Marc Hauser 4 says, "Our moral faculty is equipped with a universal set of rules, with each culture setting up particular exceptions to those rules." Aknin et al. surveyed 130 countries and found the common result that people who give more to charity are happier.

31 **So before we say that moral frameworks are just relative:** See Brown; Shweder (1991); Haidt (2012) 115; Sapolsky 498.

32 **As C. S. Lewis said, "Think of a country":** Quoted in Peterson et al. (Eds.) 243.

32 **Binmore says, "I think we care":** Binmore 15.

33 **There is a whole dimension of truly evil people and evil acts:** For an extensively documented exploration of this, see A. Miller (Ed.). See also Tancredi. Sociopathy is apparently fairly strongly heritable or genetically influenced. (Churchland (2011) 41.) Prinz 42-43 says that "psychopaths present an important test case for ethical theory. . . . They seem to comprehend moral values but they are utterly indifferent to them. . . . The psychopath can repeat the words and glibly say that he understands, and there is no way for him to realize that he does not understand." This highlights the important question: to what degree is a moral sense cognitive or affective or both? Can you really "understand" kindness or mercy if you have no desire to give it and don't feel what it would be like to need it or expect it?

33 **Thinking about morals in children was long dominated [by Piaget and Kohlberg]. Both held the view:** Hauser 16. See Piaget; Kohlberg. Piaget basically saw three moral stages in children: ages 0-5 (pre-moral); 5-9 (heteronomous, i.e. relying on parental rules); and 10+ (autonomous, i.e. beginning to formulate their own rules). Kohlberg saw six stages, but in three pairs (pre-conventional, conventional and post-conventional). They progress from an "obedience and punishment" orientation to "universal ethical principles."

34 **As brain scientist Robert Sapolsky says:** 479. See also Turiel Ch. 5.

34 **For example, Marc Hauser says that "even young children":** Hauser 21. See also Bloom (2013) 99; Kane 206; Flanagan 183-185. There is some evidence that young children have "a bias to consider actions worse than omissions" with the same effect. (Hauser 207.)

34 **Normal children by about age one or two:** For sources for this paragraph, see: Hinde 48-51; Tomasello 4; Bloom (2013) 25-29, 49-57, 98-99; Sapolsky 484; Gazzaniga 145; Warneken & Tomasello (2006); Greene 471.

34 **Even young children show some guilt over misbehavior:** Bloom (2013) 55-57.

34 **In sum, the child's "attachment [to parents] begets caring":** Churchland 149. See also Carey 169-170.

34 **Next, children develop what Tomasello calls "two person morality":** For this paragraph, see Tomasello 48, 70, 110-117; Bloom (2013) 50-56; Hauser 255-260; Hinde 48-53; Warneken & Tomasello (2006 and 2007).

35 **They also like to see rules obeyed:** Bloom (2013) 95-97; Tomasello 111; Cosmides & Tooby. They seem to judge based on who will feel bad, not the authority for the rule. Nucci.

35   **Researcher Elliot Turiel found:** Turiel 107-110. See also M. Johnson (2014) 34-40; Prinz 36-37, 116-117; Smetana & Braeges.

35   **But more recent research show that as early as age five:** Hauser 207; Haidt (2012) 11.

35   **Over time, "what grows in the child":** Hauser 263. These young children both offer and accept less in Ultimatum Game scenarios than do older children. Hauser 261.

35   **Children also learn a great deal about kindness . . . through play with other kids:** Haidt (2012) 7-9; Bloom 61-64 (2013).

35   **Importantly, kids progress from a simple notion:** Bloom (2013) 60-64, 76-82.

36   **In sum, in developing their concepts of morality:** Bloom (2013) Ch. 7; Hauser, Ch. 5; Carey 159-170; Turiel 111.

36   **As Paul Bloom explains, children develop:** Bloom (2013) 5.

36   **In time, children become . . . little "moral philosophers":** Kohlberg (1968). Many have noted that even small children understand that they should give *reasons* for their conduct. Bloom (2013) 214-217; Mercier & Sperber 291-295. See, generally, Batson.

2. Core Moral Frameworks

38   **Amusingly, the erudite website Stanford Encyclopedia of Philosophy states:** Stanford Encyclopedia of Philosophy. plato.stanford.edu/index.html. Plato, Ethics 1.

40   **An interesting if snarky tidbit:** Schwitzgebel & Rust.

40   **Through most of recorded history:** To explore what proto-moral concepts primordial humans may have been capable of *before* "recorded history," see Mithen; Klein & Edgar; D. Ross Ch. 4.

40   **Remarkably, across many times and cultures . . . the Golden Rule [emerged]:** The following are sources for the Golden Rule from a range of religious traditions. Christianity: Matthew 7:12; see also Luke 6:31. Judaism: Leviticus. 19:18; see also 19:34; Rabbi Hillel's explication of the Babylonian Talmud, Shabbat 31A. Islam: Kitab-al-Kafi, Vol. 2, 146. Hinduism: Mahabharat Brispati 13: 114.8. Buddhism: Udanavarga 5: 18. Confucianism: Analects XV.24. As to the limitations of the Golden Rule, see Churchland (2011) Ch. 7.

41   **A great historical nugget is the story:** Diodorus Siculus, *Library of History*. In their histories, both Arrian and Plutarch also recount this exchange.

41   **The Ten Commandments.** See Exodus 20:1-17; Deuteronomy 5:6-21.

42   **As a scholar of the Jewish Bible (Old Testament) says:** Claussen 86.

42   **These "points of difference [in the Bible] can actually have an enormous significance":** Ehrman (2009) 19. As leading scholar Elaine Pagels notes: "None of the narratives now called 'gospels' were written during Jesus' lifetime. Instead, they were written anonymously, some forty to sixty years after his death [by people who never knew Jesus]. . . . Authors names had been added about a hundred years after they were written when admirers of these particular 'gospels' added names familiar from Jesus' inner circle, to lend them credence." Pagels (2025) 6.

42   **Conversely, many revelatory texts later contended to be accepted:** Pagels (1979 and 2025); Ehrman (2003); White (2004); Mack (2003). Just for example, the now accepted "Synoptic Gospels" (Matthew, Mark, Luke, and John) were only consolidated around 200 CE; the now-accepted 27 books of the New Testament were not fully

assembled until about 350 CE; and even then, many disputed texts could have been included in the New Testament. Among the known ones that were excluded are the Gospels of Thomas, Philip, Mary, the Secret Book of John, and all the Nag Hammadi texts. (See Pagels (1979 and 2025); Aslan.)

Analogously, the prior Hebrew Bible "is commonly viewed as one volume, but it is an anthology of ancient Israelite texts written over the course of hundreds of years by diverse individuals, in diverse cultural contexts throughout the land of Israel. . . . Biblical authors had a wide variety of ethical perspectives, including a wide variety of political agendas." (Claussen 10.) See also Mack (1989); Ehrman (2003a and 2003b). The 4th century Papal Damasine List includes some books not now in the Hebrew Bible and rejects other texts. Even today, the seven "deutero-canonical" texts (such as Judith, Baruch, and Tobit) are recognized by the Catholic and Eastern Orthodox canons and included in their Bibles, but are not in most Protestant Bibles.

42   **After all this, it isn't surprising that the moral rules . . . within the entire Bible are not all consistent:** See generally, Bart Ehrman's several books cited in the Bibliography. See also Saunders 64; Pagels (2025). The apostle Paul's letters were dictated and copied repeatedly, over decades, with what one must assume were the usual unavoidable human errors. As one scholar says, "The Bible is replete with the most blatant and obvious errors and contradictions, just as one would expect from a document written by hundreds of hands across thousands of years." (Aslan xix.) And of course, individual believers differ in their interpretations. For example, "Christians disagree about what the Bible teaches [as to capital punishment]; some say it requires capital punishment at least for murder, and others say it was authorized in the Old Testament but not anymore." (Heimbach 432.) Evangelicals generally support the death penalty, while the Vatican formally declared it contrary to Biblical ethics in 2018. But for a different view of the consistency and authority of the Biblical text, see for example J. Wright Ch. 13.

43   **As one scholar notes, "The Bible is a collection of texts":** Collins, J. 3. As to the Hebrew Bible, see J. Wright. As Biblical scholar Burton Mack concluded: "The New Testament . . . turns out to be a very small selection of texts from a large body of literature produced by various communities during the first one hundred years after [Christ's death], . . . and these writings stem from different groups with their own histories, views, attitudes and mix of peoples." Moreover, "even among the main traditions of Christianity, the books included in the various Bibles do not agree." (Mack (1989), 456.) Another scholar notes as to the many Biblical stories: "The reading of any story from the past must respect the different layers of history and story, of then and now, that make it up. . . . We generally realize that there is not just one story—there are in fact four different accounts of Jesus life [in the four Synoptic Gospels]." This is because "They were written at different times by different authors; consequently, there is no cohesive narrative." (M. White (2004) 2.)Indeed, several of the Gospels are believed to have drawn in part from the lost-source "Q." See Mack, (2003) *The Lost Gospel.*

See also Saunders, *The Historical Jesus* 9, noting that in light of all the discrepancies, "we must, however, entertain another possibility altogether: perhaps none of the authors knew what took place (except, of course the trial and crucifixion). Possibly they had scattered bits of information, from which they constructed believable narratives which contain a fair amount of guesswork." Another view: "[To read the Bible as literal history] one must first accept the fact that the Gospels are essentially history with bits of theology that can be easily spotted and removed. One must also accept that collective memory is essentially reliable. . . . [These two assumptions] are no longer defensible." (Crook 28-29.) But for a very different, Evangelical view, see Grudem. Between 1910 and the mid-1960s, Catholic clergy, seminary professors, and religious superiors had to swear the "Oath Against Modernism" devised by Pope Pius X. It said: "I sincerely hold that the doctrine of faith was handed down to us from the apostles through the orthodox fathers in exactly the same meaning and always in the same purport. Therefore, I entirely reject the heretical misrepresentation that dogmas evolve and change from one meaning to another." This was modulated in later adoptions by the Second Vatican Council in the 1960s.

43   **Also, some evangelical Christians believe:** See, for example, Grudem. But Heimbach describes a range of views among Christians on this point, from "hard continuity" to "mild discontinuity" between the teachings of the Old Testament (Hebrew Bible) and the New Testament. (See Grudem 84-95.)

44   **The Bible accepts and at times lauds acts of enslavement . . . and so on:** The Old Testament contains many injunctions showing the wrath of a vengeful God. It contains God's sanction of death for more than 20 sins, including stoning of rebellious children (Deuteronomy 21: 18-21); blasphemy (Leviticus 24: 15-16); breaking the Sabbath (Exodus 31:14); striking a parent (Exodus 21:15); adultery (Leviticus 20:10); and owning an ox that kills someone (Exodus: 21:29). It also approves of waging war in which "you must not let any living thing survive" (Deuteronomy 20: 16). These may be understood as the rights of God, but surely not as a *literal* model for conduct by humankind.

Likewise, the New Testament contains many statements of Jesus that one would need to understand in metaphorical context to apply morally. For example, in Luke 14:26, Jesus says: "If any man comes to me and hate not his father and mother, and wife and children, and brethren, and yea, his own life also, he cannot be my disciple." Clearly, here Jesus is using "hate" in a different sense than we ordinarily do, and is referring to submission to and love of God above all else. Similarly, in Luke 19: 27, Jesus says: "But those mine enemies, which would not that I should reign over them, bring hither, and slay them before me." Or Matthew 10:34-36: "Think not that I am come to send peace on earth. I came not to send peace, but a sword." Literalism does not seem to be the message here.

44   **If one relies on the Bible as a complete guide to morals:** Peterson et al. (Eds.) 510; J. Collins 16. There is, of course, an enormous ongoing debate in Christianity over the "sufficiency" and "exclusivity" of the Bible as the fount of moral guidance. See, e.g., Heimbach Ch.3 and sources cited there; Geisler, 15-16 ("Christian ethics is a form of the divine command. . . . Moral obligations flowing from his nature are absolute"). Even a devout believer in literalism and inerrancy acknowledges that "even though Evangelicals believe God's revelation in scripture is inerrant, coherent and consistent, this does not mean we can take every command in the Bible and apply it without modification. . . . This involves . . . the science of biblical interpretation." (Heimbach 82.) See also sources cited in Id. 83-85.

44   **Some scholars believe that Jesus intentionally taught . . . by stories and parables:** Collins 16; Pagels (2025). For example, in the very first Gospel written about Jesus' works and sayings, "Mark is not writing history: he has no intention of just relating 'facts on the ground.' The story he calls 'good news' . . . mingles miracles, . . . revelations

of God, and 'wonders' . . . into everyday scenes." (Pagels (2025) 95.) Likewise, "When Luke constructs his gospel, gathering sayings from various sources, he often includes mixed messages. Luke doesn't avoid paradox. Instead, he includes sayings that directly contradict one another." (Id. 106.)

44 **The authors of the Bible never confronted these questions:** But see Grudem. On moral authority in the Jewish tradition, see Claussen 12: "Skepticism about the authority of the Bible . . . is quite ancient; even some Rabbinic sources, including within the Talmud, caution Jews not to rely on Biblical texts." Thus, "The words of the Written Torah play an important supporting role, . . . but it is the Rabbis' understanding—the Oral Torah, determined by the majority—that ultimately wins out." (Id. 32.) Accordingly, "Just as there is no singular 'Jewish ethics' that 'says' something, there is no singular Christian ethics or Islamic ethics." (Id. 2.) Some stress not only *the law* of the Torah, but also the Jewish concept of *musar*—ethical decision-making based on both piety and practicality. Thus, the Biblical Proverbs 1:8 instruct the young: "My child, heed your father's *musar*, but do not forsake your mother's Torah." Jewish ethics tends to be focused on virtues (like compassion, truthfulness, piety, generosity, and humility). It is casuistic, emphasizing moral thinking and problem solving; see Borowitz & Schwartz.

45 **Who sings the right notes?** H. Smith (1991) 2. Smith also used the analogy that God is a direction, not a specific destination. (H. Smith (2010) 3.)

45 **The challenge is different in the Jewish tradition:** Ariel 85.

46 **Despite these differences . . . a significant segment of Americans hold that you can't be a moral person without believing in God:** Compare Pew Research Center (2023) (finding about one third saying so) with Harris (2010) 146 (a majority saying so). See, generally, Gervais; D. Klein 38. For differing views, see Peterson et al. (Eds.) 584-592; Flynn et al.; and other writings on "secular humanism." So how do non-religious people decide moral issues, and do they rely on principles different from those used by religious people? A Pew Foundation survey asked them. The short answer is *that non-religious and religious people were remarkably similar*. In deciding moral issues, about 83% of the nonreligious and 82% of the religious said their prime principle was "they don't want to hurt people." About 82% of the nonreligious and 79% of the religious said they rely on "logic and reason." Some 69% of the nonreligious and 78% of the religious said they feel good when they "choose the right thing." These close similarities prevailed even though 65% of the religious people said they relied on their religious beliefs. (Pew Research Center, January 24, 2024.)

This skepticism about morality without religion is hard to square with the finding that more than 80% of people say that stealing would still be wrong—even if God did not prohibit it. Why, unless there is some other origin of "wrong"? (Prinz 145.) Nucci et al. found that religious children say that stealing would be wrong even if God didn't forbid it. Psychologist Marc Hauser argues thus: "Though equating morality with religion is commonplace, it is wrong in at least two ways. . . . Based on studies of moral judgments in a wide range of cultures, atheists and agnostics are perfectly capable of distinguishing between morally permissible and forbidden actions. More importantly, across a suite of moral dilemmas and testing situations, [adherents of various religions] and atheists and agnostics deliver the same judgments." (Hauser 421.) This is consistent with the findings in D. Xygalotas' study "Are religious people more moral?" (2017).

The highly popular scholar Will Durant became an atheist, and his scholar wife, Ariel, said she lost her original Jewish faith. But they nevertheless concluded that "there is no significant example in history, before our time, of a society effectively maintaining moral life without the aid of religion." *(The Lessons of History* 92-93.) Jonathan Sacks, former Chief Rabbi of the United Hebrew Congregations of the (British) Commonwealth, said pithily: "Religion creates community; community creates altruism." (Sacks 288.)

46   **A major survey by Pew Research Center:** Pew Research Center (2024b.)

46   **Surveys across more than 50 nations:** Pew Research Center (2025).

46   **A majority of people in Canada, Japan, Sweden, and Australia say they are not religious:** Pinker (2018) 435-436.

46   **On some indices of social caring and collaboration:** Shermer 170-172.

47   **But many people believe that another dimension of morality is critical:** A deep question probed by philosophers, since Plato in the dialogue Euthyphro, is this: Are moral rules good and to be followed because God wills them; or does God will them because they are good? Put differently, is there any meaning to "good" other than that God wills it? See Catapano & Critchley 103, 151-157; Cooper 1-17; Peterson 575-584. This conundrum recalls two maxims of Saint Augustine: "I believe so that I may understand," but also "I understand so that I may believe." From this perspective, faith and reason are allies, not opponents. Pope John Paul II, in his 1998 Fides et Ratio, declared that faith and reason are "two wings on which the human spirit rises to the constitution of truth" and that rejecting either "runs the grave risk of withering into myth or superstition."

47   **I will now do something never before attempted:** For a single comprehensive exploration of this, one cannot do better than Frederick Copleston's magisterial nine-volume *History of Philosophy*, which is staggering in its erudition and yet readable. See also Grayling; W. Durant (1926); B. Russell (1945).

48   **Indeed, various Greek philosophic schools "present themselves":** Cornford vi-vii, 6.

48   **And thus, "traditionally, [personal] conscience was given a cognitive status":** Edel 37.

48   **And bear in mind that "the Greeks" include perhaps a dozen philosophic schools:** See Copleston Vol. 1.

48   **Epitomized by some of the Dialogues of Plato:** See Cooper, Plato's Complete Works. See also Kamtekar.

48   **In Aristotle, at times called the "father of ethics":** See Nicomachean Ethics; Stanford Encyclopedia of Philosophy, Aristotle's Ethics; Aristotle (1984).

48   **As Aristotle said, "Neither by nature":** Nicomachean Ethics, Bk. 2, Ch. 1.

49   **Of who else could it seriously be said:** Soames 10.

49   **Scholars say that lay thinking in the Middle Ages was fundamentally Aristotelian:** A. Herman Ch. 14; Tarnas.

49   **Importantly, as one scholar puts it, "[E]thical debate resumed in the eighteenth century":** Grayling 454.

50   **In this chapter and the next:** Note that I discuss Kant's rationalism first, and then the empiricism of Hume, even though the latter came first in historical time. (Hume's major works were published in 1739-1758, while Kant's appeared in the 1780s and 1790s.) Kant was well acquainted with the earlier empiricism of Locke and others. But he acknowl-edged that reading Hume awakened him from his "dogmatical slumber and

gave my investigations in the field of speculative philosophy a . . . different direction." Kant (2009) 56.

50 **In Kant's view, "the ground of [moral] obligation":** Kant (2009) 56-57. Kant disdains the "mongrel" of empirical morals. (Id. 93.) More fully, he said "Everyone must admit that a [moral] law has to carry with it absolute necessity if it is to be valid morally," and "consequently, the ground of obligation must be based not on the nature of man, nor in the [empirical] circumstances of the world in which he is placed, but solidly *a priori* in the concepts of pure reason." (Id. 57.) One could argue that is just circular. Reason alone should govern *if* the purpose of morality is to serve only reason. But if instead morality's purpose is to enable people to live cooperatively in a society despite their selfish needs and desires, then empirical experience about "what works best" would be quite relevant. Kant seemed to realize this and said, albeit obliquely, that even after moral laws based on "pure reason" are discerned, "These laws admittedly require in addition a power of judgment shaped by experience." (Id., and see also 73.) He admitted this was necessary for at least two reasons: to decide subtle, hard cases where moral rules conflict, and to get real-world people to comply with moral rules. Unlike his short *Groundwork*, the later and longer *Metaphysics of Morals* contains many passages discussing the practical ("empirical") realities of feelings, life, law, and the political world, even while Kant repeats his abstract theoretical principles.

50 **As one scholar notes, "For Kant, we are free":** Stohr 19. Kant (2017) (*Metaphysics of Morals*) 19, states flatly that "a deed is right or wrong . . . insofar as it conforms with duty or is contrary to it."

50 **Moreover, Kant says that "virtue is the moral strength":** Kant (2009) 102. As many have observed, at its core, Kant's is "an ethics of duty." (E.g., Stohr 84.)

50 **Hence Kant offered a clear moral principle:** Kant (2009) 70. Likewise, Kant (2017) (*Metaphysics of Morals*) 168 says, "The Supreme principle of the doctrine of virtue is to act in accordance with a maxim of ends that it can be a universal law to have." Many have asked why this is a moral rule, rather than just a logical one, like "don't be inconsistent." See, e.g., Prinz 128-137. Why wouldn't it have been moral in some prior society to adopt a non-universal law, such as: "It is morally acceptable to steal the property of a slaveholder [i.e., free his slaves], but not for him to steal my property [such as my horses]"?

50 **Kant is a notoriously dense writer:** Kant is often described as having a "labyrinthine" writing style. Even a devoted translator says, "Kant's German, even as judged by German standards, makes difficult reading." Kant (1965) (N. Smith, Ed.) xi. A supportive scholar concedes that "the structure of his sentences are, as it were, hewn from the rock." Kant (2000) (J. Paton, Ed.) 9. But reading Kant is still not as arduous as reading Hegel, which scholar Frederick Beiser likened to "chewing gravel."

50 **But as philosopher Bertrand Russell puckishly said:** B. Russell, "Why I am not a theist" in Perry & Bratman (Eds.) 53-56.

50 **Kant aimed "to work out for once a pure moral philosophy":** Kant (2009) (*Groundwork*) 57. Kant (2017) (*Metaphysics of Morals*) 17 acknowledges the existence of "moral feelings," but insists that "in practicing laws of reason, we take no account of these feelings."

51 **For example, he said that "I can lie":** Kant (2005) (*Groundwork*) 71. But even a staunch opponent of lying like ethicist Sissela Bok says that Kant's absolute rule against

lying "has seemed too sweeping to nearly all readers and even obsessive to some." Bok 61 cites *The Metaphysics of Morals*, where she says Kant tried to avoid the problem that sometimes lying is needed to avoid harm, by declaring that "a conflict of duties and obligations is inconceivable." To reach this result, he used the legerdemain of defining some duties as "perfect" or invariable and others as "imperfect" or variable so that the former always trump the latter. Perfect duties are negative and without exception ("Never lie"), while imperfect duties include positive ones (like "Help others in peril"). But this is too simple and mechanical: if you mislead someone by mistake and they face peril, is your correcting the "lie" a perfect or imperfect duty? This distinction hardly solves the subtle conflicts of moral imperatives faced in daily life. See the sources in Heimbach Ch. 8.

51 **Kant declares that "we cannot do morality a worse service":** Kant (2009) (*Groundwork*) 76.

51 **Another of Kant's key principles:** Kant (2005) 96, 101.

51 **So "nothing in the world . . . can possibly be . . . called good without qualification except a *good will*":** Kant (2005) 61.

51 **"[Even if your intent failed entirely] it would still shine":** Kant (2009) 62. Jesus had said that doing good deeds to earn praise is not true virtue. Matthew 6:1-6. Paul echoed this: "And though I bestow all my goods to feed the poor, . . . [but] have not charity, it profits me nothing." (1 Cor: 13:3.) Conversely, it is widely understood that "the intent to do harm is an integral part of the definition of evil." (Duntley & Buss 27.)

51 **Thus, "virtue is the moral strength":** Quoted in Blackburn (1998) 32. See also Kant (2017) (*Metaphysics of Morals*) 167 ("Virtue is the strength of a human being's maxims in fulfilling his duty. . . . Ethical duties involve a constraint for which only internal lawgiving is possible.")

51 **In Kant's view, a perfect duty can never bow to an imperfect one:** Stohr 51-55. See Kant (2017) 30, 186-188.

52 **Kant also said that one must act . . . "for the sake of" the rule:** Kant (2009) (*Groundwork*) 57-58.

52 **In this spirit, modern philosopher Bernard Gert:** Gert. Ch.7. See also Hooker and Little (Eds.) 2: "One very familiar kind of generalism holds that that morality is composed of an irreducible plurality of principles that do not come in a strict order or priority." The authors cite thinkers such as Donald Davidson, Bernard Williams, Thomas Nagel, and Stuart Hampshire.

52 **The value of this approach is buoyed:** Gazzaniga (2011) 114-115. See generally Harris (2012).

52 **We yearn for clear, unconditional moral laws:** M. Johnson 164. Hare says Kant's rule is a logical, but not necessarily a moral, one. (Hare (1952) 34-35.)

52 **Interestingly, in a massive survey:** Baker 81-82.

53 **Psychological research has confirmed the unsurprising fact:** See sources cited in Chapter 6 below. Prinz 134 says, "Kant's whole enterprise is designed to liberate moral rules from the passions. I think such liberation would come at a terrible price." Note that in our legal system, we employ several quite different standards of responsibility based on intent. In criminal law, the required standard is *scienter,* i.e., actual intent. The actor must intend the act, even though he may not know for sure that it's illegal. But a crime also can be acting with *reckless disregard,* such as where person drives a car recklessly or sells a product (e.g., home-made fireworks) without actually knowing—or caring—

whether it is defectively dangerous. And in the area of civil rather than criminal wrongs (called *torts)* you can be liable even if you did not know your action would harm anyone —but you *should have known* because to the average person it would have been *reasonably foreseeable.* And different still, in certain contexts involving discrimination, you could be civilly liable for installing a *pattern or practice* that you did not foresee especially harm a given minority—but turned out to have that effect. So the moral element of intent varies.

53 **Moreover, critics charge that by insisting on consistency with universal laws:** See Mackie; Anscombe. In the *Groundwork,* Kant says "I can by no means will a universal law of lying; for by such a law there could properly be no promises at all, since it would be futile to profess a will for future action to others who would not believe . . . or who . . . would pay me back in like coin." (Kant (2005) 71.) Doesn't that refer to "consequences"? According to Foot, "There are many difficulties and obscurities in Kant's moral philosophy, and few contemporary moralists will try to defend it at all." (Foot (1997) 313.) Defend it as taken literally, perhaps. But many incline toward it and draw from it. See, e.g. Kamm, Korsgaard, Rawls, B. Herman. Kamm's intricate thought experiments illustrate how Kantian and consequentialist approaches could interweave and require reconciliation.

53 **In effect, he is saying "we must obey":** See Soames 90; S. Bok. But for many decades, the medical profession recognized a "therapeutic privilege" *not to tell the patient the worst,* if it would discourage them. An intellectual as probing as Sigmund Freud blithely stated: "When we introduce a patient to a new medical technique . . . we usually minimize its inconveniences and give him confident assurances of the success of that treatment. I think we are justified in this since by doing so we are increasing the probability of success." (Freud (1965) (*Introductory Lectures*) 15.) But today, this is largely rejected, except in cases of suicidal patients. The American Medical Association's Code of Medical Ethics, Opinion 2.1.3 (2016), states that "except in emergency situations in which a patient is incapable of making an informed decision, withholding information without the patient's knowledge or consent is ethically unacceptable." This is supported by the law known as HIPAA. See, generally, Beauchamp & Childress.

53 **Critics also ask, "Is Kant's demand for absolute, fixed moral rules":** See Mackie 87. Why couldn't rational beings choose to embrace a universal rule that *does* look to consequences and exceptions—like allowing a lie when its purpose is to save great pain, or requiring the sacrifice of one life if needed to save at least 100 lives?

53 **As Churchland says, the effort to find invariable, perfect moral rules:** Churchland (2019) 150. For some time, an influential approach was the "pluralism" of W. D. Ross, who offered not absolute moral rules but *"prima facie"* ones, i.e., the idea that some principles are presumptively good and right—until a specific situation exhibits features that warrant an exception. He offered principles such as fidelity, beneficence, and gratitude. (Ross (1930).)

54 **Karl Marx reportedly refused to give to beggars:** Baron (2006) 61.

55 **For a fascinating contrast, consider the difficult moral choices:** Drawn from Sandel (2009) 238.

56 **Thus, a loyal Kantian who wants to follow fixed rules:** Gert Ch. 7-9; Beauchamp & Childress 394-400.

56 **For example, over several decades the psychology and psychiatry profes-sions:** See *Tarasoff v. Regents of The University of California,* 17 Cal.3d 425 (CA 1976); Weinstock et al.

57 **Karen Stohr notes that to some, "Kant's theory has seemed overly abstract":** Stohr xiii. See also Churchland, quoted in Harris (2010) 226. These words recur even among Kant's admirers: "Kant's works of moral philosophy often strike readers as cold and abstract." See, for example, the editor's introduction to Kant (20017) (*Metaphysics of Morals*), L. Denis (Ed.) xii.

57 **It succumbs to what Jonathan Haidt calls:** Haidt (2012) 34. See also Searle (2001). But for a defense of Kant, see Stohr.

57 **People often lie and cheat in little ways:** Ariely (2012); Gino & Ariely.

58 **One way out of this problem traces back to the "doctrine of double effect":** Aquinas (1920) (*Summa Theologica*) 11111 Q. 64 Art 7.

59 **Marcus Luttrell, a heroic Navy SEAL:** See Luttrell.

59 **The doctrine of double effect leads to countless conundrums:** See, e.g., Jackson & Smith (Eds.) 46-47; McIntyre, "Doctrine of double effect"; Beauchamp & Childress 167-171. Some suggest that ultimately, people resort to emotion to resolve these problems. See Pizarro et al. (2003).

59 **As ethicist Jonathan Baron writes:** Baron (2006) 69. See also Beauchamp & Childress Ch. 5.

59 **For an especially consequential example, . . . consider . . . the first use of the atomic bomb:** Shermer 73. For a more comprehensive discussion, see Rhodes. Historian Thomas Childers cites the loss of perhaps 130,000 lives in the battle for Okinawa, 80,000–100,000 in the firebombing of Tokyo, and large numbers in the firebombing of other Japanese cities—none of which caused Japanese surrender. See also Groom Ch. 13 on the enormous willingness of the Japanese to accept casualties in defense of the Empire.

60 **For example, Kant acknowledges that "to be kind where one can is a duty":** Groundwork 66; *Metaphysics of Morals* 217 ("To be beneficent, . . . to promote the happiness of other human beings in need, without hoping for something in return, is everyone's duty.") See also Id. Part 2; Stohr Ch. 2.

60 **Also, modern Kantians use his approach while accommodating:** See, e.g., Korsgaard; Stohr; and others cited by them. For a particularly challenging mental ride aboard Kantian, utilitarian, and other waves, read Kamm and her myriad inventive moral conundrums. Researchers report that people who have a damaged ventromedial pre-frontal cortex in the brain become less Kantian and more utilitarian in their moral judgments. They can't see that some things are just plain wrong regardless of "justifications." (Harris (2010) 93.) Conversely, many ethical people see the Kantian approach as a critical bulwark against subjective moral decisions and wishy-washy, convenient decision-making.

60 **Thus, they argue that "[Kantian] Non-consequentialism":** Kamm 11.

61 **He said, "Two things fill the mind":** Kant, *Critique of Practical Reason*, Conclusion (1788).

3. Moral Feelings and Utilitarianism

62 **"There has been a controversy started of late":** Hume, *Enquiry* (1748) 2. (*Enquiries*, cited in the Bibliography below as Hume (1975), is the expanded later edition.)

62 **Hume said that one cannot "derive an ought from an is":** Never stated so pithily, but Hume (1978) (*Treatise*) 469-470, Bk. 3, Part 1, Sec. 1, makes the argument—and it has been universally quoted since—as "Hume's Law." See, e.g., Searle (1964); Prinz ; Corsico; M. Nelson. It is generally taken to mean that the "fact/value" distinction is unbridgeable. In fairness, that is not exactly what Hume meant. He actually said: "For as this *ought, or ought not,* expresses some new relation or affirmation, it's necessary that it should be observed and explained, and at the same time that a reason should be given." (Quoted in Stohr 136.) Thus, Hume seems to mean that you cannot derive a moral "ought" *solely* from a factual premise. Instead, you need some other connective premise, i.e., what we might call a good reason.

Thus, a moral claim might run like this: "(1) Your cousin is in need (fact); (2) If you help him now, he will likely help you if you ever need it, and if you don't help him, other family members will dislike you (connective premises); (3) You care about family and that is an inherent feature of humanness (another connective premise); (4) Therefore, you *ought* to help your cousin in need." Hume is right that you can't logically prove #4 just by #1; you must add #2 and #3.

But philosophers still refer at times to "Hume's Law" as meaning that there is a logical chasm and one can *never find a way* from facts to value propositions. And Hume gave cause for this by his frustrating inconsistency. Following the statement quoted above, he went on to say: "What seems altogether inconceivable, [is] how this new relation [the *ought*] can be a deduction from the others [the facts about what *is*], which are entirely different from it. . . . [This would] let us see that the distinction of vice and virtue is not founded merely on the relations of objects, nor is perceived by reason." (Id. 470.)

63 **For example, the fact that a person is making a promise:** Searle (1964).

63 **Instead he made "an attempt to introduce":** Hume, *Enquiry*, Introduction.

63 **He said, "Be a philosopher, but . . . be still a man":** *Enquiry* Bk. 4, p. 6.

64 **For a real-world example:** Quoted by Kahneman (2011) 135.

64 **Thus, "morality is more properly felt than justified":** *Enquiry,* Introduction, Bk. 3, p. 2.

64 **Thus, "*after* every circumstance, every relation is known":** *Enquiry*, quoted in M. Johnson 15.

64 **On the contrary, "much reasoning should precede":** *Enquiry* 1, 137, 172-173. While Hume is known for basing morality on emotional "sentiments," at times he seemed to work hard to bridge over to reason as well. He said that sentiments are not just arbitrary personal tastes but "[that] which nature has made universal in the whole species," and that "in order to pave the way for such sentiment and give a proper discernment of its object, it is often necessary, we find, that much reasoning should precede, and nice distinctions be made, just conclusions be drawn . . . complicated relations analyzed, and general facts . . . ascertained." (Quoted by Copleston Vol. 5, 329.) Those are quite *rational* processes. Yet elsewhere Hume famously said, " 'Tis not contrary to reason [for me] to prefer the destruction of the whole world to the scratching of my finger." Of course that is irrational, not just morally but practically, since you and your finger would then have no world to enjoy. Even supporters have faulted Hume for this kind of hyperbole. See Bailee 95-96.

64   **Thus, it has "seemed to many":** Baillee 10.

64   **Hume famously declared that "reason is and ought only to be the slave of the passions":** *Treatise,* Bk. 2, Pt. 3, Sec. 3, quoted in Johnson 115-116. But as we noted, Hume did not consistently deny any role for reason. He noted that "reason and sentiment concur in almost all moral deliberations and conclusions," and indeed, sentiment is that which "nature has made universal in the whole species," and not a matter of personal whim alone. (*Enquiry,* quoted in Copleston Vol. 5, x, 329.)

64   **Interestingly, Hume described himself:** B. Russell (1959) 660; see also Paton. Apparently confirmed by others, Hume described himself as "a man of mild dispositions, of command of temper, of an open, social and cheerful humor, capable of attachments, but little susceptible of enmity, and of great moderation in all my passions." *Enquiry,* Introduction.

65   **But in his moral theory, he confidently generalized:** Hume, *Treatise,* excerpted in Perry & Bratman (Eds.) 428. Thomas Hobbes and Adam Smith took a similar view.

65   **Following Hume, many philosophers:** Mackie 38.

65   **Psychologist Jonathan Haidt says Hume began:** Haidt (2012) 47, 134-135.

65   **As we'll see later in this chapter . . . Hume's empiricism is supported by extensive studies:** See, e.g., summaries in Sapolsky Ch. 13-14; Damasio (2012) Ch. 5, Ch. 7; Haidt (2001 and 2012); Churchland (2011); Tao. See also Chapter 9 below and sources cited there.

65   **Instead, they view emotions as a meeting place:** Johnson-Laird 74. See also Prinz.

66   **As one expert concludes, "People make moral judgments quickly and emotionally":** Haidt (2012) 47. But time pressure and cognitive load can affect the tendency toward Kantian versus utilitarian decisions. See Kroneisen & Heck and sources cited there.

66   **This "social intuitionist" view of moral thinking:** See, e.g., Haidt (2012); Graham et al. (2013); Sapolsky 481-487; Rozin; Tao. For a philosopher's review of "emotionism," see Prinz, who says that "moral judgments . . . ooze with sentiment" and "the good is what we regard as good, so morality is a derivative track that can be fruitfully pursued empirically." (Prinz 13.) But see Paxton & Greene; Bloom (2013) 208-210.

66   **As Antonio Damasio notes, "Contempt is often a metaphor for moral disgust":** Damasio (2012) 125; see also Tao.

66   **Thus, "someone does something lousy and selfish":** Sapolsky 41.

66   **Our gut emotions tell us:** Rozin & Nemeroff; Haidt (2006); Baron (2006) 81; Bazerman 5; Prinz 30-32. But our moral disgust can be manipulated by exposure to bad smells. (Schnall.)

66   **On the contrary, experience shows that:** Greene 62.

66   **Having studied these complexities, most psychologists:** Haidt 52. See Damasio (2012); Greene; Hauser; Prinz; Pinker (1999).

67   **Increasingly, research supports the general view:** Haidt (2006) 66; see also id. 106-107; Haidt and Kesebir.

67   **Haidt uses the metaphor that . . . reason is a small rider atop a huge elephant of emotion:** Haidt (2012) xxi.

67   **And Haidt sees that second step as largely "post hoc constructions":** Haidt (2012) xxi. Philosopher Samuel Scheffler says that "Our actual values have a more secure place in human thought and practice than any abstract conception of moral rationality that conflicts with them." (Scheffler 2.) But Julian Baggini stresses that "reason is indispensable to morality." (Baggini 156.) For assessments that do not entirely sideline reasoning, see Bloom; Paxton & Greene; Greene (2013); Mikhail (2011); Korsgaard (2009); Blackburn (1998); Churchland (2011). Mercier and Sperber offer a unique and different take: that the purpose of giving moral reasons *is not even to satisfy reason*, but rather to justify arguments that achieve socially acceptable goals. That would bring us to assess their adequacy very differently.

67   **Others point out that people genuinely wrestle with moral dilemmas:** Bloom (2013) 210. ("Moral deliberation is ubiquitous, but psychologists typically overlook it . . . because everybody loves counterintuitive findings.") See also Greene (2013); Hauser; Bloom (2016); Gabbard; Ponizovskiy et al.

67   **This recalls Pascal's comment:** *Pensees* 45.

67   **Philosopher Jesse Prinz describes the process:** See Prinz 98-99.

68   **For evolutionary reasons, we feel immediate empathy for a person who is nearby:** Ringwald & Wright; Greene (2013) 257. See, generally, Bloom (2016).

69   **"It is reason [not empathy] that leads us to recognize":** Bloom (2016) 51. See also Svoboda; Dugakin.

69   **Similarly, Jonathan Baron has outlined:** Baron (1998) 9-14. Bazerman & Moore 77; Bloom (2016).

69   **Along the same lines, consider people's moral indignation about attorneys' fees :** See Budiansky et al.

70   **Researchers have confirmed that "efforts to resolve such ambivalence":** Shermer 313 and sources cited here.

70   **Yet we routinely engage in . . . "imaginative moral deliberation":** M. Johnson 90.

71   **But psychologist William James proposed:** James, *Principles* 350, quoted by Damasio (2012) 340.

71   **In a massive 2020 survey of philosophers:** Baggini & Stangroom 181. Utilitarian weighing is what many people instinctively resort to when faced with a tough moral choice. They try to figure out what is "the best thing all-around for everybody." Thus: "Utilitarianism occupies a central place in the moral philosophy of our time. . . . [For] a much wider range of people, it is the view toward which they find themselves pressed when they try to give a theoretical account of their moral beliefs." (Scanlon 103.) Churchland (2011) 77 adds: "An enduring appeal of Mill's utilitarianism is that it acknowledges the particular importance of human happiness, as opposed to duty or some metaphysical end."

71   **As Jeremy Bentham famously enjoined, "Take reason, not custom, as your guide":** Quoted in Bruce & Barbone 53. Bentham initially expressed this idea less pithily in his 1817 *Plan of Parliamentary Reform*. Later, he stated it more fully: "The principle of utility is . . . that principle which approves or disapproves of every action whatsoever according to the tendency which it appears to have to augment or diminish the happiness of the party whose interest is in question." (*An Introduction to the Principles of Morals and Legislation,* Ch. 1.) Bentham went so far as to devise a "felicific calculus" for computing net happiness! (Reeves 35.) Before Bentham, Frances Hutcheson, in his influential *Inquiry Concerning Moral Good and Evil*, had defined good as being "the greatest happiness of the greatest number." See Durant & Durant (1965) 139.

71   **Bentham wrote that there couldn't be any absolute list:** Quoted in Beauchamp & Childress 31.

72   **Likewise, Sidgwick declared:** Preface xxii, 40. Rawls called Sidgwick's work "the first truly academic work in moral theory,modern in both method and spirit." Rawls (1997) 253.

72   **Even some of its supporters agree that utilitarianism is an "awful name":** Greene 156.

72   **By contrast, Mill wrote, "He who saves":** Mill, quoted in Cohen 343.

72   **Proponents of *act utilitarianism* believe:** See Scheffler; Beauchamp & Childress 388. As Cicero bluntly said: "Advice is judged by results, not intentions." Quoted in Herman 113. Philosopher J.C.C. Smart says that under "extreme and restricted utilitarianism," the "rightness or wrongness of keeping a promise," for example, "depends only on the goodness or badness of the consequences." (Perry & Bratman (Eds.) 505.) But for how long, and despite how many other intervening forces or events, should we measure the "consequences" of an act for which a person is thus held responsible?

72   **Others endorse *rule utilitarianism*:** Bentham, *The Principle of Utility* in Perry & Bratman (Eds.) 483. See also J. Driver. Rule utilitarianism also avoids the criticism that act utilitarianism is flawed because it means that an act can't really be declared to have been "good" if it *fails to achieve* the intended good result. (See Geisler 63.) There seems something wrong in this: trying to do good but failing is not still good? But it recalls Talleyrand's famous quip that "The murder of Caesar was worse than a crime; it was a blunder." Yes, it ended a likely tyrant, but it led to a decade of bloody civil war and then finally the ascent of Octavian to become Caesar Augustus. Thus, "Octavian was left as the sole leader of the Roman World and soon to be the Emperor of Rome. To put it another way, the assassins [of Julius Caesar] had indirectly at last brought about the very thing that they claimed to be fighting against—one man rule." (Beard 37.) So was their initial act morally good or bad?

72   **So, whereas act utilitarianism:** Elster 222.

73   **A further refinement is sometimes called *welfare utilitarianism*:** See utilitarianism.net, "Elements and Types of Utilitarianism"; Crisp, R., "Well Being" in Stanford Encyclopedia of Philosophy. To get a bit more technical: some have suggested that the goal should not be added total utility (which ignores the declining marginal utility of resources to the affluent) but rather that "To *equalize the margin* is a basic target of utilitarian theory." (Elster 212-213.) Thus, giving $1,000 to each of 1,000 poor people is far more worthy than giving a billionaire the same total of $1 million. Duh!

73   **For a more complex example, consider affirmative action:** Compare D. Bok; Bollinger & Stone; Riley; *Students for Fair Admissions v. President and Fellows of Harvard University*, 600 U.S. 181 (2023).

74   **One scholar describes it [consequentialism] as:** Scheffler 1. But how do we measure utilitarian "best"? If I am a pastor, I know it is "best" for an atheist to come to faith; but he doesn't agree.

74   **As Mill said, when a person must choose:** Mill, *Utilitarianism* Ch. 2, quoted in Gert 137.

75   **As Henry Sidgwick noted:** Sidgwick (1981) xxii, emphasis added; see also xii, xxi, 404 n.1; 486 n.1. Bernard Williams has criticized this as an unjustifiable leap in utilitarian thinking: "There is a notorious problem at this point about the transition from a supposedly indisputable aim of seeking one's own happiness, to a more disputable aim of seeking [all] other people's happiness, and the unfortunate Mill has been repeatedly beaten over the head by critics for [it]." (B. Williams (1972) 84.)

75   **As the philosopher Philippa Foot observed:** Foot, quoted in Scheffler 243.

76   **It is reported that when someone proposed to Martin Luther:** Quoted in B. Williams (1972) 76.

76   **Mill said, . . . "The only proof . . . that an object is visible":** *Utilitarianism* Ch. 4.

76   **To Russell, this is "an argument so fallacious":** B. Russell 778. See also Blackburn 136-137; Cohen xxiv; A. Fyfe. Indeed, "This passage [by Mill] has been hammered to death since its publication, and rightly so." (Reeves 326.)

77   **As Judea Pearl has said:** Pearl 10; see also Ch. 8.

77   **As I noted, a major criticism of the utilitarian approach is that it demands too much of people:** See Mackie; B. Williams (1985) 393; Carritt; Gert 20. But defenders say this isn't so, that on the contrary, utilitarianism is the most realistic moral doctrine—since it is "the only ethical theory which consistently abides by the principle that moral issues must be decided by rational tests" of net benefit, not just irrational feelings. (Harsanyi in Sen and Williams (Eds.) 40.)

77   **As psychologist Joshua Greene says:** Greene 257.

77   **In addition, if taken literally:** See Driver, *"Normative Ethics"* in Jackson and Smith (Eds.) 36. ("Thus, taking a vacation is wrong.")

78   **This is just the argument advanced:** Singer (1979, 2011, and 2023).

78   **If you think this level of altruism just isn't consistent:** Baggini 208. Kravinsky had previously given away most of his $42 million fortune.

78   **Would you be more willing to risk your life?** Kamm 15, drawing on Parfit.

78   **A related criticism is that by requiring us to be impartial:** See Nozick (1974); Nagel; B. Williams (1985).

79   **Bentham famously said, "Prejudice apart":** Bentham, *The Rationale of Reward* Ch. 9 (1830).

79   **Mill ultimately acknowledged that "some kinds of pleasure are more . . . valuable":** Perry & Bratman (Eds.) 488. Nobel Laureate John Harsanyi argues strongly that in measuring social utility, "people's irrational preferences [e.g. preferring "$3 off" to a "50% discount" on a $10 purchase] must be replaced by . . . their true preferences. [Even beyond that] . . . some preferences, which may very well be their 'true' preferences . . . must be altogether excluded. In particular, we must exclude all clearly antisocial preferences, such as sadism, envy, resentment and malice." (Harsanyi 56.)

79   **As he memorably said, "It is better to be a human being dissatisfied":** *Utilitarianism*, Ch. 2, Sec. 6.

79   **Likewise, he said that "[while] I regard utility":** Mill (1989) (*On Liberty*) Ch. 1.

79   **Bentham agreed that the "value of a pleasure or pain":** Bentham (2003) (*An Introduction*) 31.

80   **According to GiveWell:** Greene 206; see also MacAskill (2015 and 2022); GiveWell.org.

80 **But many philosophers give the concept more heft:** Kitcher 54.

80 **Most economists find calculating utility less challenging:** Elster 212, 218, citing work by Kenneth Arrow. But Churchland (2011) 178 says that "performing the required calculus in a way serious enough to qualify as maximizing happiness is a nightmare."

80 **To an economist, utilitarianism implements:** Simon 12-13; see also Harsanyi.

81 **Many moralists believe that a broad distribution of happiness would be better:** Sen 75, 209; Sen & Williams (Eds.); Rawls (1971) 26 (objecting that: "The striking feature of the utilitarian view of justice is that it does not matter, except indirectly, how this sum of satisfactions is distributed among individuals.") (See the discussion of Rawls in Chapter 4 below).

81 **Furthermore, research by Jonathan Baron and Joshua Greene:** Greene 282-283.

81 **The cognition, evaluation, and math required:** See, generally, Gert 208; Greene 166-168; Smart 504; R. Hare (1965 and 1982). On the challenges of weighing *uncertain* consequences in utilitarian assessment, see Ng et al.

81 **The liberal reformer Mill himself:** Mill (1989) (*On Liberty*) 100. This, of course, seems anti-utilitarian. During the course of his life, Mill appeared to veer away from fixed rights and more toward utilitarianism balancing. Some suggest that this was influenced in part by his brilliant social reformer wife, Harriet Taylor. (See Dworkin 259).

81 **As philosopher Thomas Nagel argues:** Nagel (2009) 154.

82 **Hence, "justice is a name for certain classes of moral rules":** Mill, quoted in Mackie 135. Rights are often seen as a sort of default code judgment, in the absence of strong counter reasons. (See Dworkin; Flanagan; Kamm.)

82 **Thus, "utilitarians make no room for justice":** Caritt 503-505. See, generally, Dworkin.

82 **Others urge that, in the end, rights can *only* be justified:** T. Scanlon in Scheffler 74.

82 **Still others say . . . :** "Appeals to 'rights' function as an intellectual free pass": Greene 302.

83 **We apply utilitarian thinking in many arenas of life:** Dworkin 98, 280; Baron; Sunstein (2025); Beauchamp & Childress.

84 **As Jonathan Baron argues:** Baron (2006) 20.

84 **Still, as Jonathan Elster notes:** Elster 238.

84 **Moreover, massive research in behavioral economics:** See Chapter 6 below. See also Gilovich et al. (Eds.); Kahneman (2011); Kahneman et al. (Eds.) (1982); Greene 279-285; Gigerenzer (2007).

86 **Research using fMRI imaging has shown:** Harris (2010) 92-94; Greene (2007); Greene et. al. (2001).

86 **His [Darwin's] son reported that Mill candidly confessed:** Quoted in Dennett 495.

86 **Joshua Greene quipped:** Greene 106-107.

86 **The esteemed philosopher Bernard Williams:** B. Williams (1972) 82-86.

87 **Bertrand Russell said Mill's theory:** B. Russell, quoted in Cohen x-xi.

87 **Another scholar says it is a "complex attitude":** Cohen xi.

87 **The eminent moralist Philippa Foot:** Foot (2009). 241.

87 **And philosopher Thomas Scanlon:** Scanlon 103.

4. Moral Justice, Virtue Ethics, Stoicism and Practical Moral Thinking

88 **During much of the twentieth century, the ascendant philosophical theory:** See works of Wittgenstein; B. Russell; Ayer; Moore; Quine; Hampshire; R. Hare (1952).

89 **Charging that philosophy lacked mathematical certainty:** Suppe 1-2, Ch. 4. The Vienna Circle included thinkers such as Otto Neurath, Moritz Schlick, Rudolf Carnap, Richard von Mises, Karl Popper, and others. But did they succeed in making philosophy scientific? Wittgenstein was a genius and offered many interesting ideas. But even geniuses can say wrongheaded things. Take Wittgenstein's example of supposing there were an omniscient person who knew everything that had ever happened in the world and "all the states of mind of all the persons who ever lived," and wrote it all down in a book. He said it would still "contain nothing that we would call an *ethical* judgment [or] . . . anything that would logically imply such a judgment"—and indeed a "murder would be on exactly the same level as any other event, for instance the falling of a stone." (Wittgenstein (1997) 67.)

But this is obviously wrong. Surely the omniscient writer would record that when stones fall, nothing follows. But when murders occur, people grieve and scurry around; police investigate; families want to take vengeance; courts convene; juries take action. This is because they agree the murder has a meaning the falling stone entirely lacks—murder has *moral significance*. Wittgenstein assumes something without proving it: that the purpose of morality is solely to satisfy deductive logic. If instead the purpose of morality is to yield social cooperation/cohesion, then the degree to which that is achieved can be empirically measured in a given society. In declaring ethical judgment an illusion, Wittgenstein might just as well have said "prestige is an illusion," "power is an illusion," or "love of family is an illusion." But if you want a "scientific" account of human society, you cannot take that view. Indeed, Wittgenstein then added "Ethics . . . is a tendency in the human mind which I personally cannot help respecting deeply and I would not for my life ridicule it." (Id. 70.)

89 **Ayer wrote that "a sentence is factually significant":** Ayer, quoted in Grayling 382. This echoed Schlick, who had declared that "the meaning of a proposition is its method of verification."

89 **A. C. Grayling summarizes the argument:** Id. 367. This view is sometimes called "emotivism," the idea that "the purpose of moral judgments is not to describe the world but to express our moral feelings or to serve as imperatives we address to ourselves and to others." The flaw here is that "expressions of feelings do not depend on reasoning from general principles, nor do they require defense by appeal to principle, whereas moral judgments do depend on reasoning." Harman (1977) 37.

89 **But then he went further, declaring that [most moral statements are] . . . "*literally meaningless*":** Ayer (1952) (*Language, Truth and Logic*) 11, 103-108). Ayer repeatedly declares this, but he also hedges. (Id. 14-15.) For an amusing example of analytic thinking reducing important concepts like "justice" to mere philology, see Sen 73 recounting a letter to Sen from Quine. And as to religion: "Widespread acceptance of the verifiability principle of meaning led many thinkers to conclude that religious claims, which are non-empirical and thus non-verifiable, are [therefore] cognitively meaningless." Peterson et al. (Eds.) 2. But later in life, Ayer had a "near death" experience, became close friends and often ruminated with the eminent Jesuit philosopher Frederick Copleston, and may have had added thoughts on the "meaning" of transcendent ideas. See D. Klein 149-152.

89   **Couldn't plenty of "sense experiences":** See Gert 189-191; Habermas 315-320; S. Bok.

90   **Moore said this was impossible:** Quoted in Copleston Vol. 8, 409. See *Principia Ethica,* excerpted in Darwall et al. (Eds.) 51-70 at 52. More recently, many have concluded that Moore's "open question argument" denying that "good" can be defined morally is "invalid . . . since it purports to refute all definitional analysis of 'good' but relies on an arbitrarily narrow definition of philosophical or scientific justification." (Darwall (1992) 3.) See also Harman (1977) 17-20. Prinz 39 notes that Moore's claim "is certainly a mistake." He points to the analogy that one can know the "essence" of something like alcohol without knowing its molecular composition. But "love" might pose an even better analogy to "good." Maybe we can't define love "metaphysically." Maybe love comes in different kinds. But we know the essence of what constitutes love. See also B. Williams (1972) 38-47, debunking Moore and, at 44, calling his claim that good could not possibly be empirical "a sad error." Another scholar says "The general opinion by now is that the [open question] argument does not work." (Verbeek 239.) Nevertheless, Moore captivated at least philosophers, and thus "Moore stopped moral theory . . . for over half of the last century." (M. Johnson 20.)

90   **In the moral realm, philosopher R. M. Hare asks:** See Edel 53. This somewhat different view is sometimes called "noncognitive prescriptivism." It asserts that moral statements are not meaningless but are just sort of impulsive "commands" to others like "Be quiet" or "Out of the way," expressing a desire but without rational moral justification. This is not the meaning embraced by General George Patton who, after decisively defeating the Vichy French forces in Morocco, nevertheless treated their military leaders with dignity, saying, "No use kicking a man when he is down." (Groom 277.)

90   **Philosopher Bernard Williams mocked the analytic school's word-based approach:** B. Williams (1972) xvii.

90   **And A. C. Grayling says:** 339.

90   **As a result of these limitations:** Baggini & Stangroom 8.

91   **As the story goes, . . . [Ayer] was entertaining a number of fashion models:** Butler-Bowden 31; D. Klein 148-149.

91   **An intellectual sibling—subjectivism:** See Harris (2010) 17. Subjectivism "is the doctrine that . . . moral judgements are [just] equivalent to reports of the speaker's own feelings or attitudes." (Mackie 17.) Basically, subjectivism means that moral judgments are purely individually derived. Relativism might say they are a bit more "objective" and not purely individual—but only with reference to a particular society. Nevertheless, if you believe that some element of morality (like reciprocity) is rationally objective or inherent in human nature, then why shouldn't it be binding on all individuals and all societies? So, subjectivism and relativism are intertwined. See Stanford Encyclopedia of Philosophy, Subjectivism Versus Moral Relativism; Kreeft; Butler.

91   **Long ago, Hobbes wrote:** Quoted in Mackie 43.

92   **Likewise, Hume said:** Quoted in Mackie 20.

91   **Philosopher J. J. Mackie confidently declares:** Mackie 105.

92   **Richard Rorty sniffs:** Quoted in Haack 9.

92   **Morals are just like quaint customs:** Mackie 105-106.

92   **But as critic Steven Pinker notes:** Pinker (2018) 406, 444.

93   **Everything I have said and done:** Mussolini, *Diaturna*, 374-377, quoted in Kreeft 18.

93   **It became their portal:** See Kreeft 28. As Simon Blackburn noted, "The relativist believes that arguing about ethical truth is like arguing about the true location of the rainbow." 298.

93   **As one philosopher observed, "Moral relativism":** Harris (2010) 45. See also Tilley.

93   **A major study of values in 2000:** Baker 85.

93   **There is some evidence that women and poor people:** Baker 144-146.

93   **Bernard Gert says that moral relativism:** Gert 308.

94   **Even a defender admits, "The term 'moral relativism' is notoriously ambiguous":** Prinz 174.

94   **As Foucault once confided:** Quoted in Saad 75.

94   **So what does relativism actually mean?** See Kitcher 139 and works cited there; Kreeft.

94   **As Nietzsche said, "There are no facts":** Quoted in Blackburn 73. See, generally, Derrida.

94   **So, "while moral truths hold objectively":** (Rovane 137.)

94   **But this wrongly confuses relativism with tolerance:** Kane 13; Blackburn Ch. 9. Prinz argues that relativism does not require toleration of evil—one could just as arbitrarily ("relatively") adopt a norm of disliking such tolerance. But he concedes that "relativism does make intolerance [of evil] difficult to sustain psychologically." Prinz 208.

94   **As Rorty said, "Anything can be made to look good or bad":** Quoted in Blackburn (1998) 288.

94   **They think many aspects of good and evil are real:** See sources cited in Chapter 6 below; Blackburn (1998) 279-310.

95   **The existentialist Sartre asserted:** Sartre (1946) (*Existentialism Is a Humanism*) 35-37.

95   **As Fletcher said, "If a lie is told not lovingly":** Fletcher 36. No guidance is given for deciding how to weigh intent, means, or effects. Even a Christian critic notes that "a one-norm ethic, especially when the norm is as broad and general as Fletcher's love norm, is in almost all (though not all) cases little better than having no norm at all. . . . [It] is no more helpful than a view that says 'Follow nature' or 'Live according to reason.'" Geisler 47-48.

95   **Fletcher also argued strenuously:** Fletcher 76-77.

95   **Accordingly, critics have dismissed situation ethics:** Fletcher 11.

95   **But research across more than 100 countries:** See Schwartz; Christakis; Edmonds; Chapter 9 below.

96   **As Joshua Greene says, "The problem with the moral relativist's answer":** Greene 149.

96   **Karl Popper noted that the relativists:** Popper (1959) 19.

96   **But if you deeply inhale the relativist doctrine:** Harris (2010) 45. For a partial defense, see Prinz 208-209.

97   **As Sam Harris observes, "Moral relativism . . . tends to be self-contradic-tory":** Harris (2010) 45.

97   **Likewise, Thomas Nagel says:** Nagel 8. For an energetic retort based on "moral realism," i.e., the argument that moral judgments can have empirical and scientific bases, see, e.g., R. Boyd. For a defense of subjectivism, see D. Wiggins.

97   **Perhaps the simplest riposte:** Cooper (Ed.), *passim.*

97   **Their rationally arguing that rational, unbiased views are impossible:** Bloom (2016) 52.

98   **"Its characteristic feature is . . . indifference to 'truth'":** Haack 9, 15. Bertrand Russell said: "I cannot see how to refute the arguments for the subjectivity of ethical values, but [nevertheless] I find myself incapable of believing that all that is wrong with wanton cruelty is that I don't see it." (Quoted in Wiggins 227.)

98   **Given all these flaws, they hope that "relativism . . . can subside":** Blackburn (1998) 308. See also A. Gibbard, arguing that moral rules are coordination principles for mutual advantage and thus are "scientifically" verifiable—either they work in society or they don't, and we ought to be able that measure that. For a lively and extended dialogue on relativism, see Kreeft.

98   **In contrast to the abstruse style of European philosophy:** Peirce (1878) ("How to Make Our Ideas Clear").

98   **As he [Peirce] said, "There is . . . no difference":** Peirce (1992) (*Essential Peirce*) Vol. 1, 131.

98   **Following this, James said:** James (1962) (*Essays*) 65. Quoted in Jonsen & Toulmin 282.

99   **James hoped that pragmatism:** Quoted in M. White (Ed.) 160. It's not clear how this dual appeal would succeed, since the "tender minded" deontological Kantians would find little that was categorical, non-empirical, and "universal" in pragmatic judgments. See, generally, Watson Ch.5.

99   **Instead, "truth *happens* to an idea":** B. Russell (1945) 816.

99   **So, "if you want to know if any kind of theory is true":** James quoted in M. White 158.

99   **In a phrase only an American philosopher . . . would employ, . . . assess a claim's "cash value" . . . in terms of results:** James (1962) 174. But Bertrand Russell says results alone are not the whole story. As to the related pragmatism of John Dewey, he said, "The main difference between Dr. Dewey and I is that he judges a belief [solely] by its effects, where I judge it by its causes [e.g., intent, goals]." B. Russell (1945) 826.

100   **But he seemed to see morality as largely a matter of "sentiment":** James (1979) 205.

100   **Richard Rorty, with his usual sarcasm:** Rorty (1982) 160, 166.

100   **In the wake of relativism, . . . John Rawls undertook a major effort to restore reasoned rules. . . . "Rawls's theory has received":** Dennett 456. See also Elster 223: "[Rawls's is] probably the greatest work in moral and political philosophy of this century"; Churchland (2011) 65: "John Rawls is arguably the most influential moral philosopher of the twentieth century." But for a mix of praise, reservations, and criticisms, see Sen; Churchland (2011).

100   **One major treatise declares:** Soames 262; Grayling 461.

100 **As he said, "Justice is the first virtue":** Rawls (1971) 3.

101 **Rawls's two basic principles of justice:** Id. 60-62. Rawls's approach has been called "Kantian contractualism." (Darwall 12-16.) Rawls was an avowed Kantian, though one who tried to construct "a connection between the first principles of justice and the concept of moral persons as free and equal." (Rawls (1997) 253.) Some see this approach as a potent antidote to pure utilitarian balancing of interests. (Hauser 443-448.)

101 **In later writings, Rawls argues for two modified principles:** Rawls (1993) 59. See also Sen 5-9; Hayek 221; Mackie 81.

102 **A leading rights theorist, Ronald Dworkin:** See Dworkin 169, 184.

102 **"The common deep structure of human fairness norms":** Binmore 15.

102 **This argument echoes Hume's criticism:** Hume (1978) (*Treatise*) Book 3, Part 2, Sec. 2; Book 3, Part 3, Sec. 5.

102 **It is, as Rawls said, "purely hypothetical":** Rawls (2001) 18.

103 **As Michael Sandel says, "Underlying the device of the veil of ignorance":** Sandel (2009) 153. For an extended assessment of the issues Rawls addresses, see Sandel (1982). Among his concerns is the view that Rawls pulls people "out of community" and common moral arguments.

103 **Rawls has been widely faulted for using an intellectual "skyhook":** Binmore 151. See also Soames 265.

103 **An example of Rawls's response:** Rawls (1971) 15.

104 **But that has been criticized:** Sen 58-59. See also Hare (1982); Dworkin Ch. 6 and 7.

104 **Dworkin proposes a distinction:** Cited in Elster 207.

104 **But others look at [unsuccessful] people . . . and "believe their ultimate causes":** Elster 207.

104 **Critics such as Robert Nozick:** Nozick Ch. 7. See also Grayling 462-466.

105 **Rawls argued that neither pure liberty nor pure reward for merit:** Rawls (1971) Sec.12.

105 **Interestingly, a new critique of merit:** See, e.g. Markovits; Sandel (2020).

106 **He acknowledged that his theory was "not intended as a comprehensive moral doctrine":** Rawls (2001) 19. See also Blackburn (1998). But see Scanlon (contractualism is a set of principles that are targeted at maximum utility and thus *would be* agreed to in an "original condition"). A later work, Rawls (1997) 253, "sketched the main idea of Kantian contractualism, which is to establish a connection between the first principles of justice and the conception of moral persons as free and equal."

105 **He noted, for example, that "utilitarianism is a teleological theory":** Rawls (2001) (rev. ed.) 26.

106 **Rawls's theory may strike some as overly "legalistic":** Jurgen Habermas objects that Rawls's theory "generates a priority of literal rights which demotes the democratic process to an inferior status." Quoted in Sen 325. See also Sandel (1982). Sen 261 has a different objection, that "Rawls [admits the importance of] special provisions for 'special needs'..., but the way he deals with this pervasive problem has quite a limited reach." Churchland argues that "legions of moral philosophers have spent their intellectual lives trying to make Rawls' approach work. [But] . . . as Owen Flanagan sums up, 'There is no such thing as universal ethical intuitions at the level Rawls was initially looking to locate them.'" (Churchland (2011) 165.) Still, as noted by Harman (1977) 59: "This idea, that there is something like a moral law, is reflected in our use of language. We speak of moral

obligations, moral duties, moral rights, and moral excuses; and these notions—duty, right, obligation, and excuse – would seem to make sense only relative to some sort of law."

106   **Another major moral framework is called *virtue ethics*:** "Virtue ethics is currently one of three major approaches to normative ethics (in addition to deontology (Kant) and consequentialism)." (Stanford Encyclopedia of Philosophy, Virtue Ethics (2022).) See also D. Russell.

106   **As the Greek Epictetus said:** Quoted in *The Daily Stoic*, Dec. 21, 2024.

106   **Lon Fuller observed that while "the morality of duty starts at the bottom":** Fuller 2.

106   **Perhaps for this reason, "in the second half of the twentieth century":** Doris and Stich 116.

107   **In his influential book:** MacIntyre (1994) (*After Virtue*); quoted in D. Russell 328.

107   **In response to abstract Platonic theorizing, [Aristotle] observed:** *Nicomachean Ethics*, Bk. 1, excerpted in Perry & Bratman (Eds.) 567.

107   **Aristotle recommended the former, practical approach:** *Nicomachean Ethics*, Bk. 2, Sec. 1.

107   **Thus, "the mark of virtue" for Aristotle:** Quoted by Harman 57.

107   **Aristotle's ethics revolved around three concepts:** Grayling 90-95.

107   **Virtue is "concerned with . . . what the man of practical wisdom":** *Nicomachean Ethics*, 1107e,

107   **The advocate of virtues William Bennett:** Bennett (1995) 10. See also Duhigg.

107   **It has been reported that the Dalai Lama:** Churchland (2019) 149.

107   **To such people, virtue ethics has "acquired a quaint veneer":** Sapolsky 504. Jonathan Sacks (2020)14 notes that in the seventeenth through nineteenth centuries it was common for "virtue" to be a stated personal goal. But it is rarely spoken of today. He observes that the Google N-gram index of word uses in published sources shows a dramatic decline since 1965 in the use of virtue-associated words like *respect, honor*, and *duty*. James Q. Wilson (1993) vii notes that "virtue has acquired a bad name. To young people it is the opposite of having fun."

108   **Thus, "what sets virtue ethics apart":** D. Russell 2. As Sacks (2020) 298 describes: "When we begin to behave toward others with care and concern, sensitivity and tact, humility and integrity, generosity and grace, forbearance and forgiveness, we start to become a different person. And such is the nature of reciprocity, itself one of the deeply ingrained instincts that is the basis of morality, that we begin to change the way others relate to us, not always, to be sure, but often." Some see virtue ethics as encompassing a range of different approaches, from focusing on self-happiness ("eudaemonist virtue ethics") to focusing on good to others ("target-focused virtue ethics"). See Heimbach 262-264 and sources cited there.

108   **Perhaps for this reason, virtue ethics has been an especially useful approach:** D. Russell 202-220. See also Beauchamp & Childress Ch. 2. (on biomedical ethics); Cohen-Almagor.

108   **As philosopher Mary Warnock writes:** Warnock 9.

108   **Reportedly, when eBay went international:** Zak 181.

108   **Moral leaders throughout history:** See, e.g., Aristotle, *Nicomachean Ethics* 1366b1; I Corinthians; Harrington & Keegan 125-126. Philosopher-humorists Cathcart and Klein

summarize the thought process thus: "I've been thinking about . . . what does 'good' mean, and I've got the answer—'good' is acting on a just principle. . . . [But] how do you determine just principles? . . . Du-uh! Just like everybody else . . . I learn them from my mom." (Cathcart & Klein 77.)

109 **Some would add the social virtues:** Johnson 64-65.

109 **Winston Churchill declared:** Wallace, *Introduction*.

109 **But some lament that "civic virtue is a fading trait":** Bauerlein & Bellow xii; Etzioni (2019); Brooks.

109 **A modern philosopher warns that "the list of mandatory virtues is notoriously subject to change:"** Flanagan 10.

109 **The leading modern proponents of virtue ethics:** See Hursthouse; Foot; Anscombe; MacIntyre; Slote; Warnock; Nussbaum. See D. Russell.

109 **As leading bioethics experts write:** Beauchamp & Childress 31.

110 **Hursthouse defends virtue ethics:** Hursthouse (1999) 17.

110 **Or they do good things on some occasions, but not always:** Ross & Nesbit; Ariely (2012).

111 **This human tendency has been called *situationism*:** See Doris & Stich and studies cited there; Prinz Ch. 4; Harman; Ariely (2012); D. Russell 394. Prinz says, "The virtues are traditionally conceived as character traits, but many social psychologists regard character traits as a defective concept. [They argue that] . . . behavior is not determined by character... but by external features of the situations that we happen to find ourselves in." Prinz 153, citing Ross & Nesbitt, Mischel, Doris, and others.

111 **Some go so far as to infer that stable character traits don't really exist:** Among these are Owen Flanagan, Walter Mischel, John Doris, and Gilbert Harman.

111 **However, it's well established that people do exhibit stable and reliable patterns of behavior:** See sources cited in Chapter 9 below; McGue; Bollich.

111 **Our virtue may be malleable to circumstances:** See Gilovich & Ross 44, 65, citing Princeton divinity student study; Svoboda; Ariely.

112 **It is a common trope that "the hero of a tragedy":** Corrigan 90.

112 **As political theorist Michael Sandel notes, "One of the great questions":** Sandel (2009) 9. This debate goes back at least to Plato and Aristotle, who favored fostering moral virtue in the polity. James Madison said, "To suppose that any form of government will secure liberty or happiness without any virtue in the people is a chimerical idea." (Cited in Brooks fn., p. 11.) More recently, the liberal political tradition has sought to acknowledge but limit such a state duty. In the 1960s, the epic H. L. A. Hart–Lord Devlin debate in Great Britain brought this to the fore. See, e.g., Hart (1958, 1963, 1968). One's position on state "promotion" of morals tends to vary depending on whether the virtues you think the state might promote are "private" moral virtues (not buying pornography) or business virtues (not producing unsafe or deceptive products) or "civic" virtues (decorum in public, or respect for the flag and the military).

112 **There is a new doctrine called *effective altruism*:** See Singer; MacAskill.

114 **Stoicism "received widespread recognition":** Grayling 112.

114 **"In ancient times, Stoicism had a kind of public relations problem":** Morris & Bassham 63.

114 **More broadly, "Stoicism is about personal freedom":** Morris & Bassham 9, quoting Matthew Arnold.

114 **As Marcus Aurelius said, "The agitations that beset you are superfluous":** Marcus Aurelius (*Meditations*) 9.32. Donald Robertson calls this "cognitive distancing." (Robertson 290.)

115 **"Keep in mind how fast things pass by":** Marcus Aurelius 5.23.

115 **One book sums up the Stoic creed:** Morris and Bassham 10. "Stoicism is the most broadly representative of the Hellenistic philosophies, possessed of a loftiness of vision and moral temper that would long leave its mark on the Western spirit." Tarnas 76.

115 **As Seneca said, "We are taught how to debate":** *Letters* 95.14.

115 **Marcus advised: "No situation is better suited":** Marcus Aurelius 1.7.

115 **We must free ourselves from pointless . . . desires:** Marcus Aurelius 3.4; Seneca (*Letters*) 59.

115 **Thus, Marcus said, "Begin each day":** Marcus Aurelius 2.1.

116 **As Marcus said: "The best revenge":** Marcus Aurelius 46.

116 **Then the Stoics emphasized what is called the "dichotomy of control":** Pigliucci & Lopez 5.

115 **As Epictetus said, "Of all existing things, some are in our power":** *Enchiridion* 1, quoted in Pigliucci 11.

116 **As Marcus Aurelius said, "How much more unconscionable":** Marcus Aurelius 11.18.

116 **Acceptance leads to more charitable views of others:** Marcus Aurelius 6.48.

116 **The venerable doctrine often used to reconcile this tension:** See Harris (2012); Stanford Encyclopedia of Philosophy, Compatibilism.

116 **Thus, "it is senseless to nurture aversion of poverty":** Pigliucci & Lopez 21.

117 **The Stoic creed was capsulized:** Epictetus, *Enchiridion* Ch. 1.

117 **The Roman Cicero called this "the brightest adornment of virtue":** Cicero (2010) (*On Duties*) 1.5.

117 **One Stoic guidebook even goes so far:** Pigliucci & Lopez 22.

118 **Seneca said, "The first thing which philosophy undertakes":** Seneca, quoted in Pigliucci & Lopez 26.

117 **And Marcus said, "Whether in a city":** Marcus Aurelius 10.15.

118 **Modern Stoic writers range:** See, e.g., William Irvine, Donald Robertson, Massimo Pigliucci, Ryan Holiday.

118 **One leading modern Stoic philosopher, Massimo Pigliucci:** Pigliucci 5. Fideler (2020) 4 lauds Stoicism thus: "This emphasis on living a good life separates Stoicism from modern academic philosophy, which has given up such practical human concerns in favor of abstract theoretical issues." Stoicism has been embraced as consistent with the "cognitive behavioral therapy" approach to mental health issues. See Fideler; Robertson.

118 **In explaining Stoicism, Ryan Holiday:** Holiday (2024) xxiii.

118 **Professor Nancy Sherman laments:** Sherman, quoted in Morris & Bassham 352.

118 **A final major approach to morality is *casuistry*:** Jonsen & Toulmin 13, quoting *The Oxford English Dictionary*.

119 **It replaces fixed rules with imaginative problem solving:** See Jonsen & Toulmin; M. Johnson 2, 90-92. Another view: "Ethics is both an art and a science because it does involve some precision like the sciences, but like art it is an inexact, intuitive discipline." (Rae 20.) See also Korsgaard (1997); Harris (2010) 8; Beauchamp & Childress 434. Dewey

(1957) 32: "Living a morally exemplary life requires developing the requisite virtues, employing the appropriate forms of inquiry, and exercising the requisite skills necessary for navigating the sociocultural landscape."

119 **Casuistry is consistent with the well-documented "dual process" theory of mind:** See Sapolsky 504-509; Kahneman (2011); Haidt (2012).

119 **"As the mind oscillates between alternatives":** Billig 144. See also M. Johnson Ch. 3.

119 **This is because "moral values and moral principles":** M. Johnson 46.

119 **Thus, "theoretical arguments are chains of proof":** Jonsen & Toulmin 34.

119 **Only as the [Roman] empire grew:** Jonsen & Toulmin 54-55.

119 **Some charge that "casuistry destroys [morality] by distinctions":** Jonsen & Toulmin 12. But these authors argue strongly the contrary, that "few intellectual activities have been more reviled than casuistry; yet few practical activities are (we shall argue) more indispensable." Id. 11.

120 **Jonathan Haidt says that when people face a moral choice:** Haidt (2001 and 2012).

120 **As Justice Oliver Wendell Holmes famously acknowledged:** *Lochner v. New York*, 198 U.S. 45 (1905).

121 **Many experts believe that bioethics . . . *requires* casuistry:** Beauchamp & Childress ix, 20-30; Baron (2006). The American Medical Association's Code of Medical Ethics (code-medical-ethics.ama-assn.org) reflects both Kantian rules, and at times the need for casuistry. See Beauchamp & Childress; Cohen-Almagor; Jonsen & Toulmin. It may also be true that "Nowhere are the lines of demarcation between the secular humanist and the Christian perspectives clearer than in biomedical issues." (Geisler 180.) The "Ethical and Religious Directives for Catholic Health Care Services" adopted by the U.S. Conference of Catholic Bishops (2009) 8 states that "while the Church cannot furnish a ready answer to every moral dilemma, there are many questions about which she provides normative guidance and direction." It then provides strong instructions as to abortion, end of life care, personal choice, suicide, and other matters. But the need for factual/ethical casuistry is evident in some other provisions, such as this: "While every person is obliged to use ordinary means to preserve his or her health, no person should be obligated to submit to a health care procedure that the person has judged, with a free and informed conscience, not to provide a reasonable hope of benefit without imposing excessive risks and burdens on the patient or excessive expense to the family or the community." Part 3, Sec. 32.

121 **Accordingly, a leading treatise on biomedical ethics:** Beauchamp & Childress ix.

121 **Philosopher Janet Radcliffe Richards agrees:** Quoted in Baggini & Stangroom 25.

121 **As Jonsen and Toulmin note:** Jonsen & Toulmin 19.

122 **Psychologist Marc Hauser explains it this way:** Hauser 418.

122 **In fact, imaging studies reveal:** See Kanai; Greene et al. (2001).

122 **So, in the broadest terms, morality is . . . "know-how":** Flanagan, cited in M. Johnson 133. Not everyone agrees. Some see "too much thinking" as eroding clear moral rules. See, e.g., William Bennett (1980): "[The] emphasis on morality as 'cognition' can lead to a series of errors in a child's understanding of in what a moral life consists. . . . The more a person has a fixed and steady disposition, the less, not the more, he has to make a decision at all." See also Bennett (1995).

122 **Thus, "moral particularism, at its most trenchant":** Stanford Encyclopedia of Philosophy, Moral Particularism (2013).

123 **Some prominent proponents of particularism:** See Dancy (1993 and 2004); McDowell; other works cited in Hooker & Little (Eds.) 160-161. One way of expressing the argument against moral "rules" is that as moral beings, "we need to weigh moral reasons against one another" and there is always a "role for judgment in order to resolve some conflicts between moral considerations." (Hooker 5.) (That seems to echo casuistry.) Likewise, Annette Baier says "I want to attack the whole idea of a moral 'theory' which systematizes and extends a body of moral judgments." Quoted in Hooker & Little (Eds.) 230.

123 **Many critics find this puzzling:** See, e.g., Crisp. For a Kantian defense of principle and a critique of Dancy, see O. O'Neil. See also Nussbaum (2000). And Margaret Little argues that even if we stop looking for fixed principles and focus on particular cases, our minds will naturally work by induction and gradually derive some patterns (what others may call principles). See Little 292-293.

123 **Martha Nussbaum notes that since antiquity:** Nussbaum (2000) 231

5. Moral Frameworks and Solving Daily Dilemmas

127 **As psychologist Paul Bloom has observed:** Bloom (2013) 162.

133 **Each of the moral frameworks we've explored has strengths and weaknesses:** Moral/ethical approaches can be divided into general categories, such as the well-known distinction between a *deontological* approach (duty-based, like Kant), *consequentialism* (results-based, like utilitarianism), and *virtue ethics* (based on good character and judgment). But scholars define the boundaries somewhat differently and there are many other approaches and subsets.

As just one example, consider this, drawn from Geisler Ch. 1. It illustrates various approaches to the question of *whether it can be morally right to lie for a good purpose*: (1) Lying is neither right nor wrong. There are no "laws," so we just need to decide based on circumstances. This is called *antinomianism* (i.e., "no-law-ism"). (2) Lying is generally wrong, but no law is absolute. This can be called *generalism*. (3) Lying is sometimes right, but the only absolute law is lovingkindness to others. This has been called *situationism* (i.e., the right thing depends on the situation). (4) Lying is always wrong. This might be called *absolutism*. (5) Lying is always wrong but forgivable. This is a *theological* view, that humans in a fallen world must do their best; they often do wrong, but God may forgive them through grace. (6) Lying may be right if done with a good heart for a moral purpose. This might be called *intentionalism*. And so on.

6. The Psychology of Morals

137 **Aristotle was ahead of his time in concluding:** *Nicomachean Ethics*, Bk. 2, 1103a25.

138 **In his famous dialogue *Phaedrus*, Plato:** Cooper (Ed.) 524-25.

138 **As I mentioned earlier, psychologist Jonathan Haidt:** Haidt (2012) xxi. See also Hauser 195. Haidt graphically said: "In a moral argument, we expect the successful rebuttal of our opponent's argument to change our opponent's mind. Such a belief is analogous to believing that forcing a dog's tail to wag by moving it with your hand should make the dog happy." (Haidt (2001) 821.) See also Uhlmann et al. (2009): "[Our] five studies demonstrate that people selectively use moral principles to rationalize preferred moral conclusions." As to the potent power of disgust, see Haidt et al. (1999); Haidt & Kesebir (citing 10 kinds of evidence). See also Luke & Gawronski on the CNI model. As to various innate capacities, see Pinker (2002).

138   **They [psychologists] have confirmed that we draw on two systems:** McPhetres et al.; Greene (2007 and 2013); Conway & Gawronski; Paxton & Greene.

138   **They disagree primarily about the balance between them:** See Hauser; Cushman; Jones; Bloom (2010 and 2016); Haidt (2012); Pinker (1999); Damasio (2012); Greene (2013); Kitcher. As one scholar notes, "The division between theorists who think feelings are essential to morality and those who see emotions as incidental is perhaps the most fundamental rift in moral psychology." (Prinz 14.) For a discussion of "emotivism," the "James/Lange" theory of emotion, and other features, see id. Ch. 2. Some, however, believe that the role of moral reasoning has been deprecated too much. See, e.g., Bloom (2013); R. Wallace; Paxton & Greene; Huebner; Sadowsky & Cogburn; Schaller & Park.

138   **For example, Leon Kass says:** Kass. For the mechanisms, see Tao et al; Landy; Rozin.

138   **And psychological researchers find that "disgust sensitivity":** Tao et al.; Landry & Goodwin; Rozin; Rozin & Nemeroff; Sapolsky 560-563; Hetherington & Weiler 19; Pizarro (2011); Chapman & Anderson; Sargent.

139   **Yet studies show that all these precautions:** See Rozin & Nemeroff; Bloom (2013); Haidt; Schnall.

139   **Likewise, if you ask people how they would feel:** Haidt (2012) 42; Bloom (2013) 148-152.

139   **Whether one denotes them as "cognitive" or "emotional":** In this section, I explore primarily what are usually discussed under the rubric of "heuristics and biases." See Gilovich et al. (Eds.); Kahneman & Tversky; Thaler (2015); Gigerenzer (2008). There is also a large literature on rationalizations, excuses, and motivated moral reasoning. See, e.g., Bartels; Bartels & Medin; Taber & Young; Baron (2006) 23; Uhlman et al. Together, these dynamics and defects lead to what is called "bounded" (i.e., limited) ethicality. See Bazerman & Moore 122-124; Chugh et al. (2005); Hastie & Davies. Also important is the phenomenon of "cognitive dissonance," in which people resist/reject information that creates psychic stress (e.g., rationalizing one's selfish act by conveniently thinking, "Oh, Mary won't really mind anyway. . . ."). See Festinger (1958).

140   **Paul Slovic and colleagues believe we use our emotions as a *heuristic* . . . for making judgments:** Slovic et al. (2002). See also Bazerman & Moore 10; Tappin & McKay; J. Johnson & Tversky. In addition, because of the emotional power of words, it is well established that "in politics, changes in the labeling of alternatives can have marked effects on public opinion." (Chong 116.) This gives rise to the "name and frame" game to tag public policy issues to sway public debate (e.g., "unguarded borders" versus "asylum for refugees"). For a vivid example of how affect can influence choice, consider the experiment Baruch Fischoff conducted (this was years before COVID). He asked respondents about a hypothetical disease with two strains. He asked if they would rather have a vaccine that "completely" protected against one strain, but with no effect on the other, or a vaccine that afforded "50% protection" against both strains. Far more people chose the first option—influenced by the emotional appeal of "completely" (but only against 50% of the risk!). (See Fischoff.)

140 **Humans have been wired by evolution to pay attention to actions:** Greene 240-245; Harris 62-63; Cushman; Armstrong et al.; Yeung et al. Gangemi & Mancini vividly capture the common disinclination to act where harm is even possible, calling it the "Do not play God" rule. In the larger public domain, we often lament "overregulation" by government. Yet as Cass Sunstein points out, it is also true that *"insufficient* [government] regulation can be a serious problem, costing both lives and money." (Sunstein (2014) 4.) See also Sunstein (2005). Likewise, Bazerman & Moore 77 notes that "Policy makers often display an irrational preference for harms of omission (e.g., letting people die) over harms of commission . . . even when the harms of inaction are much larger than the harms of action."

140 **In the words of one analyst, "We are more likely":** Hauser 11. See also Knobe (2003); Baron (1998) 1; Haidt & Baron (1996); Cushman (2000); Ritov & Baron; Duntley & Buss 27. See also *Deshaney v. Winnebago Co. Dept. of Social Services*, 489 U.S. 189 (1989) (government not liable when a government social worker *failed to act* to prevent child abuse). Yet "if you can help another person and do not have any reason not to, then it is irrational of you not to help." (Harman (1977) 72.) The help/no help bias is not dictated by logic but by the practicalities of living in society. One can state and enforce a clear rule of "don't directly impose harm." But imposing a vague "duty to help" in myriad ambiguous situations probably would not work as a social obligation.

141 **Social scientists have argued that it tends to make us too cautious:** See, e.g., Elster; Baron (1998); Sunstein (2014 and 2025); Beauchamp & Childress.

141 **Our first reaction is usually to help:** Greene (2013) Ch.2. Indeed, sole bystanders seem to help more often than do groups of people. (Wilson 36-39.) Some studies suggest that the people most likely to help are not the ones who are most empathic but those who are quick to anger and aggression: they just don't like seeing someone victimized. (Wilson 102.) See, generally, Svoboda; Franco & Zimbardo.

141 **But as the research by Nobel laureate Daniel Kahneman and Amos Tversky shows:** Since not harming is a stronger motive than helping, we are inclined not to act. See Bazerman & Moore 13, 76-80; Ritov & Baron; Baron (2006); Haidt (2012) 87-108. The physicians' Hippocratic Oath begins with *primum non nocere* –"First [or "above all"] do no harm." But that suggests that *no risk* should ever be incurred—even for a massive health benefit. That makes little sense, and of course physicians could do little good if they followed the rule in that way. Almost every medicine has some risk of an adverse reaction; all surgery carries risks.

141 **Research has shown that humans tend to rate the loss of something:** See Kahneman (2011) 284 ("The loss aversion ratio has been estimated in several experiments and is usually in the range of 1.5 to 2.5"); Thaler (2015); Sunstein (2025) Ch. 7-8. Loss is measured against some "frame" of what would otherwise exist. See, generally, Mussweiler & Stack; Bermudez.

141 **As Kahneman said in an interview:** Quoted in Harris (2020) 297.

142 **Causing harm in the future is usually felt to be less bad:** See Van Boven et al.; Huber et al.

142 **People more harshly condemn harm caused to identifiable people:** Ariely (2010) 239-241; Greene (2013) 260.

143 **Paul Bloom has argued that this is one reason:** Bloom (2016). Indeed, some argue that empathy isn't even a potent moral motivator compared to guilt or anger. See Prinz 105. See also notes, for p. 140 above, on "affect bias."

143 **This [confirmation bias] has been called "the mother of all misconceptions":** Rolf Dobelli, quoted in Duffy 65. See Nickerson; Kaanders et al.; Kahan (2013 and 2017b); Chatfield 215-218; Stanovich (2013). Confirmation bias is reinforced by the "sharp-shooter fallacy," our tendency to pay attention to and recall better the times we were right ("hit the bullseye") and forget the times we missed the target entirely. See Bazerman & Moore Ch. 8; Wikipedia, *Texas Sharpshooter Fallacy*. Confirmation bias is also related to overoptimism bias (about our own likelihood of performing to goals). See, generally, Gilovich et al. (Eds); Armor & Taylor; Dunning et al. (2002); Okamp. It is also reinforced by self-righteousness (belief that we are generally more moral than average).

143 **For example, in a classic study:** Lord et al. (1979). See also Bazerman & Moore (2009) 28-32.

143 **As a famous economist said, "Faced with the choice":** John Kenneth Galbraith. In like vein, Nicholas Taleb has said, "The person you are most afraid to contradict is yourself."

143 **Even worse, there is at times a "backfire effect":** Nyhan & Reifler; Kahneman et al. (1982) 146. See also studies cited in Marietta & Barker 158; Hetherington & Weiler 139. Related is the "false polarization effect." See Prontin et al.

144 **A related dynamic is known as *fundamental attribution bias*:** See, e.g., Nisbett & Ross; Healey; Berry.

144 **People usually get more blame for the bad side effects:** Hauser 51; Knobe (2003a and 2003b).

144 **Because evolution conditioned us to focus on danger and risk:** Sapolsky 480.

144 **This asymmetry has come to be known as the Knobe effect:** See Knobe, Id.; Feltz.

145 **Research demonstrates that most of us believe we are more moral:** Almost everyone believes they are more moral than most others. (Tappin & McKay.) This "better than average" bias has been repeatedly confirmed. See, e.g., Alicke, et al.; studies cited in Tappin & McKay. For example, people are in fact less honest than they believe. See Ariely (2012); Dunning (2016) and sources cited there; Shermer 327; Gino & Ariely 323-324 ("Research suggests that people lie and cheat on a daily basis, much more often than they care to admit. . . . An increasing amount of empirical evidence . . . demonstrates that dishonesty often results not from the actions of a few people who cheat a lot but from the actions of a lot of people who cheat a little."); Dunning (2016) 251 ("In short, we have found that people dramatically overpredict the likelihood that they will act in ethical, charitable, civic minded or socially desirable ways.")

145 **In such situations, even honest people:** Tetlock 122, 158.

146 **But research shows that people actually experience fairness:** Bazerman & Moore 116-122; Huo et al.; Engelmann & Tomasello.

148 **Research reveals that people who tend toward recursive, detailed cognition are less punitive:** This was so independent of age, education, gender, and political orientation. See Sargent; Bartels.

148   **But in the end, their stated views:** Zak 210-211, citing Darley et al. See also Prinz 103; Hauser Ch. 2. Mooney 124 cites an odd study suggesting that stronger males tend to favor the death penalty.

148   **Many believe that "consistency always has . . . [moral] force":** Baggini 162. But see Hinde Ch. 13, questioning whether consistency is a realistic moral expectation; Kurzban 4 ("The very constitution of the human mind makes us massively inconsistent"). But one must always ask "consistent on what criterion?" People usually say *they are* being consistent based on some higher-level principle or due to weighing some other criterion absent in another case. This leads to the title of Kurzban's book: *Why Everyone (Else) Is a Hypocrite.*

149   **It should upset us to know that in the real world:** See, e.g., Kahneman, Sibony & Sunstein (2021); Pink; Mlodinow; Sunstein (2025).

149   **As we all know, excuses are the most common response:** See Uhlman et al.; Uhlman & Cohen; Mulder & van Dijk. For a discussion of "ethical maneuvering" using a "fudge factor" in excusing oneself, see Gino & Ariely.

150   **Like most people, she has what experts call *bounded ethicality*:** Chugh; Bazerman & Moore 122-124 and sources cited there.

150   **An especially influential strain of recent psychological research:** See Haidt et al. (1993); Graham et al. (2011 and 2013); Haidt (2012). Moral Foundations Theory has been widely hailed and used. But it is also subject to critiques that it just "rebrands" prior concepts such as "social dominance orientation" or that it is not as supple as some other frameworks in predicting political orientation. See, e.g., McNeace & Sinn.

150   **Haidt argues strongly that these values:** Haidt (2012), at xx, and sources cited there-in.

151   **The most widely researched and accepted model for people's personality traits:** Two major versions of the Big Five Model are Costa & McCrae (1985 and 1992) and Goldberg (1990). See Kenny 9-10; Roccas et al; Parks-Leduc et al.; Parks & Guay. Recently, this framework has also been called the "Five Factor Model," with Neuroticism made more generic as "Emotional Stability": "Personality is usually defined as a collection of relatively persistent individual differences that transcend specific situations and contribute to the perceived stability of attitudes and behavior." (Huddy et al. (Eds.) 8.) More broadly, "traits, needs, motives, self-beliefs, values [and] social attitudes" all go into personality. Caprara & Vecchione 26-27.

151   **This model has been experimentally validated.** See, e.g., McCrae & Terracciano; McCrae and Costa. People can even judge your core personality traits reasonably well at first meeting. (Kenny 59, 64; Allik & McCrae.) But for analysis questioning the Big Five approach, see, e.g., Block (1995). A modification is the HEXACO model developed by Ashton and Lee, which adds a sixth major gradient, "Honesty/Humility," and reshapes some other parameters so that, for example, "Neuroticism" becomes "Emotionality." They also propose several "interstitial facets" including "altruism versus antagonism" and "negative self-evaluation." (See online at hexaco.org.)

151   **Moreover, these personality dispositions are genetically influenced:** McCrae et al. (2011); McCrae & Allik; Roberts & DelVecchio.

151   **As leading researcher Robert Plonim summarizes:** Plonim 34.

152   **For our purposes here, the most relevant finding:** McCrae et al. (1993); Caprara & Vecchione; sources cited in Chapter 9 below.

152   **Researchers have also examined the . . . CNI model of moral judgment:** See, e.g., Kroneisen & Heck and sources therein. In studying the "link of basic personality traits to moral judgments," they found that "high Honesty-Humility was selectively associated with sensitivity for norms [obeying rules], whereas high Emotionality was selectively associated with sensitivity for consequences [utilitarianism]." Luke and Gronowski say that their studies find "those higher in extraversion are less sensitive to consequences than those lower in extraversion, those higher in agreeableness are more sensitive to moral norms than those lower in agreeableness, and those higher in openness are more sensitive to consequences, more sensitive to moral norms, and show a stronger general preference for inaction versus action than those lower in openness."

152   **But one important reason that political liberals and conservatives disagree:** See E. Klein; Mooney; Hibbing et al. (2014b); Hetherington & Weiler; Appiah. As Kwame Appiah pithily noted: "A theory of ethics is tethered to the question of how a person should act. A theory of politics is tethered to the question of how a state should act. The two are intimately related." (Appiah ix.)

152   **As John Hibbing and colleagues conclude:** Hibbing et al. (2014b) 106. See also K. Smith et al. (2011 and 2012).

153   **It may surprise you, but differences in liberal and conservative biology:** As leading researcher Stanley Feldman states: "Heritability of ideology is estimated in the range of 40% to 60%. Shared environmental effects . . . are typically near zero." (Feldman (2013) 613, citing, e.g., several studies by Hatemi et al.; Block & Block; Bell et al.) See also Funk 245 ("All such studies using this index [Wilson-Patterson] have shown a substantial genetic influence on ideology (roughly 40% to 60%)"); Caprara & Vecchione 33 ("Personality differences between liberals and conservatives begin in early childhood and affect political orientations throughout life"); Sears & Brown 74 ("From age 21 on, cross twin correlations begin to be larger for monozygotic [identical] twins than for dizygotic [fraternal] twins—a key finding for the heritability view"); Hatemi & McDermott 35 ("opinions concerning 'abortion on demand,' immigration, the death penalty, euthanasia, conservatism and authoritarianism . . . have been found to be genetically influenced.") See also Fraley; K. Smith et al. (2012); Hatemi et al. (2011); Travers; Notes in this chapter and in Chapters 9-12 below.

    As to differences in personality dispositions, see Mooney 50-72, citing Kruglanski et al. (1996) and others.

    As to differences on the "startle" and "gag" reflexes and measures of disgust, see Oxley; Funk; Inbar et al. (2009a and 2009b).

    Studies show that having the DRD47R gene variant, which is thought to be associated with "novelty seeking" and "risk taking," is also correlated with having a liberal political orientation. Funk 247, citing Fowler et al.; Hatemi et al. See also Hibbing et al. (2014b) 191; Mooney 129.

    Studies show that having the NARG-1 gene variant, affecting neurotransmitter processing related to fear and social behaviors, is associated with a difference in political orientation. (Sources cited in Tuschman 7.) See also Schreiber et al.

    For studies of liberalism/conservatism across nations, see sources in Caprara & Vecchione; Feldman; Tuschman Ch.3.

153   **One large study of identical and fraternal twins:** Start with the massive "Minnesota Twins" study conducted by Block & Block, which also stratified them based on whether they were identical (same genes) or fraternal (partly shared genes), and found that genes strongly predicted later political orientations. See also Hatemi et al. (2011 and 2015); Eaves et al.; Olson et al.; Bouchard; McCourt study cited in Funk. In most of these studies, shared genes correlated .30 to .60 with political orientation. (Hatemi (2015).)

Genetic factors were more influential than environment in predicting political orientation as adults. Block & Block; Tuschman 24, 245, 428; Bouchard et al.; Hibbing et al. (2014b) 186; Hatemi (2014 and 2105); Jost et al. (2009 and 2014); Alford et al. (2005 and 2008); Funk 247; Telegen et al. Genes are more influential than, for example, gender, age, or income. Caprara & Vecchione 32. See study by Martin et al., cited in Kinder (2013) at 817; Alford et al.; Bouchard et al.; Telegen et al.

153   **Liberals and conservatives tend to have different thresholds for disgust:** See Chapter 9 below; Sapolsky 453, 560-563; Inbar et al. (2009); Smith et al.; (2011); Rozin; Rozin and Nemeroff; Zmigrod Ch.15. As to stronger gag and startle reflexes, see Oxley, et al; Inbar at al. (2009); Hibbing et al. (2014b) 161-166; sources cited in Funk 244; Bloom (2016) 48. As to the general mechanisms for disgust influencing moral judgments, see Tao et al.

153   **They usually have different levels of anxiety vigilance:** Hibbing et al. (2914bv) 129, 136, 161; sources in Chapters 9-11 below. In experiments "in which threatening images appeared, changes in skin conductance [a measure of arousal] were larger among conservatives than liberals, indicating greater threat sensitivity." (Johnston et al. 30, citing Oxley et al.) But see Zmigrod Ch. 15, raising various questions about the implications of such studies.

Liberals and conservatives also differ in their threshold for reacting to threatening or dominant faces. (Vigil; Hibbing et al. (2014b) 136; Tuschman 311 and studies cited there.) Likewise, Johnston and colleagues report that "studies find that conservatives are more likely to fixate on negative (versus positive) images, . . . to be distracted by threatening stimuli, . . . to weight negative information more heavily in opinion formation, . . . and to interpret emotionally ambiguous facial expressions as indicative of anger or hostility." (Johnston et al. 31 and sources cited there.)

Note that there is a recurring tendency in this literature to say "conservatives are more *x*" rather than "liberals are less *x*"—which may seem to imply that conservatives are the ones diverging from some proper norm. That is not accurate. These are descriptive, not normative, measures. Depending on the reality, liberals instead may be "too trusting" or "too oblivious to threat." A leading researcher Arie Kruglanski has been criticized by conservatives for research that seemed to characterize conservative psychology negatively. Yet he observes that "in times of great uncertainty, decisive leaders like Churchill and [George W.] Bush have more appeal than leaders who are full of ambiguity and indecisiveness, which is what liberals tend to be because of their makeup." Quoted in Mooney 60.

153   **Liberals and conservatives tend to differ on the Big Five:** See Jost et al. (2003 and 2014). Caprara & Vecchione 31 reports that research studies across many cultures "have shown that individuals high in openness to experience tend to prefer parties and ideologies on the left wing. People high on conscientiousness instead tend to prefer right wing and conservative ideologies." Peter Rentfrow found that in voting patterns across three U.S. presidential elections, a person's score on *openness* was *seven times more potent* in predicting Republican or Democratic voting than were factors such as income or educational level. And the states where people generally rate higher on openness tend to vote Democratic. Rentfrow. See also Tuschman 41.

In another study, Alan Gerber tested 12,000 people and found that those high on openness were more liberal than 71% of all respondents. Conservatives were somewhat more extroverted. Both groups ranked similarly overall on agreeableness, but with liberals rating higher on the empathy component and conservatives higher on the politeness component. Gerber (2010 and 2012). A meta-review of some seventy research studies found that right-wing authoritarianism was consistently and most strongly associated with low openness and low agreeableness, and more weakly correlated with conscientiousness. (Sibley & Duckitt.) See also Feldman; Caprara & Vecchione. As McCrae says, "A case can be made for saying that variations in experiential openness are the main psychological determinants of political polarities." (McCrae 1996).

153 **Conservatives tend to want to identify good or bad quickly:** Sapolsky 446-450; Hibbing et al. (2014b) 40; Johnston et al. 30-32.

153 **Liberals and conservatives tend to differ in their reflexive response:** Uhlman et al.

153 **Young political liberals are more likely to possess the DRD47R dopamine receptor gene:** Fowler et al., cited in Funk 247; see also Hatemi et al.; Hibbing et al. (2014b) 191.

154 **Cognitively, "liberals are more likely to be soft categorizers":** Hibbing et al. (2014b) 123; Shook & Fazio; Zmigrod; Taber & Young.

154 **Liberals are more likely to believe that people are inherently good:** R. Wright 13.

154 **Conservatives and liberals tend to seek and process information in somewhat different styles:** Research shows that "there is a relationship between conservatism and cognitive rigidity or high levels of cognitive structure, as well as decisiveness. . . . The implication is that quick decisions, seizing on what is most salient, most apparent, or most concretely understood, and a tendency to avoid over thinking, describe an information processing style characteristic of people on the political right." (Taber & Young 532.) Such people experience a desire for "closure," and "intolerance for ambiguity." Jost and colleagues likewise found those with right-wing political views exhibit an "existential need to maintain safety and security and minimize danger and threat" but also an "epistemic need to attain certainty." (Cited in Johnston et al. 27.) See also Caprara & Vecchione 34-36, 71; Kruglanski; Jost et al. (2003); Chirumbolo; studies cited in Mooney 68-70.

As Hibbing et al. (2014b) 139 notes, "Conservatives acquire the information they believe necessary to draw adequate conclusions, then call it a day. Liberals go on acquiring new information even if . . . they might not be able to fully absorb the information." See also Kahan (2017a and 2017b). In an inventive abstract game called "beanfest," Shook and Fazio showed people shapes that looked like potatoes or beans with various patterns of dots on them. To make a long (research) story short: some people got comfortable with the patterns from beans they "knew" and wanted to stick with them; other people were more willing to fool around with beans that they had "never met before." You guessed it: the first group were more likely to be politically conservative and the latter to be liberal. Shook & Fazio (1997) concludes that this points to "fundamental differences in how individuals with varying ideologies approach their social world [and] acquire information."

In some contexts, liberals are more apt to seek situational explanations for behavior, while conservatives look to simpler, more consistent "character" explanations. (Sapolsky 447.) Indeed, "the conservative dislike of ambiguity has been demonstrated in numerous apolitical contexts." (Id. 450.) But for contrary or non-confirming views, see Ruisch; Zmigrod 167-169; Sadowski & Cogburn.

154 **Liberal and conservative brains may develop . . . differently:** Kanai et al.; Hibbing et al. (2014b) 153-158; Mooney 111-115; Zmigrod; Sapolsky Ch. 13; Westen et al (2006); Amodeo et al.; Zamboni; Taber & Young 542-546 and sources cited there; Mosely 158-159; Schreiber; Johnston et al. 31 ("In a replication study, [Kanai et al.] . . . were able to correctly classify 72 percent of their subjects in ideological terms using grey matter volume in the ACC [anterior cingulate cortex] alone. Thus, tendencies for liberals to engage more with uncertain or unfamiliar stimuli and for conservatives to be more sensitive to threatening stimuli may be reflected in their brain anatomy.")

154 **Scholar George Lakoff explains that as they develop:** For this paragraph, see Lakoff (1996) Ch. 5-6. For testing of this model, see, e.g., Fraley; Feinberg et al.; McAdams et al.

A different and widely cited model of parenting style conceives of it as having two main axes: the degree of authority and the degree of responsiveness. Thus, there are four main types of parents: (1) *authoritative* (high demand and high response: children are given rules and expectations but are listened to and encouraged to give feedback); (2) *authoritarian* (high demand but low responsiveness: children are told what to do and are punished if they don't comply); (3) *permissive* (low demand but high responsiveness: children's feelings are paramount; they set the agenda and are rarely sanctioned); and (4) *neglectful* (low demand and low responsiveness: children are left mainly on their own without much expectation or response). These parenting styles naturally have lifelong effects on the children's outlook and values. See Baumrind et al; Feinberg et al.

155 **John Hibbing and colleagues summarize the research findings:** Hibbing et al. (2014b) 107. In their book *Open Versus Closed*, at 6-7, Christoper Johnston, Howard Lavine, and Christopher Federico report on extensive research on "dispositional sorting." They find that "liberalism and conservatism are rooted in stable individual differences in the ways people perceive, interpret and cope with *threat and uncertainty.*" (Italics in original.) More-over, because "emotionally laden cultural and lifestyle issues have become more central to partisan branding," this has "created an alignment between political identity and dispositional openness [one of the Big Five gradients]." (Id 11.) Hibbing (Id.) 110 says: "Evidence exists that a range of seemingly nonpolitical tastes and preferences correlate with political temperament. . . . [T]hey range from occupational preferences to leisure pursuits to sensitivity to disgust, as well as personality traits, moral foundations, personal values, culinary choices . . . [etc.]" See, generally, Marietta & Barker.

155 **In fact, both liberals and conservatives rely on all of the main moral frameworks:** See Kurzban; Baker Ch. 3; Mooney; Hibbing et al. (2014b); Hochschild 40, 61. Binmore 93 says philosophical liberals tend more toward a utilitarian view while conservatives tend toward a Kantian approach. Zmigrod 251 disagrees.

158   **Haidt and some other MFT advocates:** Haidt, quoted in Hibbing et al. (2014b) 107. See Graham et al. Actually, they have different *food taste receptors*! See Hibbing (Id.) 91-94, 112-113.

158   **Haidt has proposed a chart to depict:** Haidt (2012) 182-188.

158   **In many situations, liberals tend to focus on the fact of pain or harm:** Haidt (2012) 182-188, 350-358; Hibbing (Id.) 106-107.

158   **As John Hibbing and colleagues summarize:** Hibbing (Id.) 106.

158   **Sam Harris concludes that "conservatives have the same morality":** Harris (2010) 181. How strong is this difference? On many measures, 25 or 50 percent of the variation between people's political attitudes is due to inborn differences in personality dispositions. (See Notes for this chapter above; Haidt 324; Funk.) This is stronger than many factors usually cited. Thus "whether you end up on the right or the left of the political spectrum turns out to be just as heritable as most other traits; genetics explain between a third and a half of the variability among people on their political attitudes. Being raised in a liberal or conservative household accounts for much less." (Haidt 324, citing Alford.) See also Funk; Taber & Young.

158   **And philosopher Bernard Gert offers:** Gert 373.

159   **There is lots of research showing female/male differences:** See, e.g., Baron-Cohen; Weisberg et al.; Costa (2001); Susan Pinker (2008) Ch. 18; Sapolsky 211-222; Tancredi Ch.7; J. Williams (2025); Schwartz & Rubel; Bloom (2013) 49 ("[There is a] broader body of research suggesting greater empathy and compassion, on average, in females"). Some research finds that women tend to score higher on agreeableness, neuroticism, and openness to feelings, while men tend to score higher on assertiveness and excitement seeking. (Weisberg.) Some studies suggest that men are more utilitarian in their morals. See Friesdorf.

159   **Gilligan criticized the biased approach she saw:** She said this often in interviews. See, for example, "Why Psychological Theories Are Incomplete," *The Institute of Art and Ideas*, Sept. 25, 2024.

159   **In contrast, "the female experience was said to be more . . . caring":** Driver 57. In children, Bloom reports that "girls are more likely to soothe than boys, which meshes with a broader set of research suggesting greater empathy and compassion on average in females." (Bloom (2016) 99.) See also Tannen Ch. 6.

159   **Thus, "some researchers have proposed that women prefer care reasoning":** See Gilligan; Noddings; Langton et al.; Prinz 193; Wilson 65; but see also Haack; Flanagan. It has been noted that women philosophers are especially prominent in the arena of virtue ethics, which is seen as relying less on strict rules and more on humane character. But others remain Kantian, for example. See, e.g., Stohr; Korsgaard; B. Herman. Some researchers suggests that men and women may tend to value different inputs in assessing fairness and resolving interpersonal disputes. (Wilson 185-187.) Others suggest that differences are primarily because women more often encounter certain kinds of situations. See also Haack, questioning the philosophical differences and arguing, e.g., that "the rubric 'feminist epistemology' is incongruous on its face." (Haack 1254.) See also Longino; Anderson.

160   **In a major survey across 67 nations:** Atari et al. (2020); see also Niazi et al. Based on their review of the research literature, Sidanius and Kurzban, at 221, say that "[research shows] males to be more militaristic, ethnocentric, xenophobic, ethnically discriminatory, anti-egalitarian, punitive and positively disposed . . . to the exploitation of out-groups than are women."

160   Some studies have reported that women tend to have a stronger . . . "moral identity": Kennedy et al.

160   A meta-analysis conducted on 470 experimental studies: Gerlach et al. See also Niazi et al. Tancredi Ch. 9 describes how men and women lie for different motives—men usually to enhance their standing and women usually to protect themselves from harm.

160   Some studies . . . suggest that women and men tend to react differently to [the] Trolley Problem: See Bartels & Pizarro (2011) ("Many researchers have documented that men are more willing than women to outcome-maximizing harm.") But others report few differences. (Hauser 124.) For a broader study of similar "crisis" scenarios, see Armstrong et al. The authors found that "women scored higher than men on deontological tendencies [i.e., duty], and this difference was enhanced [when it involved] . . . a harmful action rather than acting to prevent harm. . . . Gender differences in deontological inclinations are affected by both harm aversion and action aversion." What this means is that women inclined more to the Kantian view of "do what is moral" and "don't harm" rather than to a utilitarian "do what's good overall, even if unfortunately, you need to hurt somebody." See also Zamzow & Nichols (finding male/female differences), and Seyedsayamdost et al. (finding little difference).

160   Does all this add up to a significant difference?: Some argue that any differences have probably been exaggerated. (Hinde 6; Mikhail.) But there are diverse results. (Reporting some differences, see Zamzow & Nichols.) Zak 84 reports that in the studies of Ultimatum/Dictator "trust games," women typically give 40 percent while men give only 25 percent. But see Seyedsayamdost. Overall, Prinz 193 summarizes the situation thus: "Men and women in the same community often seem to have subtly different moral values. Relevant findings include the following: men are slightly more concerned with justice than women and women are slightly more concerned with care. . . . Men tend to be more in favor of violent punishment than women . . . and women are significantly more deontological than men in their responses to trolley dilemmas [citations in source omitted]."

161   An entire bookcase could be filled with books [about runaway trolley cars]: See, e.g., Edmonds; Kamm; Hauser; Greene (2013); Unger; Foot (1976); Thompson (1985); Bauman et al.; Cushman et al.; Ng. et al. Appiah says that the vast and complicated Trolley Problem literature "makes the Talmud look like Cliff Notes." (Quoted in Bloom (2013) 169.) Some may feel that the trolley examples are too artificial to reveal what people actually would do in life-saving situations. If so, then consider the choices that are actually faced by a physician who must allocate time and resources among patients in a hospital's trauma service, COVID ward, or an intensive care unit after a natural disaster. Does she divide her time equally among all the patients, trying to save all (which may result in several deaths) or does she "economize" on the time spent on the one most severely compromised, in order to devote more time to saving all the other patients? See G. Harman (1971); Beauchamp & Childress. As another example: In a German movie called *Terror*, an air force pilot is put on trial for deciding to shoot down a plane and thus kill 164 passengers—to avoid its crashing into a soccer stadium with 70,000 people. About 87 percent of the German viewers said this was morally justified. (Cited in Kroneisen & Heck.) See also Uhlman et al.

161 **This literature was spawned by an elegant ethical mind game:** Foot (1978). See also Thompson (1976 and 1985).

162 **Over the years, scholars have devised many variations of the Trolley Problem:** See, e.g., Kamm; Edmonds; Hauser.

162 **These and related scenarios have now been presented to *hundreds of thousands of people:*** Greene Ch. 9; Mikhail; Prinz Ch. 7; Edmonds 92-94; Hauser; Cushman et al.; Gazzaniga 169. (See the report of a BBC poll cited in Edmonds 92.)

162 **The start of an answer emerges from a key 2001 research study:** Greene et al.

163 **As Paul Bloom summarized the results:** Bloom (2013) 167, 169.

163 **Greene finds that three factors combine to influence:** Greene (2013) 222-223; Greene (2007); See also Cushman et al.

163 **In another scenario, instead of pulling the switch:** Kamm 21.

163 **In this scenario, you can save the five people. . . . but:** Greene (2013) 217-222.

164 **In saving human lives, why should race matter?:** See Bloom (2013) 169; Mooney 78; Edmonds 130-132. Uhlman et al. (2009) also finds illogical reversals of moral preferences: it made a big difference whether the lives to be sacrificed were U.S. versus Iraqi civilians. In a later study, political conservatives displayed this difference, but liberals didn't. In a related study judging whether one person could be sacrificed to save others, only 13 percent of subjects said the race of the sacrificed person mattered; 20 percent said gender; 49 percent said health; 62 percent said age; and 54 percent used social distance (in-group or out-group). In another study, Petrinovich asked people to decide the Trolley Problem—but with the identity of the victims made clear. As Marc Hauser describes, they favored saving "kin over non-kin, friends over strangers, humans over non-humans, and politically safe or neutral individuals over politically abhorrent" ones. (Hauser 122-123.) Which of these do you see as morally defensible criteria? Preferring kin makes sense. But would you really prefer to save the life of someone because they are in your political party?

164 **In the trolley scenario, would you kill your spouse or child to save five strangers?:** Harris (2010) 260.

164 **As Sapolsky says, "Somebody with damage to . . . part of the brain":** Quoted in Harris (2020) 260.

165 **This explains why people who have a damaged vmPFC:** Greene 125. See also Greene 116-131; Gazzaniga 170-171; Harris (2010) 260. See, generally, Zmigrod; Damasio (2006). Some research also suggests that "higher levels of psychopathy are associated with a greater preference for utilitarian over deontological [Kantian] judgments." (Luke et al.)

165 **Some have criticized the Trolley Problem as artificial:** Churchland (2011) 110-111, citing Zimbardo; see also Levine & Wilson.

165 **Analogously, most people say:** Miller (Ed.) Ch. 16 and 22; Svoboda.

165 **In one study, researchers found that "public health officials":** Greene conducted a study confirming this mode of thinking. (Greene (2013) 129-131.)

165 **Philosopher Gilbert Harman posed two examples:** Harman (1977) 3-4. In a study by Hauser: 98 percent of subjects said the second scenario was morally wrong. (Hauser 110.) But what exactly is the criterion of moral difference? For an empirical exploration of how people see such dilemmas, see Ng at al.

166   **Recall the example … conjured by Tversky and Kahneman:** Tversky & Kahneman (1981). See discussions by Harris (2010) 141; Bermudez 20-23, 198; Pinker (1999) 193. For a re-peat study with some variations, see Druckman.

168   **A leading researcher explains that when we think:** Sapolsky 45-55, 505. See also Zak 174-178.

168   **As Hauser vividly says:** Hauser 418-420.

7. Arguing Morals Well: Facts, Logic, and Words

170   **As Aristotle said, "We must know . . . the facts":** *Rhetoric*, Bk. 2, 1396a 4-6.

171   **In a historic break from the pursuit of objective reason:** See Kronman 93; Liautaud 135, 153; Bloom (2016) 6.

170   **In this world, "there are no universal truths":** Kakutani 18. For a deeper philosophical reflection, see Putnam. Of course, beyond ignorance, we must now navigate the perilous shoals—especially online—of mistaken information, factoids, intentional disinformation, counterknowledge, and manipulation. See, e.g., Sunstein (2025); Edmans; Nichols; Grimes.

172   **To answer that, we need to know the facts about how . . . organs are allocated:** See for example: United Network for Organ Sharing, unos.org; HRSA, "Organ Donation Legislation and Policy," www.organdonor.gov; *Wikipedia,* Organ Donation; Organ Trans-plantation.

173   **In 2023 and 2024, both the American Library Association and PEN America:** American Library Assn., 2024 Book Ban Data (4,200 books banned in 2023); PEN America (10,000 books banned in 2023 and 6,800 in 2024). The actual number is surely higher since some states did not report. The most often banned author was Stephen King. See also Lukianoff and Schott 150-158.

174   **But before a person decides about the morality of vaccine refusal:** See, e.g., Paris; Dirusso & Stansberry; Liautaud 181. COVID-19 vaccination rates varied among counties from about 9 to 96 percent. And parents obtaining "vaccine exemptions" for other vaccines are far more common in Republican-voting states. Perhaps oddly, the areas where people core highest on "conservative" values like loyalty to community yield low vaccination rates. Reimer et al.

175   **As Simon Blackburn notes: "Today's relativists":** Blackburn (2005) xiv.

175   **This is the opposite of the classic wisdom:** Hume, *Enquiry*, Section 10.

175   **Making matters worse, . . . most of us know a lot less than we think:** See Kinder & Kalmoe; Chong (2013 and 2019); Boghossian & Lindsay 213; O'Connor; O'Connor & Wetherall; Hochschild & Einstein; Lawson & Kakkar; Bauerlein; Kakutani; Kuklinski & Quirk; Kavanagh & Rich; McIntyre (2018); Gilovich & Ross; Rosling; Shermer; Sowell; Sloman & Fernbach. There is also the problem of "noise"—information that is distracting or misleading. More generally, see Lupia et al. Ch. 3. As Kahneman, Sibony, and Sunstein (2020) note, a number of social policy-salient systems inherently are afflicted with "noisy," distorted decisioning. These include medical care, child custody, bail hearings, and hiring for jobs.

175   **Unfortunately, as the leading researcher on expert forecasting:** Tetlock & Gardner 74. See also Marietta & Barker xvii-xiv; Greener & Greve; Jacoby. This is not patronizing. There are many subjects on which the average person knows a lot of practical wisdom—and their opinions are probably the best information that exists. But that often is not true of technical or specialized policy issues.

175 **In time, the well-documented *Dunning-Kruger effect*:** See Dunning; Dunning et al.

175 **In the words of the old saying:** This witticism is usually attributed to Mark Twain. See marktwainhouse.org. But it probably should be ascribed to nineteenth-century humorist Josh Billings. Few people care, because poor Billings is no longer as famous as Twain. See Levitin 125-128.

175 **Here are just a few examples of the kinds of misconceptions:** Data is from Duffy. See also E. Klein 107-108; L. McIntyre (2013 and 2018).

177 **As Aldous Huxley said, "Facts don't cease to exist":** Huxley, *Complete Essays*, Vol. 2.

178 **As Boghossian and Lindsay conclude:** Boghossian & Lindsay 213.

178 **Logic has been described as a system:** Black & Murphy (1982) 7. See also Lee 2; Toulmin et al. 3-4. See, generally, Tindale; Copi; Toulmin & Reike; Sinott-Armstrong; Sinott-Armstrong & Fogelin; Walton (2008 and 2017); Cheng. As Hume said, "The sole end of logic is to explain the principles and operations of our reasoning capacity." (*Enquiry* 184.)

178 **Indeed, its "rational force is . . . psychological":** Baggini 129. Unfortunately, we are quite poor at many elements of logic, especially "conditional" propositions (e.g., "If A, then B, but if C, then not D.") See Prinz 264-268. A very intelligent, logically analytic man, the eminent lawyer Clarence Darrow, reportedly said: "I don't like spinach, and I'm glad I don't, because if I did, I'd eat it, and I hate the stuff." So much for logic.

178 **As Bertrand Russell said, "If the law of contradiction were . . . false":** B. Russell (1957) 71.

179 **As relevant here, there are two principal types of logic:** These are deductive (formal) and inductive (informal) logic. But there are subtypes (such as Bayesian, and abductive, which are forms of inductive logic). And there are specialized forms, such as symbolic logic and mathematical logic, not relevant here. See, generally, Johnson-Laird Parts 3-4; Lee Ch. 4-6.

For discussions of formal deductive logic, see Lee; Copi; Cheng. The validity of a deductive statement is a *relation* of the premises and conclusion, not a *property* of the conclusion. Thus, a syllogism can be logically *valid* even though a premise is false and thus leads to a false conclusion (e.g., "Every nation's capital must be within the nation. Paris is the capital of Spain. Therefore, Paris is within Spain.") But a syllogism is not called *sound* unless it has true premises *as well as* logical validity. See Lee 14-15.

179 **In Aristotle's words, a syllogism is a "discourse in which":** *Prior Analytics*, 24a 19-22.

180 **Then there is the problem of *fallacies*:** Hamblin 12; Walton (1987 and 2008); Arp et al.; Hansen & Pinto; Thoughtco.com; Tindale 9, 172 ("The basic problem with fallacies has always been that once you look at them closer, . . . [they] can evidently in some cases be a correct—or at least not unreasonable–form of argument.")

181 **The second main type of logic is *informal* or *inductive logic*:** See Walton (2008). The key difference: "In deductive logic, correctness is an all or nothing affair. Deductive inferences are either totally valid or totally invalid. . . . [But] inductive

correctness does admit of degrees; one inductive conclusion may be more strongly supported than another." (Salmon 237.)

181   **Bertrand Russell said that without induction:** Russell (1945) 674.

181   **Layers and layers of induction can at best lead:** Lee Ch. 3; Salmon. This is in contrast to deduction. "The deductive standard is [absolute] validity. The inductive standard is [relative persuasive] strength." Sinott-Armstrong 180. As to the practical variant called "abduction" or "inference to the best explanation," see Stanford Encyclopedia of Philosophy, Abduction (I. Douven); Lipton. Induction is sometimes allied with Bayesian statistical analysis, in which one constantly updates one's "priors" with new information to obtain probabilistic judgments. See van de Schoot et al. (2014); van de Schoot (2021).

182   **In the pages that follow, I'll explain some common fallacies.** For more on these and others, see Hansen & Pinto; Walton (1987); Hamblin; Gula; Bruce & Barbone.

186   **Recognizing fallacies when other people use them:** For readable explorations of logic, see Cheng; Lee; Hamblin; Black; Hansen & Pinto.

187   **"Words matter":** Tannen iv; See, generally, Leith. For a philosophical exploration, see Grice.

187   **As one commentator says, "Language is like fire":** Luntz xxv.

189   **But what exactly does it mean to "cause" something?:** See Pearl; Bunge; Beebe et al.; Hall. See also Kahneman et al. (1982) Part 3; Anscombe (1999); Beauchamp & Childress Ch. 5; Pinker (2007); Pizarro et al. (2003)

189   **But Aristotle devised an early typology [of causes] that has rarely been improved upon:** See *Physics*, Bk. 2, Ch. 3; *Metaphysics,* Bk. 5, Ch 2.

8. Overlapping Mandates: Customs, Morals, and Law

192   **As Mark Twain said, "Laws are sand; customs are rock":** marktwainhouse.org.

193   **In many traditional societies, violating custom:** See Shweder; Boehm; Henrich et al. (2004); Prinz 71-72; Johnson 38.

193   **As one scholar puts it, "The moral domain varies by culture":** Haidt (2012) 30. See his discussion of the debate between Shweder and Turiel on this issue. (Id. 21-30.) But the moral boundary must be known. As Bernard Gert notes, "Everyone about whom moral judgments can be correctly made must know what kind of behavior morality prohibits." (Gert 7.) The social function of morality requires that.

197   **Many . . . professions have developed specialized codes of ethics:** See, e.g.: for lawyers: American Bar Association, *Model Rules for Professional Conduct*; for doctors, American Medical Association, *Code of Medical Ethics*; for psychologists, American Psychological Association, *Ethical Principles of Psychologists and Code of Conduct*; for physical therapists: American Physical Therapy Association, *Code of Ethics for the Physical Therapist*; for accountants, AICPA, *Code of Professional Conduct*; for mechanical engineers: American Society of Mechanical Engineers, *Code of Ethics.*

198   **Let's be honest: Many people think [business ethics] is an oxymoron:** But on the other hand, "nearly all business ethicists believe, not surprisingly, that there is such a thing as business ethics." (D. Russell 245.) See also Cook.

198   **For example, Google's Code of Conduct:** abc.xyz/investor/google-code-of-conduct.

198   **That is why the annual lists of "most admired companies":** See Kornferry.com.

199 **One treatise says, "Business ethics is about how you make your money":** Brennan et al. 15.

199 **One author asks her Stanford students each year:** Liautaud 27.

199 **Here are some commonly cited principles:** See, generally, Brennan et al.; Ferrell; Vogel. As to *indirect* harm via strategic choices, see Bazerman & Moore 132-133.

201 **Some experts believe that company directors must make stockholder welfare their sole end:** See, e.g., Bainbridge.

201 **Others disagree, and the U.S. Supreme Court has said:** *Burwell v. Hobby Lobby Stores*, 573 U.S. 682 (2014).

201 **They believe that the fiduciary duty of directors:** *Ebay Domestic Holdings v. Newmark,* 16 A.3d 1 (Del. Ct. Chancery 2009). See, generally, Vogel; Zhao & Murrell. Legal scholar Lynn Stout, author of the book *The Shareholder Value Myth*, says, "There is a common belief that corporate directors have a duty to maximize corporate profits, even if this means skirting ethical rules, damaging the environment or harming employees. That belief is utterly false." *New York Times,* April 16, 2015. See also Vogel; Zhao & Murrell; A. Lipton; Hart & Zingales; LoPucki.

201 **Yet legal commentators continue to express the concern:** Bainbridge.

201 **In 2019, about 200 CEOs:** Frydman et al.; A. Lipton.

202 **Sometimes, when a big corporate error harms people:** See Liautaud.

203 **As one expert says, "Ethics are an early-stage endeavor":** Liautaud 52.

203 **He recommends "strategic stalling":** Badaracco (2003a) 7.

203 **Another scholar says that corporate morality:** Nash 45.

203 **It also runs up against another business reality:** Andrews 76.

203 **Both ethical and "unethical business practice reflects the values":** Paine 86; Badaracco (2003b) 139-164.

203 **Another practical difference is that individuals can try to be saints :** Badaracco (2003a) 1-18. But see Paine. For a distinctly Christian take on this, see Grudem Ch. 40. For a more general view of good and not-so-good corporate behavior, see Brief & Smith-Crowe in Miller (Ed.) 390-414. For an argument that even good ethics "rules" won't suffice and we need a more operational process, an "ethics of practice," see Woermann.

9. The Broader Domain of Values

205 **Basically, values are described by psychologists:** Rokeach (1968) 124. See also Rokeach (1973); Roccas; Parks & Guay; Parks-Leduc; Kenny; Russo.

208 **Let's dig a little deeper into what values are:** For Schwartz's definition, see Schwartz (1992) 4; Schwartz (1994); Baier & Rescher 36-47. A classic definition by Rokeach described values as "abstract ideals, positive or negative, not tied to any specific attitude, object or situation, representing a person's beliefs about ideal modes of conduct and ideal terminal goals of life." Rokeach (1968) 24. See also Baier & Rescher 36; Parks-Leduc at al. 3; Bar-Tal 109. See generally Maio. Values differ from but overlap somewhat with personality traits. "Traits describe how individuals tend to feel, think and believe. They are therefore summaries of an individual's responses and behaviors." Unlike traits, "values express a person's motivations that may or may not be reflected in behaviors." Parks-Leduc et al. 5.

To see the difference, consider a person who may greatly *value* creativity, but whose *traits* (endowments) just don't enable him to be especially creative. An early researcher, Gordon Allport, referred to traits as "temperament" and to values as "character," which captures well the commonsense difference. (Allport, *passim.*) See also Roccas; Parks & Guay. But some researchers do not see them as that separate; see Parks-Leduc 5. In the end, "values include an evaluative component lacking from personality [traits]. Values relate to what we believe we ought to do, while personality relates to what we naturally tend to do." Parks & Guay 677. Yet "people who consistently exhibit a behavioral trait are likely to increase the degree to which they value the goals the trait services." (Roccas 791.) For example, if you are dispositionally inclined to conformity and obeying rules, and you make yourself comply most of the time, you tend to value that in others and want to punish violators. This is known as "value justification" or "value instantiating beliefs." For an interesting study of it, see Ponizovskiy et al.

208 **He [Schwartz] identified ten core values that recur across all [nations and cultures]:** Schwartz (1992); Bardi & Schwartz. Later he and colleagues refined this to 19 values, but the added ones are basically splits of the initial ones.

208 **Values give rise to more specific norms of behavior:** Feldman (2013) 602-603. Indeed, "moral judgments . . . ooze with sentiment. *We are passionate about our values* [emphasis added]." (Prinz 13.) Accordingly, "People who consistently exhibit a behavioral trait are likely to increase the degree to which they value the goals the trait services." (Roccas 791.)

210 **Note just one large-scale example: About 65 percent of all the firefighters . . . are volunteers:** U.S. Fire Administration, 2025.

210 **The long-dominant *rational choice theory*:** As Nobel laureate economist Gary Becker flatly stated: "All human behavior can be viewed as involving participants who (1) maximize their utility; (2) form a stable set of preferences; and (3) accumulate an optimal amount of information." (Becker 14.) But much research since has undermined belief that we humans function in this idealized way. See, e.g., Thaler; Kahneman (2011); Kahneman et al. (Eds.) (1982); Sloman & Fernbach; Gigerenzer; Pinker (2021); Stanovich et al. (2016); Lupia et al.; Gintis; Redlawsk & Lau.

Huddy et al. 5-6, 9 observes that "rational choice theory is built on a set of basic assumptions about human behavior: first, individuals have consistent preferences over their goals, which are often defined as the pursuit of economic self-interest; second, individuals assign a value or utility to these goals; and third, probabilities are assigned to the different ways of achieving these goals. . . . [Thus, rational choice] is making the choice that maximizes one's expected utility . . . [But such] pure rationality is something of a fiction when applied to human behavior . . . In myriad ways, cognitive psychology has undermined the rational choice model." That's not because people are dumb. It's because in many situations, all the alternatives aren't clear; all the facts aren't available; the probability of each outcome is uncertain; choices have second-order consequences; and so on.

People are in fact beset by a raft of mental habits and glitches that limit our effective decision-making. Just for example: we routinely violate basic rules of rational choice like "transitivity" by preference reversals. Thus, if you prefer *a* to *b* and prefer *b* to *c*, then logically you *must* prefer *a* to *c*. But in choosing wines, buying houses, and voting for candidates, we sometimes don't do this. Also, we don't seek out information neutrally, but instead succumb to "confirmation bias." We use heuristics to save time—even when they don't really "fit" the problem. We engage in "motivated reasoning" distorted by emotion. We have only "bounded" rationality. And so on. See Lord et al.; Kahan (2006); Kahan & Braman; Gilovich et al. (Eds.); Mooney; Kahneman (2011); Sunstein (2025).

If we then turn to the larger public sphere, political scientists Lodge and Taber explain the problem thus: "Grounded in an Enlightenment view of Rational Man, political science has been dominated by models of conscious control and political democracy. Rational and intentional reasoning, in this conventional view, *causes* political behavior. [But] this is a book about unconscious thinking and its influence on political attitudes and behavior." (Lodge & Taber 1.) Huddy et al. 752 explains that "in contrast to material interests focused on tangible economic . . . concerns, social identity theory shifts the focus to the defense of group status as a source of political concern. There is ample evidence that symbolic concerns can increase political cohesion." See also Sunstein (2014) 5.

210 **What's more, every "National Election Study has shown":** Tuschman, Introduction, citing Jost et al.(2006). See also Sears & Funk.

210 **Across the presidential elections spanning 1996–2004:** Tuschman 41. In 2009, the average household income in Congressional districts that voted Democratic was $3,000 *less* than in districts voting Republican (poorer areas voted Democratic). But by 2023, that had reversed: average income was $12,000 *higher* in Democratic districts (wealthier areas voted Democratic). *The Week,* Nov. 7, 2025, 16.

210 **A 2024 Pew Research Center study found that Democrats:** Pew Research Center (2024a and 2024b). See also Citrin & Green.

210 **A leading expert says that while exceptions exist:** See Johnston et al. Ch.7; Lodge & Taber.

211 **"Lots of evidence indicates that people do not simply vote their economic self- interest":** See Williams Ch.16. In her book *Outclassed,* Joan Williams describes the new ascendent group of "Scaffles"—working-class folks who are "socially conservative and financially liberal." They react negatively to what they see as left-liberal attacks on religion, hard work, gender identity, masculinity, etc., while favoring some liberal social programs. Others note that "emotionally-laden cultural and lifestyle issues have become more central to partisan branding," and "this has created an alignment between identity and dispositional openness [for example]." Johnston et al. 11.

211 **As Joan Williams wrote in 2025:** J. Williams 5.

211 **Leading scholars find that "compared to self-interest":** See Chong (2013) 101; Chong & Druckman; Cave 13; Hardin 17; Taber & Young; Sears & Funk: Etzioni (1988) 58; Kat & Zupan. Indeed, "There are powerful reasons to question the empirical importance of self-interest. . . . [If] self-interest is defined in a reasonably tangible and material way, . . . then self-interest turns out in study after study to have remarkably little to do with public opinion on a wide range of political issues." (Taber & Young 529.) Another leading researcher finds that "compared to self-interest, people's values and their [social] . . . evaluations are better predictors of their views [on political issues like] . . . government spending, law and order, race and gender issues, social welfare policy and foreign affairs." (Chong (2013) 101.) See also Citrin & Green. In reality, instead of trying to evaluate each policy issue one by one to decide how it will benefit them, most voters use a shorthand proxy—"party identification" or response to strong "value themes" in candidates' appeals. (Taber & Young.) See also Redlawsk; Redlawsk & Lau.

211   **This is no secret to political campaign experts:** Tuschman 35, citing Glaser & Ward ("Economic opinions don't seem to respond to economic interests" but instead represent "motivated signals of partisan identity"). See also J. Williams; Lupia et al. Some assert that people actually do vote in an economically rational way—but they focus on long-term rather than short-term economic interests. The theory is that wise elite people know, for example, that society will be more prosperous and civilized in the long run if they are taxed to support the "safety net" and make society more equitable; and wise working-class people know that lower taxes will stimulate economic growth and jobs, so they will ultimately gain more than they lose in lesser social programs.

Some people may reason this way, but it still assumes that people are primarily rational calculators of what the economists call the "discounted present value of future utilities." That may not reflect how people make most decisions—even on economic issues. See for example Kahneman & Tversky (2002); Gigerenzer (2008); Thaler; Sunstein (2025). But for a more positive view, see Popkin. Nobel Laureate Richard Thaler says this wrongly sees people as idealized "econs"; he then methodically shows how we are cognitively and emotionally flawed human deciders, not purely rational econ deciders.

211   **The polarization of politics in recent decades:** See E. Klein. Kahan and Braman's research indicates that conservatives tend to be more individualistic and hierarchical, while liberals tend to be more communitarian and egalitarian. Kahan & Braman. See also Mooney 80-81; Marietta & Barker Ch. 7. But others conclude that we are not as polarized as we think. In their book *Neither Liberal nor Conservative,* Kinder and Kalmoe review massive data from the ANES survey of opinions. They conclude that most Americans have clear views on only a handful of issues, and they don't usually cohere into a political philosophy. "Sentinel" or polarizing issues like immigration or abortion can move the electorate. But they say Americans' views are far more "in play" than a settled political philosophy would ordain. See also Lupia et al. and works cited there.

212   **But in reality, value change happens often:** This section draws greatly on Rescher, and on Russo et al. See also Alwin et al.

213   **"The experience of members of a generation in adolescence":** Baker 3.

214   **A *Wall Street Journal*/NORC poll compared:** A. Zitner (Mar. 7, 2023).

214   **Still, a major survey surprisingly finds that "American values are more traditional":** Baker 34-35. See also Inglehart & Wetzel; Schuck & Wilson (Eds.)

214   **Your values then become bound up in your identity:** Sears & Brown.

214   **People who know you well can describe your values:** Kenny 89-90.

215   **So, not surprisingly, our values tend to be quite durable:** Sloman & Fernbach 160.

217   **While individuals vary, in general, the politically conservative tribe are in fact *more likely*:** Tuschman 57-59; Marietta & Barker; Hetherington & Weiler; Hibbing et al. (2014b) 91-96, 112-114.

217   **Some scholars depict values as falling into "radial categories":** See Lakoff (1996).

217   **The Schwartz Value Scale (SVS) uses:** See Schwartz (2012).

218   **As we will see, the SVS even helps predict political orientations:** Schwartz & Boenke.

218   **The SVS value structure has been shown to be largely consistent with the Big Five model:** Vecchione; Dobewell et al.; Parks-Leduc et al. (2015). Importantly, Schwartz found empirical evidence supporting the depiction of common value patterns in a chart—a segmented circle with *opposite poles* being, for example, universalism versus power over others. People who score high on holding a given value (like universalism) typically score low on its polar opposite (power). Likewise, people who score high on self-direction tend to be low on the antipode of obeying rules or seeking security. The SVS chart also helps explain how values that are *adjacent* to one another sometimes fuse together, like conformity and security. Thus, people who worry a lot about external threats also tend to want a high degree of internal conformity to norms. Likewise, the values of benevolence and universalism are adjacent, so kind people tend to worry about how to extend kindness to everyone.

218   **The SVS also ties into the moral foundations theory:** Haidt (2012); Graham et al.; McNeace & Sinn. It may surprise people, but massive research suggests that a person's dispositions on the moral foundations scales powerfully predict their *political* views. (See main text p. 152.) See also Marietta and Barker 123. And for a bizarre, tendentious but revealing account, see the book authored by "Anonymous Conservative."

219   **Another fruitful and widely used framework:** Feldman (1988). Liberals and conservatives differ in their instincts about child rearing. Remarkably, an analogous divergence is seen in preferences for *dogs*. Liberals tend to say they want a gentle and sociable dog; conservatives say they want an obedient and loyal dog. Hibbing et al. (2014b) 107-108 The dogs' political opinions have not been reported.

219   **Marc Hetherington and Jonathan Weiler see:** Hetherington and Weiler 13-21.

219   **Scholars have administered the Feldman questions:** Id 18.

220   **Another effort to organize value orientations:** Lakoff (1996).

220   **Researchers David Barker and James Tinnick found:** See Barker& Tinnick. See also Stenner 195; Feldman ("The McAdams et al. study suggests that when liberals and conservatives in the United States are asked to describe important events in their lives, they use concepts consistent with Haidt's and Lakoff's theoretical frameworks"). Importantly, Lakoff did not propose anything so crude as "if you had a strict father, then your politics will be such and such." The Strict Father/Nurturant Mother paradigm is a metaphor to depict people's ultimate value orientations, not a theory of developmental psychology. And a person might have a nurturing father and a very strict mother, instead of the converse.

220   **The broader values associated with Lakoff's two paradigms:** The Lakoff model differs from but recalls in some respects William James's depiction of the "tough-minded" versus the "tender-minded" temperaments. James (1962 and 1979). Tough-minded people tend to want facts. They are skeptics, atheists, or materialists, and have an engineering approach to organizing the world via markets or social mechanisms. In contrast, the tender-minded tend to focus on ideals, religion, and morality; they believe in organizing the world based on virtuous principles. See Dewey (1960) 147-150; Harman 538-529. Consider the vivid description given by Richard Hofstadter in his influential 1964 book *Anti-Intellectualism in American Life:* The tender-minded intellectual was an "egghead," "overemotional," and "feminine," exhibiting a "self-consciousness so given to examining all sides of a question that he becomes thoroughly addled." (Hofstader 9-10.) Note the then negative epithet "feminine" applied to the intellectual, in contrast to the "tough-minded," masculine, practical thinker. This silly pejorative continues to echo though current public debate.

222 As one expert notes, "We tend to value things as a function of how we frame them": Bermudez 10, 226. See also Chong & Druckman; Druckman. As Kahan & Braman 149 says, "Cultural commitments are prior to facts on highly charged political issues." In his widely lauded book *The Nature and Origins of Mass Opinion*, John Zaller says, "Every opinion is a marriage of information and predisposition: information to form a mental picture of a given issue and predisposition to motivate some conclusion about it." (Quoted in Marietta & Barker 46.) He cast doubt on whether opinion surveys can reveal durable beliefs. Instead, he saw a three-step process by which citizens *receive* messages (and frame them); *accept* them (subject to consistency with prior beliefs); and then *sample* how they "fit" with then current issues. Framing affects thinking, but it is not necessarily the end of thinking. As Prinz 32 explains, "We might say that people have no reasons for their basic values, but it would be better to say that basic values are implemented in our psychology in a way that puts them outside certain practices of justification [i.e., logical proof]." But there are other forms of justification for some beliefs.

224 It is well documented that "in politics, changes in the labeling": Chong (2013) 116-119. This is just one factor that fuels polarization. See Kleinfeld.

224 In a famous study, people were asked whether a political extremist group: Kahan et al. (2006). See also Chong (2019).

226 Our political leanings are significantly genetically and biologically influenced: See Alford et al. (2005 and 2008); Johnston et al.; Jost et al. (2009 and 2014); Fraley; Funk. Indeed, the Big Five dispositions predict political orientation better than income or education. Scores on the Big Five accounted for more in predicting left-wing affiliation than "demographic variables such as gender, age, income, and educational level, [which are] typically used as predictors of political behavior." Caprara & Vecchione 32, 36. See also Tuschman 30, 41-22, 430-432; Gerber; Gerber et al.; Mooney 96.

226 fMRI studies show that liberals tend: See Amodeo; Kanai; Johnston et al. 31.

226 In a repeat study, the authors "were able to correctly classify": Kanai et al.; see also studies cited in Funk, and in Taber & Young.

226 Liberals' genetic makeup leads them to be less attentive to danger signals: See Hibbing et al. (2014b); Kanai, et al.; Schreiber; Tuschman 311; Hetherington & Weiler, Ch. 6. Conservatives are more likely to interpret a face as threatening or angry. (Vigil (2010); Vigil & Strenth (2001); Johnston et al. 32; Hibbing (Id.) 135-136.)

226 As one scholar summarized, "These relationships hold up across time": See Hibbing et al. (2014b) 104. See also Tuschman 23; Johnston et al. As John Hibbing (Id.) colorfully says: "Two of the Big Five [personality traits] . . . consistently correlate with political orientations: openness and conscientiousness. . . . Those open to new experience are not just hanging Jackson Pollock prints in disorganized bedrooms while listening to techno-pop reinterpretations of Bach. . . . They are also more likely to identify themselves as liberals. [In contrast,] high conscientiousness types are not just hanging up patriotic posters in neat and tidy offices while listening to their favorite elevator music. They are also more likely to identify as conservatives." Conservatives collect less "stuff" and have neater rooms than liberals. Their stuff tends to have less related to other countries. (Id. 95; Tuschman 77.)

226 As shown in the massive "Minnesota Twins" study: Block & Block. See also Bouchard et al.; Tuschman 24-27; Hibbing et al. (2014b) 185-190; Hatemi & McDermott; Jost et al. (2009); Alford et al. (2005 and 2008); Funk 243-247, citing studies by

McCourt, and Scarr and Weinberg. In a large Australian study of identical and fraternal twins, "the analysis suggested not just a genetic component to conservatism, but a large genetic component; more than half of the observed variation in conservatism was attributed to genetic difference." (Kinder in Huddy et al. (Eds.) 817, citing study by Martin and colleagues.) Moreover, "other studies, employing different designs, samples, and statistical techniques, arrive at essentially the same conclusion." (Id., citing Alford et al. (2005); Bouchard et al.; Telegen et al; Eaves et al.; Olson et al.) See also Fraley et al.

227 **In a later study, Alford asked some 9,000 twins:** Alford et al. (2005); Tuschman 26. Twin studies show that "heritability of ideology is estimated in the range of 40% to 60%. Shared environmental effects . . . are typically near zero." (Feldman 613.) See also Hatemi et al. (2014), which extends the analysis to families without twins.

227 **Differences on Chromosome 4 and a gene called NARG1:** Hatemi et al. (2014).

227 **Teenagers and young adults who possess the DRD47R variant :** Fowler at al. cited by Funk 247. See also Hibbing et al. (2014b) 191; Mooney 244.

227 **After exposing subjects to even a single "disgusting" image:** Churchland (2019) 112-114. Conservatives tend to have stronger automatic "gag" and "startle" reflexes and disgust response. Oxley; Hibbing et al. (2014b) 162-165 and sources cited there; Funk 244; K. Smith et al. (2011); Alford et al. (2008).

227 **In studies of the brain's ACC:** Amodeo et al., cited in Johnston et al. 31. See also Zmigrod Ch.15.

227 **As shown in many studies, liberals tend to be more open, trusting:** See, e.g., Taber & Young 532 ("The finding that experimental openness is associated with liberalism versus conservatism is now firmly established"). See also Johnston et al., 11, 17; Funk; Caprara & Vecchione 31 (Studies in both the U.S. and Europe "have shown that individuals high in openness to experience tend to prefer parties and ideologies located on the left wing. . . . People high in conscientiousness tend to prefer right wing and conservative ideologies, parties and issues"). People high on openness are more liberal than about 70% of all people. (Mooney 66, citing Gerber study.) Importantly, the Big Five scoring accounted for more of the results than gender, age, income and educational level. Caprara & Vecchione 32. Neuroticism is also positively correlated to liberal attitudes. Taber & Young 532.

227 **As previously mentioned, researchers say, "We found we could turn [it] . . . on and off":** Zak ix.

228 **Overall, a large body of research now shows that genes likely set the potential for inclinations:** See Johnston et al. 6-7; 20-22. "Two major components of conservatism—resistance to change and inequality endorsement—are essentially uncertainty reducing." (Taber & Young 534, citing works by Jost et al. In addition, "Liberals score higher on neophilia (also known as 'openness to experience') not just for new foods but also for new people, music and ideas. Conservatives are higher on neophobia [dislike of the new]; they prefer to stick with what's tried and true, and they care a lot more about guarding borders, boundaries and traditions." (Haidt 172, citing McCrae (1996).) See also Mooney 16. Johnston et al. 11, 17 says: "The extension of partisan conflict to issues touching on race, ethnicity, gender, sexuality, nationalism and religion has created an alignment between political identity and dispositional openness." Thus, "engaged citizens who score low on openness forge right-leaning political identities . . . whereas those who score high on openness do the opposite." Conservatives are more accepting of inequality. Jost

et al. (2003); Jost (2006); Glasser; Kruglanski & Webster; Hatemi & McDermott. Another study sought to assess whether the Schwartz value scales, or moral foundations theory gradients (discussed earlier), are better predictors of liberalism versus conservatism. It tended to favor the former. (McNeace & Sinn.)

228 In addition, strong liberals and strong conservatives differ in how they . . . process information: Caprara & Vecchione and sources cited there; Taber & Young; Ruisch; Shook & Fazio.

228 This is crucial because it can affect all the issues: Caprara & Vecchione 32-33, citing work by Kruglanski, Jost, Glaser, Chirumbolo, and others. See also Taber & Young 531; Mooney 69. There is an often-reported "epistemic need to attain certainty" among political conservatives. (Johnston et al. 23-26, citing, for example, work by Jost and colleagues.) But is that "need" calibrated to be excessive or just appropriate, and by what standard?

228 A "substantial body of research" confirms extreme conservatives': Hibbing et al. (2014b) 105.

228 As one scholar finds: "Conservatives acquire the information they believe necessary": Hibbing et al. (2014b) 139-141; Shook & Fazio.

228 Liberals may at times keep endlessly "noodling" an issue: Kahan et al. (2013 and 2017b).

228 This cognitive difference is important to public debate over [science]: See Ridley; McIntyre; Mooney; Kahan et al. (2017a). See Conservapedia.com, which casts doubt on even the most well-established scientific principles such as Einstein's theory of relativity. A clever study tracked the party affiliation of physicians in various specialties. The Republican-leaning specialties included surgery, orthopedics, and anesthesiology—which are generally viewed as more "cut and dried' and appealing to "fixed" rather than "fluid" personalities. Conversely, the Democratic-leaning specialties were psychiatry, infectious disease, and internal medicine, which are more reflective/cognitive and appeal to fluid personalities. Probably none of that surprised you. (Hersh & Goldenberg, cited in Hetherington & Weiler 73-74.)

229 But as top COVID adviser Anthony Fauci later noted: *Scientific American*, April 2025, 80-82.

229 Conservatives often have a faster and stronger tendency to categorize: Mooney 71-76; Shook & Fazio; but see Zmigrod 167.

229 Liberals tend to be softer categorizers: Hibbing et al. (2014b) 123-124; Taber & Young.

229 Interestingly, research reveals this difference not just when: See Shook & Fazio. See also Feldman.

229 Conservatives also tend to prefer simpler, more direct explanations: Taber & Young 535-536.

229 Keith Stanovich and colleagues describe the difference: Stanovich et al. and sources cited there.

229 But even moderate conservatives tend to seek more certainty: Caprara & Vecchione and sources cited there.

229 A major review by John Jost and colleagues: Jost et al. (2003). See also Caprara & Vecchione 39-40; Carney et al.; Mooney 59-64. Philip Tetlock has examined this association between preference for integrative complexity and political orientation across nations and various policy issues. (Tetlock (2017).) See also sources cited in Caprara & Vecchione.

229 Consider a typical grenade lobbed: Quoted in Mooney 60.

229 A liberal might reply in the famous words: Learned Hand, "The Spirit of Liberty."

230 As we have seen, liberals and conservatives each tend to bring to any issue a framework: See, generally, Lakoff (1996 and 2008); Hibbing et al. (2014b); Hetherington & Weiler; Feinberg at al. See notes above to page 154, describing the Baumrind et al. typology of parenting styles.

   As to conservative values, see William Bennett: "Conservatism . . . seeks to conserve the best elements of the past. It understands the important role that traditions, institutions, habits and authority can have in our social life together, and recognizes that our national institutions are products of principles developed over time by custom, lessons of experience and consensus." (Bennett (1992) 35.) Conservative parenting author Kevin Dobson wrote that "the main reason for the overwhelming success of capitalism is that hard work and personal discipline are rewarded. . . . The great weakness of socialism is the absence of reinforcement. . . . Some parents implement a miniature system of socialism at home. The children's wants and desires are provided by the 'State' and are not linked to diligence or discipline." (Dobson 88-89.) An arch-conservative tract declares: "Conservatives think like lions; liberals think like lambs." Thus, liberals "exhibit a psychological aversion to . . . competition with peers and the competitive environment. . . . Conservatives favor competition . . . and accept that such competition will produce disparate outcomes which will be based on inherent ability and effort." (Anonymous Conservative 4-5.)

232 An important and provocative thesis advanced by Jonathan Haidt: Haidt (2012) Ch.8. at 214 states flatly: "Liberals have a two foundation morality, based on the Care and Fairness foundations [only], whereas conservatives have a five-foundation morality [adding Loyalty, Authority and Sanctity]." He believes that strongly aids conservatives in shaping public opinion on policy issues.

232 For example, Lakoff had proudly proclaimed: Lakoff (2008) 47.

232 For an interesting and well-documented exploration: As to "Scaffles", see J. Williams (2025) 17.

235 Theodore Adorno described the "authoritarian personality": This framework has been widely used and yet often criticized. See, e.g., Kinder (2013) 817-819; Tuschman Ch.4; Rosier & Willig (recounting critiques, but concluding that the "central thesis remains sound"). Some scholars (such as Hans Eysenck and Milton Rokeach) noted that Adorno worried about right authoritarianism but not so much the left-wing version. And yet Adorno's work has been widely used, studied, and called "the best post-War work on moral psychology and still one of the chief works in the history of the field." (Flanagan 182.) But many feel that the later work by Stenner, Feldman, and others is more applicable to the current political continuum.

235 Robert Altemeyer later described the "authoritarian attitude syndrome": Altemeyer's scale primarily pivoted around authoritarian submission to authority, aggressiveness, and conventionalism as to norms. See Altemeyer (1966 and 1981); Caprara & Vecchione 37-39; Stenner 21-25. Duckitt and Sibley say that RWA entails "beliefs in coercive social control, in obedience and respect for existing authorities and in conforming to traditional moral and religious morals and values." (Quoted in Caprara & Vecchione

38.) Feldman (2013) 597 explains that "underlying RWA is a personality that emphasizes social conformity and a corresponding view of the world as a dangerous place. . . . [John Jost's model sees] conservatism as a motivated response to psychological insecurity. Duckitt traces the origins of SDO [social dominance orientation] to a tough-minded personality that produces a view of the world as a competitive jungle." In studies across diverse nations, "when RWA scores rise, conscientiousness goes up and openness goes down." (Tuschman 51.) In addition, "The strongest personality effect on SDO came from agreeableness—higher scores on that trait are associated with lower levels of SDO." (Feldman (2013) 611.)

235 Then in the 1960s, Glenn Wilson and William Patterson: See Hibbing et al. (2014b) 113.

235 Later, Rokeach found that those high on the authoritarianism scale: Rokeach (1960) 16. See also Zmigrod 128 ("[In research studies,] I found that the individuals who are most cognitively rigid have a genetic predisposition that concentrates less dopamine in their prefrontal cortex, the decision-making part of the brain, and more dopamine in their striatum, the midbrain structure that controls our rapid instincts.") Zmigrod expresses doubts that this aligns more with conservatism.

235 They suffer from what Russell Hardin called: Hardin, quoted in Breton (2010) 32.

235 More recently, John Jost and colleagues conducted major reviews: High SDO reflects an acceptance of social hierarchy, inequality and in- versus out-group dominance. See Sidanius & Pratto; Sidanius & Kurzban; Duckitt & Sibley. Hatemi et al. found a significant overlap between RWA and SDO.

236 Especially illuminating is the extensive research by Janet Stenner: Stenner 24, 195.

236 As Stenner concludes, this disposition: Stenner 1, and sources cited there. Stenner's work is statistically detailed, including an assessment of (1) the largest U.S. database of social attitudes (the Cumulative General Social Survey (GSS) 1972-1994); (2) the National Elections Survey (NES-1992); (3) large surveys across 60 nations (World Values Survey 1992-1998); and (4) her own interview research in New York and North Carolina. The patterns yielded by the data help explain why political views on seemingly disparate issues "go together"—like concern over immigration, gay rights, and crime. Stenner says, the "regularity with which these things 'go together' . . . suggests [that] individuals possess fairly stable dispositions to intolerance of difference, that is, varying degrees of willingness to 'put up with' differing people, ideas and behaviors. Our attitudes toward minorities, immigrants and foreigners could not be predicted from our views on dissidents, deviants and criminals (and vice versa) if not for some relatively enduring [psychological] predisposition to be intolerant of all manner of difference." (Stenner 2.)

236 Among other data, she cites the surprising findings from a real-world . . . experiment: Stenner 162-163. Of course, genes matter, but so does culture. One might ask: are the genetic profiles of the citizenry in Finland really very different from nearby Northern Russia, or in the Netherlands, from in Northern Germany, or in Morocco versus Algeria, or in North versus South Korea? But we do know that their historic levels of tolerance have at times differed.

236 A series of later German studies of twin pairs: Spinath, et al.

237 **Importantly, "authoritarian" does not mean "conservative":** "This process probably begins for most people with some general desire to transfer sovereignty to and commit self and others to conformity with some collective order." (Stenner 141.) See also Mooney 90-92; Chirumbolo. Some disagree, believing that conservatism is central to authoritarianism. But conservatism has a number of strains, including "status quo" conservatism which is generally *not* authoritarian, and libertarianism which is strongly *anti*-authoritarian. It is said that conservatives want to conserve the good from the past and limit change, while authoritarians want to limit divergence from the dominant norm. These can overlap or diverge. There is also *laissez faire* conservatism which seeks to rely largely on markets. Often overlooked is the strong strain of liberal or progressive authoritarianism. The liberal narrative is that only conservatives want to "tell people how to live their lives." But rampant political correctness, "wokeness," and "reform" do so as well.

237 **It would be a sad irony if the American progressive movement:** See, e.g., Lukianoff & Schott.

237 **Most progressives would be shocked to learn:** Stenner 167.

237 **Political scientists Marietta and Barker's data:** Marietta & Barker 266. And this has accelerated markedly since their book appeared in 2019.

238 **On the other hand, Jost and colleagues reviewed:** See studies by Jost et al. See also Stenner Ch.6 for evolving data.

238 **When all factors are considered, there appears to be a moderately strong correlation:** Stenner 167.

238 **Stenner concludes: "Authoritarianism can provide the most complete account":** Id. 189-195.

239 **Many other factors influence one's political posture.** See Brader; Marietta & Barker; J. Williams; Mason; Marsden; Schuck & Wilson (Eds.)

239 **It has been found that in the U.S., non-Hispanic Catholics:** Pew Research Center (2017 and 2024).

239 **On world values surveys, eight of the top ten:** Baker. See also Huntington.

239 **People in the following four industries:** Saad 136.

239 **The most Republican job categories:** See Verdantlabs.com; Voronai.com.

240 **This phenomenon has been called the Big Sort.** Bishop. See also Glaser & Ward.

240 **Americans are now "sorting" ourselves into psychological tribes by our choices of where to live:** Marietta & Barker; Mooney; E. Klein; Baker; Mason; Rentfrow et al.

240 **Not only that, but the gap . . . is widening:** Klein; Mason; J. Williams.

240 **What's more, "the increase in partisan ideological *identity differences*":** Mason 28.

241 **This verbal warfare is dangerous:** See Mason; Sloman & Fernbach 160; Lapore; Huntington.

10. The Morality of Fairness

248 **Thus, "many modern accounts [focus on] contrasting":** Tomasello 1-2. See, generally, Sandel; Rawls.

248 **Fairness—or its related concept, justice:** For a range of perspectives, see, e.g. Sun; Binmore; Rawls; Miller & Walzer (Eds.); Davies; Hauser Ch.2; Bazerman & Moore. In a narrower context, see the extensive research on perceptions of fairness in "bargaining" games like the Ultimatum Game and the Dictator Game; e.g., Hauser; Henrich; Avelino-Silva; Engel. "There is surprising cross-cultural consistency in the way people play the ultimatum game. [Henrich et al.] . . . conducted studies that included the game in fifteen global societies. [Not self-interest but] . . . fairness was found to be an important factor in these economic games in each of the societies tested. . . . Fairness appears to be a universal concept affecting decisions, but implementation of fairness depends on cultural norms." (Bazerman & Moore 118-119.)

253 **There you have 25 good—but different—meanings of "fair."** See Elster; Hayek; Rawls; Avelino-Silva; Gaus; Beauchamp & Childress. For a wonderful survey of how various claims about "fairness" are determined under the law, see Chemerinsky.

253 **Kenneth Binmore, author of two volumes:** Binmore vii.

254 **They say (drum roll): "Equal opportunity":** Luntz 208. For a readable overview, see J. Johnson. Other cultures differ. See Henrich et al. (2005 and 2010).

253 **Sometimes, we identify an outcome we desire:** See Pizarro, et al. (2003); Uhlman; Uhlman & Cohen; Beauchamp & Childress.

258 **Yet people evidently judge fairness compared to the reference price:** See, e.g., Scott & Lizieri; Steinberg et al.; Montevirgen; Hauser 93; Bazerman & Moore Ch.7; Thaler 60-63.

263 **Judges often lament that prior decisions "have not been a model of consistency":** *Edmondson v. Leesville Concrete Co.*, 500 U.S. 632 (1991). See also Chemerinsky 538, 733. On inconsistency in bail, criminal sentencing, and parole, for example, see Kahneman et al. (2021); Guentert & Gerber; Epps; Halvorsen. On other social policies, see Fiske.

263 **Legal theorist Ronald Dworkin suggests: Follow** *principles, not rules***:** Dworkin Ch. 2-3.

264 **Johathan Elster's excellent book** *Local Justice***:** Ask yourself this: If you could order that certain people would be given a preference in receiving some social benefit, would you favor minorities, poor, elderly, women, veterans, handicapped people, the young, brilliant computer geeks, profoundly gifted artists—or who instead? What's your principle of justification?

264 **Let's consider how, as a society, we mix and match fairness criteria :** See, e.g., Sandel; Elster; Hayek; Beauchamp & Childress 267-300.

265 **Many believe that resources should be allocated based on relative benefit:** Elster 86-87; Christakis 267; Beauchamp & Childress, *passim.*

266 **These court rulings did not settle the issue:** See *Regents of The University of California v. Baake*, 438 U.S. 265 (1978); *Grutter v. Bollinger,* 539 U.S. 306 (2003); *Gratz v. Bollinger,* 539 U.S. 244 (2003); *Fisher v. University of Texas,* 579 U.S. 365 (2016). Finally, see *Students for Fair Admission v. President and Fellows of Harvard University,* 600 U.S. 181 (2023).

266 **But the Supreme Court has ruled that this practice:** *Teamsters v. U.S.,* 431 U.S. 324 (1977).

268 **Stated in broad terms, "if you care more about false negatives":** Cheng 26. The Supreme Court has said, "Even if the classification involved here [a mandatory retirement age] is in some context both underinclusive and overinclusive, and hence the law drawn by Congress is imperfect, it is nevertheless the rule that . . . perfection is by no means required [in setting rules]." *Vance v. Bradley,* 440 U.S. 93, 108 (1979).

269 As Jonathan Baron observes, "People often take some simple principle": Baron (1998) 67.

268 Binmore provides a useful reminder: Binmore 21. This, of course, recalls Rawls.

11. Pathways to Effective Moral Thinking and Arguing

270 If you're looking for a way to explain [fairness norms] to a friend: Beauchamp & Childress 386- 388. Of course, one can be using a given moral framework with or without being intentionally committed to it. See Conway et al. (2013); Kroneisen & Heck; Gawronski et al.

273 The deeply Christian scholar C. S. Lewis said: "Right and Wrong as a Clue to the Meaning of the Universe," in Lewis (1958).

276 But taking moral initiative in some way is an important feature of a moral life: See Bregman.

Bibliography

Adorno, T. et al. (1950). *The authoritarian personality*. Harper.

Aknin, L. et al. (2010). Prosocial spending and cross-cultural evidence of a psychological universal. *Harvard Business School Working Paper* 11-038.

Ale, S. et al. (2013). Evolution of cooperation. *PLoS One*, 8(5) e6376.

Alexander, R. (1987). *The biology of moral systems*. Aldine De Gruyter.

Alford, J. et al. (2005). Are political orientations genetically transmitted? *American Political Science Review*, 99(2), 734-49.

Alford, J. et al. (2008). Beyond liberals and conservatives to political genotypes and phenotypes. *Perspectives on Politics*, 6, 321-328.

Alicke, M. (2001). The "better than myself" effect. *Motivation and Emotion*, 25, 7-22.

Allik, J. & McCrae, R. (2004). Toward a geography of traits: Patterns of profiles across 36 cultures. *Journal of Cross-Cultural Psychology*, 35(1):13-28.

Allport, G. (1938). *Personality: A psychological interpretation*. Holt.

Altemeyer, R. (1981). *Right wing authoritarianism*. University of Manitoba Press.

Altemeyer, R. (1996). *The authoritarian specter*. Harvard University Press.

Alwin, D. et al. (1994). *Aging, personality and social change: The stability of individual differences over the adult lifespan*. Routledge.

American Bar Association. (1983). *Model rules for professional conduct*.

American Library Association. (2025). *2024 book ban data*.

American Medical Association. (2025). *Code of medical ethics*.

American Physical Therapy Association. (2025). *Code of ethics for the physical therapist*.

American Psychological Association. (2017). *Ethical principles of psychologists and code of conduct*.

Amodeo, D. et al. (2007). Neurocognitive correlates of liberalism and conservatism. *Nature Neuroscience*, 10(10), 1246-1247.

Annas, G. (2003). Virtue ethics and social psychology. *A Priori*, 2, 20-59.

Anderson, E. (1999). Knowledge, human interest and objectivity in feminist epistemology. In J. Perry & M. Bratman (Eds.), *Introduction to philosophy* (pp. 284-304). Oxford University Press.

Andrews, K. (2003). Ethics in practice. *Harvard Business Review on Corporate Ethics* (pp. 62-84).

Anonymous Conservative. (2017). *The evolutionary biology behind politics.* Federalist Publications.

Anscombe, E. (1958). *Intention.* Harvard University Press.

Anscombe, E. (1999). Causality and determinism. In J. Perry & M. Bratman (Eds.), *Introduction to philosophy* (pp. 252-262). Oxford University Press.

Appelman, L. (2015). A tragedy of errors: Blackstone, procedural asymmetry and criminal justice. *Harvard Law Review,* 120, 91.

Appiah, K. (2005). *The Ethics of identity.* Princeton University Press.

Aquinas. See Thomas Aquinas, Saint.

Ariel, S. (1995). *What do jews believe?* Schocken Books.

Ariely, D. (2008). *Predictably irrational.* Harper Perennial.

Ariely, D. (2010). *The upside of irrationality.* Harper Perennial.

Ariely, D. (2012). *The (honest) truth about dishonesty.* Harper.

Ariely, D. & Garcia-Rada, X. Contagious dishonesty. *Scientific American,* Sept. 2019, 63-66.

Aristotle. (1984). *The Complete works of Aristotle: The revised Oxford translation.* Vols 1-2 (J. Barnes, Ed.). Princeton University Press.

Aristotle. (Garver E., ed.) (2005). *Poetics and rhetoric.* Barnes & Noble.

Armor, D. & Taylor, S. (2002). When predictions fail: The dilemma of unrealistic optimism. In Gilovich, T. et al. (Eds.), *Heuristics and biases: The psychology of intuitive judgment* (pp. 334-347). Cambridge University Press.

Armstrong, J. et al. (2018). Clarifying gender differences in moral dilemma judgments. *Social Psychology and Personality Science,* 10(3), 287-294.

Arp, R. et al. (2019). *Bad arguments.* Wiley Blackwell.

Arrow, K. (1963). *Social choice and individual values.* (2d. ed.) Wiley.

Ashton, M. & Lee, K. (2007). Empirical, theoretical and practical advantages of the HEXACO model of personality structure. *Personality and Social Psychology Review,* 11, 150-166.

Aslan, R. (2013). *Zealot.* Random House.

Atari, M. et al. (2020). Sex differences in moral judgments across 67 countries. *Proceedings of the Royal Society B: Biological Sciences,* 287 (1937), 2020124.

Atari, M. et al. (2023). The paucity of morality in everyday talk. *Scientific Reports,* 13 (5967).

Avelino-Silva, T. et al. (2023). Fairness: From the guts to the brain. *Frontiers in Psychology,* 14, 1241125.

Axelrod, R. (1984). *The evolution of cooperation.* Basic Books.

Axelrod, R. & Hamilton, W. (1981). The evolution of cooperation. *Science,* 211, 1390-1396.

Ayer, A. (1952). *Language, truth and logic.* Dover Publications.

Bachman, J. (1995). Appeal to authority. In H. Hansen & R. Pinto (Eds.), *Fallacies: Classical and contemporary readings* (pp.274-286). Penn State University Press.

Badaracco, J. (2003a). We don't need another saint. In *Harvard Business Review of Corporate Ethics*, 1-18.

Badaracco, J. (2003b). The discipline of building character. In *Harvard Business Review of Corporate Ethics*, 139-164.

Baggini, J. (2016). *The edge of reason.* Yale University Press.

Baggini, J. & Stangroom, J. (Eds.). 2003. *What philosophers think.* Barnes & Noble

Baier, A. (1989). Doing without a moral theory. In S. Clarke & E. Simpson (Eds.), *Anti-Theory in Ethics and Moral Conservatism* (pp. 00-00). SUNY Press.

Baier, K. & Rescher, N. (1969). *Values and the future.* Free Press.

Baillie, J. (2000). *Hume on morality.* Routledge.

Bainbridge, S. (2023). *The profit motive: Defining shareholder value maximization.* Cambridge University Press.

Baker, W. (2005). *America's crisis of values.* Princeton University Press.

Bardi, A. & Schwartz, S. (2003). Values and behavior: Strength and structure of relations. *Personality and Social Psychology Bulletin, 29*(10), 1207-1220.

Barker, D. & Tinnick, J. (2006). Competing views of parental roles and internal constraints. *American Political Science Review, 100*(12), 249-263.

Baron, J. (1998). *Judgment misguided.* Oxford University Press.

Baron, J. (2006). *Against bioethics.* MIT Press.

Baron-Cohen, J. (2003). *The essential difference.* Penguin.

Bar-Tal, D. & Staub, E. (1997). *Patriotism in the lives of individuals and nations.* Nelson-Hall.

Bartels, D. (2008). Principled moral sentiments and the flexibility of moral judgments and decision making. *Cognition,* 108, 381-417.

Bartels, D. & Medin, D. (2007). Are morally motivated decisionmakers insensitive to the consequences of their choices? *Psychological Science,* 18, 24-28.

Bartels, D. & Pizarro, D. (2011). The mismeasure of morals: Antisocial personality traits predict utilitarian responses to moral dilemmas. *Cognition,* 121(1), 154-161.

Batson, D. (2011). *Altruism in humans.* Oxford University Press.

Batson, D. et al. (2016). Benefits and liabilities of empathy-induced altruism. In A. Miller (Ed.), *The social psychology of good and evil* (pp. 443-466). Guilford Press.

Bauerlein, M. (2008). *The dumbest generation.* Tarcher.

Bauerlein, M. & Bellow, A. (2015). *The state of the American mind.* Templeton Books.

Bauman, C. et al. (2014). Revisiting external validity: Concerns about trolley problems and other sacrificial dilemmas in moral psychology. Journal of *Social and Personality Psychology,* 8, 536-554.

Baumrind, D. (1967). Child care practices anteceding three patterns of preschool behavior. *Genetic Psychology Monographs,* 75(1), 43-88.

Bazerman, M. & Moore, D. (2009). *Judgment in managerial decision-making.* Wiley.

Bazerman, M. et al. (2001). *You can't enlarge the pie.* Basic Books.

Beard, M. (2024). *Emperor of Rome.* Liveright.

Beauchamp, T. & Childress, J. (2019). *Principles of biomedical ethics.* Oxford University Press.

Becker, G. (1976). *The economic approach to human behavior.* University of Chicago Press.

Becker, L. (1990). *Reciprocity.* University of Chicago Press.

Beebe, H. et al. (Eds.). (2009). *The Oxford handbook of causation.* Oxford University Press.

Bell, E. et al. (2009). The origins of political attitudes and behavior: An analysis using twins. *Canadian Journal of Political Science.* 42(4), 855-879.

Benedict, R. (1934). *Patterns of culture.* Houghton Mifflin.

Bennett, W. (1980). The teacher, the curriculum and values education development. In M. McBee (Ed.), *Rethinking college responsibilities for values* (pp. 27-34). Jossey Bass.

Bennett, W. (1992). *The devaluing of America: The fight for our culture and our children.* Simon & Schuster.

Bennett, W. (1995). *The children's book of virtues.* Simon & Schuster.

Bentham, J. (1948). *An introduction to the principles of morals and legislation.* Harper.

Bentham, J. (2005). *Deontology and the source of morality.* Adamant Media.

Bermudez, J. (2021). *Frame it again: New tools for rational decision-making.* Cambridge University Press.

Berreby, D. (2008). *Us and them: The science of identity.* University of Chicago Press.

Berry, Z. (2015). Explanation and implications of the fundamental attribution error: A review and proposal. *Journal of Integrated Social Sciences,* 5(1), 44-57.

Billig, M. (1996). *Arguing and thinking.* Cambridge University Press.

Binmore, K. (2005). *Natural justice.* Oxford University Press.

Biologos. biologos.org.

Bishop, R. (2008). *The big sort: Why the clustering of like-minded Americans is tearing us apart.* Houghton Mifflin.

Black, M. (1962). *Models and metaphors.* Cornell University Press.

Black, M. & Murphy, A. (1982), *Critical thinking.* Prentice-Hall.

Blackburn, S. (1998). *Ruling passions.* Clarendon Press.

Blackburn, S. (2005). *Truth.* Oxford University Press.

Block, J. (1995). A contrarian view of the five-factor approach to personality description. *Psychological Bulletin,* 17(2), 187-215.

Block, J. & Block, J. H. (2006). Nursery school personality and political orientation two decades later, *Journal of Research in Personality,* 40(5), 734-749.

Bloom, A. (1987). *The closing of the American mind.* Simon & Schuster.

Bloom, P. (2013). *Just babies: The origins of good and evil.* Broadway Books.

Bloom, P. (2016). *Against empathy: The case for rational compassion.* Ecco/Harper Collins.

Boas, F. (1887). Museums of ethnology and their classification. *Science,* 9, 589.

Boehm, C. (2012). *Moral origins.* Basic Books.

Boghossian, P. (2006). *Fear of knowledge.* Clarendon.

Boghossian, P. & Lindsay, J. (2019). *How to have impossible conversations.* Hachette.

Bok, D. (2024). *Attacking the elites.* Yale University Press.

Bok, S. (1978). *Lying.* Vintage.

Bollich, K. (2016). Eavesdropping on character: Analyzing everyday relationships. *Journal of Research on Personality,* 61, 15-21.

Bollinger, L. & Stone, G. (2022). *A legacy of discrimination.* Oxford University Press.

Borowitz, E. & Schwartz, F. (1999). *The Jewish moral virtues.* The Jewish Publication Society.

Bouchard, T. & McCrae, M. (2003). Genetic and environmental influence on human psychological differences. *Developmental Neurobiology,* 54(1), 4-45.

Bouchard, T. et al. (1990). Sources of human psychological difference: The Minnesota study of twins reared apart. *Science,* 250 (4978), 223-228.

Bouchard, T. et al. (2003). Evidence for the construct validity and heritability of the Wilson-Patterson conservatism scale: A reared-apart twins study of social attitudes. *Personality and Individual Differences,* 34(6), 959-969.

Boyd, E. & Richerson, P. (2005). *The origin and evolution of cultures.* Oxford University Press.

Boyd, R. (1997). How to be a moral realist. In S. Darwall et al.(Eds.), *Moral discourse and practice: Some philosophical approaches* (pp. 105-136). Oxford University Press.

Brader, T. (2006). *Campaigning for hearts and minds.* University of Chicago Press.

Brandom, R. (1994). *Making it explicit: Reasoning, representing and discursive commitment.* Harvard University Press.

Bregman, R. (2025). *Moral ambition.* Little Brown.

Brennan, J. et al. (2021). *Business ethics for better behavior.* Oxford University Press.

Breton, A. et al. (Eds.) (2010). *Political extremism and rationality.* Cambridge University Press.

Breton, C. (2016). Benefits and liabilities of empathy. In A. Miller (Ed.), *The social psychology of good and evil* (pp. 443-466). Guilford Press.

Brief, A. & Smith-Crowe, K., (2016). *Organizations matter.* In A. Miller (Ed.), *The social psychology of good and evil* (pp. 390-414). Guilford Press.

Brooks, A. (2024). America's crisis of civic virtue. *Journal of Democracy*, 35(2), 23-39.

Brosnan, S. & de Waal, F. (Sept. 2003). Monkeys reject unfair pay. *Nature*, 425 (6955), 297-299.

Brown, D. (1999). *Human universals.* McGraw Hill.

Bruce, M. & Barbone, S. (2011). *Just the arguments.* Wiley Blackwell.

Budiansky, S. et al. (1995). How lawyers abuse the law. *U.S. News & World Report,* Jan. 30, 1995.

Bunge, M. (1959). *Causality.* The World Publishing Co.

Burwell v. Hobby Lobby Stores, 573 U.S. 682 (2014).

Butler, C. (2002). *Postmodernism: A very short introduction.* Oxford University Press.

Butler-Bowdon, T. (2013). *50 philosophy classics.* Nicholas Brealey.

Caprara, G. & Vecchione, M. (2013). Personality approaches to political behavior. In L. Huddy et al. (Eds.), *The Oxford handbook of political psychology* (pp. 24-58). Oxford University Press.

Caprara, G. et al. (2006). Personality and politics: Values, interests and political choices. *Political Psychology*, 27, 1-28 .

Carey, S. (2009). *The origin of concepts.* Oxford University Press.

Carney, D. et al. (2008). The secret lives of liberals and conservatives: Personality profiles, interaction styles, and things they leave behind. *Political Psychology*, 29(6), 807-840.

Carritt, E. (1999). Criticisms of utilitarianism. In J. Perry & M. Bratman (Eds.), *Introduction to philosophy* (pp. 503–505). Oxford University Press.

Caspi, A. et al. (2005). Personality development: Stability and change. *Annual Review of Psychology,* 56, 453-484.

Catapano, P. & Critchley, S. (2017). *Modern ethics in 77 arguments.* W.W. Norton.

Cathcart, T. & Klein, D. (2004). *Plato and a platypus walk into a bar.* Penguin.

Chapman, G. & Johnson, E. (2002). Incorporating the irrelevant: Anchors in judgments of belief and value. In T. Gilovich et al. (Eds.), *Heuristics and biases: The psychology of intuitive judgment* (pp. 120-138). Cambridge University Press.

Chapman, H. & Anderson, A. (2013). Things rank and gross in nature: A review and synthesis of moral disgust. *Psychological Bulletin,* 139(2), 300-327.

Chatfield, T. (2018). *Critical thinking.* Sage.

Chemerinsky, E. (2019). *Constitutional law.* Wolters Kluwer.

Cheng, E. (2018). *The art of logic in an illogical world.* Basic Books.

Chong, D. (2013). Degrees of rationality in politics. In L. Huddy et al. (Eds.), *The Oxford handbook of political psychology* (pp. 96-129). Oxford University Press.

Chong, D. (2019). Competitive framing in political decision-making. Oxfordre.com. Sept. 30, 2019.

Chong, D. & Druckman, J. (2007). Framing public opinion in competitive democracies. *American Political Science Review*, 101(4), 637-655.

Chong, D. & Druckman, J. (2008). The influence of democratic competition on public opinion. *American Political Science Review* (48-pp. ms., pdf posted July 30, 2007).

Childers, T. (1998). *World war two: A military and social history*. The Teaching Company.

Chirumbolo, A. (2002). The relation between need for cognitive closure and political orientation: The mediating role of authoritarianism. *Personality & Individual Differences.*, 32, 603-610.

Christakis, N. (2019). *Blueprint: The evolutionary origins of a good society*. Little Brown Spark.

Chugh, D. et al. (2005). Bounded ethicality as a psychological barrier to recognizing conflicts of interest. In D. Moore et al., *Challenges and solutions in business, law, medicine and public policy* (pp. 74-96). Cambridge University Press.

Churchland, P. (2018). *Braintrust: What neuroscience tells us about morality*. Princeton University Press.

Churchland, P. (2019). *Conscience*. W.W. Norton.

Cicero, M. (2010). *On duties*. Editorium.

Cicero, M. (2016). *How to win an argument* (J. May, Ed.). Princeton University Press.

Citrin, J. (2008). Political culture. In P. Schuck & J. Wilson (Eds.), *Understanding America: The anatomy of an exceptional nation* (pp. 147-180). Perseus/Public Affairs.

Citrin, J. & Green, D. (1990). The self-interest motive in American public opinion. *Research in Micropolitics*, 3(1), 1-28.

City of Richmond v. J.A. Croson Co., 488 U.S. 469 (1989).

Claussen, J. (2025). *Jewish ethics*. Routledge.

Cohen, M. (Ed.) (1961). *The philosophy of John Stuart Mill*. Modern Library.

Cohen-Almagor, R. (2017). On the philosophical foundations of medical ethics. *Ethics, Medicine and Public Health*, 3(4), 436-444.

Collins, F. (2006). *The language of God*. Free Press.

Collins, J. (2019). *What are biblical values?* Yale University Press.

Conservapedia (website). Conservapedia.com.

Conway, P. & Gawronski, B. (2013). Deontological and utilitarian inclinations in moral decision making: A process dissociation approach. *Journal of Personality and Social Psychology*, 104, 216-235.

Cook, M. (2025). *What is business ethics? Principles, examples and why it matters*. American College of Education.

Cooper, J. (Ed.) (1997). *Plato's complete works*. Hackett Publishing Co.

Copi, I. (1961). *An introduction to logic*. MacMillan.

Copleston, F. (1962-1977). *History of philosophy*. Nine vols. Image/Doubleday.

Cornford, F. (2004). *From religion to philosophy*. Dover.

Corsico, P. (2025). Is Hume's law a valid argument against empirical bioethics? *Bioethics*, 39(5), 512-518.

Cosmides, L. & Tooby, J. (2004). Knowing thyself: The evolutionary psychology of moral reasoning and moral sentiments. www.the-brights.net.

Costa, P. & McCrae, N. (1985). *The NEO personality inventory manual.* Psychological Assessment Resources.

Costa, P. & McCrae, N. (1992). *Revised NEO personality inventory.* Psychological Assessment Resources.

Crisp, R. (2000). Particularizing particularism. In B. Hooker & M. Little (Eds.), *Moral particularism* (pp. 23-47). Clarendon.

Crisp, R. Well-being. In Stanford Encyclopedia of Philosophy. Last edited Sept. 15, 2021.

Crisp, R. & Slote, M. (Eds.) (1997). *Virtue ethics.* Oxford University Press.

Crook, Z. (Summer 2005). The quest for John the Baptist. *Biblical Archeology Review,* 28-29.

Cushman, F. et al. (2006). The role of conscious reasoning and intuition in moral judgment. *Psychological Science,* 17, 1082-1089.

Damasio, A. (2012). *Self comes to mind.* Vintage.

Dancy, J. (1993). *Moral reasons.* Blackwell.

Dancy, J. (2000). The particularist's progress. In B. Hooker & M. Little (Eds.), *Moral particularism* (pp. 130-156). Clarendon.

Dancy, J. (2004*). Ethics without principles.* Clarendon.

Dancy, J. Moral Particularism. In Stanford Encyclopedia of Philosophy. Last edited Sept. 22, 2017.

Darley, J. & Batson, C. (1973). From Jerusalem to Jericho: A study of situational and dispositional variables in helping behavior. *Journal of Personality and Social Psychology,* 27(1), 100-108.

Darley, J. et al. (2000). Incapacitation and just deserts as motives for punishment. *Law & Human Behavior,* 24, 659-683.

Darwall, S. (1992). Toward fin de siècle ethics: Some trends. In Darwall et al. (Eds.) *Moral discourse and practice: Some philosophical approaches* (pp.3-47). Oxford University Press.

Darwall, S. et al. (Eds.) (1997). *Moral discourse and practice: Some philosophical approaches.* Oxford University Press.

Darwin, C. (1992). *The descent of man and selection in relation to sex.* Princeton University Press.

Davies, H. (2000). *What works: Evidence based policy and practice in public service.* Policy Press.

Dawes, R. et al. (2002). Clinical versus actuarial judgment. In T. Gilovich et al (Eds.), *Heuristics and biases: The psychology of intuitive judgment* (pp.716-729). Cambridge University Press.

Dennett, D. (1995). *Darwin's dangerous idea: Evolution and the meaning of life.* Simon & Schuster.

Derrida, J. (1978). *Writing and difference.* University of Chicago Press.

Deshaney v. Winnebago Dept. of Social Services, 489 U.S. 189 (1989).

de Waal, F. (1996). *Good natured: The origins of right and wrong in humans and other animals.* Harvard University Press.

de Waal, F. (2005). *Our inner ape.* Riverhead Books.

de Waal, F. (2007). *Chimpanzee politics: Power and sex among apes.* Johns Hopkins University Press.

de Waal, F. et al. (2006). *Primates and philosophers.* Princeton University Press.

Dewey, J. (1957). *Human nature and conduct.* Modern Library.

Dewey, J. (1960). *The quest for certainty.* G.P. Putnam's Sons.

DiRusso, C. & Stansberry, K. (2022). Unvaxxed: A cultural study of the online anti-vaccination movement. *Qualitative Health Research,* 32(2), 317-329.

Dobewall, H. et al. (2014). A comparison of self–other agreement in personal values versus the Big Five personality traits. *Journal of Research in Personality,* 50, 1-10.

Dobson, J. (1992). *Dare to discipline.* Tindale House.

Doris, J. & Stich, S. (2005). As a matter of fact: Empirical perspectives on ethics. In F. Jackson & M. Smith (Eds.), *The Oxford handbook of contemporary philosophy* (pp. 114-154). Oxford University Press.

Douven, I. Abduction. In Stanford Encyclopedia of Philosophy. Last edited June 18, 2025.

Driver, J. (2005) Normative ethics. In F. Jackson & M. Smith (Eds.), *The Oxford handbook of contemporary philosophy* (pp. 31-62). Oxford University Press.

Druckman, J. (2001). The implications of framing effects for citizen competence. *Political Behavior,* 23(3), 225-256.

Duckitt, J. & Sibley, C. (2009). A dual process model of ideological attitudes and system justification. In J. Jost et al. *Social and psychological bases of identity and system justification.* Oxford University Press.

Duckitt, J. & Sibley, C. (2010). Personality, ideology, prejudice and politics. *Journal of Personality,* 78, 1861-1893.

Duffy, B. (2018). *Why we're wrong about nearly everything.* Basic Books.

Dugatkin, L. (2006). *The altruism equation: Seven scientists search for the origins of goodness.* Princeton University Press.

Duhigg, C. (2012). *The power of habit.* Random House.

Dunbar, R. et al. (1997). Human conversational behavior. *Human Nature,* 8(3), 231-246.

Dunning, D. (2016). False moral superiority. In A. Miller (Ed.), *The social psychology of good and evil* (pp. 249-269). Guilford Press.

Dunning, D. et al. (2002). Ambiguity and self-evaluation: The role of idiosyncratic role definitions in self-serving assessments of ability. In T. Gilovich et al. (Eds.), *Heuristics and biases: The psychology of intuitive judgment* (pp. 324-333). Cambridge University Press.

Duntley, J. & Buss, D. (2016). The evolution of good and evil. In A. Miller (Ed.), *The social psychology of good and evil* (pp. 17-40). Guilford Press.

Durant, W. (1926). *The story of philosophy.* Garden City Publishing Co.

Durant, W. & Durant, A. (1946). *The lessons of history.* Simon & Schuster.

Durant, W. & Durant, A. (1965). *The story of civilization.* MJF Books.

Dworkin, R. (1977). *Taking rights seriously.* Harvard University Press.

Dwyer, S. et al. (2010). The linguistic analogy: Motivations, results and expectations. *Topics in Cognitive Science,* 2(3), 486-410.

Eaves, L. et al. (2011). Modeling the cultural and biological inheritance of social and political views in twins and nuclear families. In P. Hatemi & R. McDermott, *Man is by nature a political animal* (pp. 101-184). University of Chicago Press.

Edel, A. (1955). *Ethical judgment.* Free Press of Glencoe.

Edgerton, R. (1992). *Sick societies: Challenging the myth of primitive harmony.* Free Press.

Edmans, A. (2024). *May contain lies.* University of California Press.

Edmonds, D. (2014). *Would you kill the fat man?* Princeton University Press.

Edmondson v. Leesville Concrete Co., 500 U.S. 632 (1991).

Edwards, P. (1958). *The logic of moral discourse.* Free Press.

Ehrman, B. (2003a). *Lost scriptures.* Oxford University Press.

Ehrman, B. (2003b). *Lost Christianities.* Oxford University Press.

Ehrman, B. (2005). *Misquoting Jesus.* Harper.

Ehrman, B. (2009). *Jesus interrupted.* Harper Collins.

Ehrman, B. (2018). *The triumph of Christianity.* Simon & Schuster.

Einhorn, H. (1982). Learning from experience and suboptimal rules in decision making. In D. Kahneman et al. (Eds.), *Judgment under uncertainty: Heuristics and biases* (pp. 268-283). Cambridge University Press.

Elster, J. (1992). *Local justice.* Russell Sage Foundation.

Engel, C. (2011). Dictator games: A meta-study. *Experimental Economics, 14,* 583-610.

Engelmann, J. & Tomasello, M. (2019). Children's sense of fairness as equal respect. *Trends in Cognitive Science,* 23(6), 454-463.

Epps, D. (2015). The consequences of error in criminal justice. *Harvard Law Review, 128,* 1067.

Etzioni, A. (1988). *The moral dimension: Toward a new economics.* Free Press.

Etzioni, A. (2019). *Reclaiming patriotism.* University of Virginia Press.

Fehr, E. & Gachter, S. (2002). Altruistic punishment in humans. *Nature, 415,* 137-145.

Feinberg, M. & Willer, R. (2019). Moral reframing: A technique for effective and persuasive communication across political divides. *Social and Personality Psychology Compass,* 13(12), e12501.

Feinberg, M. et al. (2019). Measuring moral politics: How strict and nurturing family values explain individual differences in conservatism, liberalism and the political middle. *Journal of Personality and Social Psychology,* 118(4), 777-804.

Feldman, S. (1988). Structure and consistency in political opinion: The role of core beliefs and values. *American Journal of Political Science,* 32, 416-440.

Feldman, S. (2003). Enforcing social conformity: A theory of authoritarianism. *Political Psychology,* 24(1), 41-74.

Feldman, S. (2013). Political ideology. In L. Huddy et al. (Eds.), *The Oxford handbook of political psychology* (pp. 591-626). Oxford University Press.

Feltz, A. (2007). The Knobe effect: A brief overview. *Journal of Mind and Behavior,* 28(3-4), 265-277.

Ferrell, O. et al. (2022). *Business ethics (13th ed.).* Centgage.

Festinger, L. (1957). *Theory of cognitive dissonance.* Stanford University Press.

Fideler, D. (2022). *Breakfast with Seneca: A stoic guide to the art of living.* W.W. Norton.

Fischoff, B. (1977). Knowing with certainty: Extreme confidence. *Journal of Experimental Psychology,* 3(4), 552-564.

Fisher v. University of Texas, 579 U.S. 365 (2016).

Fiske, S. (2016). Categories, intent and harm, in A. Miller (Ed.), *The social psychology of good and evil* (pp. 52-68). Guilford Press.

Flanagan, O. (1991). *Varieties of moral personality.* Harvard University Press.

Fletcher, J. (1966). *Situation ethics: The new morality.* John Knox Press.

Flynn, T. et al. (Eds.) (2012). *Secular humanism and its commitments.* Council for Secular Humanism.

Foot, P. (1978). The problem of abortion and the doctrine of double effect. In P. Foot, *Virtues and vices and other essays in moral philosophy* (pp. 9-32). Basil Blackwell Press.

Foot, P. (1997), Morality as a system of hypothetical imperatives. In S. Darwall et al. (Eds.), *Moral discourse and practice: Some philosophical approaches* (pp. 313-322). Oxford University Press.

Foot, P. (2001). *Natural goodness.* Oxford University Press.

Foot, P. (2009). Utilitarianism and the virtues. In S. Scheffler (Ed.), *Consequentialism and its critics* (pp. 224-242). Oxford University Press.

Foucault, M. (1966). *The order of things.* Gallimard.

Fraley, R. et al. (2012). Developmental antecedents of political ideology: A longitudinal investigation from birth to 18 years. *Psychological Science,* 20(10), 1-7.

Francis (pope) (2014). *National Catholic Reporter,* Oct. 27, 2014.

Franco, Z. & Zimbardo, P. (2016) *The psychology of heroism.* In A. Miller (Ed.), *The social psychology of good and evil* (pp. 494-523). Guilford Press.

Franco, Z. et al. (2011). Heroism: A conceptual analysis and differentiation between heroic acts and altruism. *Review of General Psychology,* 15(2), 99-113.

Frede, D. Plato's Ethics. In Stanford Encyclopedia of Philosophy. Last edited Feb. 1, 2023.

Freud, S. (1965). *New introductory lectures on psychoanalysis.* W.W. Norton.

Friesdorf, R. et al. (2015). Gender differences in response to moral dilemmas: A process dissociation analysis, *Personality and Social Psychology Bulletin,* 41, 696-713.

Frydman, C. et al. (2019). Is maximizing shareholder value a thing of the past? *Kellogg Insight,* Sept. 9, 2019.

Fuller, L. (1964). *The morality of law.* Yale University Press.

Funk, C. (2013). Genetic foundations of political behavior. In L. Huddy et al. (Eds.), *The Oxford handbook of political psychology* (pp. 237-261). Oxford University Press.

Furnham, A. & Boo, H. (2011). A literature review of the anchoring effect. *Journal of Socio-Economics,* 40(1), 35-42.

Fyfe, A. (2011). Mill's proof of utilitarianism. In B. Bruce & S. Barbone (Eds.), *Just the arguments* (pp. 222-228). Wiley Blackwell.

Gabbard, A. (1997). Wise choices: Apt feelings. In S. Darwall et al. (Eds.), *Moral discourse and practice: Some philosophical approaches* (pp. 179-198). Oxford University Press.

Gangemi, A. & Mancini F. Moral choice: The influence of the "do not play God" principle. www.apc.it.

Gaus, G. (2016). *The tyranny of the ideal: Justice in a diverse society.* Princeton University Press.

Gawronski, B. & Beer, J. (2017). What makes moral dilemma judgments "utilitarian" or "deontological"? *Social Neuroscience,* 12, 626-632.

Gawronski, B. et al. (2017). Consequences, norms and generalized inaction in moral dilemmas: The CNI model of moral decision-making. *Journal of Personality & Social Psychology,* 113, 343-376.

Gay, P. (1969). *Enlightenment: The science of freedom.* W.W. Norton.

Gazzaniga, M. (2011). *Who's in charge? Free will and the science of the brain.* Harper Collins.

Gazzaniga, M. (2014). *The ethical brain.* Dana Press.

Geisler, N. (2010). *Christian ethics: Contemporary issues and options.* Baker Academic.

Gerber, A. (2010). Personality and political attitudes: Relationships across issue domains and political contexts. *American Political Science Review,* 104(1), 1-23.

Gerber, A. et al. (2012). Personality and the strength and direction of partisan identification. *Political Behavior, 34,* 653-685.

Gerlach, P. et al. (2019). The truth about lies: A meta-analysis of dishonest behavior. *Psychological Bulletin,* 145(1), 1-10.

Gert, B. (2005). *Morality.* Oxford University Press.

Gervais, W. (2017). Global evidence of extreme intuitive moral prejudice against atheists. *Nature Human Behavior, 1,* 0151.

Gibbs, R. (1994). *The poetics of mind.* Cambridge University Press.

Gigerenzer, G. (2007). *Gut feelings: The intelligence of the unconscious.* Penguin.

Gigerenzer, G. (2008). *Rationality for mortals.* Oxford University Press.

Gigerenzer, G. & Selten, R. (2007). *Bounded rationality: The adaptive toolbox.* MIT Press.

Gilovich, T. (1991). *How we know what isn't so.* Basic Books.

Gilovich, T. & Griffin, D. (2002). Introduction: Heuristics and biases: Then and now. In T. Gilovich et al. (Eds.) *Heuristics and biases: The psychology of intuitive judgment* (pp. 1-18). Cambridge University Press.

Gilovich, T. & Ross, C. (2013). *The wisest man in the room.* Free Press.

Gilovich, T. et al. (Eds.) (2002). *Heuristics and biases: The psychology of intuitive judgment.* Cambridge University Press.

Gino, F. & Ariely, D. (2016). Dishonesty explained: What leads moral people to act immorally? In A. Miller (Ed.), *The social psychology of good and evil* (pp. 322-342). Guilford Press.

Gintis, H. et al. (Eds.) (2005). *Moral sentiments and material interests.* MIT Press.

Glaser, E. & Ward, B. (2005). Myths and realities of American political geography. *Journal of Economic Perspectives,* 20(2), 119-144.

Glasser, B. (1999). *The culture of fear: Why Americans are afraid of the wrong things.* Hachette/Basic Books.

Goldberg, L. (1990). An alternative description of personality: The big 5 factor structure. *Journal of Personality and Social Psychology, 59,* 1216-1222.

Goodpaster, T. (2022). *Times of insight: Conscience, corporations and the common good.* Springer.

Graham, J. (2011). Mapping the moral domain. *Journal of Personality and Social Psychology,* 101(2), 366-385.

Graham, J. et al. (2009). Liberals and conservatives rely on different sets of moral foundations. *Journal of Personality and Social Psychology,* 96(25), 1029-1046.

Graham, J. et al. (2013). Chapter two of moral foundations theory: The pragmatic validity of moral pluralism. *Advances in Experimental Social Psychology, 47,* 55-130.

Grannan, C. What's the difference between morality and ethics? *Brittanica,* retrieved Oct. 25, 2025.

Grant, E. (1978). Authoritarianism and the longevity of the liberal world view. *History of Science, 16,* 93-106.

Gratz v. Bollinger, 539 U.S. 244 (2003).

Grayling, A. (2019). *The history of philosophy.* Penguin.

Greene, J. (2007). Why are vmPFC patients more utilitarian? A dual process theory of moral judgment explains. *Trends in Cognitive Science,* 11(8), 322-323.

Greene, J. (2013). *Moral tribes.* Penguin.

Greene, J. et al. (2001). An fMRI investigation of emotional engagement in moral judgment. *Science,* 293, 2105-2108.

Greener, I. & Greve, B. (2014.) *Evidence and evaluation in social policy.* Wiley Blackwell.

Grice, P. (1989). *Studies in the way of words.* Harvard University Press.

Grimes, D. (2019). *Good thinking.* The Experiment.

Groom, W. (2015). *The generals.* National Geographic Society.

Grudem, W. (2024*). Christian ethics.* Crossway.

Grutter v. Bollinger, 539 U.S. 306 (2003).

Guala, F. & Mittone, L. (2010). Paradigmatic experiments: The dictator game. *Journal of Socio-Economics,* 39(5), 578-584.

Guentert, C. & Gerber, R. (2019). A judge's attempt at sentencing consistency after Booker: Judge Jack. B. Weinstein's guidelines for sentencing. *Cardozo Law Review,* 41(1); article 3, 1-83.

Gula, R. (2002). *Nonsense: A handbook of logical fallacies.* Axios Press.

Haack, S. (1998). *Manifesto of a passionate moderate.* University of Chicago Press.

Habermas, J. (1984). *The theory of communicative action.* Beacon Press.

Haidt, J. (2001). The emotional dog and its rational tail: A social intuitionist approach to moral judgment. *Psychological Review,* 108(4), 814-834.

Haidt, J. (2012). *The righteous mind.* Vintage Books.

Haidt, J. & Kesebir, S. (2010). Morality. In S. Fiske et al (Eds.), *Handbook of social psychology* (5th ed.) (pp. 797-832). John Wiley & Sons.

Haidt, J. et al. (1993). Affect, culture and morality: Or is it wrong to eat your dog? *Journal of Personality and Social Psychology,* 15, 613-628.

Hall, N. (2005). Causation. In F. Jackson & M. Smith (Eds.), *Oxford Handbook of Contemporary Philosophy* (pp. 508-533). Oxford University Press.

Halvorsen, V. (2004). Is it better to let ten guilty persons free than one innocent person be convicted? *Criminal Justice Ethics,* 23, 3-13.

Hamblin, C. (1970). *Fallacies.* Methuen.

Hamilton, W. (1964). The genetical evolution of social behavior. *Journal of Theoretical Biology,* 7, 1-16.

Hamlin, J. et al. (2007). Social evaluation by proverbial infants. *Nature,* 450, 557-559.

Hampshire, S. (1959). *Thought and action.* Viking.

Hand, L. (1944). *The spirit of liberty.* www.digitalhistory.uh.edu.

Hansen, H. & Pinto, R. (1995). *Fallacies: Classical and Contemporary Readings.* Pennsylvania State University Press.

Hardin, R. (2010). The crippled epistemology of extremism. In Breton et al. (Eds.), *Political extremism and rationality* (pp. 3-22). Cambridge University Press.

Hare, B. (2007). Tolerance allows bonobos to outperform chimpanzees on a cooperative task. *Current Biology,* 17(7), 617-623.

Hare, R. (1952). *The language of morals.* Oxford University Press.

Hare, R. (1965). *Freedom and reason.* Oxford University Press.

Hare, R. (1982). Ethical theory and utilitarianism. In A. Sen & B. Williams (Eds.), *Utilitarianism and beyond* (pp. 23-38). Cambridge University Press.

Hare, R. (2003). *Manual for the revised psychopathy checklist.* Multi-Health.

Harman, G. (1977). *The nature of morality.* Oxford University Press.

Harman, G. (1997). Ethics and observation. In S. Darwall et al. (Eds.), *Moral discourse and practice: Some philosophical approaches* (pp. 83-88). Oxford University Press.

Harman, G. & Thomson, J. (1996). *Moral relativism and moral obligation.* Blackwell.

Harrington, D. & Keenan, J. (2010). *Paul and virtue ethics.* Rowan & Littlefield.

Harris, S. (2010). *The moral landscape.* Free Press.

Harris, S. (2012). *Free will.* Free Press.

Harris, S. (2020*). Making sense.* Harper Collins.

Harsanyi, J. (1982). Morality and the theory of rational behavior. In A. Sen & B. Williams (Eds.), *Utilitarianism and beyond* (pp. 39-62). Cambridge University Press.

Hart, H. (1958). Positivism and the separation of law and morals. *Harvard Law Review*, 71, 593.

Hart, H. (1963). *Law, liberty and morality.* Vintage.

Hart, H. (1968). *Punishment and responsibility.* Oxford University Press.

Hart, O. & Zingales, L. (2017). Companies should maximize shareholder welfare not market value. *Journal of Law, Finance and Accounting*, 2, 247-274.

Hastie, R. & Dawes, R. (2010). *Rational choice in an uncertain world: The psychology of judgment and decision making.* Sage.

Hatemi, P. & McDermott, R. (2011). *Man is by nature a political animal.* University of Chicago Press.

Hatemi, P. et al. (2009). Genetic and environmental transmission of political attitudes over a life time. *The Journal of Politics*, 71(3), 1141-1156.

Hatemi, P. et al. (2011). A genome wide analysis of liberal and conservative political attitudes. *Journal of Politics*, 73(1), 271-285.

Hatemi, P. et al. (2014). Not by twins alone: Using extended family design to investigate genetic influence on political beliefs. *American Journal of Political Science,* 54, 798-814.

Hatemi, P. et al. (2015). Genetic influences on political ideologies: Twin analyses of 19 measures. *Behavioral Genetics*, 44(3), 282-294.

Hauser, M. (2006). *Moral minds: The nature of right and wrong.* Harper Perennial.

Hayek, F. (2011). *The constitution of liberty.* University of Chicago Press.

Healey, P. (2017). The fundamental attribution error: What it is and how to avoid it. *Harvard Business School Online*, June 8, 2017.

Health Resources and Services Administration. (2025). *Organ donation legislation and policy.* www.organdonor.gov.

Heck, D. et al. (2018). Who lies? A large scale reanalysis linking basic personality traits to unethical decision-making. *Judgment and Decision Making,* 13, 356-371.

Heimbach, D. (2002). *Fundamental Christian ethics.* B & H Academic.

Henrich, J. et al. (2001). In search of homo economicus: Behavioral experiments in fifteen small scale societies. *American Economic Review,* 91, 73-78.

Henrich, J. et al. (2004). *Foundations of human sociality.* Oxford University Press.

Henrich, J. et al. (2005). Economic man in cross-cultural perspective: Behavioral experiments in 15 small scale societies. *Behavioral and Brain Sciences*, 28(6), 795-815.

Herman, A. (2013). *The cave and the light.* Random House.

Herman, B. (1993). *The practice of moral judgment.* Harvard University Press.

Hersh, E. & Goldenberg, M. (2016). Democratic and Republican physicians provide different care on polarized health issues. *Proceedings of the National Academy of Sciences,* 113(42), 11811-11816.

Heterodox Academy. heterodoxacademy.org.

Hetherington, M. & Weiler, J. (2018). *Prius or pickup.* Houghton Mifflin Harcourt.

Hibbing, J. et al. (2014a) Differences in negativity bias underlie variations in political identity. *Behavioral and Brain Sciences,* 37(3), 297-350.

Hibbing, J. et al. (2014b). *Predisposed.* Routledge.

Hinde, R. (2002). *Why good is good: The sources of morality.* Routledge.

Hobbes, T. (2019). *Leviathan.* W.W. Norton.

Hochschild, J. (2021). *Genomic politics.* Oxford University Press.

Hochschild, J. & Einstein, K. (1993). *Do facts matter?* University of Oklahoma Press.

Hoffman, M. (2000). *Empathy and moral development.* Cambridge University Press.

Hofstadter, R. (1963). *Anti-intellectualism in American life.* Knopf.

Holiday, R. (2022). *Right thing, right now.* Portfolio/Penguin.

Holiday, R. The Daily Stoic (website). dailystoic.com.

Hooker, B. and Little, M. (Eds.). (2000). *Moral particularism.* Clarendon Press.

Horowitz, M. et al. (2019). Anthropology's science wars: Insights from a new survey. *Cultural Anthropology,* 60(5), 674-679.

Huber, M. et al. (2011). Whom to help: Immediacy bias in judgments and decisions about humanitarian aid. *Organizational Behavior and Human Decision Processes,* 115(2), 283-293.

Huddy, L. et al. (Eds.). (2013). *The Oxford handbook of political psychology.* Oxford University Press.

Huebner, B. at al. (2009). The role of emotion in moral psychology. *Trends in Cognitive Sciences,* 13, 1-6.

Hume, D. (1975). *Enquiries concerning human understanding and concerning the principles of morals.* L. Selby-Bigge & P. Nidditch (Eds.). Clarendon.

Hume, D. (1978). *A treatise on human nature.* L. Selby-Bigge & P. Nidditch (Eds.). Oxford University Press.

Huntington, S. (2004). *Who are we? The challenge to American identity.* Simon & Schuster.

Huo, Y. et al. (2010). The interplay between fairness and the experience of respect: Implications for group life. *Research on Managing Groups and Teams,* 13, 95-120.

Hursthouse, R. (1999). *On virtue ethics.* Oxford University Press.

Hursthouse, R. Virtue Ethics. In Stanford Encyclopedia of Philosophy. Last edited Oct. 11, 2022.

Hursthouse, R. et al. (1995). *Virtues and reasons.* Oxford University Press.

Huxley, T. (1980). *Evolution and ethics.* Princeton University Press.

Inbar, Y. et al. (2009a). Conservatives are more easily disgusted than liberals. *Cognition and Emotion,* 23(4), 714-725.

Inbar, Y. et al. (2009b). Disgust sensitivity predicts disapproval of gays. *Emotion* 9(3), 435-439.

Inglehart, R. & Wetzel, C. (2023). World Values Survey. worldvaluessurvey.org.

Jackson, F. & Smith, M. (Eds.). 2005. *The Oxford handbook of contemporary philosophy.* Oxford University Press.

Jacoby, S. (2008) *The age of American unreason.* Pantheon Books.

James, W. (1962). *Essays on faith and morals.* New York: World Publishing Co.

James, W. (1963). *Pragmatism and other essays.* Washington Square Press.

James, W. (1971). *The essential writings* (B. Wilshire, Ed.). Harper Toprchbooks.

James, W. (1979). *The will to believe and other essays.* Harvard University Press.

Jensen, C. (2016). *Moral development in a global world: Research from a cultural developmental perspective.* Cambridge University Press.

John Paul II (pope). (2006). *Fides et ratio.* Catholic Education Resource Center.

Johnson, E. & Tversky, A. (1983). Affect generalization and the perception of risk. *Journal of Personality and Social Psychology, 45*(1), 20-31.

Johnson, J. (2023). The psychology of equality and fairness. *Psychology Today*, Sept, 27, 2023.

Johnson, M. (2014). *Morality for humans.* University of Chicago Press.

Johnson, R. (2012). *Manifest rationality.* Routledge.

Johnson-Laird, P. (2006). *How we reason.* Oxford University Press.

Johnston, C. et al. (2017). *Open versus closed.* Cambridge University Press.

Jones, K. (2005). Moral epistemology. In F. Jackson and M. Smith (Eds.), *The Oxford handbook of contemporary philosophy* (pp. 86-113). Oxford University Press.

Jonsen, A. & Toulmin, S. (1988). *The abuse of casuistry.* University of California Press.

Jost, J. et al. (2003). Political conservatism as motivated social cognition. *Psychological Bulletin, 129*(3), 339-375.

Jost, J. et al. (2006). The end of the end of ideology. *American Psychologist, 61*(7), 651-670.

Jost, J. et al. (2009). *Social and psychological bases of identity and system justification.* Oxford University Press.

Jost, J. et al. (2014). Political neuroscience: The beginning of a beautiful friendship. *Advances in Political Psychology, 35*(1), 3-42.

Journal of Jewish Studies. The Pennsylvania State University Press.

Joyce, R. Moral Subjectivism Versus Moral Relativism. In Stanford Encyclopedia of Philosophy. Last edited Winter 2022.

Kaanders, P. et al. (2022). Humans actively sample evidence to support prior belief. *Elife*, 11, e71768.

Kahan, D. & Braman, D. (2006). Cultural cognition and public policy. *Yale Law Journal*, 24, 147.

Kahan, D. et al. (2006). They saw a protest: Cognitive illiberalism and the speech-conduct distinction. *Stanford Law Review*, 64, 851.

Kahan, D. (2013). Ideology, motivated reasoning, and cognitive reflection. *Judgment and Decision Making, 8*(11), 407-424.

Kahan, D. et al. (2017a). Science curiosity and political information processing. *Political Psychology, 38*(51), 175-199.

Kahan, D. et al. (2017b). Motivated numeracy and enlightened self-interest. *Behavioral Health Policy*, 1, 54-86.

Kahane, G. (2015). Sidetracked by trolleys: Why sacrificial moral dilemmas tell us little (or nothing) about utilitarian judgment. *Social Neuroscience*, 10, 551-560.

Kahneman, D. (2011). *Thinking fast and slow.* Farrar Straus and Giroux.

Kahneman, D. & Frederick, S. (2002). Representativeness revisited: Attribute substitution in intuitive judgment. In T. Gilovich et al. (Eds.), *Heuristics and biases: The psychology of intuitive judgment* (pp. 49-81). Cambridge University Press.

Kahneman, D. & Miller, D. (2002). Norm theory: Comparing reality to its alternatives. In T. Gilovich et al. (Eds.), *Heuristics and biases: The psychology of intuitive judgment* (pp. 348-366). Cambridge University Press.

Kahneman. D. & Tversky, A. (2002). Extensional versus intuitive reasoning: The conjunction fallacy in probability judgment. In T. Gilovich et al. (Eds.), *Heuristics and biases: The psychology of intuitive judgment* (pp. 19-48). Cambridge University Press.

Kahneman, D. & Tversky, A. (1982). On the psychology of prediction. In Kahneman et al. (Eds.), *Judgment under uncertainty: Heuristics and biases* (pp. 48-68). Cambridge University Press.

Kahneman, D. et al. (Eds.) (1982). *Judgment under uncertainty: Heuristics and biases.* Cambridge University Press

Kahneman, D. et al. (2021). *Noise: A flaw in human judgment.* Little Brown Spark.

Kaiser, I. et al. (2012). Theft in an ultimatum game: Chimpanzees and bonobos are Insensitive to fairness. *Biology Letters,* 15(8), 942-945.

Kakutani, M. (2018). *The death of truth.* Crown Penguin.

Kamm, F. (2007). *Intricate ethics.* Oxford University Press.

Kamtekar, R. (2018). *Plato's moral psychology: Intellectualism, the divided soul, and the desire for the good.* Oxford University Press.

Kanai, R. et al. (2011). Political orientation is correlated with brain structure in young adults. *Current Biology,* 21(8), 677-680.

Kane, R. (1996). *Through the moral maze.* Northcastle Books.

Kant, I. (1965). *Critique of pure reason* (N. Smith, Ed.). St. Martin's Press.

Kant, I. (2009). *Groundwork of the metaphysics of morals.* (H. Paton, Trans.). Harper Perennial.

Kant, I. (2015). *Critique of practical reason.* Cambridge University Press.

Kant, I. (2017). *The metaphysics of morals.* (L. Denis, Ed.). Cambridge University Press.

Kass, L. (1977). The wisdom of repugnance. *The New Republic,* June 2, 1977, 20.

Kavanagh, J. & Rich, M. (2018). *Truth decay: An explanation of the diminishing role of facts and analysis in American public life.* Rand Corporation.

Kay, J. (2015). Has internet-fueled conspiracy mongering crested? In M. Bauerlein & A. Bellow, *The state of the American mind* (pp. 137-49). Templeton Books.

Keller, T. (2008). *The reason for God.* Penguin.

Kennedy, J. et al. (2017). A social-cognitive approach to understanding gender differences in negotiating tactics: The role of moral identity. *Organizational Behavior and Human Decision Process,* 138, 28-44.

Kenny, D. (2020). *Interpersonal Perception.* Guilford Press.

Kildoff, G. (2016). Whatever it takes to win: Issues in unethical behavior. *Academy of Management Journal,* 59, 1508-1534.

Kinder, D. (2013) Prejudice and politics. In L. Huddy et al. (Eds.), *The Oxford handbook of political psychology* (pp. 812-851). Oxford University Press.

Kinder, D. & Kalmoe, N. (2017). *Neither liberal nor conservative: Ideological innocence in the American public.* University of Chicago Press.

Kitcher, P. (2011). *The ethical project.* Cambridge University Press.

Klein, D. (2015). *Every time I find the meaning of life, they change it.* Penguin.

Klein, D. & Edgar, B. (2002.) *The dawn of human culture.* John Wiley & Sons.

Klein, E. (2020). *Why we're polarized.* Avid Reader Press.

Kleinfeld, R. (2023). *Polarization, democracy and political violence in the United States: What the research says.* Carnegie Endowment for International Peace.

Knobe, J. (2003a). Intentional action in folk psychology: An experimental investigation. *Philosophical Psychology, 16*(2), 309-325.

Knobe, J. (2003b). Intentional action and side effects in ordinary language. *Analysis, 63*(3), 190-194.

Kohlberg, L. (1968). The child as amoral philosopher. *Psychology Today, 2,* 25-30.

Kohlberg, L. (1981). *Essays on moral development, Vol 1: The philosophy of moral development.* Harper & Row.

Korner, A. et al.(2020). Using the CNI model to investigate individual differences in moral dilemma judgments. *Journal of Personality and Social Psychology, 46*(9), 1392-1407.

Kornferry.com (website). Fortune and Korn Ferry reveal the 2025 world's most admired companies list. Jan. 29, 2025.

Korsgaard, C. (1997). Skepticism and practical reason. In Darwall, S. et al. (Eds.) *Moral discourse and practice: Some practical approaches* (pp. 373-387). Oxford University Press.

Korsgaard, C. (2006). Morality and the distinctness of human action. In de Waal (Ed.), *Primates and philosophers* (pp. 98-119). Princeton University Press.

Korsgaard, C. (2009). *Self-constitution: Agency, identity and integrity.* Oxford University Press.

Kraut, R. Aristotle's Ethics. In Stanford Encyclopedia of Philosophy. Last edited July 2, 2022.

Kreeft, P. (1999). *A reflection on moral relativism.* St. Ignatius Press.

Kroneisen, M. & Heck, D. (2019). Interindividual differences in the sensitivity for consequences, moral norms and preferences for inaction: Relating basic personality traits to the CNI model. *Personality and Social Psychology Bulletin, 46*(7), 1013-1026.

Kronman, A. (2019). *The assault on American excellence.* Free Press.

Kruger, J. & Dunning, D. (1999). Unskilled and unaware of it: How difficulties in recognizing one's own incompetence lead to inflated self-assessments. *Journal of Personality and Social Psychology, 77*(6), 1121-1134.

Kruglanski, A. & Webster, D. (1996). Motivated closing of the mind: Seizing and freezing. *Psychological Bulletin, 103,* 263-283.

Kruglanski, A. et al. (1993). Motivated resistance and openness to persuasion in the presence or absence of prior information. *Journal of Personality and Social Psychology, 65*(5), 861-876.

Kuklinski, J. & Quirk, P. (2000). Reconsidering the rational public: Cognition, heuristics and mass opinion. In A. Lupia et al. (Eds.), *Elements of reason* (pp. 153-182). Oxford University Press.

Kundie, Z. (1990). The case for motivated reasoning. *Psychological Bulletin, 108,* 480-498.

Kurzban, R. (2010). *Why everyone (else) is a hypocrite.* Princeton University Press.

Lakoff, G. (1996). *Moral politics.* University of Chicago Press.

Lakoff, G. (2008). *The political mind.* Viking.

Lakoff, G. & Johnson, M. (1999). *Philosophy in the flesh.* Basic Books.

Lakoff, G. & Johnson, M. (2003). *Metaphors we live by.* University of Chicago Press.

Landy, J. & Goodwin, G. (2015). Does incidental disgust amplify moral judgment? A meta-analytic review of experimental evidence. *Perspectives on Psychological Science, 10*(4), 518-536.

Langton, R. (2005). Feminism in philosophy. In F. Jackson and M. Smith (Eds.), *The Oxford handbook of contemporary philosophy* (pp. 231-257). Oxford University Press.

Lapore, J. (2019). *This America*. John Murray.

Lavin, C. et al. (2013). The anterior cingulate cortex: An integrative hub for human socially driven interactions. *Frontiers of Neuroscience, 7, 64.*

Lawson, A. & Kakker A. (2022). Fake news sharers. *Scientific American*, April 2022, 78.

Lee, S. (2017) *Logic: A complete introduction.* Hachette.

Lefebvre, J. & Krettenhauer, T. (2020). Is the true self truly moral? Identity intuitions across domains of sociomoral reasoning and age. *Journal of Experimental Child Psychiatry,* 192, 104679.

Leith, S. (2012). *Words like loaded pistols.* Basic Books.

Less Wrong (website). www.lesswrong.com.

Levine, M. & Wilson, N. (2016). Bystanders and emergencies. In A. Miller (Ed.), *The social psychology of good and evil* (pp. 345-366). Guilford Press.

Levi-Strauss, C. (1962). *The savage mind.* University of Chicago Press.

Levitin, D. (2019). *A field guide to lies.* Dutton.

Lewis, C. S. (1958). *Mere Christianity.* MacMillan.

Liautaud, S. (2021). *The power of ethics.* Simon & Schuster.

Lilla, M. (2017). *The once and future liberal.* Harper.

Lipton, A. (2024). Will the real shareholder primacy please stand up? *Harvard Law Review,* 137, 1584.

Lipton, P. (1991). *Inference to the best explanation.* Routledge.

Little, M. (2000). Moral generalities revisited. In B. Hooker & M. Little (Eds.), *Moral particularism* 276-304. Clarendon.

Lochner v. New York, 198 U.S. 45 (1905).

Locke, J. (1975). *Essay concerning human understanding* (P. Nidditch, Ed.). Oxford University Press.

Lodge, M. & Taber, C. (2013). *The rationalizing voter.* Cambridge University Press.

Lombrozo, T. (2013). Are moral philosophers better people? NPR.org. Jan. 7, 2013.

Longino, H. (1994). In search of feminist epistemology. *Monist*, 77, 472-485.

LoPucki, L, (2023). The end of shareholder wealth maximization. *University of California–Davis Law Review,* 56, 2017 (2023).

Lord, C. et al. (1979). Biased assimilation and attitude polarization. *Journal of Personality and Social Psychology,* 37(11), 2098-2109.

Luke, D. & Gawronski, B. (2022). Big five personality traits and moral dilemma judgments: Two preregistered studies using the CNI Model. *Journal of Research in Personality,* 101, 104297.

Luke, D. et al. (2022). Psychopathy and moral-dilemma judgment: An analysis using the four-factor model of psychopathy and the CNI model of decision-making. *Clinical Psychological Science*, 10(3), 553-569.

Lukianoff, G. & Haidt, J. (2018). *The coddling of the American mind.* Penguin.

Lukianoff, G. & Schlott, R. (2023). *The cancelling of the American mind.* Simon & Schuster.

Luntz, F. (2007). *Words that work.* Hachette.

Lupia, A. et al. (2000). Beyond rationality: Reason and the study of politics. In A. Lupia et al. (Eds.), *Elements of reason: Cognition, choice and the bounds of rationality* (pp. 1-22). Cambridge University Press.

Luttrell, M. (2007). *Lone survivor*. Little Brown.

Lynch, M. (2012). *In praise of reason*. MIT Press.

MacAskill, W. (2015). *Doing good better*. Avery/Penguin.

MacAskill, W. (2022). *What we owe to the future*. Basic Books.

MacGiolla, E. et al. (2019). Sex differences in personality are larger in gender-equal countries: Replicating and extending a surprising finding. *International Journal of Psychology, 54*(6), 705-711.

MacIntyre, A. (1994). *After virtue*. Notre Dame Press.

MacIntyre, A. Doctrine of Double Effect. In Stanford Encyclopedia of Philosophy. Last edited July 27, 2023.

Mack, B. (1989). *Who wrote the New Testament?* Harper.

Mack, B. (2003). *The lost gospel: The book of Q and Christian origins*. Harper.

Mackie, J. (1977). *Ethics: Inventing right and wrong*. Penguin.

Maio, G. (2017). *The psychology of human values*. Routledge.

Marcus Aurelius (2006). *Meditations*. (M. Hammond, Trans.). Penguin.

Marietta, M. & Barker, C. (2019). *One nation: Two realities*. Oxford University Press.

Markovits, D. (2019). *The meritocracy trap*. Penguin Books.

Mark Twain House (website). Marktwainhouse.com.

Marsden, P. (2012). *Social trends in American life*. Princeton University Press.

Mason, L. (2018). *Uncivil agreement*. University of Chicago Press.

Masserman, J. et al. (1964). Altruistic behavior in rhesus monkeys. *American Journal of Psychiatry, 121*(6), 584-585.

Masterpiece Cakeshop, Ltd. v. Colorado Civil Rights Commission, 584 U.S.617 (2018).

McAdams, P. et al. (2008). Family metaphors and moral intuitions: How conservatives and liberals navigate their lives. *Journal of Personality and Social Psychology, 95*(4), 978-990.

McCrae, R. (1996). Social consequences of experiential openness. *Psychological Bulletin, 120*(3), 323-337.

McCrae, R. & Allik, J. (2002). *The five factor model of personality across cultures*. Kluwer Academic.

McCrae, R. & Costa, P. (2011). The five factor theory of personality. In O. John et al. (Eds.), *Handbook of personality theory and research* (pp.159-181). Guilford Press.

McCrae, R. & Terraciano, A. (2005). Universal features of personality traits from the observer's perspective: Data from 50 cultures. *Journal of Personality and Social Psychology, 85*(3), 547-561.

McDonnell, B. (2022). Doctor Leo and Justice Strine. *University of Pennsylvania Law Review, 24,* 855.

McDowell, J. (1979). Virtue and reason. *The Monist, 62,* 331-350.

McGue, M. et al. (1993). Personality stability and change in early adulthood: A behavioral genetic analysis. *Developmental Psychology, 23*(1), 96-109.

McInerny, D. (2005). *Being logical*. Random House.

McIntyre, L. (2013). *Rejecting truth: Willful ignorance in the internet age*. Routledge.

McIntyre, L. (2018). *Post truth*. MIT Press.

McKenna, M. Compatibilism. In Stanford Encyclopedia of Philosophy. Last edited Feb. 25, 2015.

McNeece, M. & Sinn, J. (2018). Moral foundations theory and Schwartz values theory: Which theory better explains ideological differences? *Winthrop McNair Research Bulletin,* 4(6), 00-00.

McPhetres, J. et al. (2018). Reflecting on God's will: Reflective processing contributes to religious people's deontological dilemma responses. *Journal of Experimental Social Psychology,* 79, 301-314.

Mead, M. (1928). *Coming of age in Samoa.* William Morrow and Co.

Mercier, H. & Sperber, D. (2017). *The enigma of reason.* Harvard University Press.

Mikhail, J. (2007). Universal moral grammar: Theory, evidence and the future. *Trends in Cognitive Sciences,* 11(4), 143-152.

Mikhail, J. (2011). *Elements of moral cognition.* Oxford University Press.

Mill, J. (1965). *The philosophy of John Stuart Mill.* (M. Cohen, Ed.) Modern Library.

Mill, J. (1989). *On liberty.* Cambridge University Press.

Miller, A. (Ed.). (2016). *The social psychology of good and evil.* Guilford Press.

Miller, D. & Taylor, B. (2002). Counterfactual thought, regret and superstition: How to avoid kicking yourself. In T. Gilovich et al. (Eds.), *Heuristics and biases: The psychology of intuitive judgment* (pp. 367-378). Cambridge University Press.

Miller, D. & Walzer, M. (2002). *Pluralism, justice and equality.* Oxford University Press.

Mithen, S. (1996). *The prehistory of the mind.* Thames and Hudson.

Mittelman, A. (2012). *A short history of Jewish ethics: Content and character in the context of covenant.* Wiley Blackwell.

Mlodinow, L. (2023). *Emotional: How our feelings shape our thinking.* Vintage.

Monevirgen, K. (2025). Dynamic pricing: Fair market surge or gouging? *Brittanica Money.*

Mooney, C. (2011). *The Republican brain.* John Wiley & Sons.

Moore, G. (1922). *Principia ethica.* Cambridge University Press.

Moral Sense Test (website). www.moralsensetest.com.

Morris, T. & Bassham, G. (2024). *Stoicism for dummies.* Wiley.

Mosely, R. (2019). *Morality: A natural history.* Friesen Press.

Mulder, L. et al. (2020). Moral rationalization contributes more strongly to escalation of unethical behavior among low moral identifiers than among high moral identifiers. *Frontiers of Psychology,* 10, Jan. 7, 2020.

Mussweiler, T. & Stack, F. (1998). Hypothesis consistent testing and semantic priming in the anchoring paradigm: A selective accessibility model. *Journal of Experimental and Social Psychology,* 35, 136-64.

Nagel, T. (1970). *The possibility of altruism.* Princeton University Press.

Nagel, T. (2009). Autonomy and deontology. In S. Scheffler (Ed.), *Consequentialism and its critics* (pp. 142-172). Oxford University Press.

Nash, L. (2003). Ethics without a sermon. In *Harvard Business Review of Corporate Ethics* (pp. 19-48).

Nelson, C. (2016). *Pearl Harbor: From infamy to greatness.* Scribner's.

Nelson, M. (2019). Is/ought fallacy. In R. Arp et al. (Eds). *Bad arguments* (pp. 360-364). Wiley Blackwell.

Ng, N. et al. (2022). Moral judgment under uncertainty: A CNI model analysis. *European Journal of Social Psychology,* 53(6), 1055-1077.

Niazi, F. et al. (2020). Accuracy of consensual stereotypes in moral foundations: A gender analysis. *PLOS One,* 15(3), e0229926.

Nichols, T. (2017). *The death of expertise.* Oxford University Press.

Nickerson, R. (1998). Confirmation bias: A ubiquitous phenomenon in many guises. *Review of General Psychology,* 2(2), 175-220.

Niebuhr, R. (1935). *An interpretation of Christian ethics.* Harper & Row.

Nisbett, R. & Ross, E. (1980). *Human inference: Strategies and shortcomings of social judgment.* Prentice-Hall.

Niv, Y. (2022). An empirical perspective on moral expertise: Evidence from a global study of philosophers. *Bioethics,* 36(9), 926-935.

Noddings, N. (1989). *Caring: A feminist approach to ethics and moral education.* University of California Press.

Nowak, M. (2012). Five rules for the evolution of cooperation. *Science,* 314(5565), 1560-1563.

Nozick, R. (1974). *Anarchy, state and utopia.* Basic Books.

Nozick, R. (1993). *The nature of rationality.* Princeton University Press.

Nucci, L. (2001). *Education in the moral domain.* Oxford University Press.

Nussbaum, M. (1999). Virtue ethics: A misleading category. *Journal of Ethics,* 3(3), 163-201.

Nussbaum, M. (2000). Why practice needs ethical theory. In B. Hooker & M. Little (Eds.), *Moral particularism* (pp. 227-255). Clarendon.

Nyhan, B. & Reifler, J. (2010). When corrections fail: The persistence of political misperceptions. *Political Behavior,* 32(2), 303-330.

O'Connor, C. & Wetherall, J. (2019). *The misinformation age.* Yale University Press.

O'Connor W. (2019). Why we trust lies. *Scientific American,* Sept. 2019, 54-61.

O'Donovan, O. (2020). *Resurrection and moral order.* Inter-Varsity Press.

Okamp, S. (1982). Overconfidence in case study judgments. In D. Kahneman et al. (Eds.), *Judgment under uncertainty: Heuristics and biases* (pp. 285-293). Cambridge University Press.

Oliner, S. & Oliner, P. (1988). *The altruistic personality.* Free Press.

Olson, J. (2001). The heritability of attitudes: A study of twins. *Journal of Personality and Social Psychology,* 80(6), 845-860.

O'Neil, P. & Petrinovich, L. (1998). A preliminary cross-cultural study of moral intuitions. *Evolution and Human Behavior* 19(6), 349-367.

O'Neill, O. (1996). *Towards justice and virtue: A reconstructive account of practical reasoning.* Cambridge University Press.

Oosterbeck, H. (2004). Cultural differences in ultimatum game experiments: Evidence from a meta-analysis. *Experimental Economics,* 7(2), 171-178.

Orsi, F. (2008). The dualism of the practical reason: Some interpretations and responses. *Ethics and Politics,* 10(2), 19-41.

Ortoney, A. (Ed.). (1993). *Metaphor and thought.* Cambridge University Press.

Our World in Data (website). ourworldindata.org.

Oxford English Dictionary (website). www.oed.com.

Oxford Learning College (website). Ethics versus morals: What's the difference. www.oxfordcollege.ac.

Oxley, D. et al. (2008). Political attitudes vary with physiological traits. *Science,* 321 (5896), 1667-1670.

Pagels, E. (1979). *The gnostic gospels.* Vintage.

Pagels, E. (2025). *Miracles and wonder: The historical mystery of Jesus.* Doubleday.

Paine, L. (2003). Managing for corporate integrity. In *Harvard Business Review on Corporate Ethics* (pp. 85-112).

Parfit, D. (1984). *Reason and reasons*. Oxford University Press.

Paris, F. (2025). Unvaxxed. *The New York Times*, Jan. 13, 2025.

Parks, L. & Guay, R. (2009). Personality, values and motivation. *Personality and Individual Differences*, 47(7), 675-684.

Parks-Leduc, L. et al. (2015). Personality traits and personal values: A meta-analysis. *Personality and Social Psychology Review,* 19(1), 3-29.

Paxton J. & Greene, J. (2010) Moral reasoning: Hints and allegations. *Topics in Cognitive Science* 2(3), 511-527.

Pearl, J. & Mackenzie, D. (2018). *The book of why*. Basic Books.

Peirce, C. (1878). How to make our ideas clear. *Popular Science Monthly*, 12, 286-302.

Peirce, C. (1992-1994). *The essential Peirce* (N. Houser & C. Kloesel, Eds.). Indiana University Press.

Pen America. *Book Bans*. pen.org/book-bans/.

Perry, J. & Bratman, M. (Eds.) (1999). *Introduction to philosophy*. Oxford University Press.

Peterson, M. et al. (2001). *Philosophy of religion*. Oxford University Press.

Pew Research Center (2017). *Political typology: views on religion and social issues.*

Pew Research Center (2023). J. Fetterolf & S. Austin, *Many people in U.S., other advanced economies say it is not necessary to believe in God to be moral.* June 20, 2023.

Pew Research Center (2024a). Religious "nones" in America: Who are they and what do they believe? Jan. 24, 2024.

Pew Research Center (2024b). *How do "nones" think about morality?*

Pew Research Center. (2025). Hackett, C. *How the global religious landscape changed from 2010 to 2020.*

Piaget, J. (1932). *The moral judgment of the child*. Free Press.

Pigliucci, M. (2010). *Nonsense on stilts*. University of Chicago Press.

Pigliucci, M. & Lopez, G. (2019). *A handbook for new stoics*. The Experiment.

Pink, D. (2008). *When: The scientific secrets of perfect timing*. Riverhead.

Pinker, S. (1999). *How the mind works*. W.W. Norton.

Pinker, S. (2002). *The blank slate*. Penguin.

Pinker, S. (2007). *The stuff of thought*. Penguin.

Pinker, S. (2011). *Better angels of our nature*. Penguin.

Pinker, S. (2018). *Enlightenment now*. Viking.

Pinker, S. (2021). *Rationality*. Viking.

Pinker, Susan (2008). *The sexual paradox*. Scribner.

Pizarro, D. et al. (2003). Causal deviance and the attribution of responsibility. *Journal of Experimental Social Psychology,* 39(6), 653-660.

Pizarro, D. et al. (2011). On disgust and judgment. *Emotion Review*, 3(3), 267-268.

Plato (1997). *The complete works* (J. Cooper, Ed.). Hackett Publishing.

Plomin, R. (2018). *Blueprint: How DNA makes us what we are*. Penguin.

Plomin, R. et al. (Eds.) (4th Ed. 2001). *Behavioral genetics*. Worth.

Ponizovskiy, V. et al. (2019). Social construction of the value-behavior relation. *Frontiers in Psychology*, 10, 934.

Popkin, S. (1991). *The reasoning voter*. University of Chicago Press.

Popper, K. (1959). *The logic of scientific discovery*. Routledge.

Popper, K. (1966). The *open society and its enemies*. Princeton University Press.

Premack D. & Premack, A. (1997). Infants attribute value to the goal directed actions of self-propelled objects. *Journal of Cognitive Neuroscience,* 9(6), 848-856.

Prinz, J. (2007). *The emotional construction of morals*. Oxford University Press.

Prontin, E. et al. (2002). Understanding misunderstanding: Social psychological perspectives. In T. Gilovich et al. (Eds.) *Heuristics and biases: The psychology of intuitive judgment.* (pp. 636-665.) Cambridge University Press.

Prothero, S. (2010). *God is not one*. Harper One.

Purzycki, B. (2016). Moralistic gods, supernatural punishment and the expansion of human sociality. *Nature,* 530(7590), 327-330.

Putnam, H. (2002). *The collapse of the fact-value distinction and other essays*. Harvard University Press.

Quine, W. (1991). *Word and object*. MIT Press.

Rae, S. (2018). *Moral choices: An introduction to ethics*. Zondervan.

Rauch, J. (2021). *The constitution of knowledge: A defense of truth*. Brookings Institution.

Rawls, J. (1971). *A theory of justice*. Harvard University Press.

Rawls. J. (1993). *Political liberalism*. Columbia University Press.

Rawls, J. (1997). Kantian constructivism in moral theory. In S. Darwall et al. (Eds.) *Moral discourse and practice: Some philosophical approaches* (pp. 247-266). Oxford University Press.

Rawls, J. (2001). *Justice as fairness: A restatement*. (E. Kelly, Ed.). Harvard University Press.

Redlawsk, D. & Lau, R. (2013). Behavioral decision-making. In L. Huddy et al. (Eds.), *The Oxford handbook of political psychology* (pp. 130-164). Oxford University Press.

Reeves, R. (2007). *John Stuart Mill: Victorian firebrand*. Atlantic Books.

Regents of the University of California v. Baake, 438 U.S. 265 (1978).

Reimer, N. et al. (2022). Moral values predict county-level COVID-19 vaccination rates in the United States. *American Psychologist* 77(6), 743-759.

Rentfrow, J. et al. (2009). Statewide differences in personality predict voting patterns in 1996-2004 U.S. presidential elections. In J. Jost et al. (Eds.), *Social and psychological bases of ideology and system justification* (pp. 314-347). Oxford University Press.

Rentfrow, P. (2010). Statewide differences in personality: Toward a psychological geography of the United States. *American Psychologist* 65(6), 548-558.

Rescher, N. (1969). *What is value change? A framework for research*. In K. Baier & N. Rescher (Eds.), *Values and the future* (pp. 68-89). The Free Press.

Reuter, M. et al. (2013). The influence of dopaminergic gene variants on decision making in the ultimatum game. *Frontiers in Human Neuroscience,* 4(7), 242.

Rhodes, R. (1996). *The atomic bomb*. Simon & Schuster.

Richerson, P & Boyd, R. (2000). *Not by genes alone: How culture transformed human evolution*. University of Chicago Press.

Ridley, M. (1996). *The origins of virtue*. Penguin.

Riley, J. (2025). *The affirmative action myth*. Basic Books.

Ringwald, W. & Wright, A. (2020). The affiliative role of empathy in everyday interpersonal interactions. *European Journal of Personality* 35(2), 197-211.

Ritov, J. & Baron, J. (1990). Reluctance to vaccinate: Omission bias and ambiguity. *Journal of Behavioral Decision Making,* 3(4), 263-277.

Roberts, B. & Delvecchio, W. (2000). The rank order consistency of personality from childhood to old age: A quantitative review of longitudinal studies. *Psychological Bulletin*, 126(1), 3-25.

Robertson, D. (2019). *How to think like a Roman emperor*. Griffin.

Roccas, S. et al. (2002). The big five personality factors and personal values. *Personality and Social Psychology Bulletin* 289, 789-801.

Rokeach, M. (1960). *The open and closed mind*. Basic Books.

Rokeach, M. (1968). *Beliefs, attitudes and values*. Harvard University Press.

Rokeach, M. (1973). *The nature of human values*. Free Press.

Rokeach, M. (1975). *Understanding human values: Individual and societal*. Free Press.

Rorty, R. (1982). *Consequences of pragmatism*. University of Minnesota Press.

Rorty, R. (1989). *Contingency, irony, solidarity*. Cambridge University Press.

Rosier, M. & Willig, C. (2002). The strange death of the authoritarian personality: 50 years of psychological and political debate. *History of the Human Sciences*, 15(4): 71-96.

Rosling, H. (2021). *Factfulness*. Flatiron Books

Ross, D. (1999). *A history of the world's religions*. Prentice Hall.

Ross, L. & Anderson, C. (1982). Shortcomings in the attribution process: On the origins and maintenance of erroneous social assessments. In D. Kahneman et al. (Eds.), *Judgment under uncertainty: Heuristics and biases* (pp. 129-152). Cambridge University Press.

Ross, L. & Nesbitt, R. (1991). *The person and the situation*. Temple University Press.

Ross, W. (1930). *The Right and the Good*. Oxford University Press.

Rovane, C. (2017). Moral dispute or cultural difference. In P. Catapano & S. Critchley, *Modern ethics in 77 arguments* (pp. 134-138). W.W. Norton.

Rozin, P. (1999). The CAD triad hypothesis. *Journal of Personality and Social Psychology*, 76(4), 574-586.

Rozin, P. & Nemeroff, C. (2002). Sympathetic magical thinking: The contagion and similarity heuristics. In T. Gilovich et al. (Eds.), *Heuristics and biases: The psychology of intuitive judgment* (pp. 201-216). Cambridge University Press.

Ruisch, C. et al. (2021). Of unbiased beans and slanted stocks: Neural stimuli reveal the fundamental relation between political ideology and exploratory behavior. *British Journal of Psychology*, 112(1), 358-361.

Russell, B. (1945). *The history of western philosophy*. Simon & Schuster.

Russell, B. (1957). *Mysticism and logic*. Anchor Books.

Russell, B. (1959). *The problems of philosophy*. Oxford University Press.

Russell, B. (1999). Why I am not a theist. In J. Perry & M. Bratman (Eds.), *Introduction to Philosophy* (pp. 53-56). Oxford University Press.

Russell, D. (Ed.). (2013). *Virtue ethics*. Cambridge University Press.

Russo, C. et al. (2022). Changing personal values through value manipulation tasks: A systematic literature review based on Schwartz's theory of basic human values. *European Journal of Investigation in Health, Psychology and Education*, 12(7), 692-715.

Saad, G. (2020). *The parasitic mind*. Regnery Press.

Sacks, J. (2019). *Seven moral rules found all around the world*. The Institute of Cognitive and Evolutionary Anthropology.

Sacks, J. (2020). *Morality: Restoring the common good in divided times*. Basic Books.

Sadowsky, L. & Cogburn, H. (1997). Need for cognition in the big-five factor structure. *The Journal of Psychology: Interdisciplinary and Applied*, 131(3), 307-312.

Salmon, W.(1999). The problem of induction. In J. Perry & M. Bratman (Eds.), *Introduction to philosophy* (pp. 230-251). Oxford University Press.

Sandel, M. (1982). *Liberalism: The limits of justice.* Cambridge University Press.

Sandel, M. (2009). *Justice.* Farrar, Straus and Giroux.

Sandel, M. (2020). *The tyranny of merit.* Farrar, Straus and Giroux.

Sanfey, H. et al. (2003). The neural basis of economic decision-making in the ultimatum game. *Science,* 300 (5626), 1755-1758.

Sapolsky, R. (2017). *Behave: The biology of humans at our best and worst.* Penguin.

Sargent, M. (2004). Less thought, more punishment: Need for cognition predicts support for punitive responses to crime. *Personality and Social Psychology Bulletin,* 30(11), 1485-1493.

Sartre, J. (1946). *Existentialism is a humanism.* Methuen.

Saunders, E. (1993). *The historical figure of Jesus.* Penguin.

Seyedsayamdost, H. (2010). On normativity and epistemic intuitions: Failure of replication. *Episteme,* 12(1), 95-116.

Scanlon, T. (1982). Contractualism and utilitarianism. In A. Sen and B. Williams (Eds.), *Utilitarianism and beyond* (pp. 103-128). Cambridge University Press.

Schaller, M. & Park, J. (2011). The behavioral immune system (and why it matters). *Current Directions in Psychological Science,* 20(2), 99-103.

Scheffler, S. (Ed.) (2009). *Consequentialism and its critics.* Oxford University Press.

Schnall, S. et al. (2008). Disgust as embodied moral judgment. *Personality and Social Psychology Bulletin,* 34(8), 1096-1109.

Schreiber, D. et al. (2013). Red brain, blue brain: Evaluative processes differ in Democrats and Republicans. *PLOS One,* 8(2), e52970.

Schuck, P. & Wilson, J. (Eds.). (2008). *Understanding America.* Perseus/Public Affairs.

Schwarz, N. (2002). Feelings as information: Moods influence judgments and processing strategies. In T. Gilovich et al. (Eds.), *Heuristics and biases: The psychology of intuitive judgment* (pp. 534-547). Cambridge University Press.

Schwartz, S. (1992). Universals in the content and structure of values: Theoretical advances and empirical tests in 20 countries. *Advances in Experimental Social Psychology,* 25(1), 1-65.

Schwartz, S. (1994). Are there universal aspects in the structure and content of human values? *Journal of Social Issues,* 50(4), 19-45.

Schwartz, S. (2012). An overview of the Schwartz theory of basic values. *Online Readings in Psychology & Culture,* 2(1).

Schwartz, S. & Boenke, K. (2004). Evaluating the structure of human values with confirmatory factor analysis. *Journal of Research in Personality,* 38(3), 230-255.

Schwartz, S. & Rubel, T. (2005). Sex differences in value priorities: Cross-cultural and multi-method studies. *Journal of Personality and Social Psychology,* 89(6), 1010-1028.

Shweder, R. (1991). *Thinking through cultures: Expeditions in cultural psychology.* Harvard University Press.

Shweder, R. (2003). *Why do men barbecue: Recipes for cultural psychology.* Harvard University Press.

Schweinfurth, M. & Call, J. (2019). Revisiting the possibility of reciprocal help in non-human primates. *Neuroscience & Behavioral Reviews* 104, 73-86.

Schwitzgebel, E. & Rust, J. (2009). The moral behavior of ethicists: Peer opinion. *Mind,* 118 (472), 1043-1059.

Scott, P. & Lizieri, C. (2011). Consumer price judgments: New evidence of anchoring and arbitrary coherence. *Journal of Property Research,* 29(1), 49-68.

Scruton, R. (1994). *Modern philosophy: An introduction and a survey.* Penguin.

Searle, J. (1964). How to derive an ought from an is. *The Philosophical Review,* 73(1), 42-58.

Searle, J. (1980). Minds, brains and programs. *Behavioral and Brain Sciences,* 3(3), 417-424.

Searle, J. (1983). *Intentionality.* Cambridge University Press.

Searle, J. (1995). *The construction of social reality.* The Free Press.

Searle, J. (2001). *Rationality in action.* MIT Press.

Searle, J. (2002). *Consciousness and language.* Harvard University Press.

Sears, D. & Funk, C. (1991). The role of self interest in social and political attitudes. *Advances in Experimental Social Psychology,* 24(1), 1-91.

Sears, D. & Brown. C. (2013). Childhood and adult development. In L. Huddy et al. (Eds.), *The Oxford handbook of political psychology* (pp. 59-95). Oxford University Press.

Sen, A. (2009). *The idea of justice.* Harvard University Press.

Sen, A. & Williams, B. (Eds.). (1982). *Utilitarianism and beyond.* Cambridge University Press.

Seneca (2015). *Letters from a stoic.* Penguin.

Shermer, M. (2015). *The moral arc.* Henry Holt & Co.

Shook, N. (1975). Pragmatism and the tragic sense of life. In R. Corrigan (Ed.), *Tragedy: Vision and form* (pp. 56-75). Chandler Publishing.

Shook, N. & Fazio, R. (2009). Political ideology and exploration of novel stimuli and attitude formation. *Journal of Experimental Social Psychology,* 45(4), 995-998.

Sibley C. & Duckitt, S. (2008). Personality and perspective: A meta-analysis and theoretical review. *Personality and Social Psychology Review,* 12(3), 248-279.

Sidanius, J. & Pratto F. (1999). *Social dominance.* Cambridge University Press.

Sidanius, J. & Kurzban, R. (2013). Toward an evolutionarily informed political psychology. In L. Huddy et al. (Eds.), *Oxford handbook of political psychology* (pp. 205-236). Oxford University Press.

Sidgwick, H. (1981). *The methods of ethics.* Hackett Publishing.

Silk, J. et al. (2005). Chimpanzees are indifferent to the welfare of unrelated group members. *Nature,* 437 (7063), 1357-1359.

Simon, H. (1983). *Reason in human affairs.* Stanford University Press.

Singer, P. (1979). *Practical ethics.* Harvard University Press.

Singer, P. (1999). Famine, affluence and morality. In F. Perry and M. Bratman (Eds.), *Introduction to philosophy* (pp. 521-528). Oxford University Press.

Singer, P. (2011). *The expanding circle: Ethics, evolution and moral progress.* Princeton University Press.

Singer, P. (2023). *Ethics in the real world.* Princeton University Press.

Singer, T. et al. (2006). Empathic neural responses are modulated by the perceived fairness of others. *Nature,* 439 (7075), 466-469.

Sinnott-Armstrong, W. (2018). *Think again: How to reason and argue.* Oxford University Press.

Sinnott-Armstrong, W. & Fogelin, E. (2015). *Understanding Arguments.* Cengage.

Sloman, S. & Fernbach, P. (2017). *The knowledge illusion.* Riverhead Books.

Slote, M. (1992). *From morality to virtue*. Oxford University Press.

Slote, M. (2001). *Morals from motives*. Oxford University Press.

Slovic, P. et al. (2002). The affect heuristic. In T. Gilovich et al. (Eds.), *Heuristics* and *biases: The psychology of intuitive judgment* (pp. 397-420). Cambridge University Press.

Smart, J. & Williams, B. (1973). *Utilitarianism: for and against*. Cambridge University Press.

Smetana, J. & Braeges, J. (1990). The development of toddler's moral and conventional judgments. *Merrill-Palmer Quarterly, 36*(3), 329-346.

Smith, A. (1969). *The theory of moral sentiments*. Clarendon Press.

Smith, C. (2003). *Moral believing animals: Human personhood and culture*. Oxford University Press.

Smith, F. (2005). Meta-ethics. In F. Jackson and M. Smith (Eds.), *The Oxford handbook of contemporary philosophy* (pp. 3-30). Oxford University Press.

Smith, H. (1991). *The world's religions*. Harper.

Smith, H. (2001). *Why religion matters*. Harper.

Smith, K. et al. (2011). Disgust sensitivity and neurophysiology of left-right political orientations. *PLOS One*, 2011(6)(10) e25552.

Smith, K. et al. (2011) Linking genetics and political attitudes: Reconceptualizing political ideology. *Political Psychology, 32*(3), 369-397.

Smith, K. et al. (2012). Biology, ideology and epistemology: How do we know political attitudes are inherited and why should we care? *American Journal of Political Science* 56(1),17-33.

Soames, S. (2019). *The world philosophy made*. Princeton University Press.

Sowell, T. (2007). *Economic facts and fallacies*. Basic Books.

Spinath, F., et al. (2002). German observational study of adult twins (GOSAT): A multimodal investigation of personality, temperament and cognitive ability. *Twin Research,* 5 (5), 372-375.

Spinoza, B. (2018). *The ethics*. Dover.

Stanford Encyclopedia of Philosophy. (E. Zalta et al., Eds.). plato.stanford.edu/index.html.

Stanley, L. (2020). The centrality of remembered moral and immoral actions in constructing personal identity. *Memory* 28(2), 278-284.

Stanovich, K. & West, R. (2000). Individual differences in reasoning: Implications for the rationality debate. *Behavioral and Brain Sciences*, 23(5), 645-665 (discussion 665-726).

Stanovich, K. et al. (2013). My-side bias, rational thinking and intelligence. *Current Directions in Psychological Science, 22*(4), 259-264.

Stanovich, K. et al. (2016). *The rationality quotient*. MIT Press.

Staw, B. (1989). Understanding behavior in escalation situations. *Science* 246(4927), 216-220.

Steinberg, K., et al. (2020). Big data and personalized pricing. *Business Ethics Quarterly* 30(1), 97-117.

Stenner, K. (2005). *The authoritarian dynamic*. Cambridge University Press.

Stohr, K. (2024). Choosing freedom: A Kantian guide to life. Oxford University Press.

Stout, L. (2015a). *The shareholder value myth*. Cambridge University Press Online.

Stout, L. (2015b). Corporations don't have to maximize profits. *The New York Times*, April 16, 2015.

Strine, L. (2014). Making it easier for directors to 'do the right thing.' *Harvard Business Law Review*, 4, 235.

Strine, L. (2021a). Caremark and ESG: Perfect together: A practical approach to implementing an integrated, efficient and effective Caremark and ESG Strategy. *Iowa Law Review*, 106, 1885.

Strine, L. (2021b). Our continuing struggle with the idea that for-profit corporations seek profit. *Wake Forest Law Review* 47, 135.

Students for Fair Admissions v. President and Fellows of Harvard College, 600 U.S. 181 (2023).

Sulloway, F. (1996). *Born to rebel.* Vintage.

Sun, L. (2013). *The fairness instinct.* Prometheus.

Sunstein, C. (2005). Moral heuristics. *Behavioral and Brain Sciences,* 28(4), 531-542.

Sunstein, C. (2009). *Going to extremes.* Oxford University Press.

Sunstein, C. (2014). *Valuing life.* University of Chicago Press.

Sunstein, C. (2023). *Decisions about decisions.* Cambridge University Press.

Sunstein, C. (2025). *Manipulation.* Cambridge University Press.

Suppe, S. (Ed.) (1977). *The structure of scientific theories* (2d ed.). University of Illinois Press.

Svoboda, E. (2013). *What makes a hero?* Penguin.

Swanton, C. (2003). *The virtue ethics: A pluralistic view.* Oxford University Press.

Taber, C. & Lodge, M. (2006). Motivated skepticism in the evaluation of political beliefs. *American Journal of Political Science* 50(3), 755-769.

Taber, C. & Young, E. (2013). Political information processing. In L. Huddy et al. (Eds.), *Oxford handbook of political psychology* (pp. 525-558). Oxford University Press.

Taleb, N. (2010). *The bed of Procrustes: Philosophical and practical aphorisms.* Random House.

Tancredi, L. (2005). *Hardwired behavior: What neuroscience reveals about morality.* Cambridge University Press.

Tannen D. (1998). *The argument culture.* Ballantine Books.

Tao, D. et al. (2022). Effects of core disgust and moral disgust on moral judgment: An event related potential study. *Frontiers in Psychology,* 13: 806784.

Tappin, B. & McKay, R. (2017). The illusion of moral superiority. *Social Psychological and Personality Science,* 8(6), 623-631.

Tappin, B. et al. (2017). The heart trumps the head: Desirability bias in political belief. *Journal of Experimental Psychology: General,* 146(8), 1143-1149.

Tarasoff v. Regents of the University of California, 17 Cal.3d 425 (CA 1976).

Tarnas, R. (1991). *The passion of the western mind.* Ballantine.

Taylor, S. & Brown, J. (1988). Illusion and well-being: Social and psychological perspectives on mental health. *Psychological Bulletin,* 10093, 193-210.

Tellegen, A. et al. (1988). Personality similarity in twins reared apart and together. *Journal of Personality and Social Psychology,* 54(6), 1031-1039.

Tetlock, P. (1983). Cognitive style and political ideology. *Journal of Personality and Social Psychology,* 45(1), 118-126.

Tetlock, P. (2017). *Expert political judgment.* Princeton University Press.

Thaler, R. (2015). *Misbehaving: The making of behavioral economics.* W.W. Norton.

Thomas Aquinas, Saint. (1920). *Summa theologica.* New Advent.

Thomson, J. (1976). Killing, letting die and the trolley problem. *Monist,* 59(2), 204-217.

Thomson, J. (1985). The trolley problem. *Yale Law Journal,* 94, 1395.

Thoughtco.com (2025). *How a fallacy invalidates any argument.*

Tilley, J. (2000). Cultural relativism. *Human Rights Quarterly*, 22(2), 501-547.

Tindale, C. (2007). *Fallacies and argument appraisal.* Cambridge University Press.

Todorov, A. (2017). *Face value.* Princeton University Press.

Tomasello, M. (2016). *A natural history of human morality.* Harvard University Press.

Tomasello, M. & Carpenter, M. (2007). Shared intentionality. *Developmental Science*, 10(1), 121-125.

Toulmin, S. et al. (1984). *Introduction to reasoning (2d Ed).* Macmillan.

Travers, M, (2024). A psychologist explains the politics-genetics link. *Forbes,* May 14, 2024.

Trivers, R. (1971). The evolution of reciprocal altruism. *Quarterly Review of Biology*, 46(1), 35-57.

Trivers, R. (2011). *The folly of fools.* Basic Books.

Turiel, E. (1983). *The development of social knowledge.* Cambridge University Press.

Turiel, E. (2002). *The culture of morality.* Cambridge University Press.

Tuschman, A. (2013). *Our political nature.* Prometheus.

Tversky, A. & Kahneman, D. (1981). The framing of decisions and the psychology of choice. *Science,* 211: 453-458.

Tversky, A. & Kahneman, D. (1982a). Judgment under uncertainty: Heuristics and biases. In D. Kahneman et al. (Eds.), *Judgment under uncertainty: Heuristics and biases* (pp. 3-20). Cambridge University Press.

Tversky, A. & Kahneman, D. (1982b). Causal schemas in judgments under uncertainty. In D. Kahneman et al. (Eds.), *Judgment under uncertainty: Heuristics and biases* (pp. 117-128). Cambridge University Press.

Uchii, S. *Darwin on the evolution of morality.* philsci-archive.pitt.edu.

Uhlman, E. & Cohen, G. (2005). Constructed criteria: Redefining merit to justify discrimination. *Psychological Science,* 16(4), 474-480.

Uhlman, E. et al. (2009). The motivated use of moral principles. *Judgment and Decision Making,* 4(6), 476-491.

Unger, P. (1996). *Living and letting die.* Oxford University Press.

United Network for Organ Sharing, unos.org.

United States Conference of Catholic Bishops (2018). *Ethical and religious directives for Catholic health care services* (6th ed.)

United States Fire Administration.

Utilitarianism.net

Van Biema, D. (2005). Can you believe in God and evolution? *Time Forum,* Aug. 7, 2005.

Van Boven, L. et al. (2009). Immediacy bias in emotion perception. *Journal of Experimental Psychology: General,* 138(3), 368-382.

Van de Schoot, R. et al. (2014). A gentle introduction to Bayesian analysis: Applications to developmental research. *Child Development,* 85(3), 842-860.

Van de Schoot, R. et al. (2021). Bayesian statistics and modelling. *Nature Reviews Methods Primers,* (1), 3.

Vanopal, L. (2010). These are the most common arguments married couples have. *Health & Science.* Aug. 6, 2019, 558.

Vecchione, M. (2023). The five factors of personality and personal values: An update with the refined theory. *Personality and Individual Differences,* 203(1), 112033.

Verbeek. B. (2011) Moore's open question. In M. Bruce and S. Barbone [Eds.], *Just the arguments* (pp. 237-239). Wiley Blackwell.

Verdantlabs.com. (2025). Democratic versus Republican occupations.

Vigil, J. (2010). Political leanings vary with facial expression processing and psychosocial functioning. *Group Processes & Intergroup Relations*, 13(5), 547-558.

Vigil, J. & Strenth, C. (2001). Facial expression judgments support a socio-relational model, rather than a negativity bias model of political psychology. *Behavioral and Brain Sciences*, 37(3), 331-332.

Vogel, D. (2005). *The market for virtue: The potential and limits of corporate social responsibility*. Brookings Institution.

Vollhardt, J. (2011). Inclusive altruism born of suffering: The relationship between adversity and prosocial attitudes and behavior toward disadvantaged groups. *American Journal of Orthopsychiatry*, 81(3), 307-315.

Voronai.com. (2024). *Political leaning by occupation*. Dec. 12, 2024.

Wallace, B. et al. (2007). Heritability of ultimatum game responder behavior. *Proceedings of the National Academy of Sciences,* 104(40), 15631-15634.

Wallace, C. (2005). *Character: Profiles in presidential courage*. Rugged Land.

Wallace, R. (2005). Moral psychology. In F. Jackson and M. Smith (Eds.), *The Oxford handbook of contemporary philosophy* (pp. 86-113). Oxford University Press.

Wall Street Journal/NORC (2023). America pushes back from values that once defined it: WSJ/NORC Poll finds. *The Wall Street Journal*, Mar. 7, 2023.

Walton, D. (1987). *Informal fallacies*. John Benjamins.

Walton, D. (2008). *Informal logic: A pragmatic approach*. Cambridge University Press.

Walton, D. (2017). *A rulebook for arguments* (5th Ed.). Hackett Publishing.

Walzer, M. (1983). *Spheres of justice*. Basic Books.

Warneken, F. & Tomasello, M. (2006). Altruistic helping in human infants and young chimpanzees. *Science,* (3)311 (5765), 1301-1303.

Warneken, F. & Tomasello, M. (2007). Helping and cooperation at 14 months of age. *Infancy,* 11(3), 271-294.

Warneken, F. et al. (2007). Spontaneous altruism by chimpanzees and young children. *PLOS Biology,* July 2007, 5(7) e184.

Warnock, M. (2004). *An intelligent person's guide to ethics*. Duckworth.

Watson, P. (2001). *The modern mind*. Harper Collins.

The Week, Nov. 7, 2025. theweek.com.

Weinstock, P. et al. (2014). No duty to warn In California: Now unambiguously solely a duty to protect. *Journal of the American Academy of Psychiatry and The Law.* 42(1), 101-108.

Welch, B. (2008). *State of confusion*. St. Martin's Press.

Westen, D. (2007). *The political brain: The role of emotions in deciding the fate of the nation*. Perseus/Public Affairs.

Westen, D. et al. (2006). Neural bases of motivated reasoning: An fMRI study of emotional constraints on partisan political judgment in the 2004 U.S. presidential election. *Journal of Cognitive Neuroscience,* 18(1), 1947-1958.

White, M. (Ed.) (1959). *The age of analysis*. Mentor Books.

White, M. (2004). *From Jesus to Christianity*. Harper.

Wierzbicka, A. (2007). Moral sense. *Journal of Social, Evolutionary and Cultural Psychology,* 1(3), 66-85.

Wiggins, D. (1997). A sensible subjectivism. In S. Darwall et al. (Eds.), *Moral discourse and practice: Some philosophical approaches* (pp. 227-244). Oxford University Press.

Wikipedia. Organ donation, and Organ transplantation

Wikipedia. Reciprocal altruism.

Wikipedia. Texas sharpshooter fallacy.

Wikipedia. Ultimatum game.

Williams, B. (1972). *Morality: An introduction to ethics.* Cambridge University Press.

Williams, B. (1985). *Ethics and the limits of philosophy.* Harvard University Press.

Williams, J. (2025). *Outclassed.* St. Martins.

Wilson, J. (1993). *The moral sense.* Free Press.

Wittgenstein, L. (1958). *The blue and the brown books.* Harper Torchbooks.

Wittgenstein, L. (1997). A lecture on ethics. In S. Darwall et al. (Eds.), *Moral discourse and practice: Some philosophical approaches* (pp. 65-70). Oxford University Press.

Woermann, M. (2013). *On the (im)possibility of business ethics.* Springer.

Wright, J. (2023). *Why the Bible began.* Cambridge University Press.

Wright, N. (2006). *Simply Christian: Why Christianity makes sense.* Harper.

Wright, R. (1994). *The moral animal.* Pantheon.

Xygalatas, D. (2017). Are religious people more moral? *Culture Lab*, Dec. 6, 2017.

Your Morals (website). www.yourmorals.org.

Yueng, S. et al. (2022). Action and inaction in moral judgments and decisions: Meta-analysis of omission bias, omission-commission asymmetries. *Personality and Social Psychology Bulletin*, 48(10), 1499-1515.

Zak, P. (2012). *The moral molecule: How trust works.* Penguin/Plume.

Zaller, J. (1992). *The nature and origins of mass opinion.* Cambridge University Press.

Zamboni, G. et al. (2009). Individualism, conservatism and radicalism as criteria for processing political beliefs: A parametric fMRI study. *Social Neuroscience,* 4(5), 367-383.

Zamzow, L. & Nichols, S. (2009). Variations in ethical intuitions. *Philosophy Issues,* 19(1), 368-388.

Zhao, X. and Murrell, A. (2022). Does a virtuous circle really exist? Revisiting the causal linkage between CSP and CTP. *Journal of Business Ethics,* 177(5), April 2022.

Zimbardo, P. (2007). *The Lucifer effect.* Random House.

Zmigrod, L. (2025). *The ideological brain.* Henry Holt and Company.

Index

References are to the text page number, or to note page followed by the text page.

About the Author

Cliff Stromberg attended public schools, won a National Merit Scholarship to attend Yale, from which he graduated *summa cum laude*, and a scholarship to Harvard Law School. He then served as law clerk to a federal judge. A few years later, the President appointed him as Deputy Executive Secretary of the U.S. Department of Health and Human Services, overseeing the policy coordination staff. He was later an advisor to the Federal Trade Commission.

Cliff is the coauthor of several books and was the founding editor-in-chief of a monthly magazine on the health care industry. He served on the board and then was elected chair of the American Bar Association's Civil Rights and Social Justice Section. He also coached traveling AAU youth basketball teams for many years. Cliff is a partner in one of the world's largest law firms, and during his career he has advised many of the nation's leading universities, health care systems, and other health organizations. He has a lifelong passion for philosophy, science, and history.